MAXIMUM RIDE

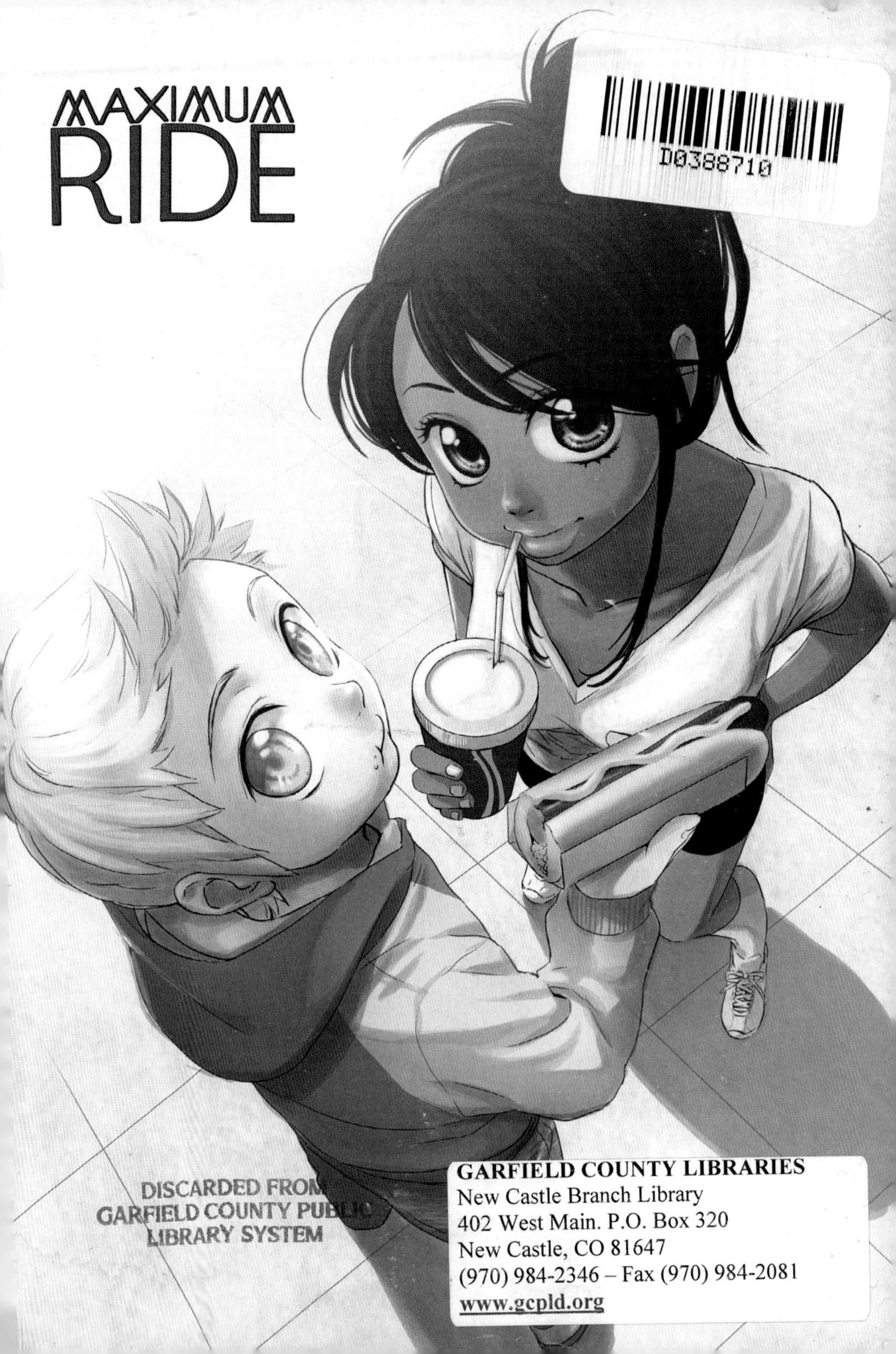

WHAT CAME BEFORE

Max and her "flock" appear at a glance to be normal kids...that is, if you don't notice the wings!

Instilled with avian DNA in a lab known as the "School," Max and her family escaped confinement with the help of scientist Jeb Batchelder, who they believed perished assisting them. When the youngest of the flock, Angel, is abducted by the lab's foot soldiers – shape-shifting men and women infused with lupine DNA called Erasers – led by Jeb's son, Ari, Max discovers that Jeb is not only alive, but still working with the School! Rescuing Angel, the flock heads to New York City to find the "Institute," which they believe holds the secrets to their past. While raiding the facility, though, they are again confronted by Jeb and his Erasers. The flock manages to get away, but not before Max accidentally kills Ari!

Now the flock is off to Washington, D.C., following up a lead on their parents, but Max can't escape the mysterious voice that's begun whispering inside her head – or Jeb's haunting words that in killing Ari, she may have killed her own brother...

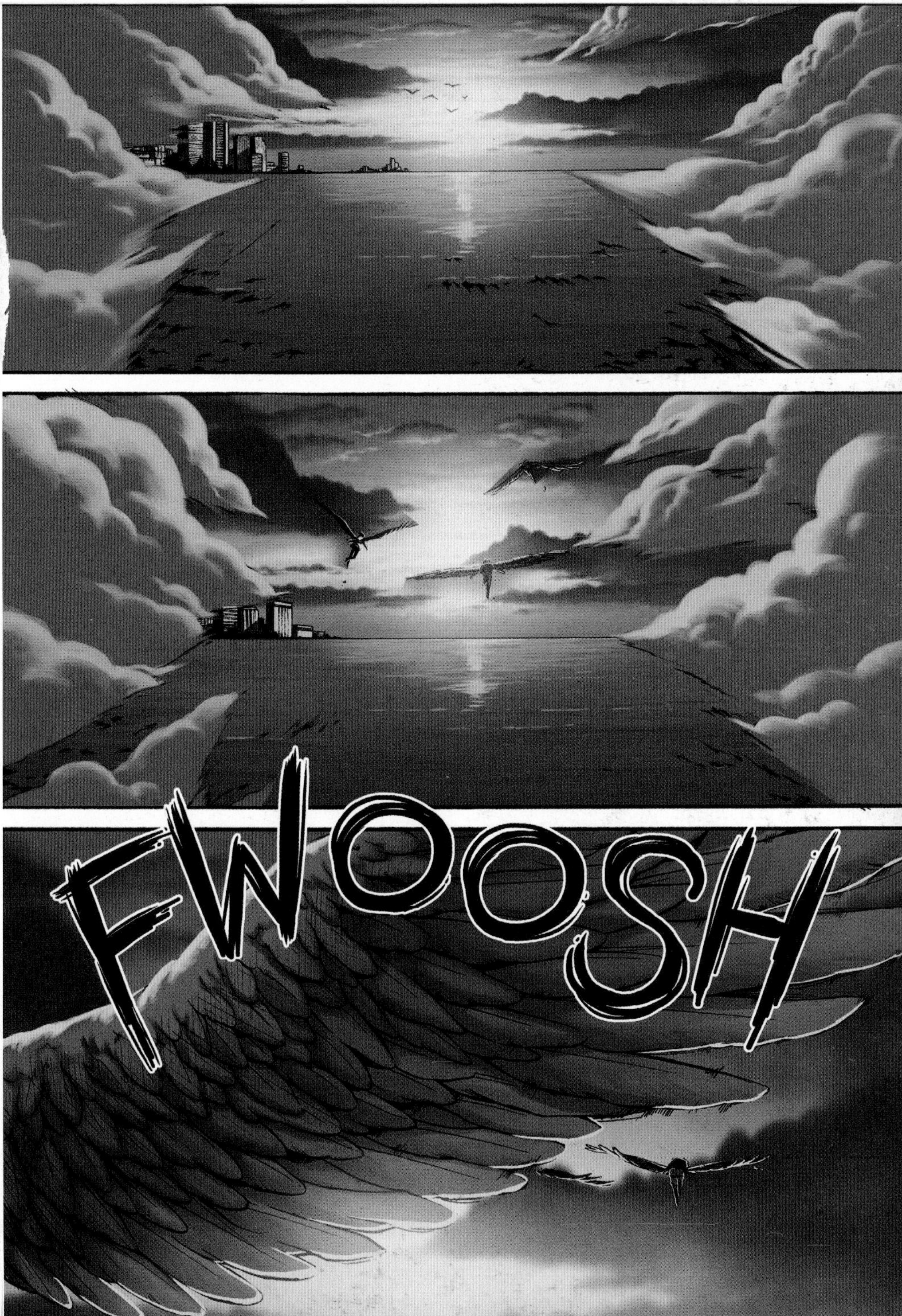
FWOOSH

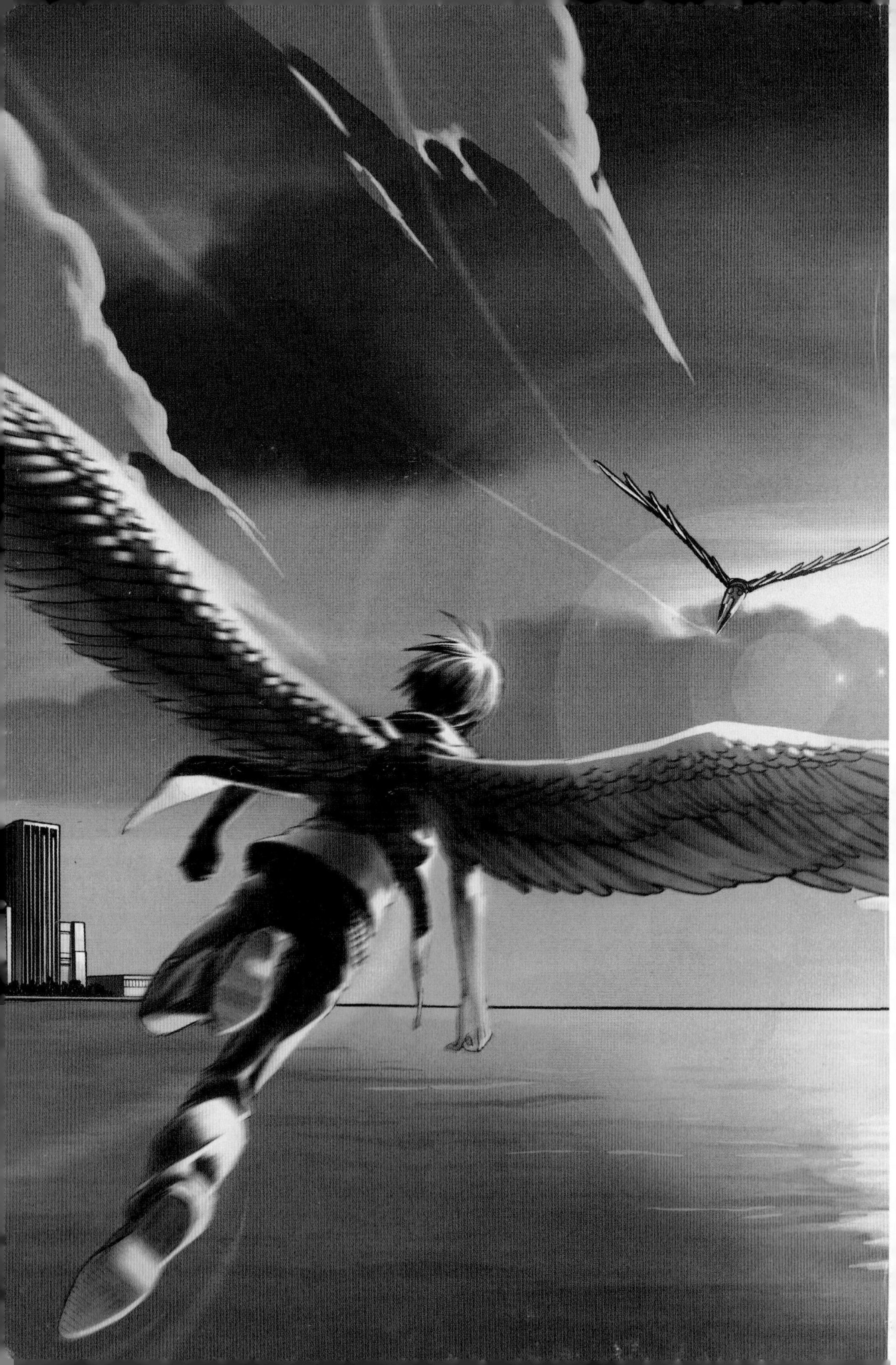

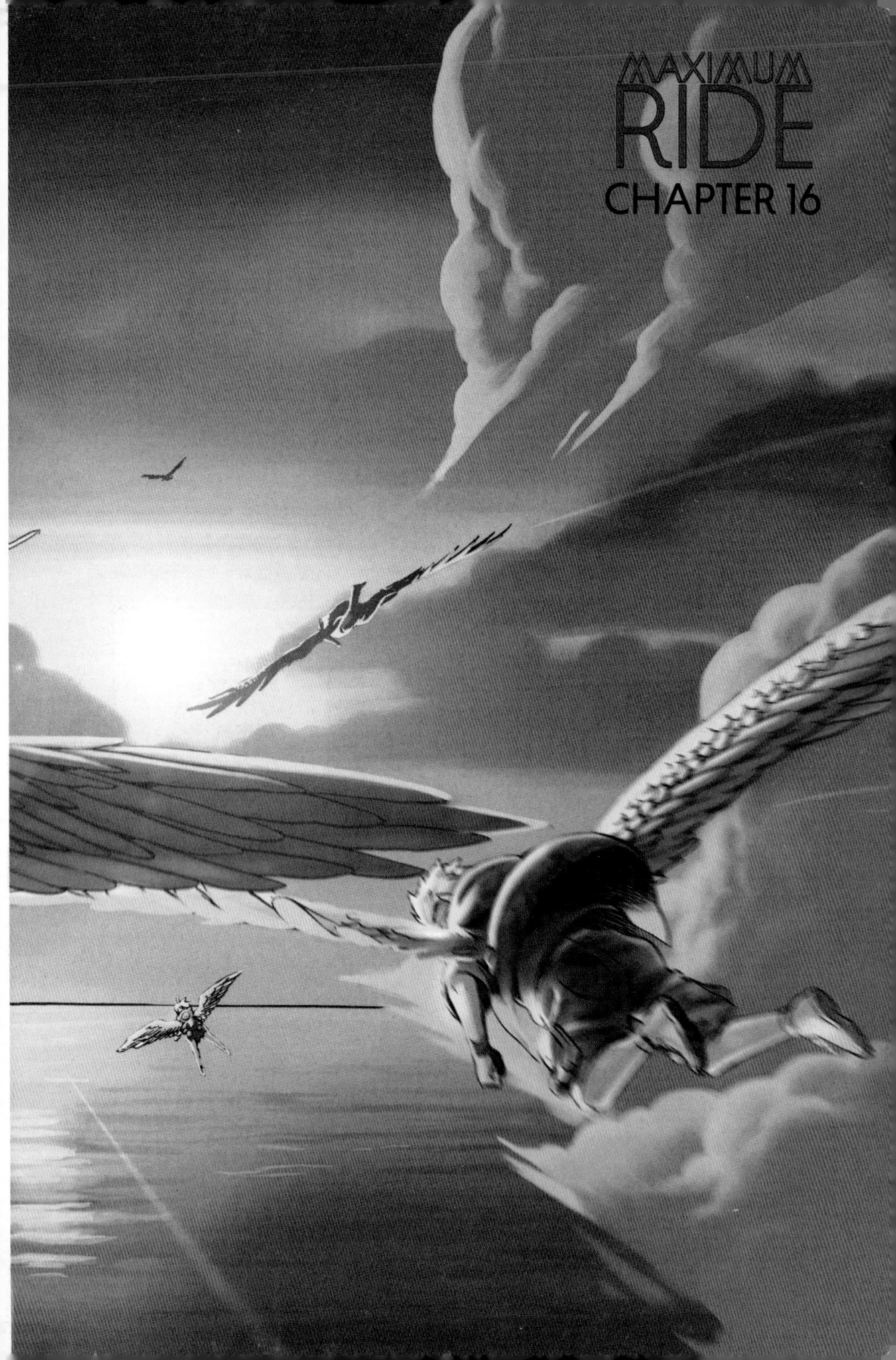
MAXIMUM RIDE
CHAPTER 16

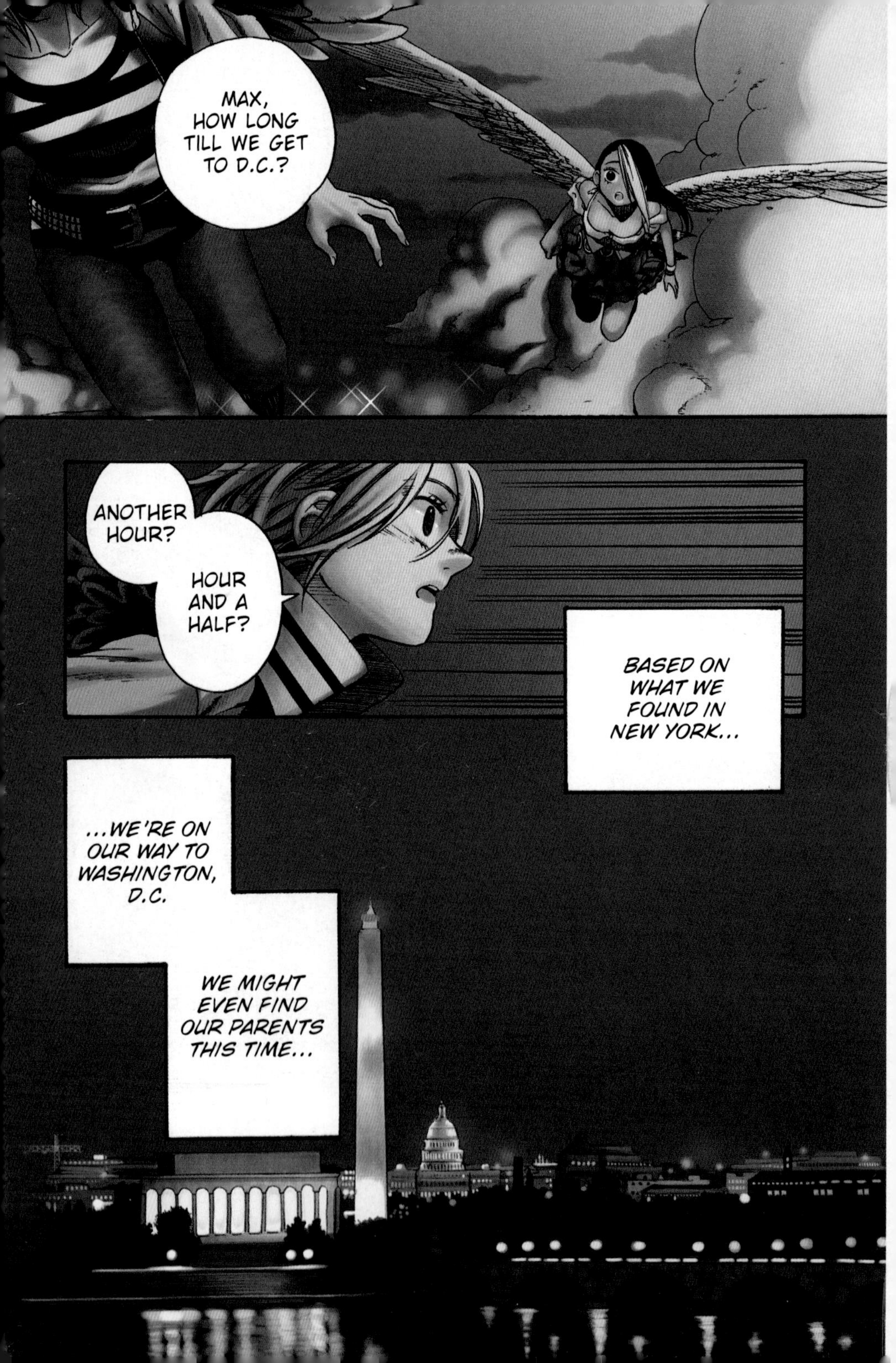
MAX, HOW LONG TILL WE GET TO D.C.?
ANOTHER HOUR?
HOUR AND A HALF?
BASED ON WHAT WE FOUND IN NEW YORK...
...WE'RE ON OUR WAY TO WASHINGTON, D.C.
WE MIGHT EVEN FIND OUR PARENTS THIS TIME...

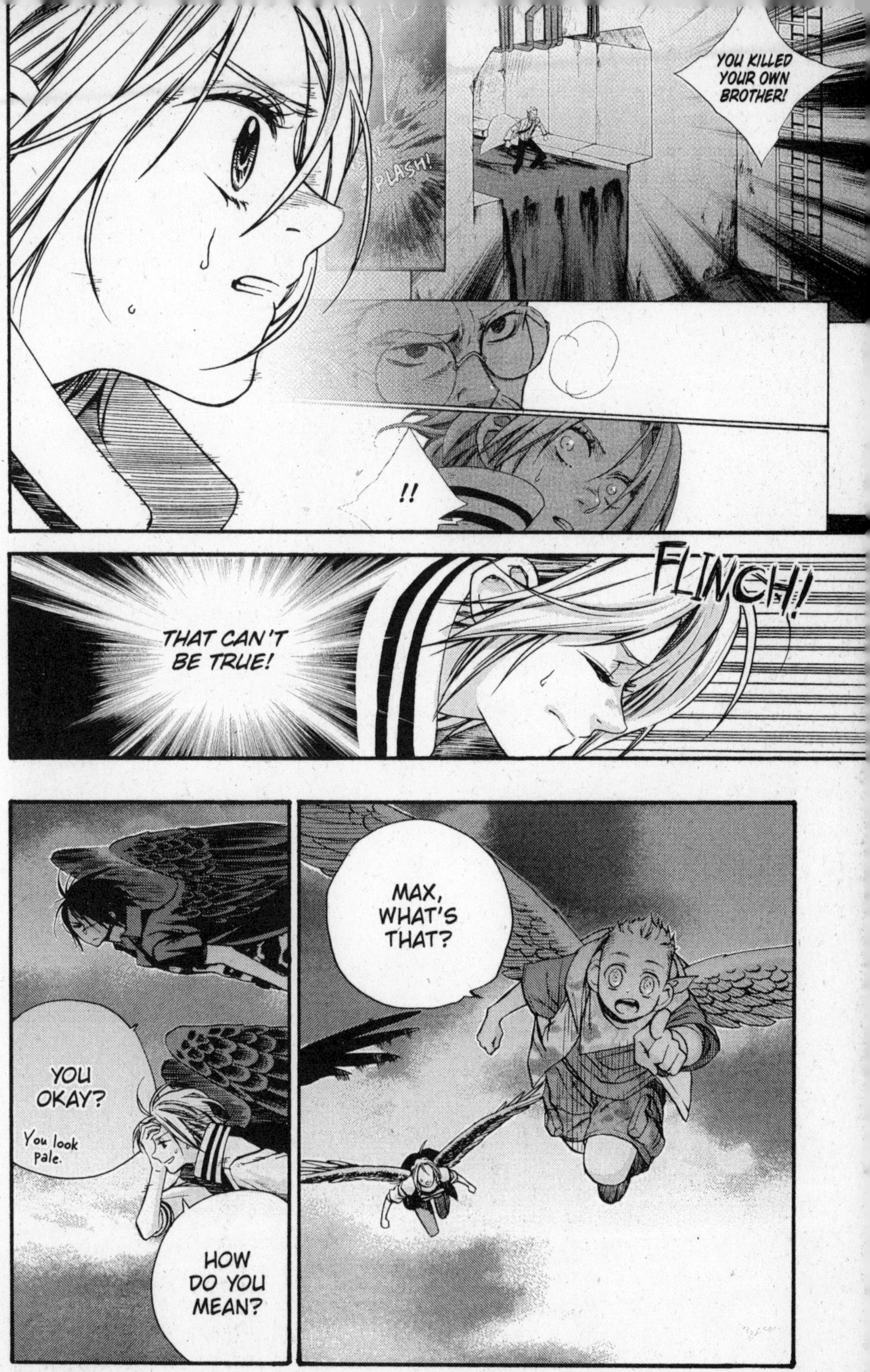

SPLASH!
YOU KILLED YOUR OWN BROTHER!
!!
THAT CAN'T BE TRUE!
FLINCH!
YOU OKAY?
You look pale.
HOW DO YOU MEAN?
MAX, WHAT'S THAT?

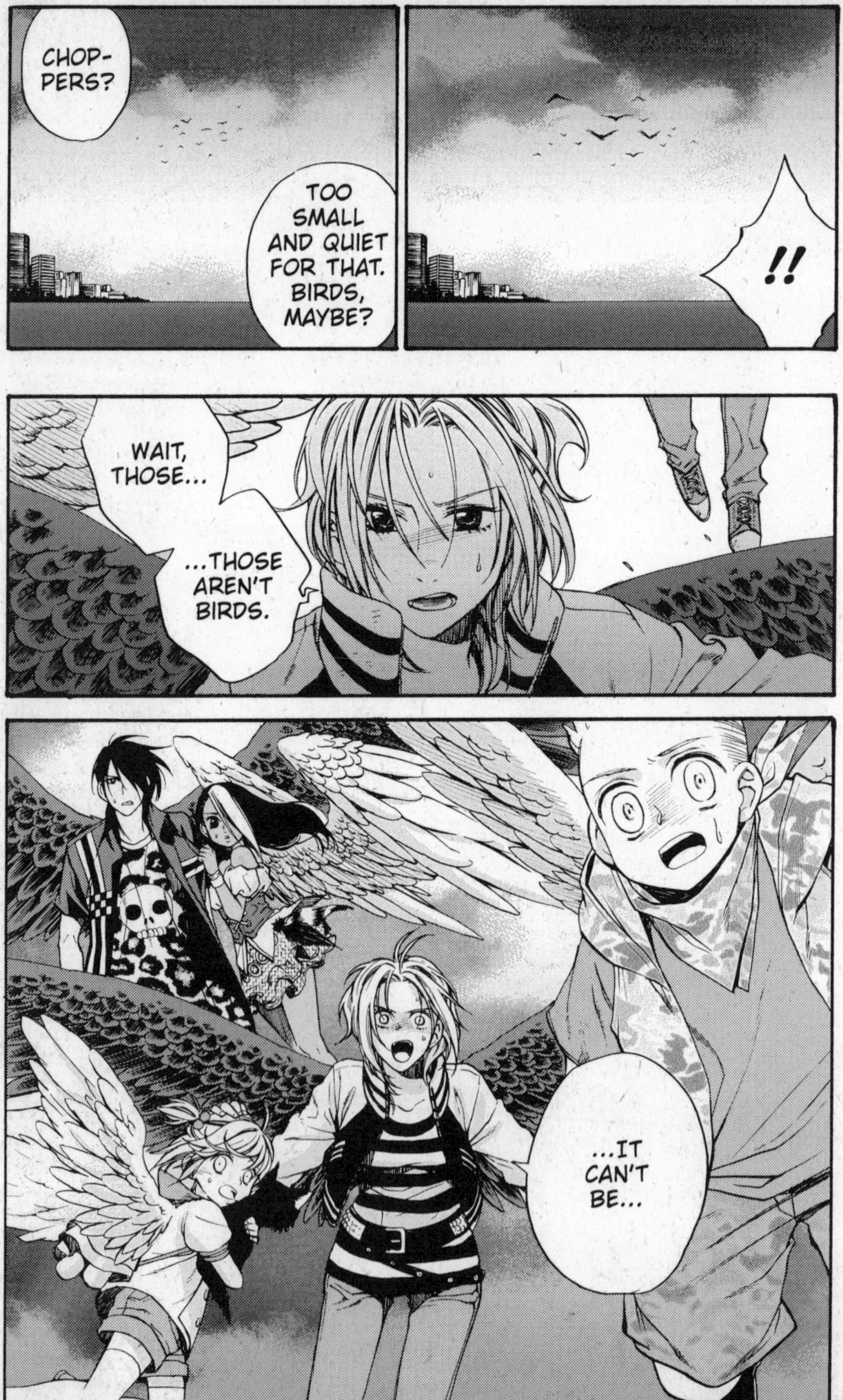
CHOP-
PERS?
TOO SMALL AND QUIET FOR THAT. BIRDS, MAYBE?
!!
WAIT, THOSE...
...THOSE AREN'T BIRDS.
...IT CAN'T BE...

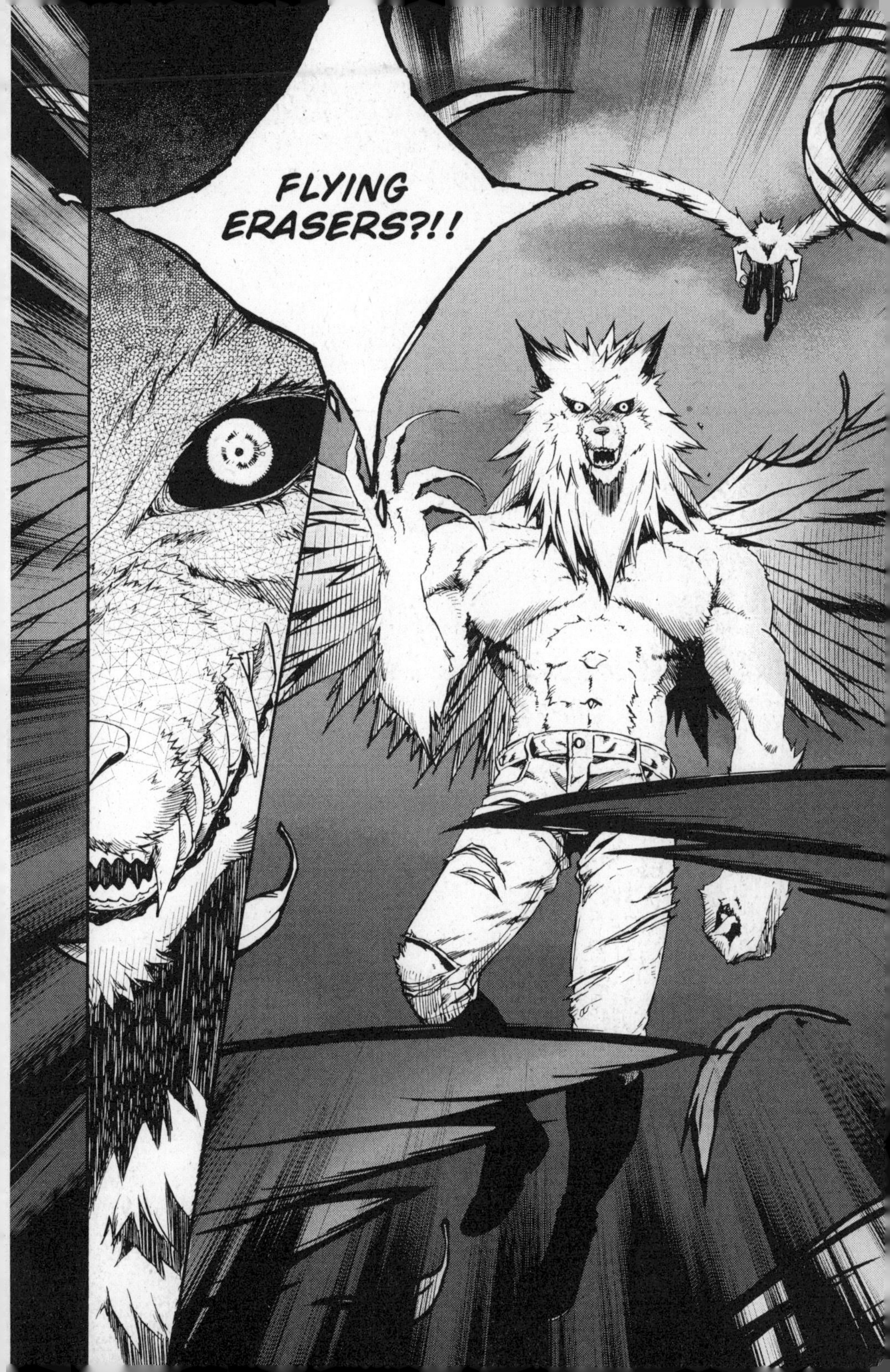
FLYING ERASERS?!!

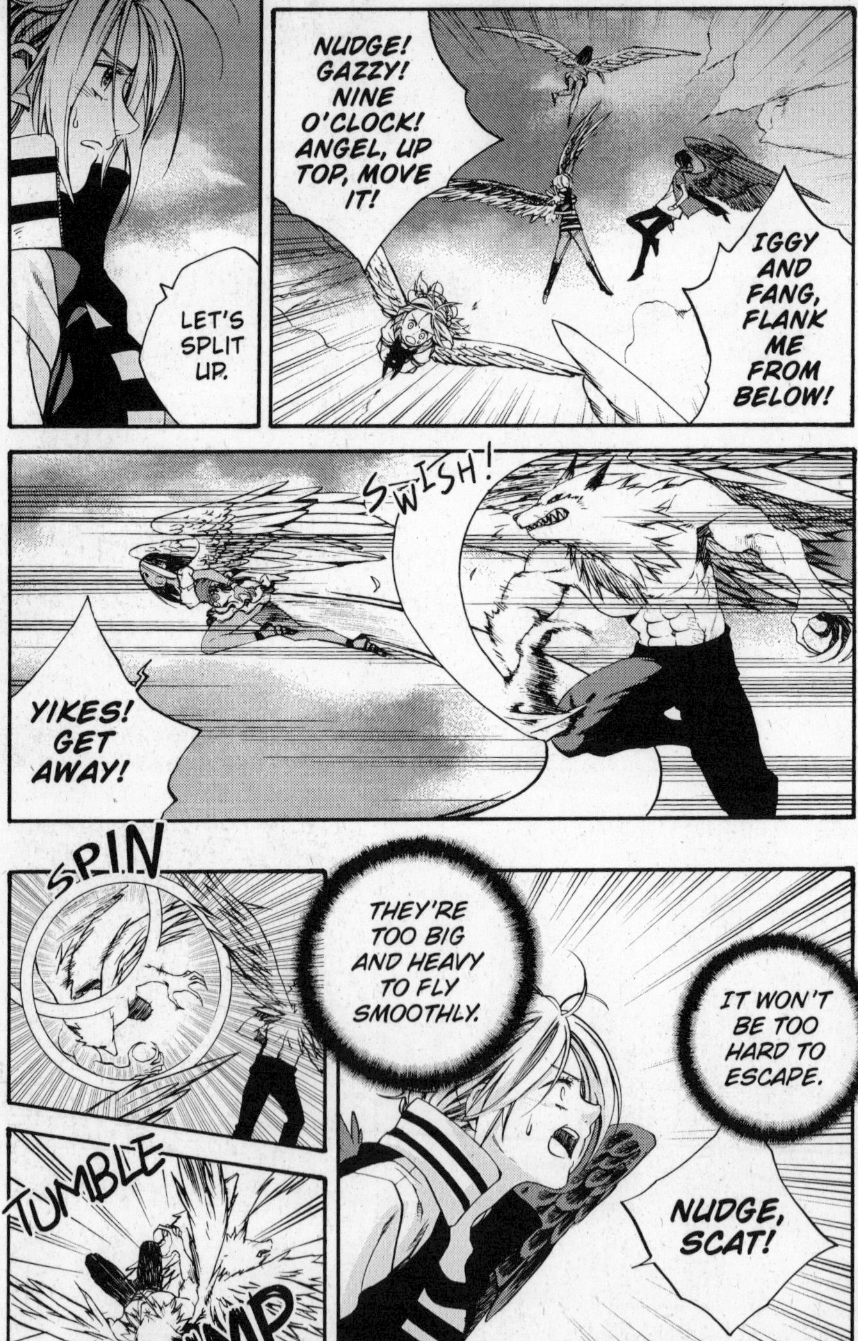
LET'S SPLIT UP.
NUDGE! GAZZY! NINE O'CLOCK! ANGEL, UP TOP, MOVE IT!
IGGY AND FANG, FLANK ME FROM BELOW!
SWISH!
YIKES! GET AWAY!
SPIN
TUMBLE
BUMP
THEY'RE TOO BIG AND HEAVY TO FLY SMOOTHLY.
IT WON'T BE TOO HARD TO ESCAPE.
NUDGE, SCAT!

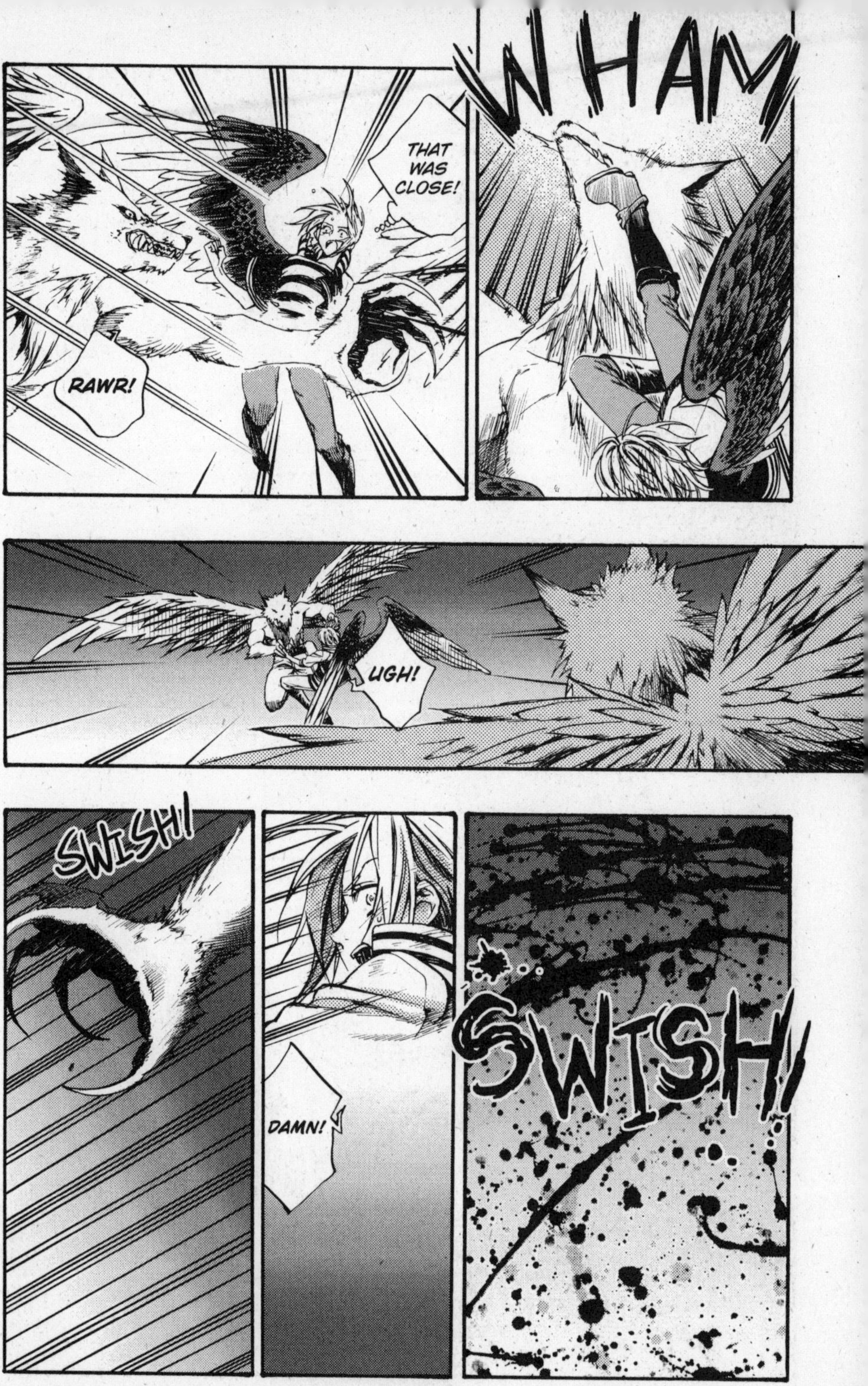
THAT WAS CLOSE!
RAWR!
WHAM
UGH!
SWISH!
DAMN!
SWISH!

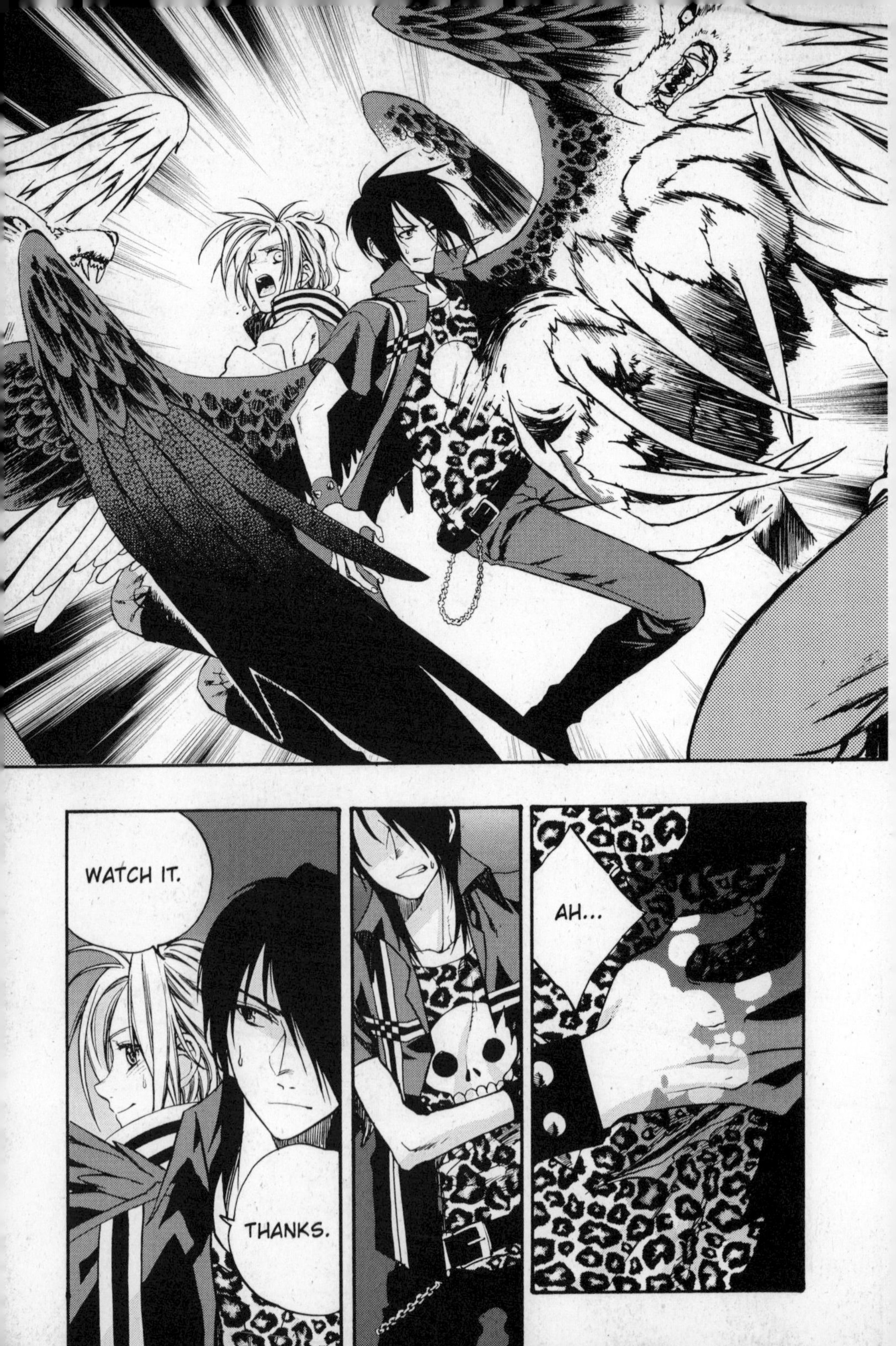
WATCH IT.
THANKS.
AH...

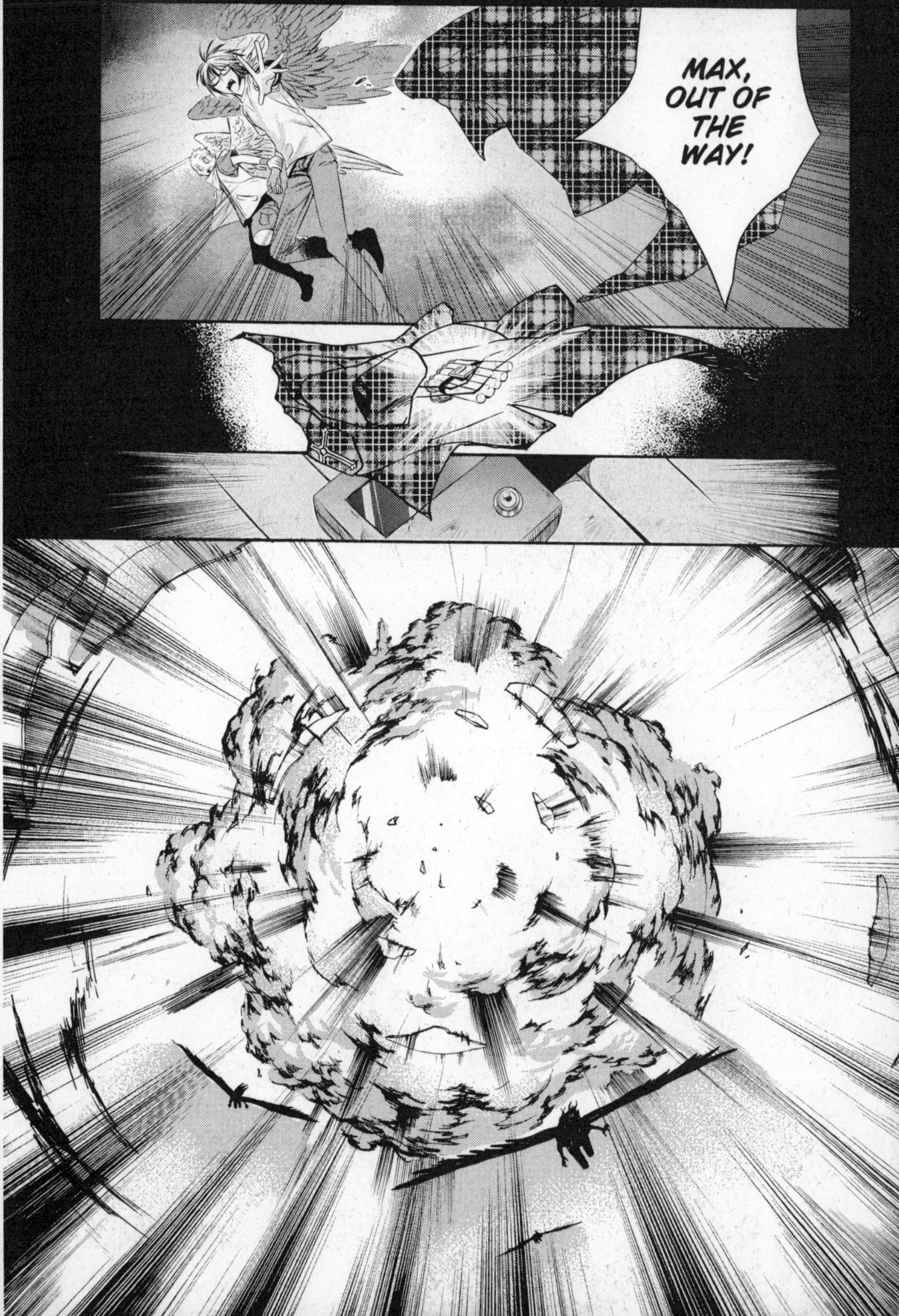
MAX, OUT OF THE WAY!

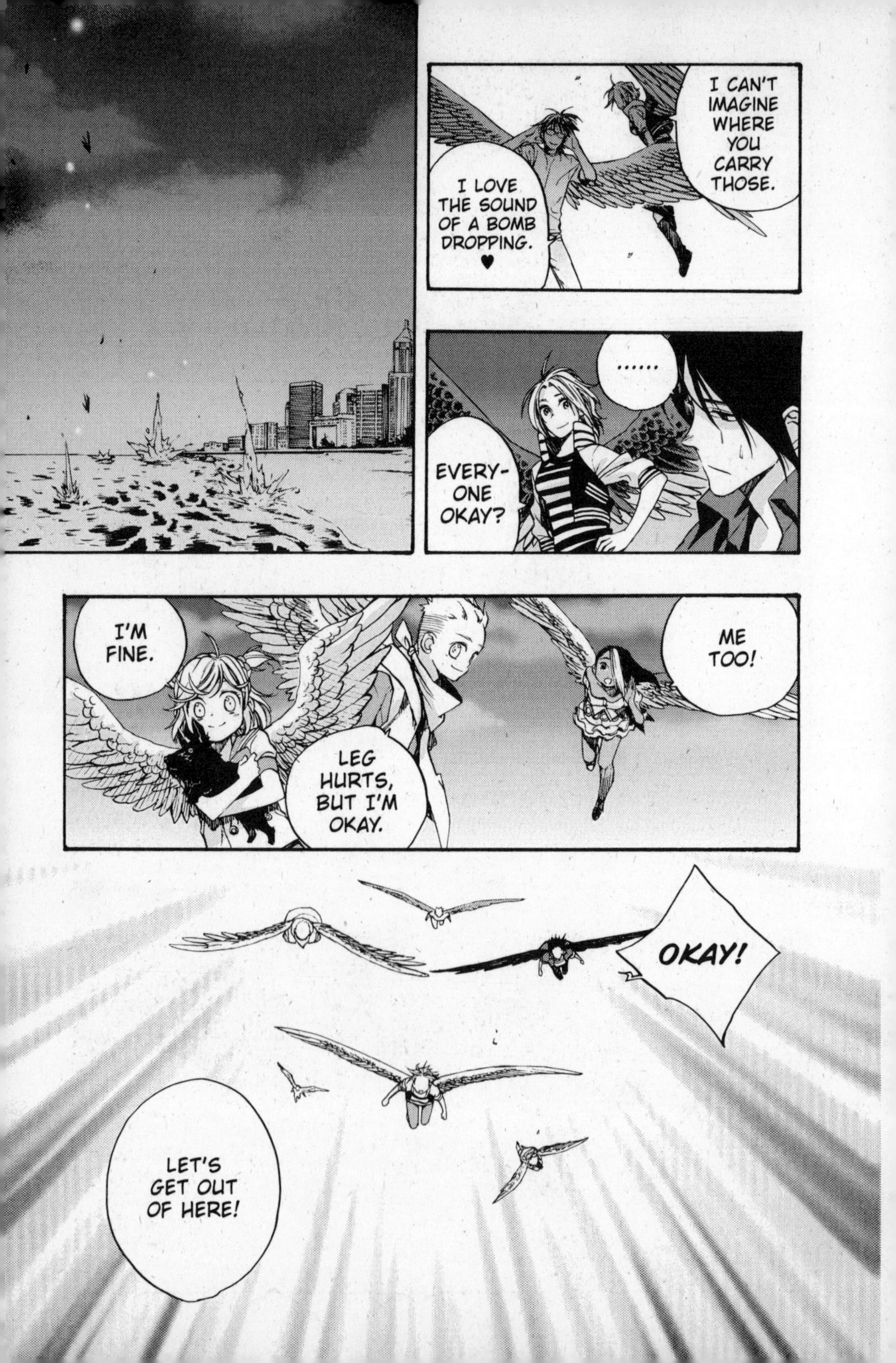
I LOVE THE SOUND OF A BOMB DROPPING. ♥
I CAN'T IMAGINE WHERE YOU CARRY THOSE.
EVERY-ONE OKAY?
......
I'M FINE.
LEG HURTS, BUT I'M OKAY.
ME TOO!
LET'S GET OUT OF HERE!
OKAY!

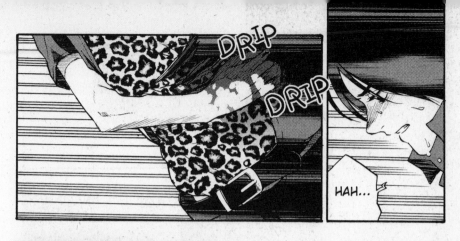

DRIP
DRIP

HAH...

I'M GUESSING A NEW PROTOTYPE.

SO...WHAT WAS WITH THE FLYING ERASERS?

BUT, MAN, THEY'RE FAILURES. THEY WERE HAVING A HARD TIME FLYING AND FIGHTING AT THE SAME TIME.

THEY WERE REALLY BAD FLIERS.

YEAH, THEY WERE LIKE A BUNCH OF IDIOTS TRYING TO DANCE.

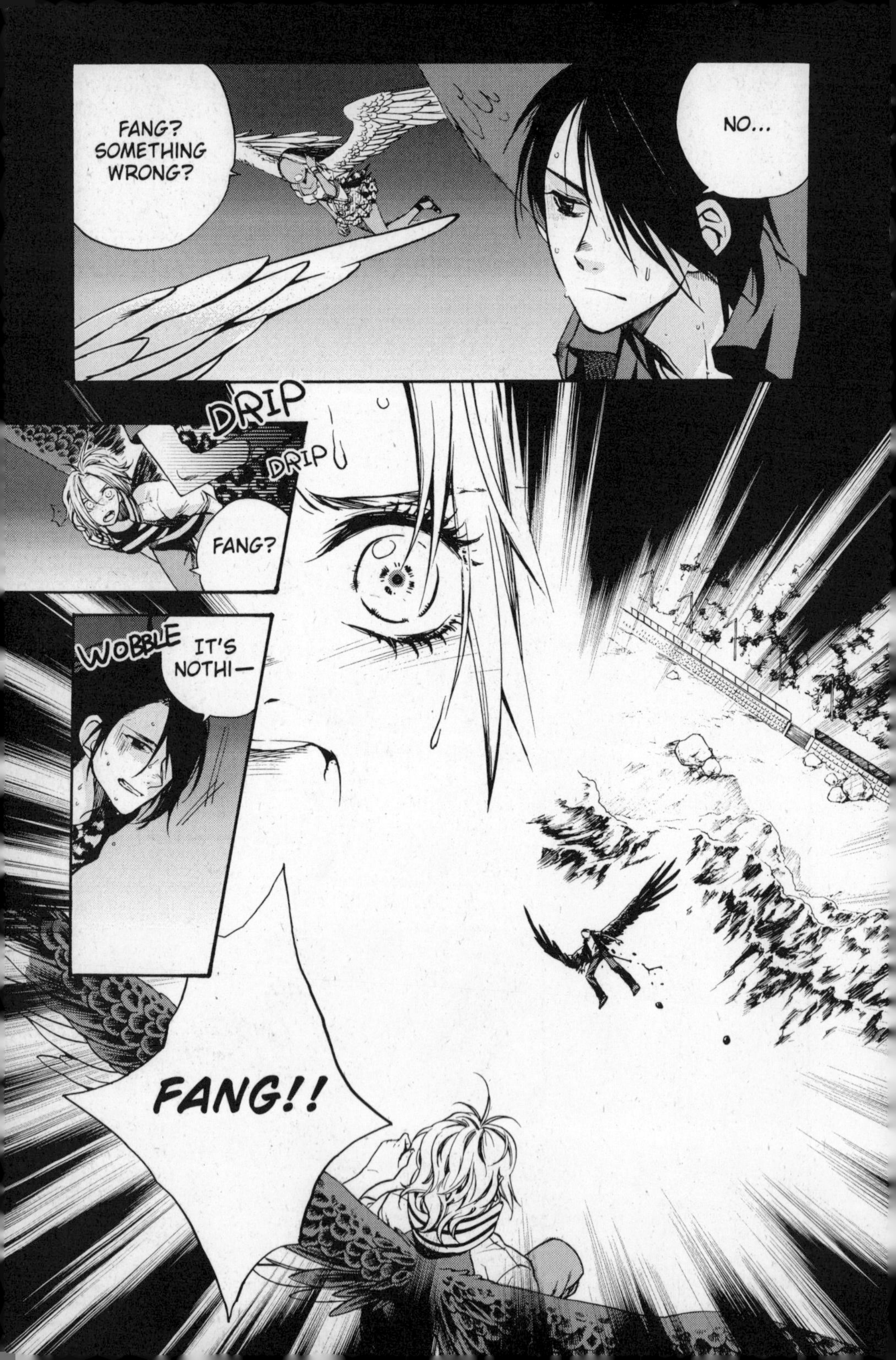
FANG? SOMETHING WRONG?
NO...
DRIP
DRIP
FANG?
WOBBLE
IT'S NOTHI—
FANG!!

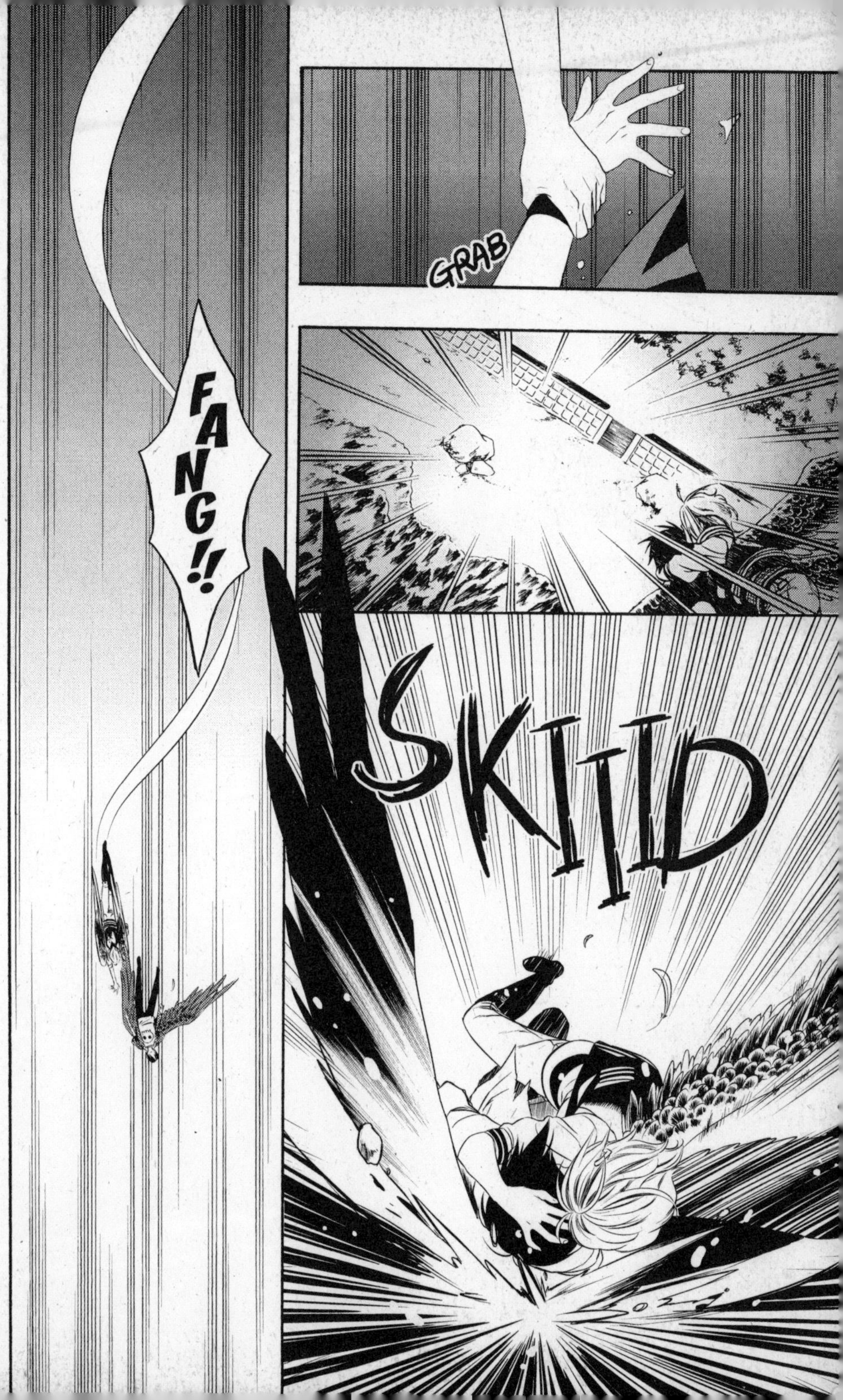
FANG!!
GRAB
SKIID

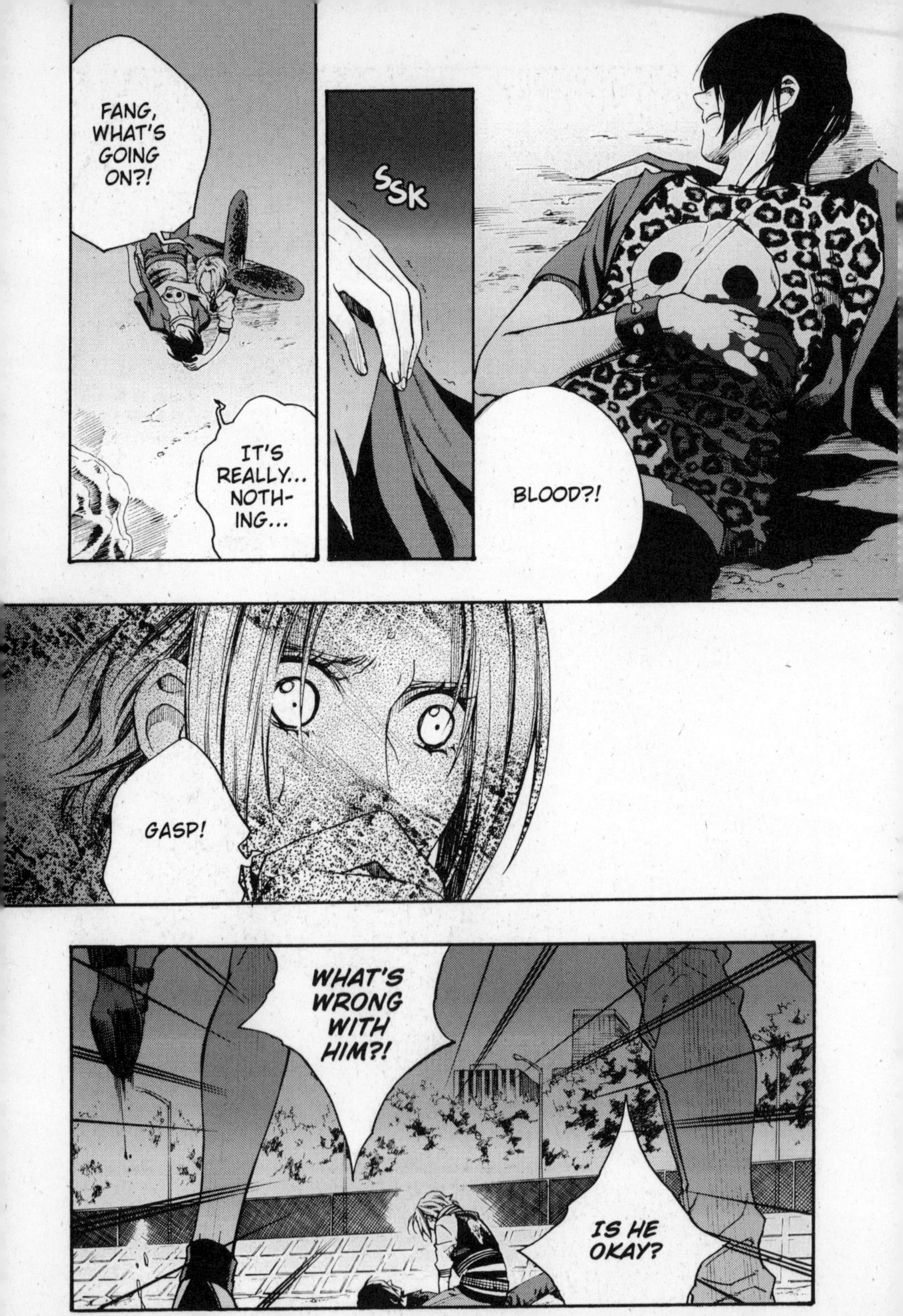
FANG, WHAT'S GOING ON?!
IT'S REALLY... NOTHING...
SSK
BLOOD?!
GASP!
WHAT'S WRONG WITH HIM?!
IS HE OKAY?

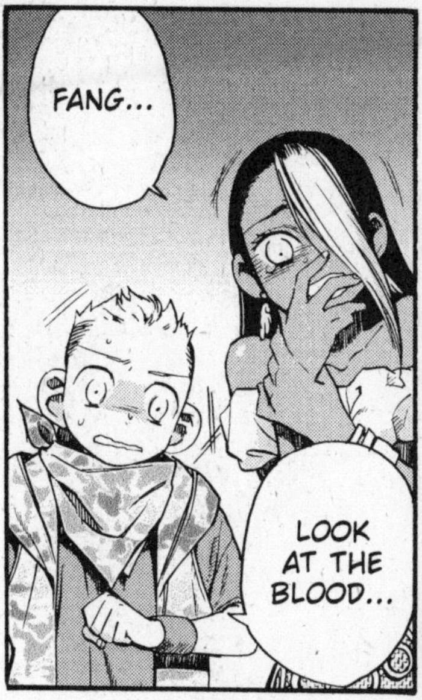
FANG...
LOOK AT THE BLOOD...

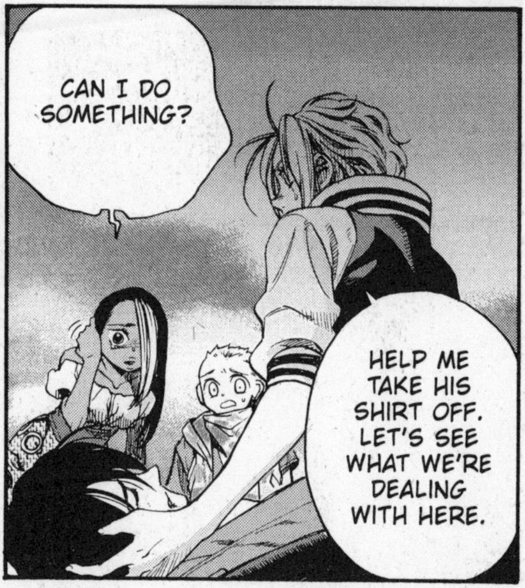
CAN I DO SOMETHING?
HELP ME TAKE HIS SHIRT OFF. LET'S SEE WHAT WE'RE DEALING WITH HERE.

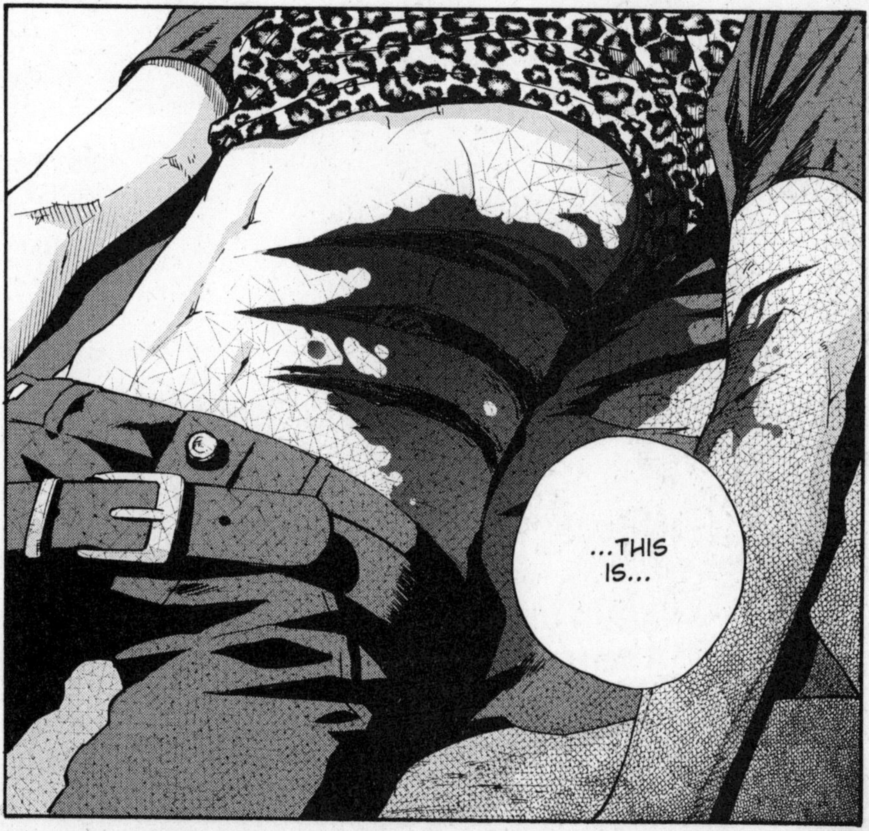
...THIS IS...

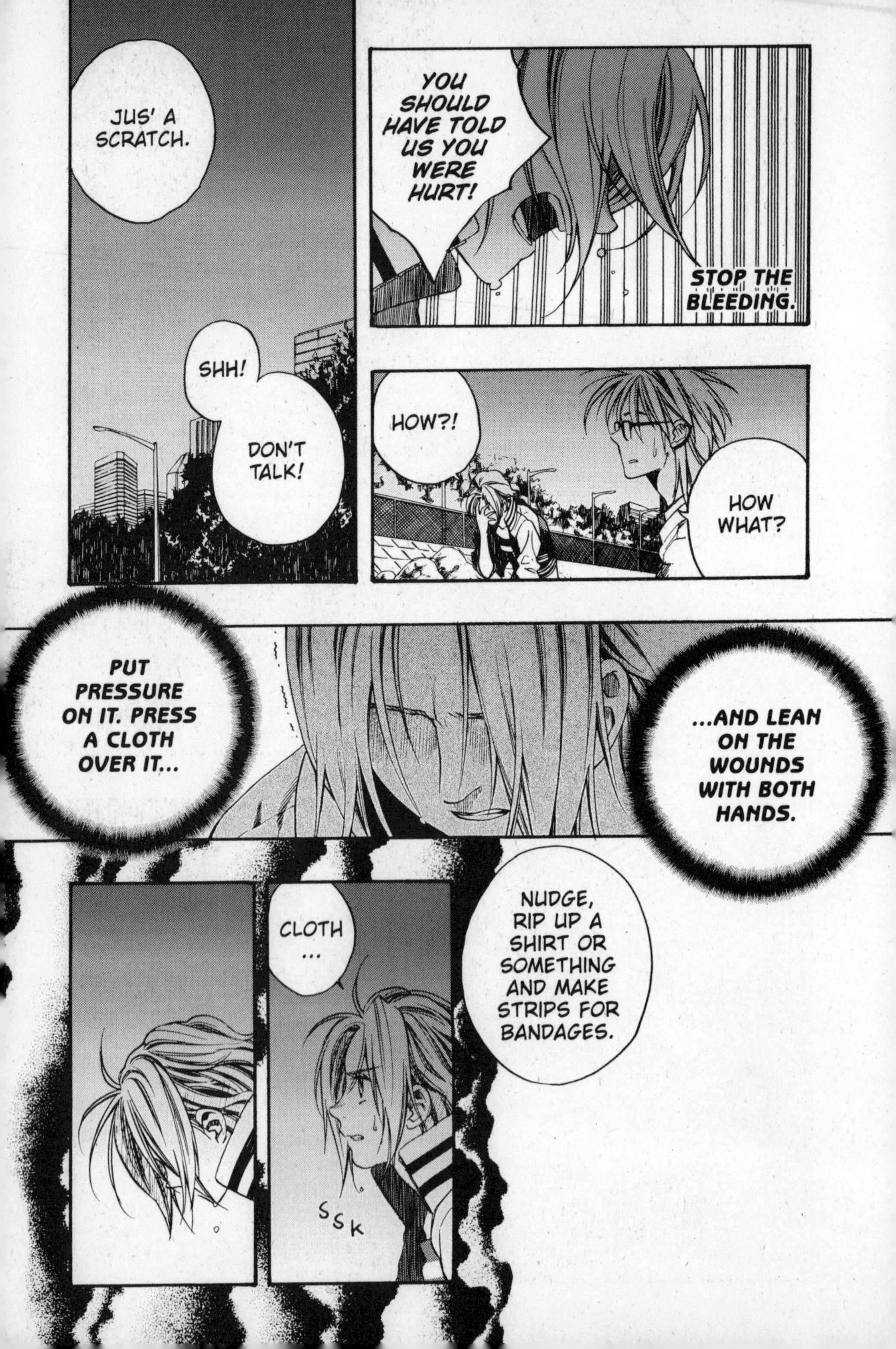
JUS' A SCRATCH.
SHH!
DON'T TALK!
YOU SHOULD HAVE TOLD US YOU WERE HURT!
STOP THE BLEEDING.
HOW?!
HOW WHAT?
PUT PRESSURE ON IT. PRESS A CLOTH OVER IT...
...AND LEAN ON THE WOUNDS WITH BOTH HANDS.
CLOTH ...
NUDGE, RIP UP A SHIRT OR SOMETHING AND MAKE STRIPS FOR BANDAGES.
SSK

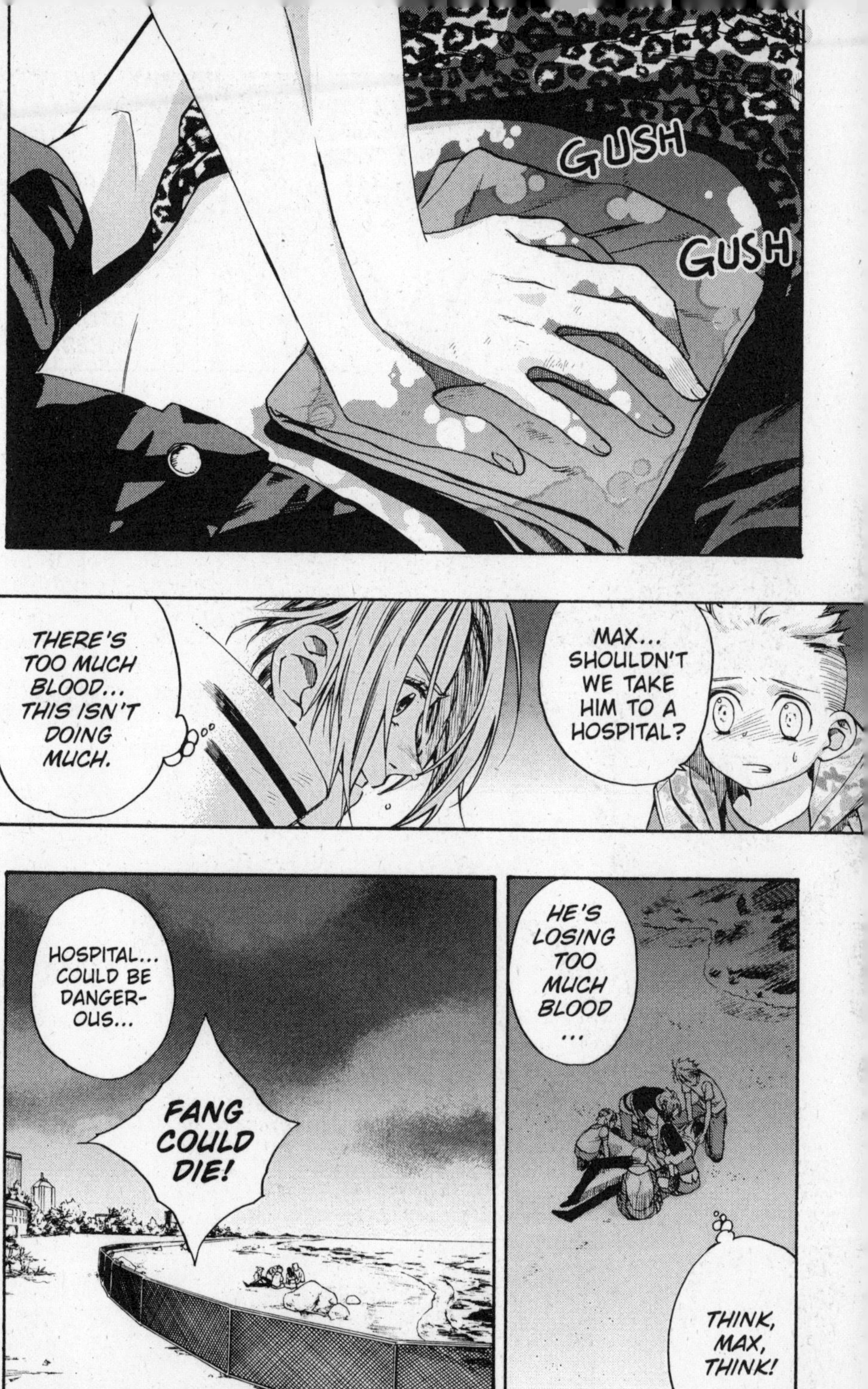
GUSH
GUSH
THERE'S TOO MUCH BLOOD... THIS ISN'T DOING MUCH.
MAX... SHOULDN'T WE TAKE HIM TO A HOSPITAL?
HOSPITAL... COULD BE DANGER-OUS...
FANG COULD DIE!
HE'S LOSING TOO MUCH BLOOD...
THINK, MAX, THINK!

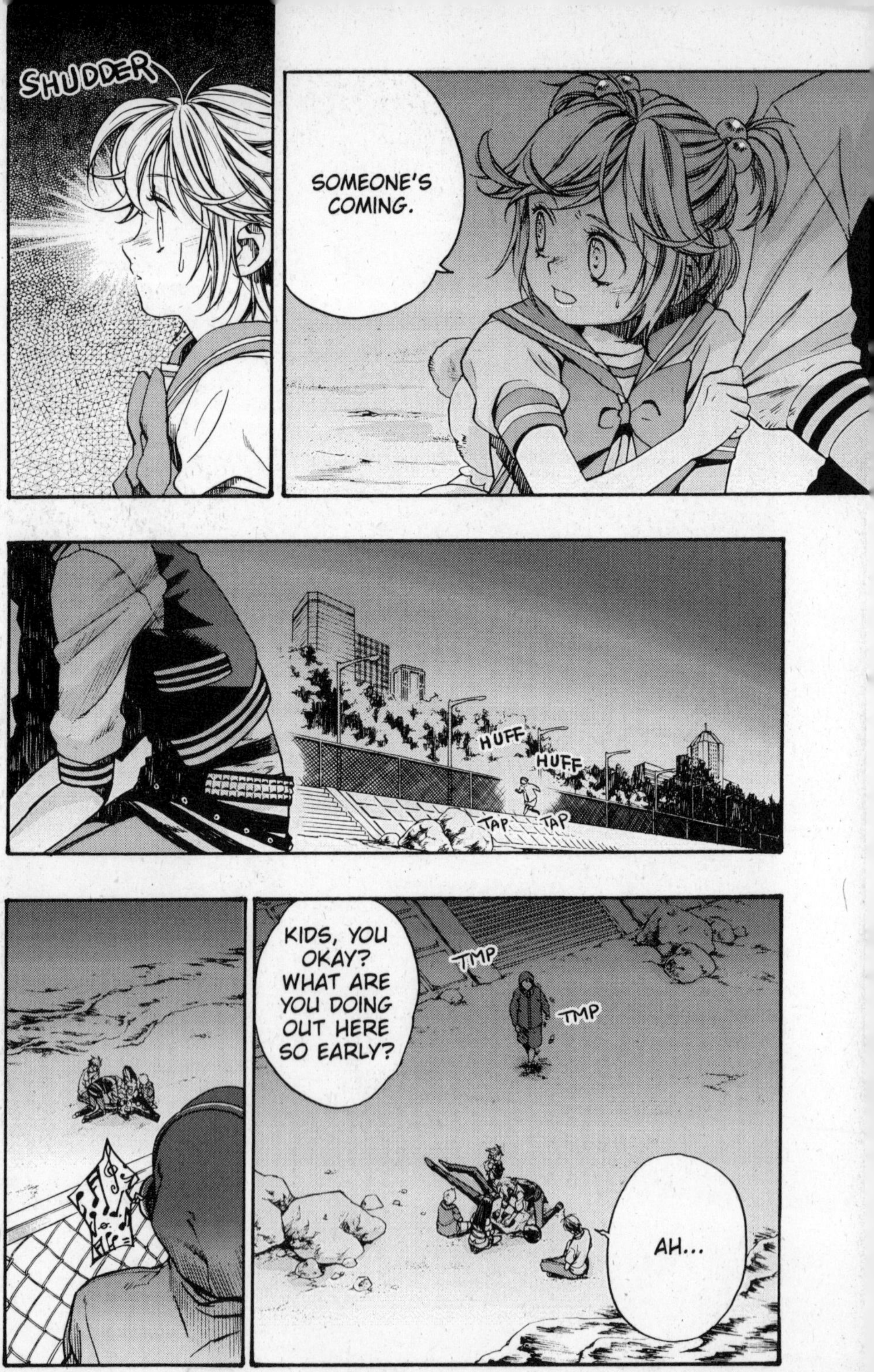
SHUDDER
SOMEONE'S COMING.
HUFF
HUFF
TAP
TAP
KIDS, YOU OKAY? WHAT ARE YOU DOING OUT HERE SO EARLY?
TMP
TMP
AH...

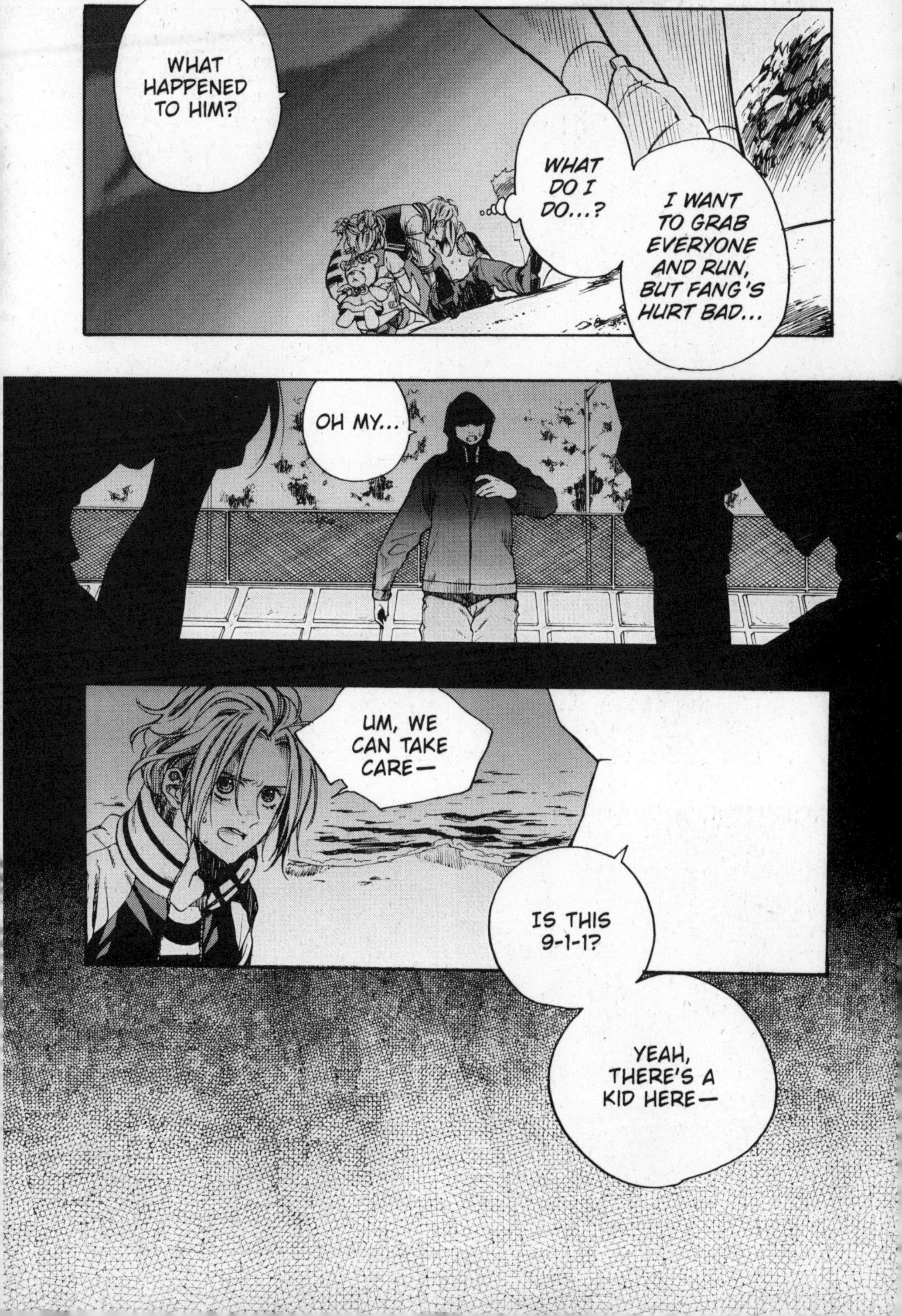
WHAT HAPPENED TO HIM?
WHAT DO I DO...?
I WANT TO GRAB EVERYONE AND RUN, BUT FANG'S HURT BAD...
OH MY...
UM, WE CAN TAKE CARE—
IS THIS 9-1-1?
YEAH, THERE'S A KID HERE—

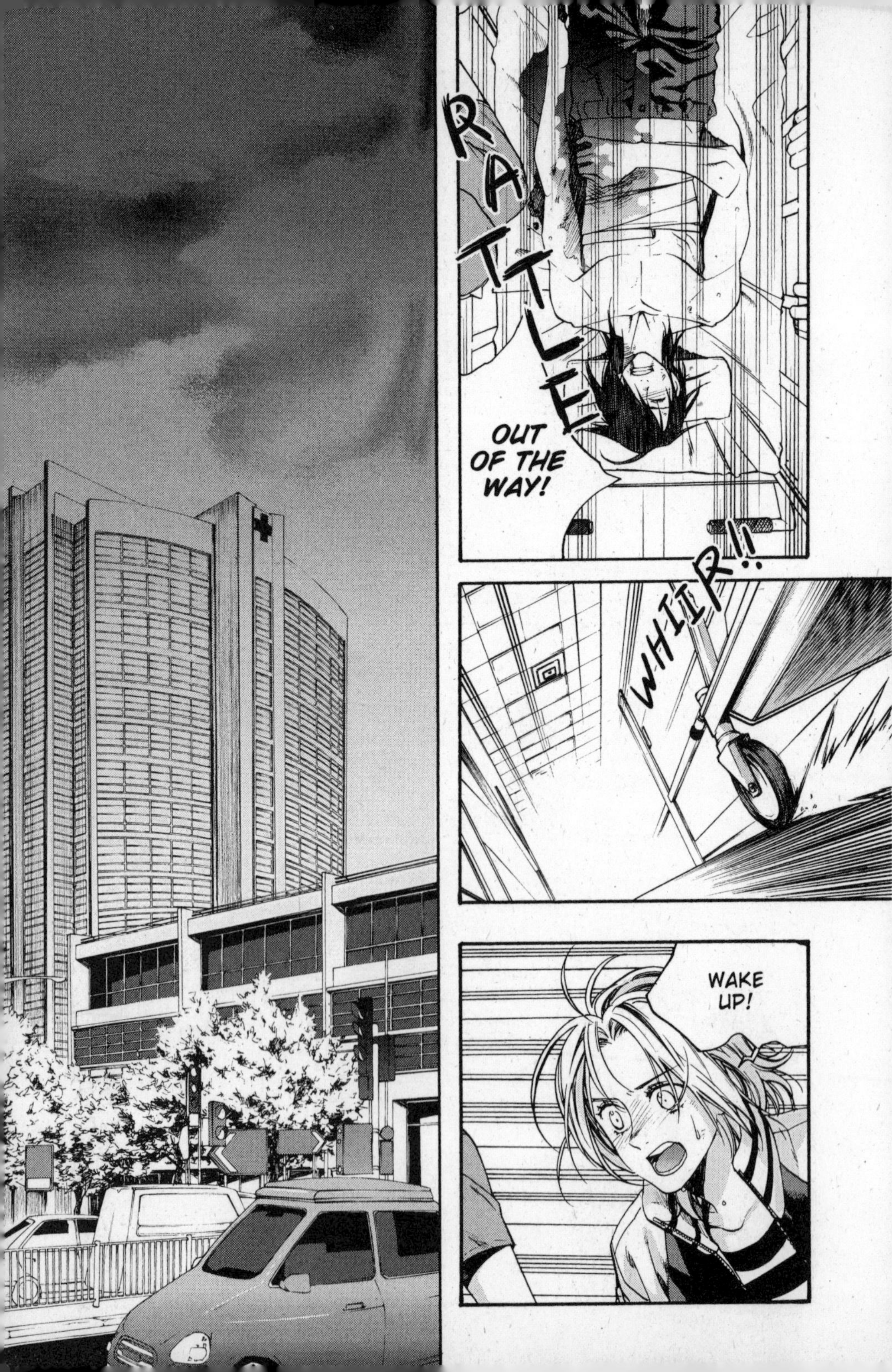
RATTLE
OUT OF THE WAY!
WHIIR!!
WAKE UP!

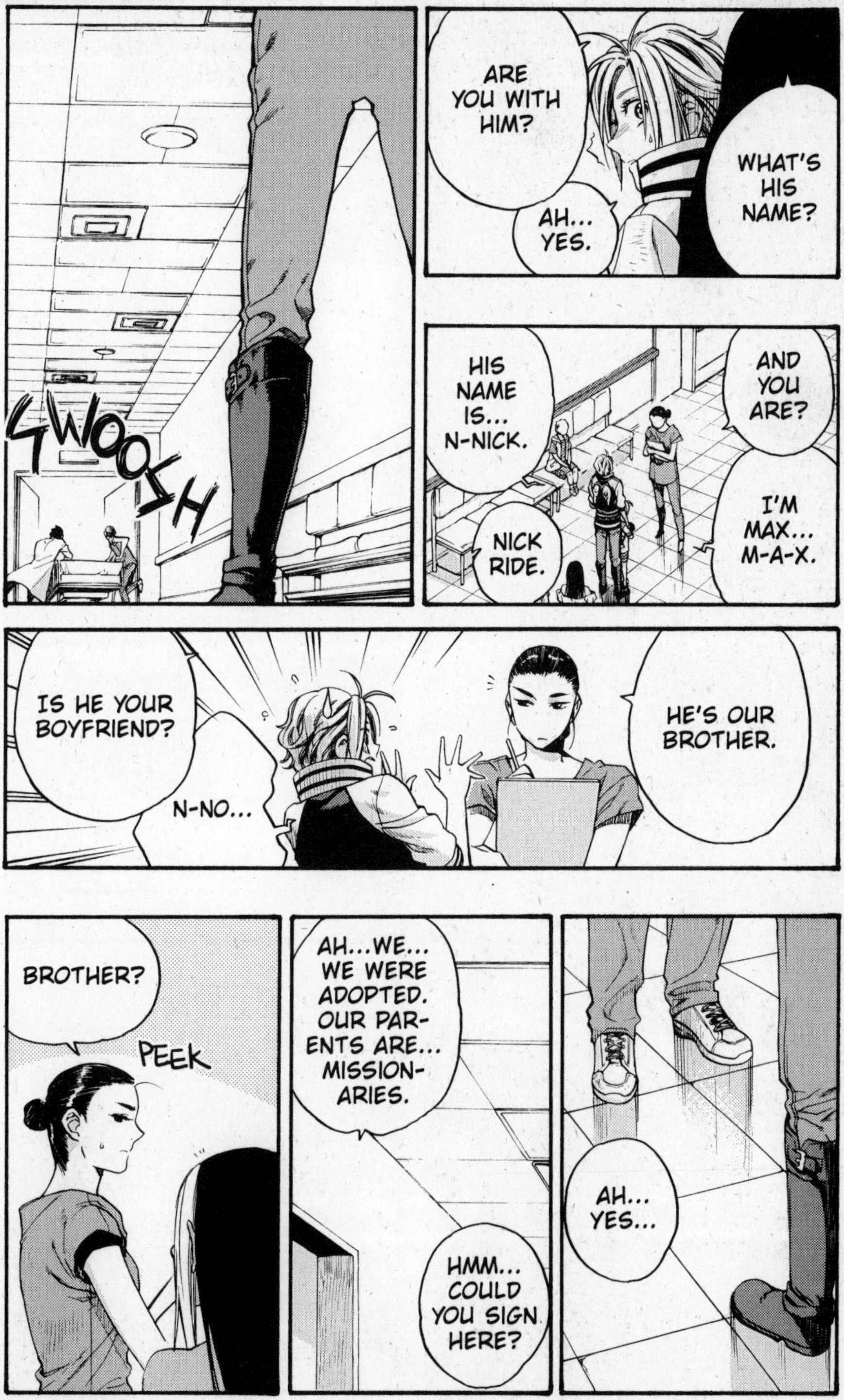
SWOOSH
ARE YOU WITH HIM?
AH... YES.
WHAT'S HIS NAME?
HIS NAME IS... N-NICK.
NICK RIDE.
AND YOU ARE?
I'M MAX... M-A-X.
IS HE YOUR BOYFRIEND?
N-NO...
HE'S OUR BROTHER.
BROTHER?
PEEK
AH...WE... WE WERE ADOPTED. OUR PAR-ENTS ARE... MISSION-ARIES.
HMM... COULD YOU SIGN HERE?
AH... YES...

OH MY, DOCTOR!

......?

I THINK YOU NEED TO TAKE A LOOK AT THIS.

......!

TH- THIS IS...!!

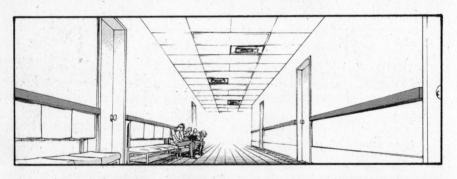

ARE YOU NICK'S SISTER?

AH...

YES, I AM.

WHISPER

ARE YOU— *LIKE* HIM?

WHISPER

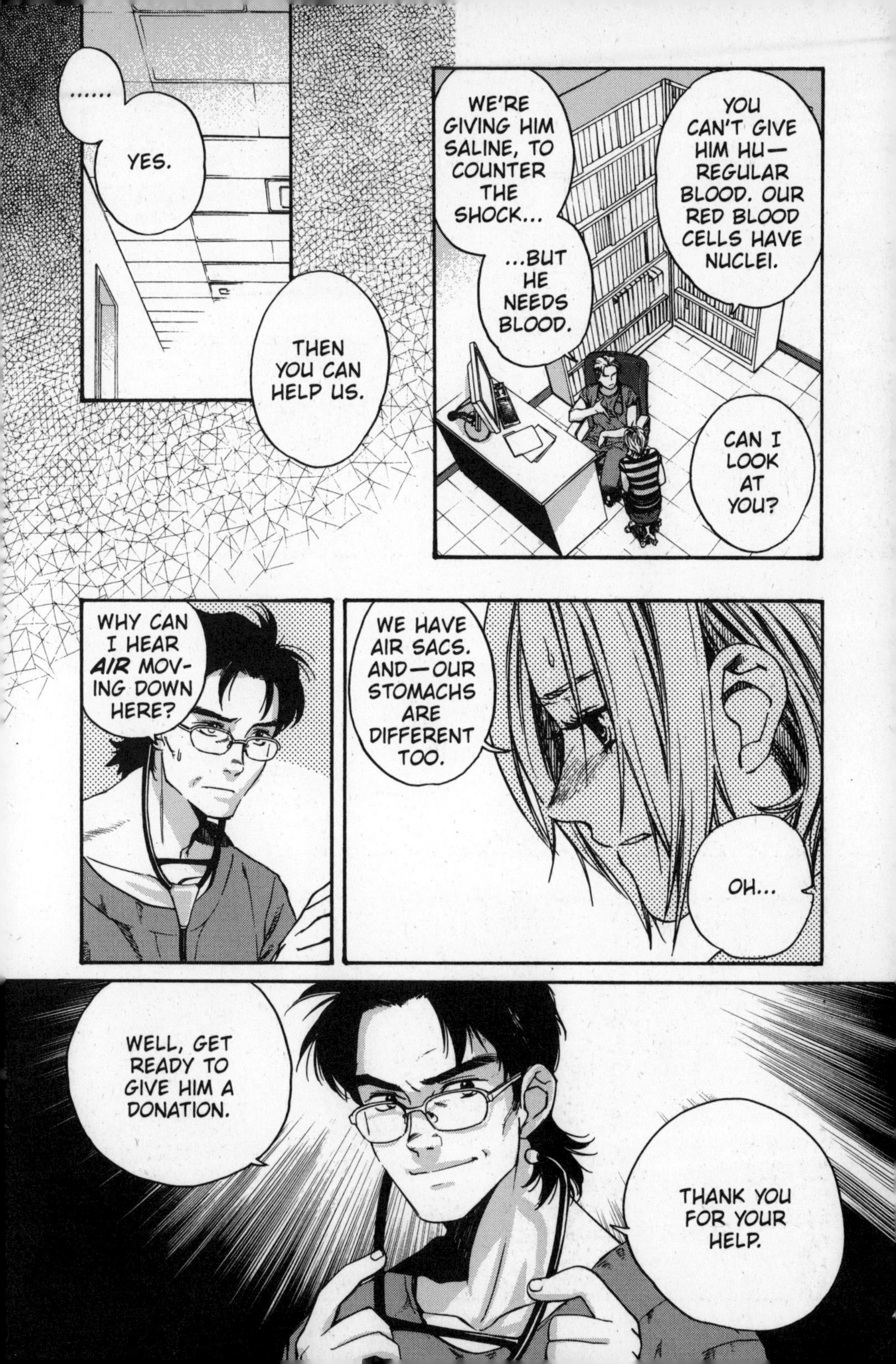
......
YES.
THEN YOU CAN HELP US.
WE'RE GIVING HIM SALINE, TO COUNTER THE SHOCK...
...BUT HE NEEDS BLOOD.
YOU CAN'T GIVE HIM HU—REGULAR BLOOD. OUR RED BLOOD CELLS HAVE NUCLEI.
CAN I LOOK AT YOU?
WHY CAN I HEAR *AIR* MOVING DOWN HERE?
WE HAVE AIR SACS. AND—OUR STOMACHS ARE DIFFERENT TOO.
OH...
WELL, GET READY TO GIVE HIM A DONATION.
THANK YOU FOR YOUR HELP.

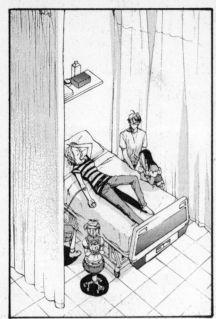

HOW DO YOU FEEL?

DIZZY AS A DODO BIRD.

KNOCK KNOCK

HUH? WHO IS IT?

CREAK

CAN WE TALK TO YOU FOR A MOMENT?

ERASERS?!

YOU MUST BE MAX, RIGHT?

NO... SOMETHING'S DIFFERENT.

WE'RE FROM THE FEDERAL BUREAU OF INVESTIGATION.

MY NAME IS ANNE WALKER.

FBI

AND WE'RE ON YOUR SIDE. WE JUST BECAME AWARE THAT YOU WERE HAVING SOME TROUBLE HERE...

...SO WE CAME TO SEE IF WE COULD HELP.

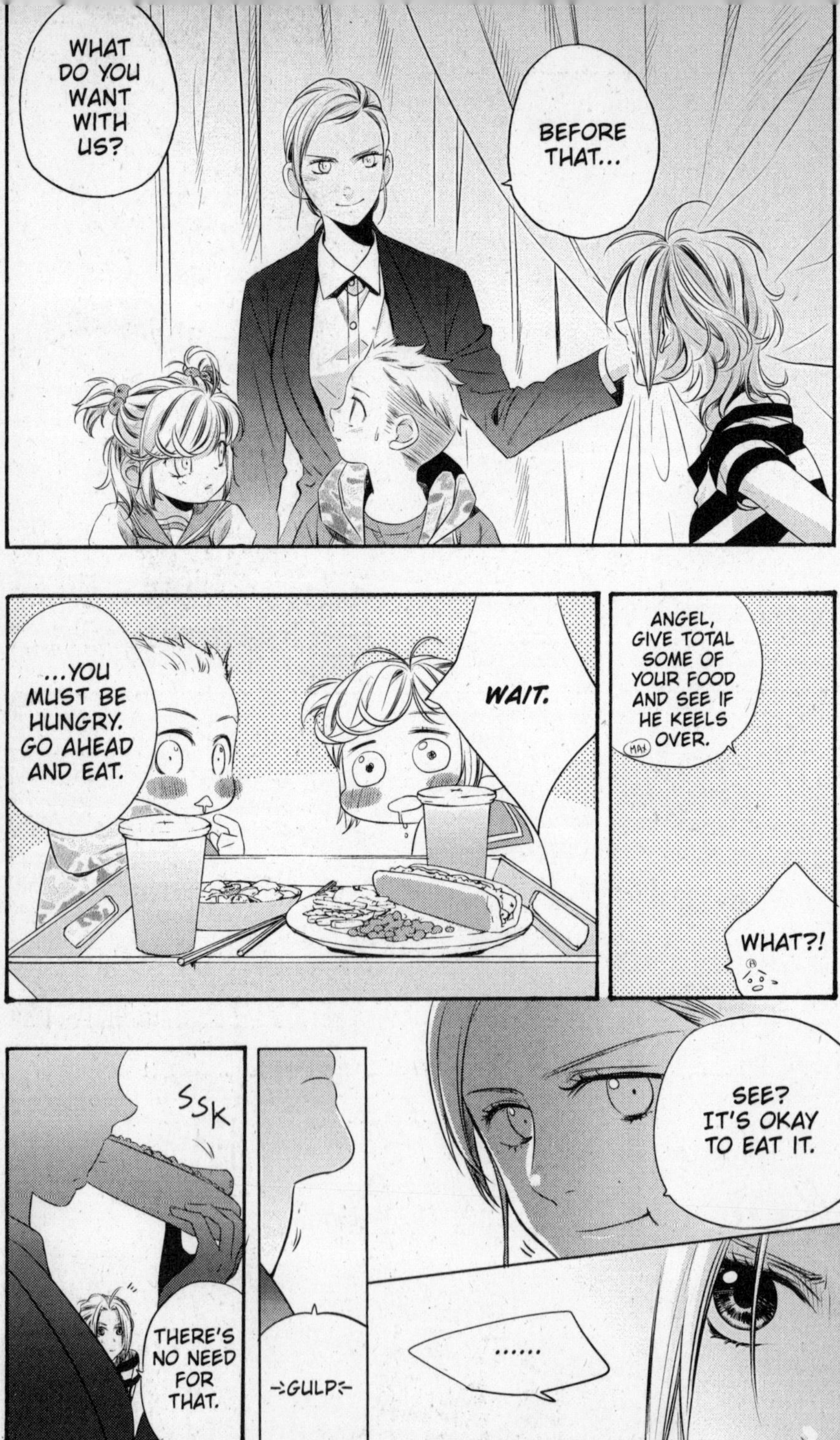
WHAT DO YOU WANT WITH US?
BEFORE THAT...
...YOU MUST BE HUNGRY. GO AHEAD AND EAT.
WAIT.
ANGEL, GIVE TOTAL SOME OF YOUR FOOD AND SEE IF HE KEELS OVER.
WHAT?!
SSK
THERE'S NO NEED FOR THAT.
GULP
SEE? IT'S OKAY TO EAT IT.
......

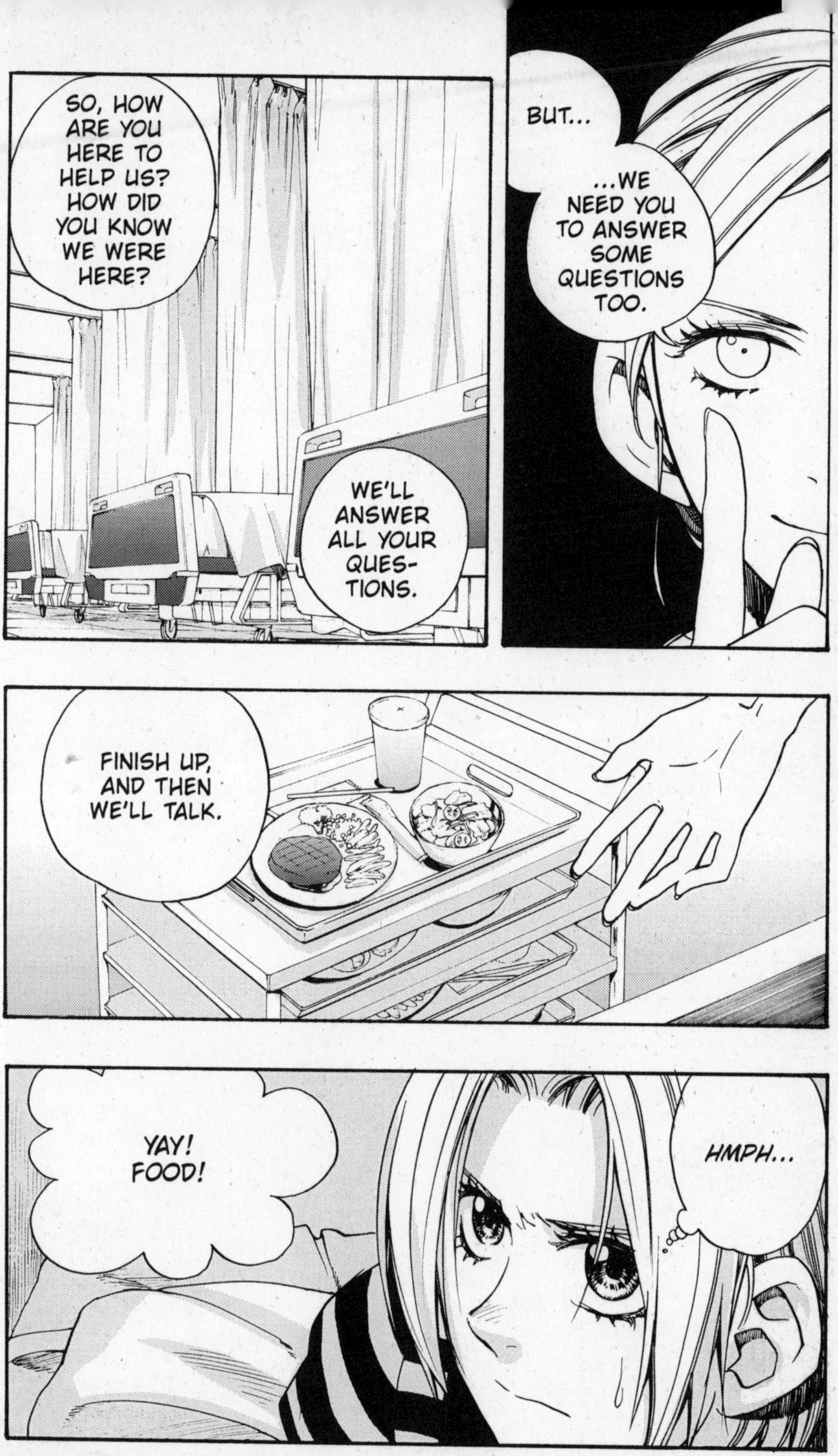
SO, HOW ARE YOU HERE TO HELP US? HOW DID YOU KNOW WE WERE HERE?
WE'LL ANSWER ALL YOUR QUES-TIONS.
BUT...
...WE NEED YOU TO ANSWER SOME QUESTIONS TOO.
FINISH UP, AND THEN WE'LL TALK.
YAY! FOOD!
HMPH...

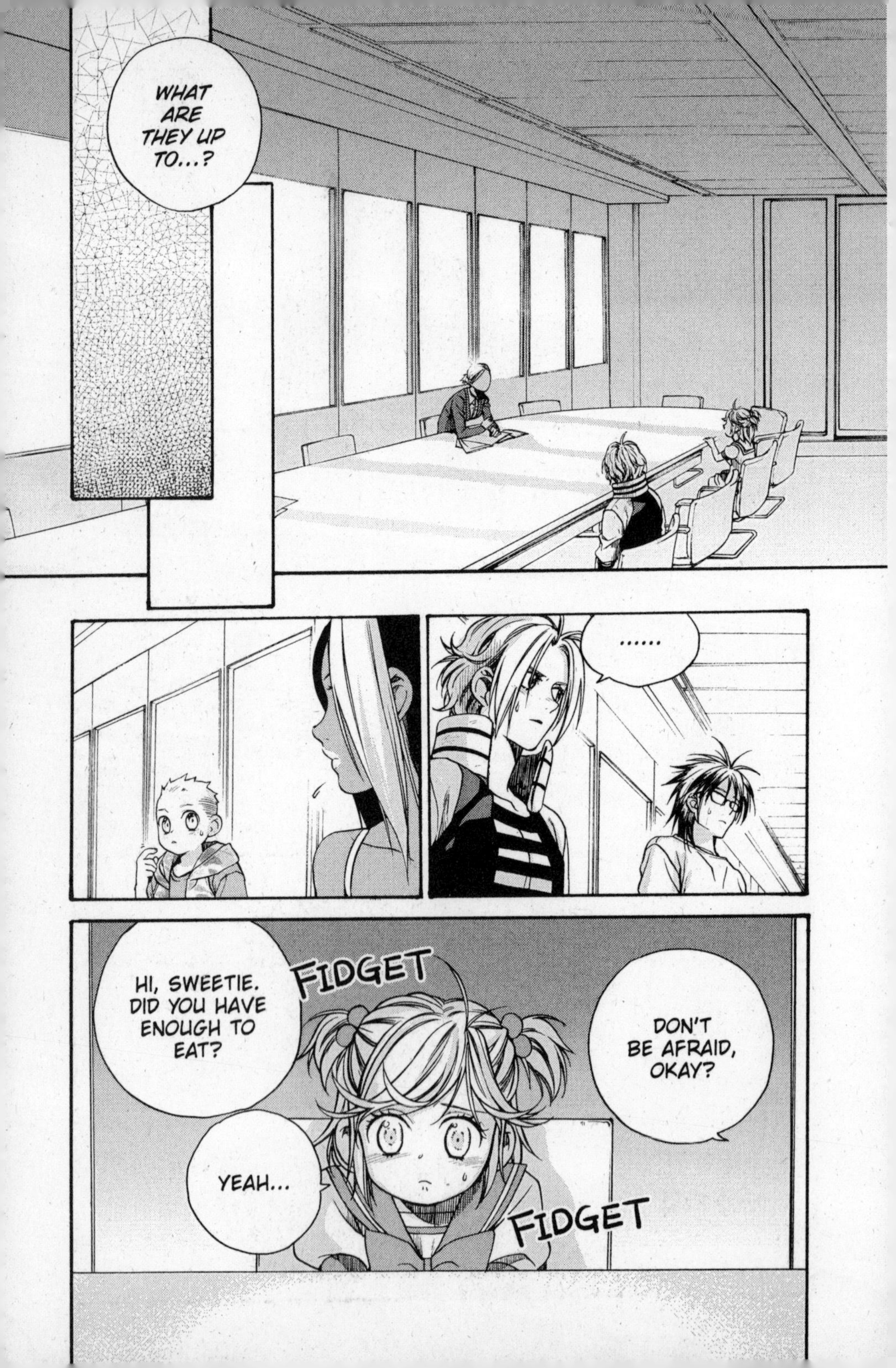
WHAT ARE THEY UP TO...?
......
HI, SWEETIE. DID YOU HAVE ENOUGH TO EAT?
FIDGET
DON'T BE AFRAID, OKAY?
YEAH...
FIDGET

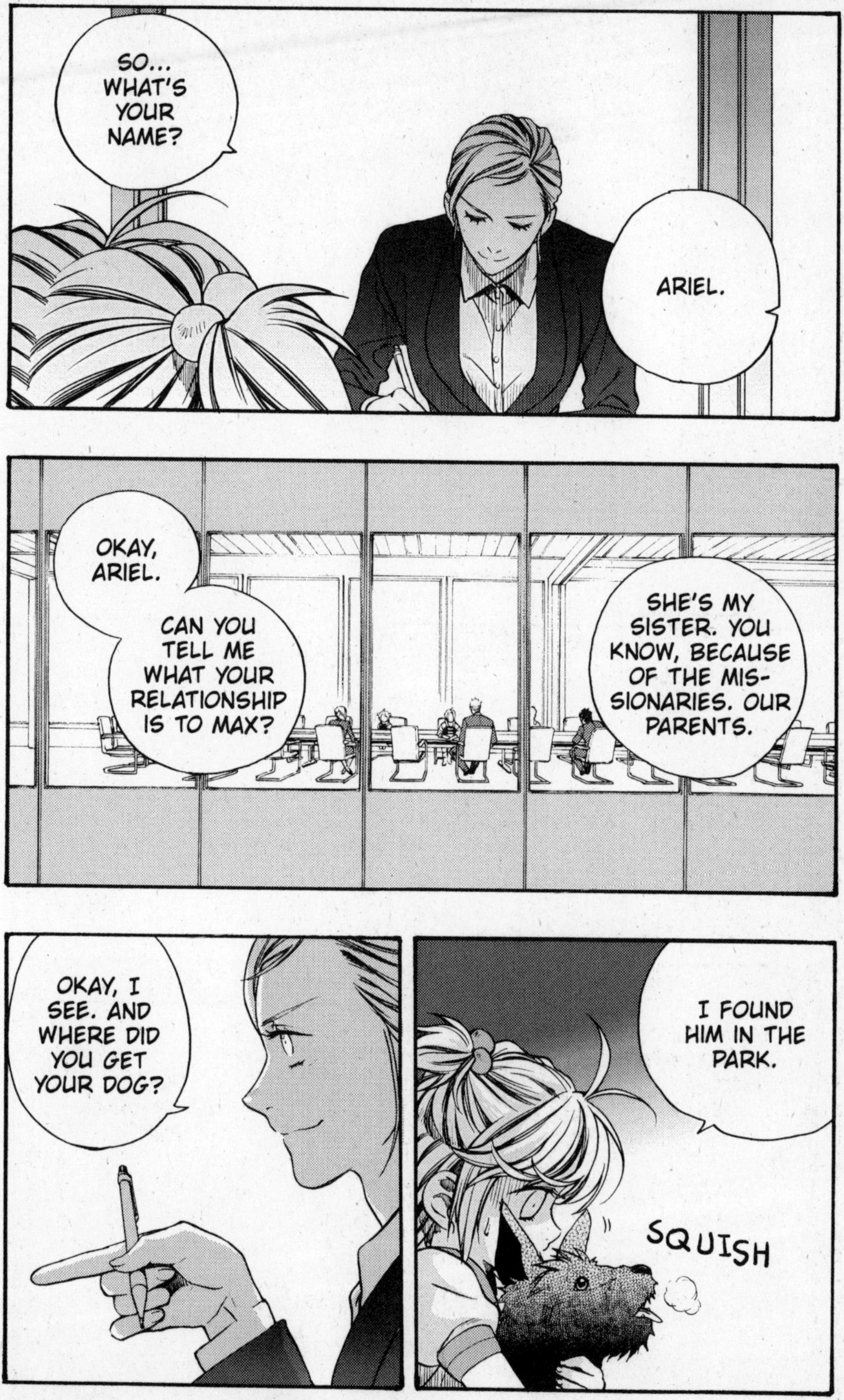
SO... WHAT'S YOUR NAME?
ARIEL.
OKAY, ARIEL.
CAN YOU TELL ME WHAT YOUR RELATIONSHIP IS TO MAX?
SHE'S MY SISTER. YOU KNOW, BECAUSE OF THE MIS- SIONARIES. OUR PARENTS.
OKAY, I SEE. AND WHERE DID YOU GET YOUR DOG?
I FOUND HIM IN THE PARK.
SQUISH

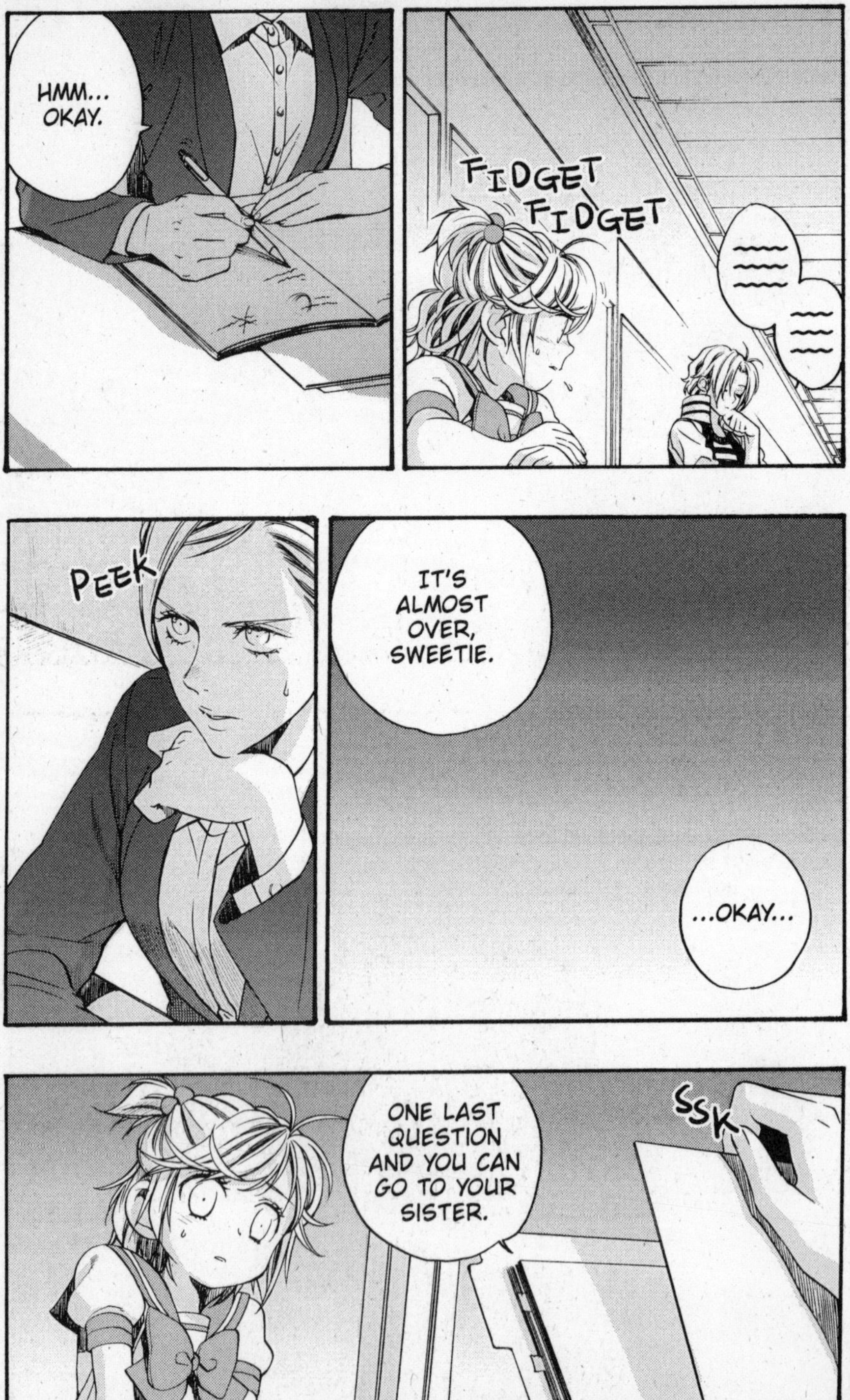
HMM... OKAY.
FIDGET FIDGET
......
......
PEEK
IT'S ALMOST OVER, SWEETIE.
...OKAY...
ONE LAST QUESTION AND YOU CAN GO TO YOUR SISTER.
SSK

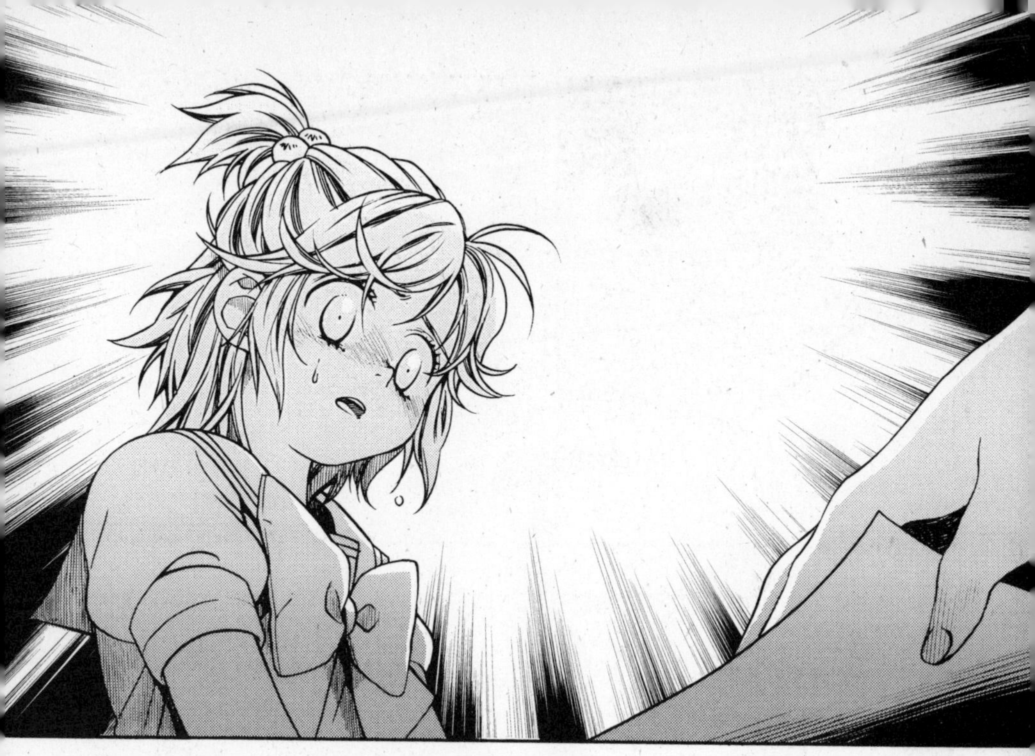

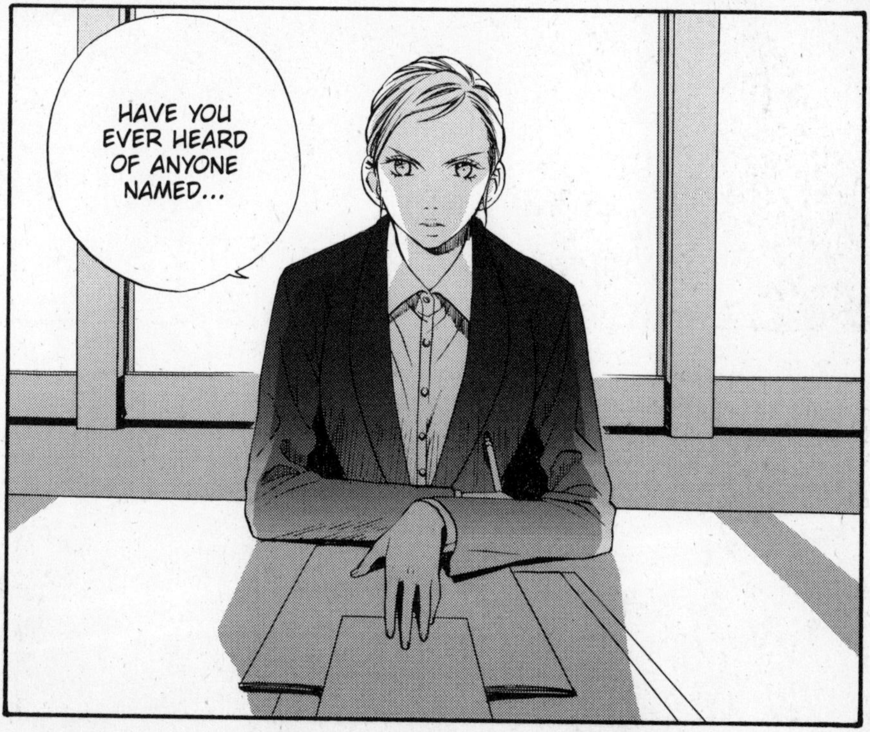
HAVE YOU EVER HEARD OF ANYONE NAMED...

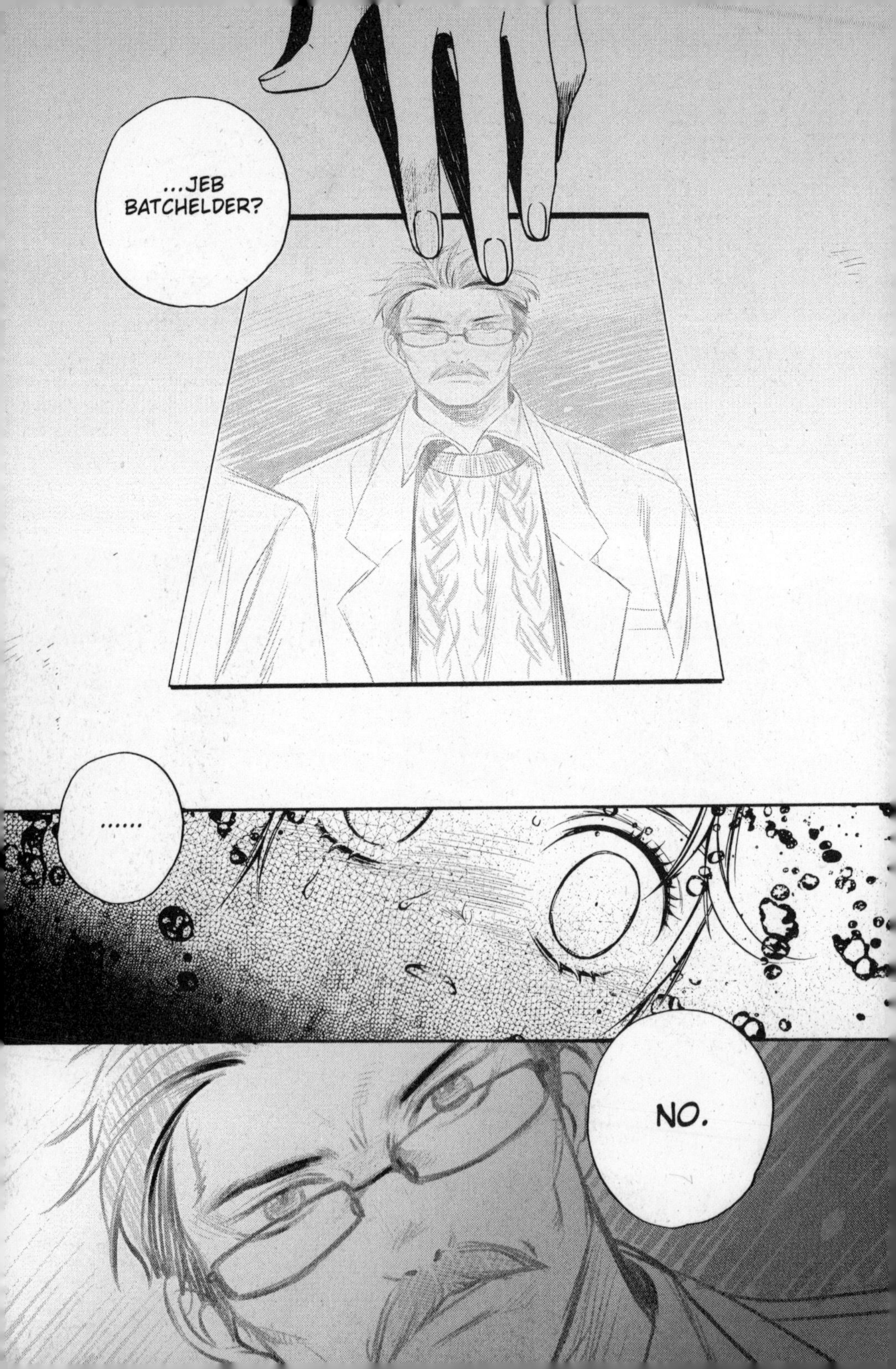
...JEB BATCHELDER?
......
NO.

MAXIMUM RIDE
CHAPTER 17

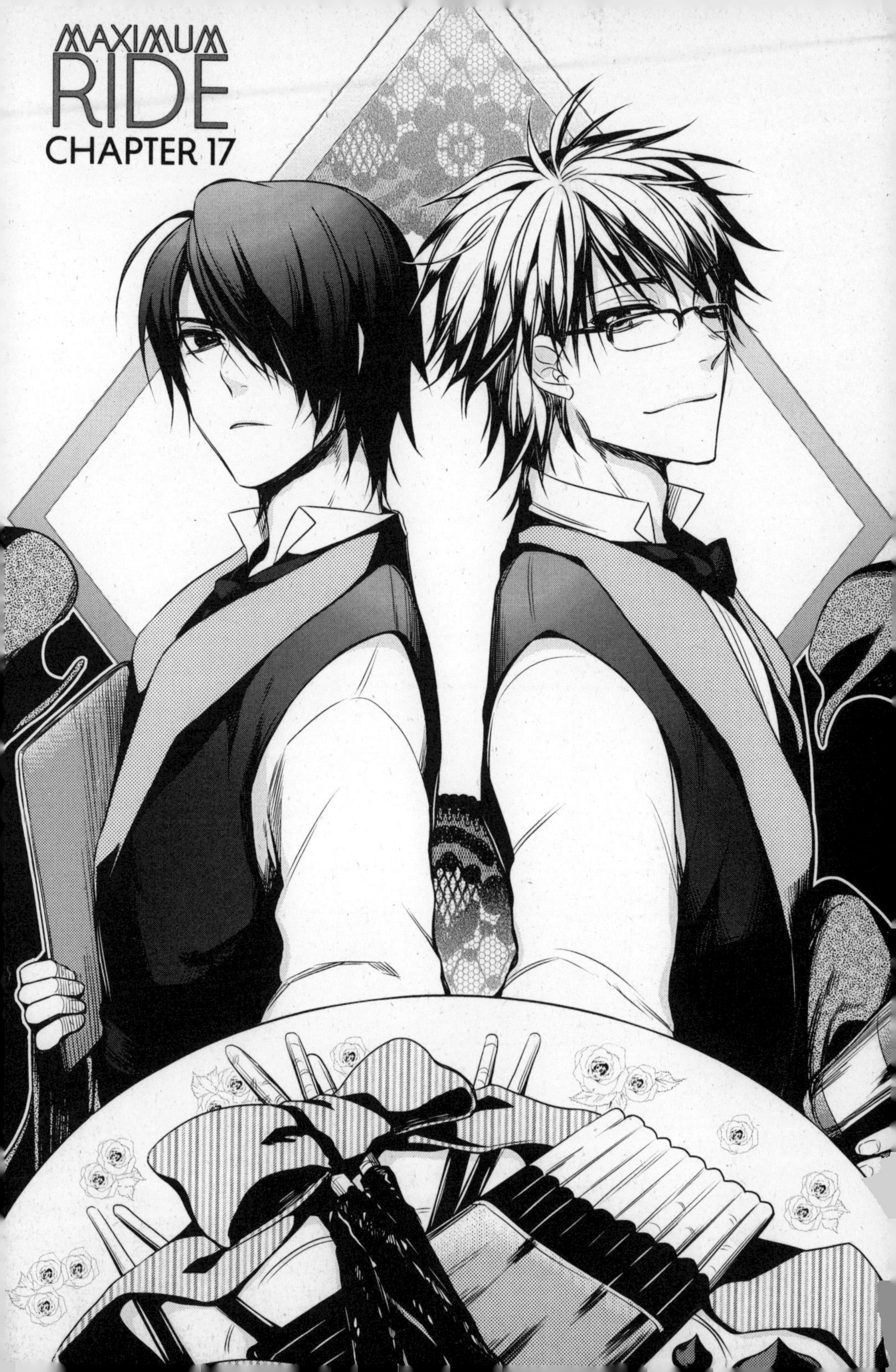

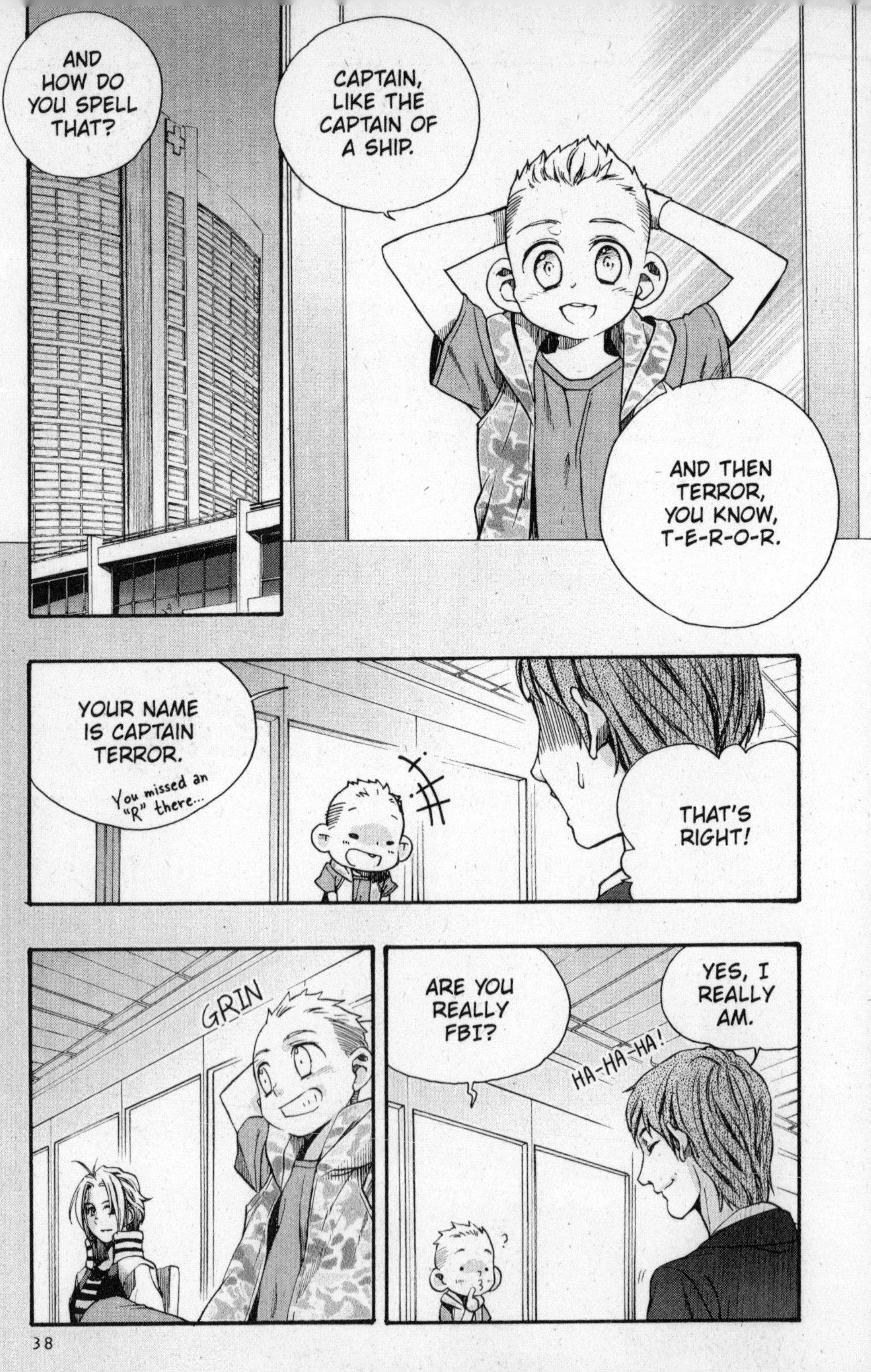
AND HOW DO YOU SPELL THAT?
CAPTAIN, LIKE THE CAPTAIN OF A SHIP.
AND THEN TERROR, YOU KNOW, T-E-R-O-R.
YOUR NAME IS CAPTAIN TERROR.
You missed an "R" there...
THAT'S RIGHT!
GRIN
ARE YOU REALLY FBI?
YES, I REALLY AM.
HA-HA-HA!

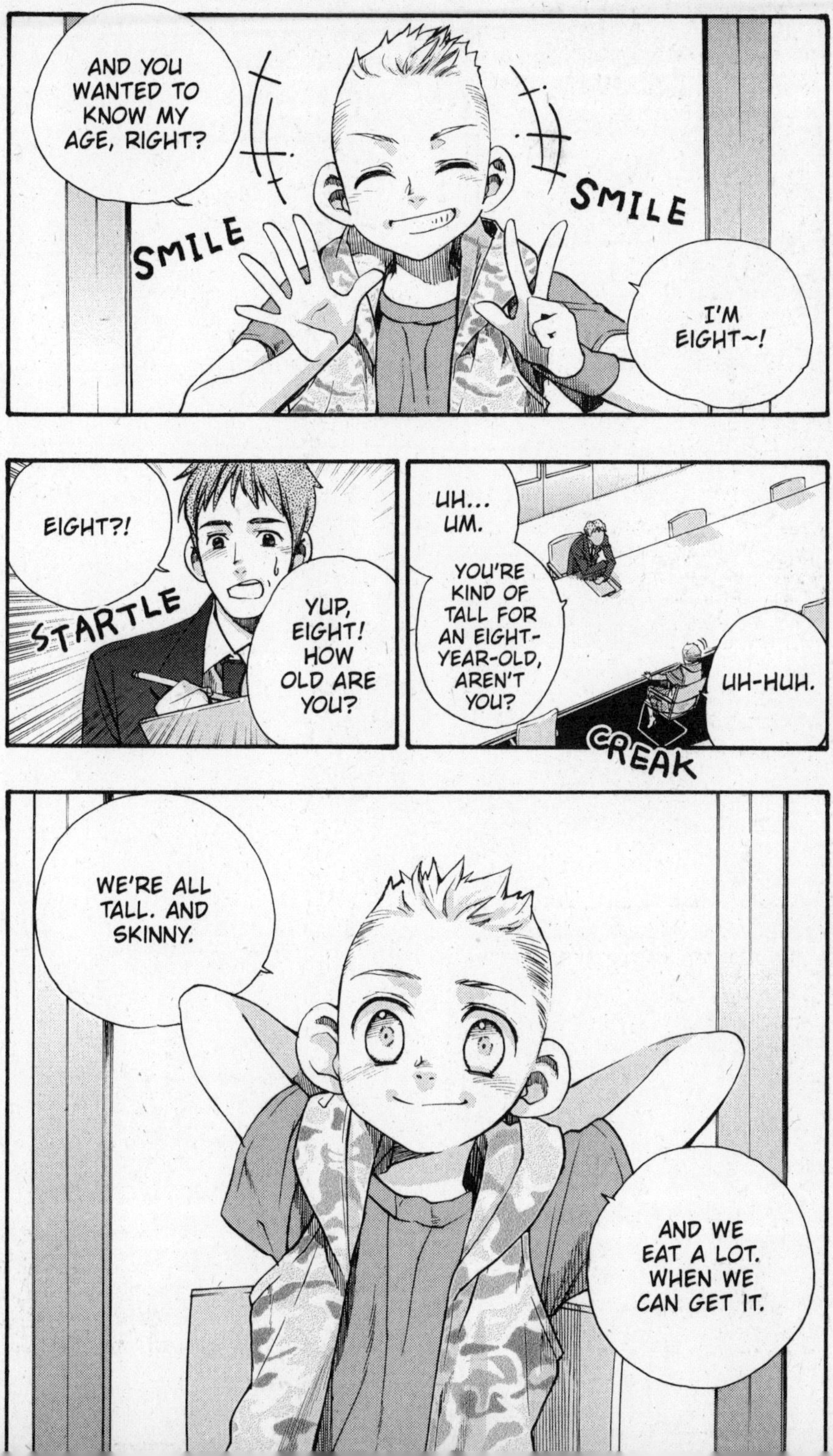
AND YOU WANTED TO KNOW MY AGE, RIGHT?
SMILE
SMILE
I'M EIGHT~!
EIGHT?!
STARTLE
YUP, EIGHT! HOW OLD ARE YOU?
UH... UM.
YOU'RE KIND OF TALL FOR AN EIGHT-YEAR-OLD, AREN'T YOU?
UH-HUH.
CREAK
WE'RE ALL TALL. AND SKINNY.
AND WE EAT A LOT. WHEN WE CAN GET IT.

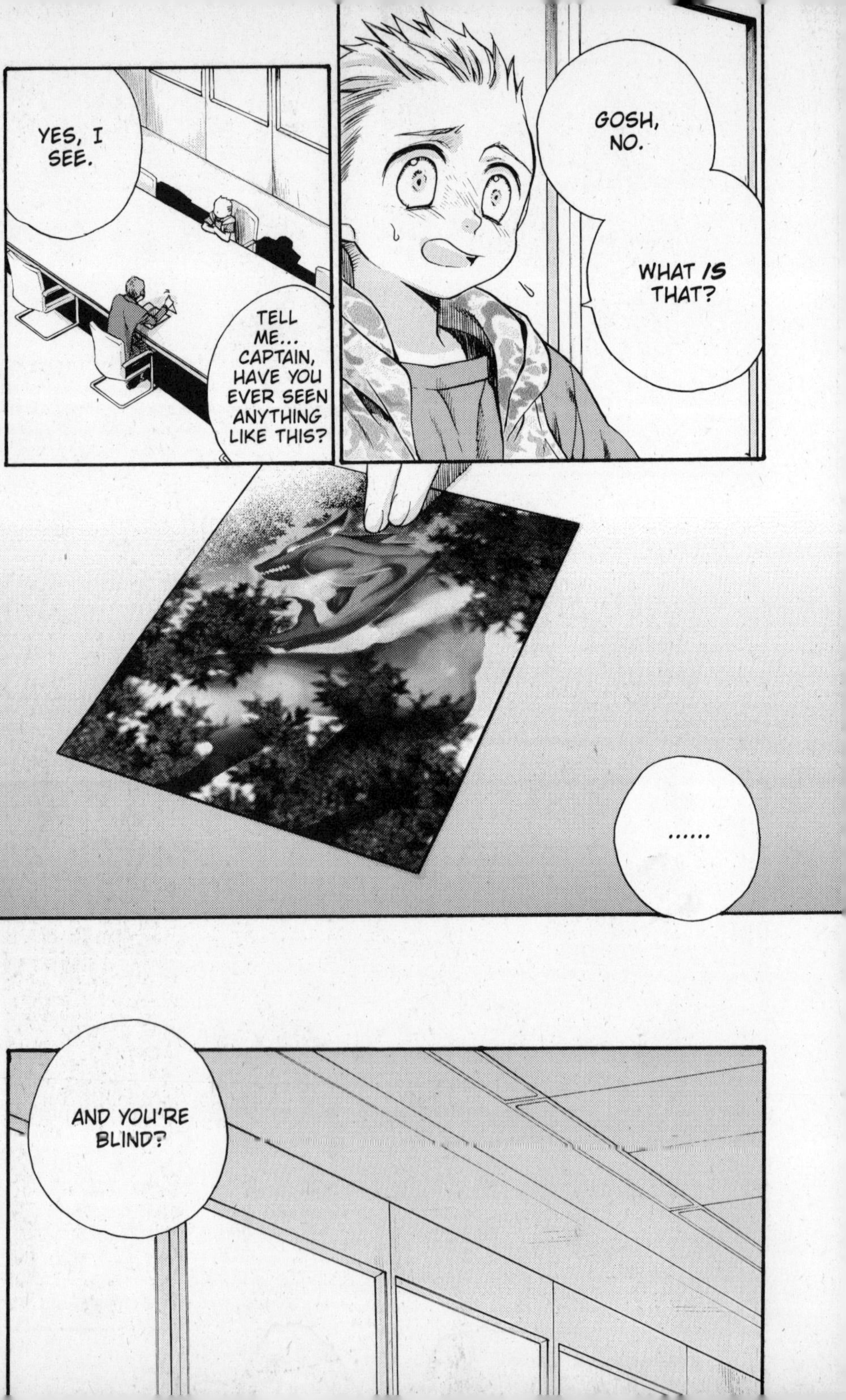
YES, I SEE.
TELL ME... CAPTAIN, HAVE YOU EVER SEEN ANYTHING LIKE THIS?
GOSH, NO.
WHAT IS THAT?
......
AND YOU'RE BLIND?

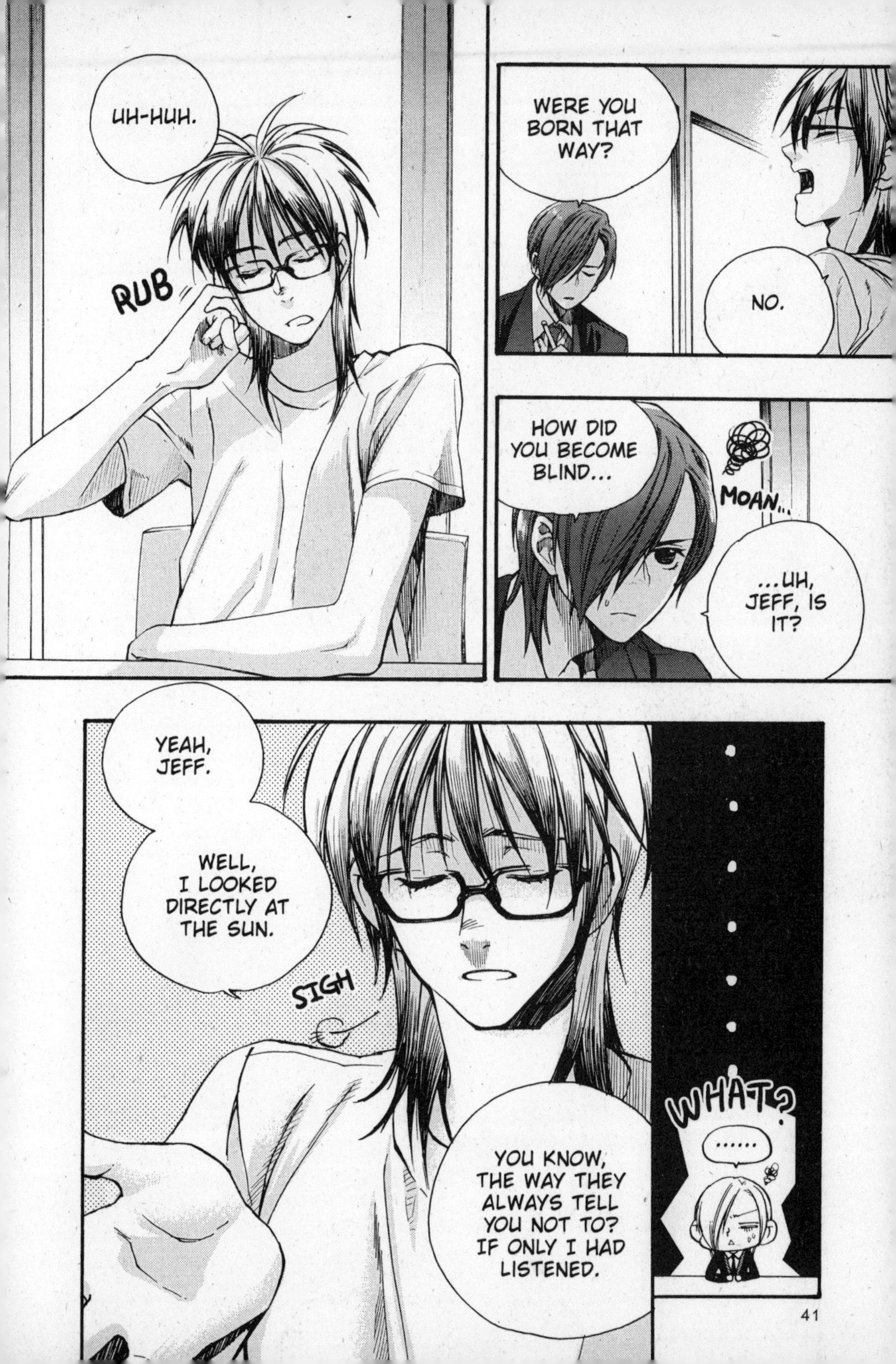
UH-HUH.
RUB
WERE YOU BORN THAT WAY?
NO.
HOW DID YOU BECOME BLIND...
MOAN..
...UH, JEFF, IS IT?
YEAH, JEFF.
WELL, I LOOKED DIRECTLY AT THE SUN.
SIGH
YOU KNOW, THE WAY THEY ALWAYS TELL YOU NOT TO? IF ONLY I HAD LISTENED.
WHAT?
......

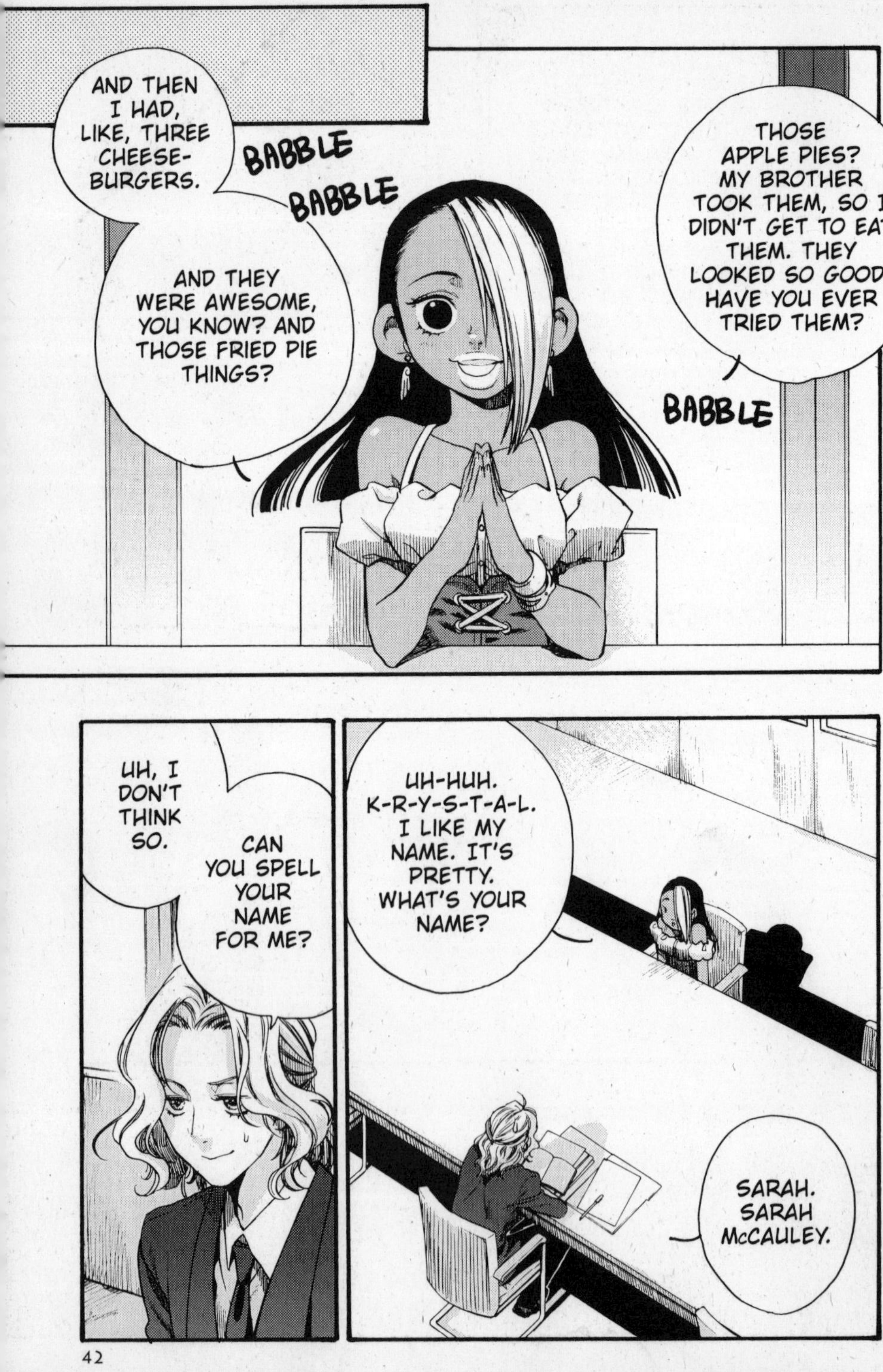
AND THEN I HAD, LIKE, THREE CHEESE-BURGERS.
BABBLE
BABBLE
AND THEY WERE AWESOME, YOU KNOW? AND THOSE FRIED PIE THINGS?
THOSE APPLE PIES? MY BROTHER TOOK THEM, SO I DIDN'T GET TO EAT THEM. THEY LOOKED SO GOOD. HAVE YOU EVER TRIED THEM?
BABBLE
UH, I DON'T THINK SO.
CAN YOU SPELL YOUR NAME FOR ME?
UH-HUH. K-R-Y-S-T-A-L. I LIKE MY NAME. IT'S PRETTY. WHAT'S YOUR NAME?
SARAH. SARAH McCAULEY.

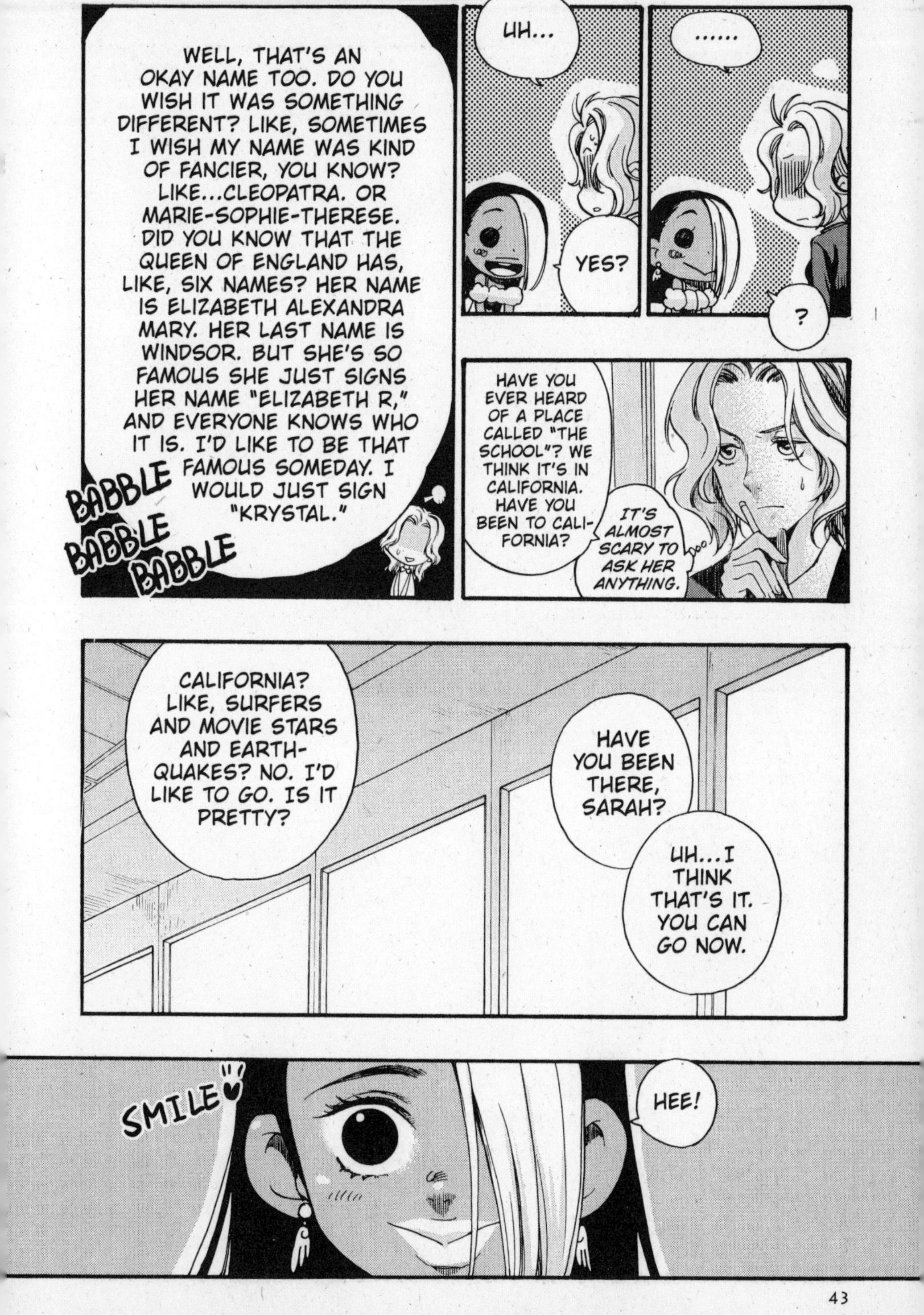
WELL, THAT'S AN OKAY NAME TOO. DO YOU WISH IT WAS SOMETHING DIFFERENT? LIKE, SOMETIMES I WISH MY NAME WAS KIND OF FANCIER, YOU KNOW? LIKE...CLEOPATRA. OR MARIE-SOPHIE-THERESE. DID YOU KNOW THAT THE QUEEN OF ENGLAND HAS, LIKE, SIX NAMES? HER NAME IS ELIZABETH ALEXANDRA MARY. HER LAST NAME IS WINDSOR. BUT SHE'S SO FAMOUS SHE JUST SIGNS HER NAME "ELIZABETH R," AND EVERYONE KNOWS WHO IT IS. I'D LIKE TO BE THAT FAMOUS SOMEDAY. I WOULD JUST SIGN "KRYSTAL."
BABBLE BABBLE BABBLE
UH...
YES?
....
?
HAVE YOU EVER HEARD OF A PLACE CALLED "THE SCHOOL"? WE THINK IT'S IN CALIFORNIA. HAVE YOU BEEN TO CALIFORNIA?
IT'S ALMOST SCARY TO ASK HER ANYTHING.
CALIFORNIA? LIKE, SURFERS AND MOVIE STARS AND EARTHQUAKES? NO. I'D LIKE TO GO. IS IT PRETTY?
HAVE YOU BEEN THERE, SARAH?
UH...I THINK THAT'S IT. YOU CAN GO NOW.
SMILE
HEE!

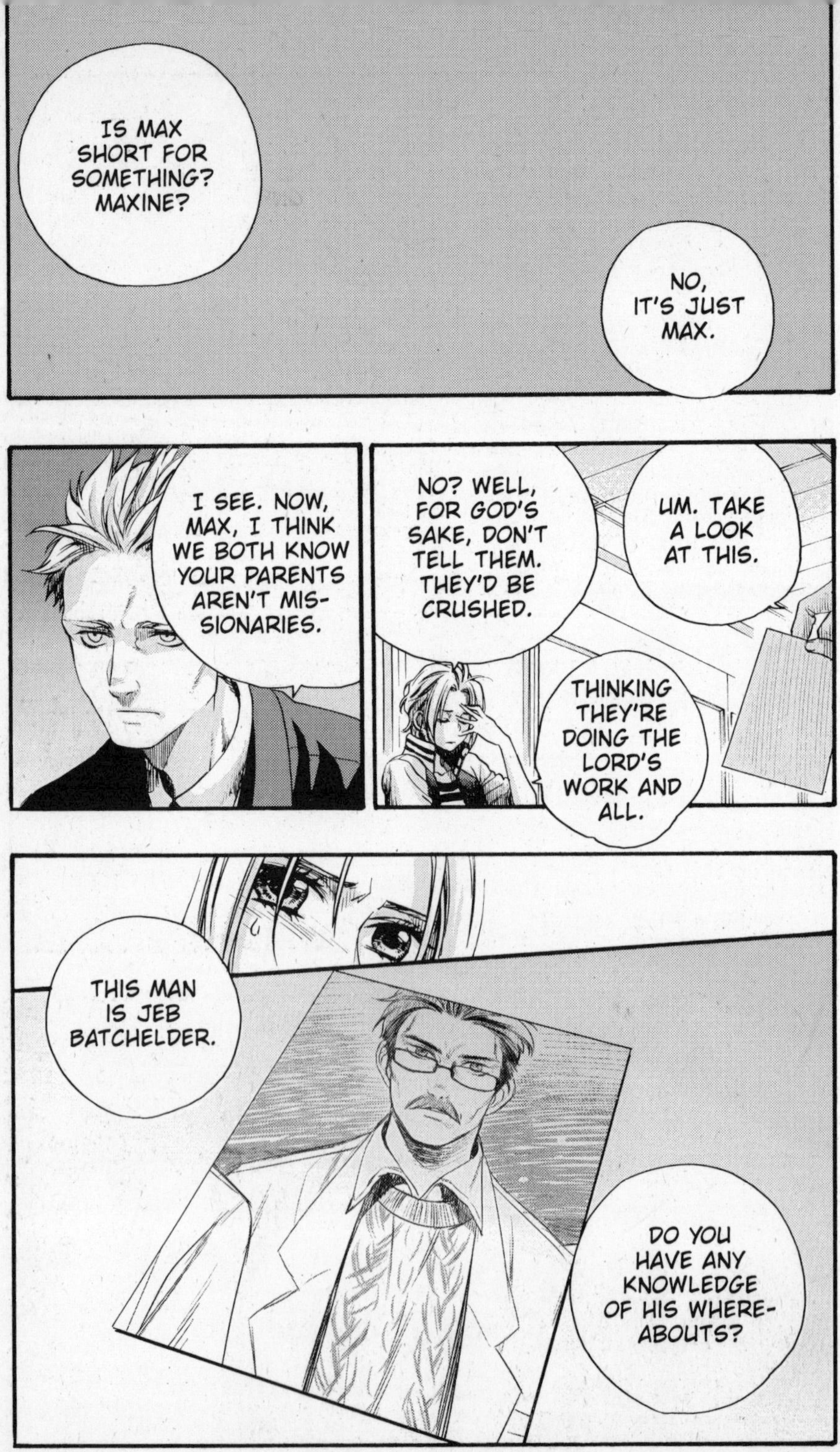
IS MAX SHORT FOR SOMETHING? MAXINE?
NO, IT'S JUST MAX.
I SEE. NOW, MAX, I THINK WE BOTH KNOW YOUR PARENTS AREN'T MIS-SIONARIES.
NO? WELL, FOR GOD'S SAKE, DON'T TELL THEM. THEY'D BE CRUSHED.
THINKING THEY'RE DOING THE LORD'S WORK AND ALL.
UM. TAKE A LOOK AT THIS.
THIS MAN IS JEB BATCHELDER.
DO YOU HAVE ANY KNOWLEDGE OF HIS WHERE-ABOUTS?

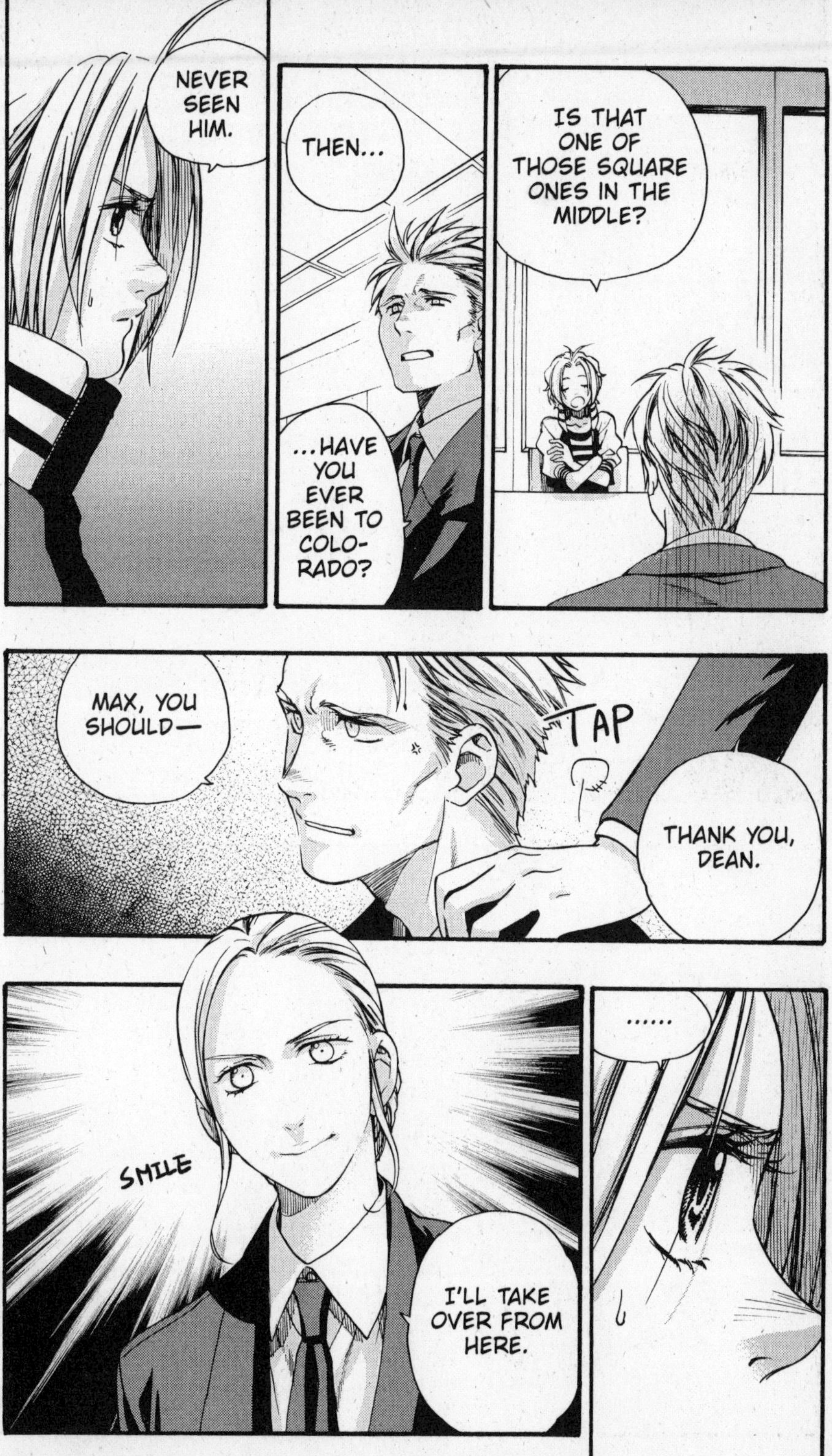
NEVER SEEN HIM.
THEN...
...HAVE YOU EVER BEEN TO COLO-RADO?
IS THAT ONE OF THOSE SQUARE ONES IN THE MIDDLE?
MAX, YOU SHOULD—
TAP
THANK YOU, DEAN.
SMILE
I'LL TAKE OVER FROM HERE.
......

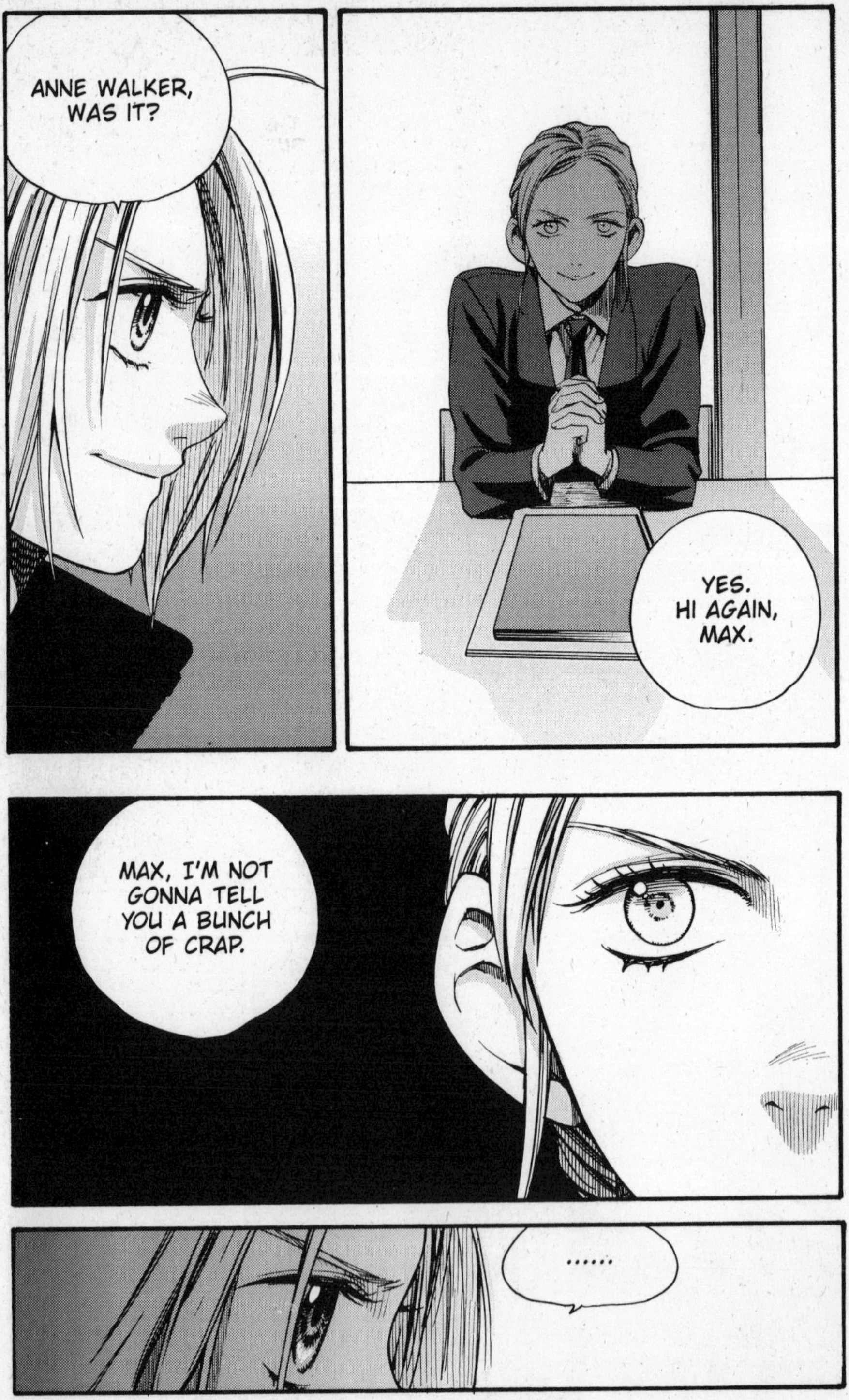
ANNE WALKER, WAS IT?
YES. HI AGAIN, MAX.
MAX, I'M NOT GONNA TELL YOU A BUNCH OF CRAP.
......

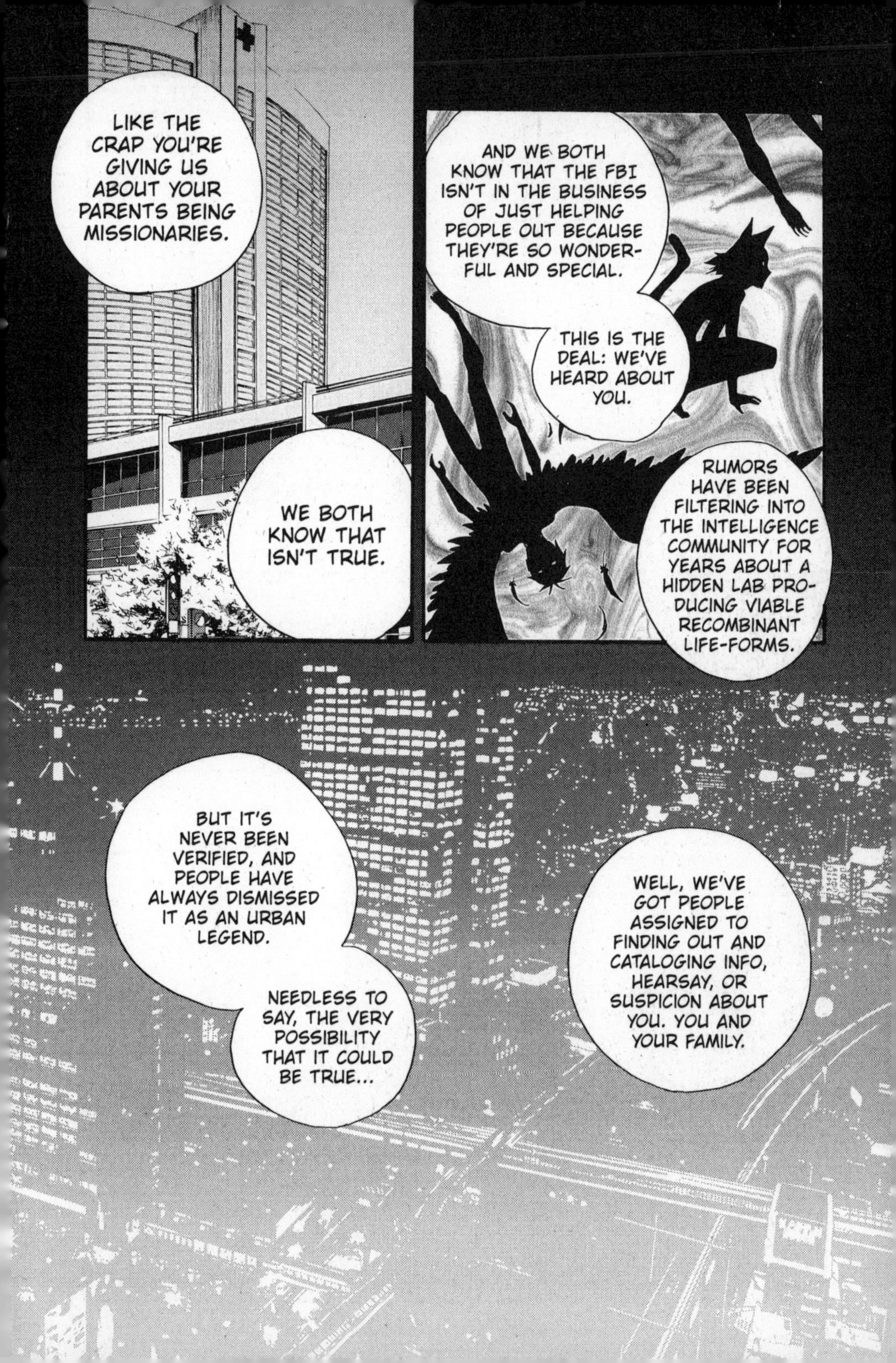
LIKE THE CRAP YOU'RE GIVING US ABOUT YOUR PARENTS BEING MISSIONARIES.
WE BOTH KNOW THAT ISN'T TRUE.
AND WE BOTH KNOW THAT THE FBI ISN'T IN THE BUSINESS OF JUST HELPING PEOPLE OUT BECAUSE THEY'RE SO WONDERFUL AND SPECIAL.
THIS IS THE DEAL: WE'VE HEARD ABOUT YOU.
RUMORS HAVE BEEN FILTERING INTO THE INTELLIGENCE COMMUNITY FOR YEARS ABOUT A HIDDEN LAB PRODUCING VIABLE RECOMBINANT LIFE-FORMS.
BUT IT'S NEVER BEEN VERIFIED, AND PEOPLE HAVE ALWAYS DISMISSED IT AS AN URBAN LEGEND.
NEEDLESS TO SAY, THE VERY POSSIBILITY THAT IT COULD BE TRUE...
WELL, WE'VE GOT PEOPLE ASSIGNED TO FINDING OUT AND CATALOGING INFO, HEARSAY, OR SUSPICION ABOUT YOU. YOU AND YOUR FAMILY.

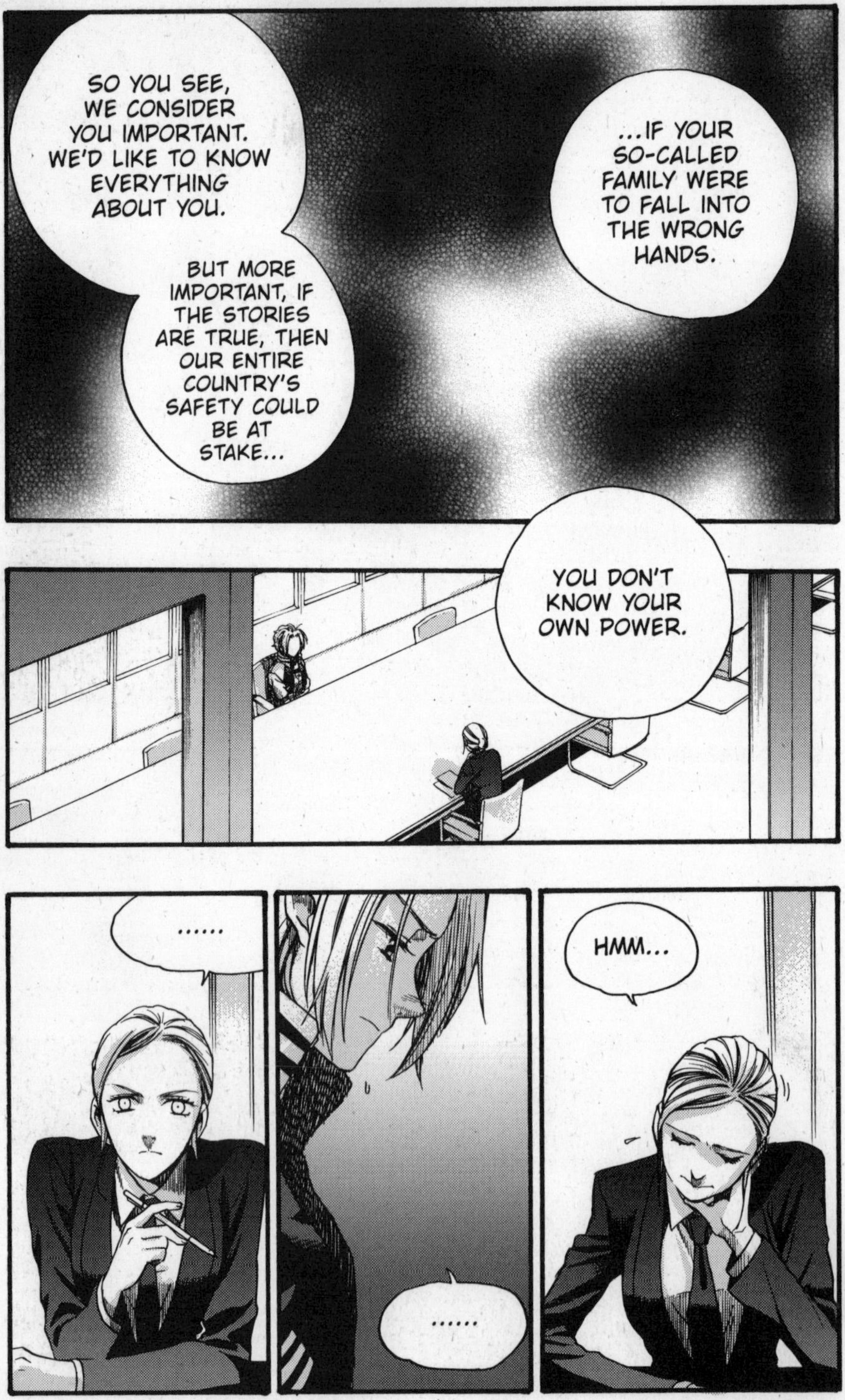
SO YOU SEE, WE CONSIDER YOU IMPORTANT. WE'D LIKE TO KNOW EVERYTHING ABOUT YOU.
BUT MORE IMPORTANT, IF THE STORIES ARE TRUE, THEN OUR ENTIRE COUNTRY'S SAFETY COULD BE AT STAKE...
...IF YOUR SO-CALLED FAMILY WERE TO FALL INTO THE WRONG HANDS.
YOU DON'T KNOW YOUR OWN POWER.
......
......
HMM...

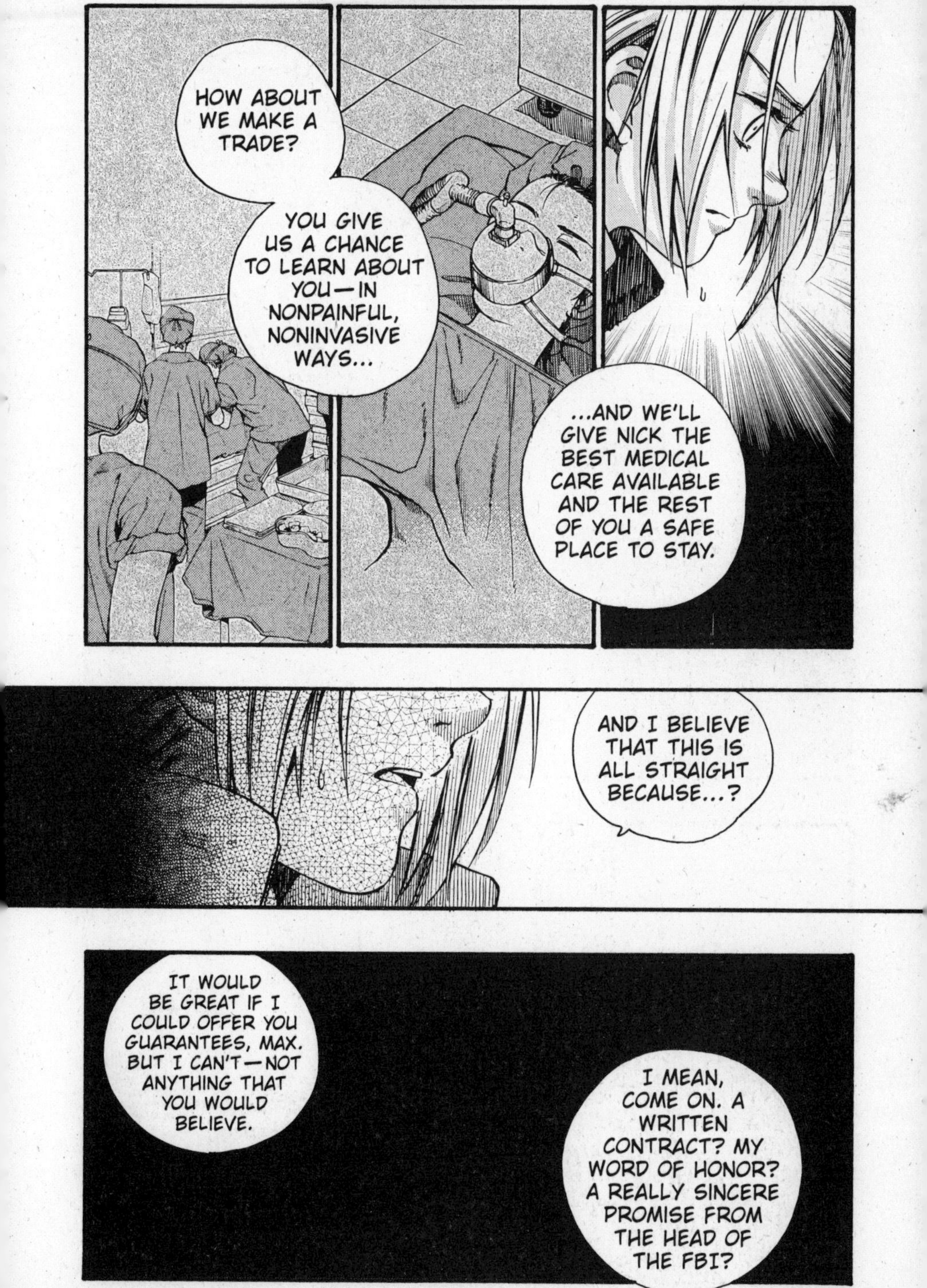
HOW ABOUT WE MAKE A TRADE?
YOU GIVE US A CHANCE TO LEARN ABOUT YOU—IN NONPAINFUL, NONINVASIVE WAYS...
...AND WE'LL GIVE NICK THE BEST MEDICAL CARE AVAILABLE AND THE REST OF YOU A SAFE PLACE TO STAY.
AND I BELIEVE THAT THIS IS ALL STRAIGHT BECAUSE...?
IT WOULD BE GREAT IF I COULD OFFER YOU GUARANTEES, MAX. BUT I CAN'T—NOT ANYTHING THAT YOU WOULD BELIEVE.
I MEAN, COME ON. A WRITTEN CONTRACT? MY WORD OF HONOR? A REALLY SINCERE PROMISE FROM THE HEAD OF THE FBI?

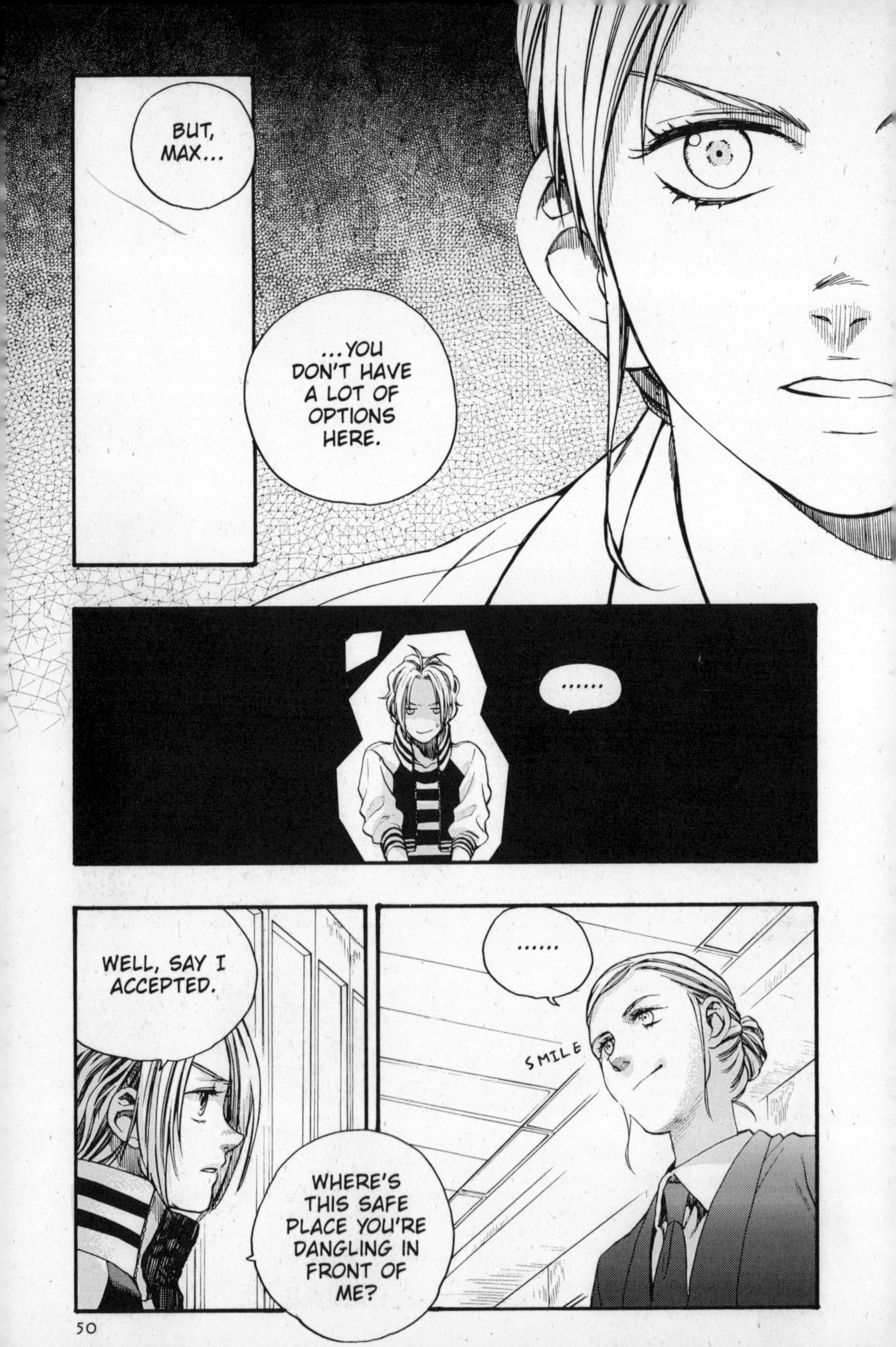
BUT, MAX...
...YOU DON'T HAVE A LOT OF OPTIONS HERE.
......
WELL, SAY I ACCEPTED.
WHERE'S THIS SAFE PLACE YOU'RE DANGLING IN FRONT OF ME?
......
SMILE

MY HOUSE.

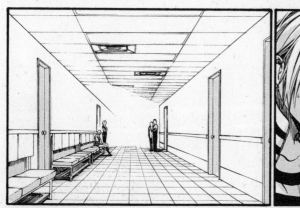

WHAT DO I DO...?

CREAK

MAX,
IS IT?

YES.
HOW DID
IT GO?

YOUR
BROTHER NICK—
IT WAS A LITTLE DICEY
FOR A WHILE. WE GAVE
HIM SEVERAL UNITS OF
BLOOD SUBSTITUTE, AND
IT BROUGHT HIS BLOOD
PRESSURE UP TO A
SAFE RANGE.

WE WERE
ABLE TO PATCH
UP HIS SIDE,
STOP ALL THE
HEMORRHAGING. A
MAIN ARTERY HAD
BEEN HIT, AND
ONE OF HIS...
AIR SACS.

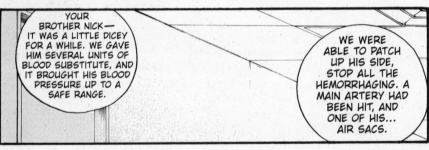

SO
HOW IS HE
NOW?!

FIDGET
FIDGET

HE'S
HOLDING
STEADY.

PHEW...

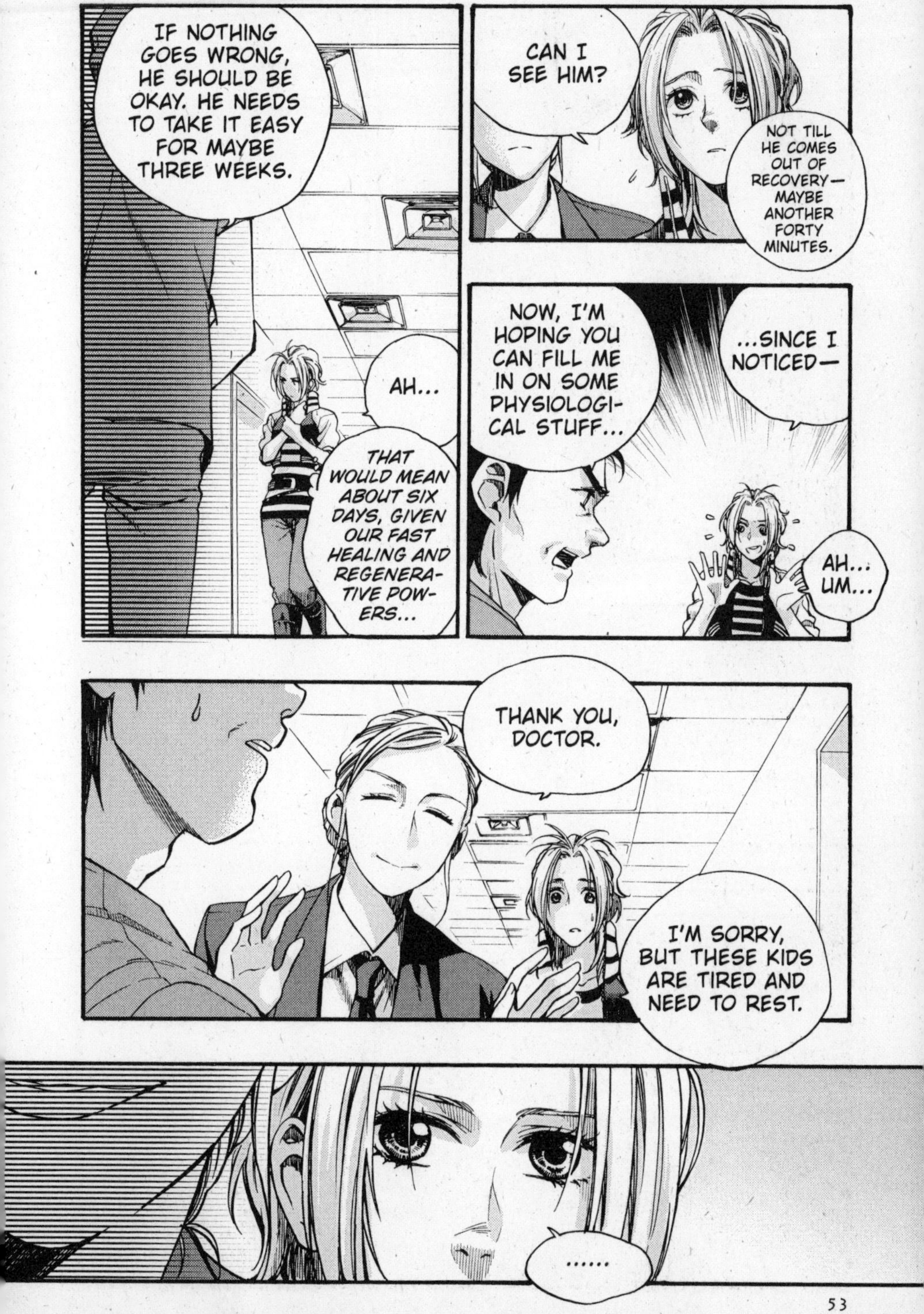
IF NOTHING GOES WRONG, HE SHOULD BE OKAY. HE NEEDS TO TAKE IT EASY FOR MAYBE THREE WEEKS.
AH...
THAT WOULD MEAN ABOUT SIX DAYS, GIVEN OUR FAST HEALING AND REGENERA-TIVE POW-ERS...
CAN I SEE HIM?
NOT TILL HE COMES OUT OF RECOVERY— MAYBE ANOTHER FORTY MINUTES.
NOW, I'M HOPING YOU CAN FILL ME IN ON SOME PHYSIOLOGI-CAL STUFF...
...SINCE I NOTICED—
AH... UM...
THANK YOU, DOCTOR.
I'M SORRY, BUT THESE KIDS ARE TIRED AND NEED TO REST.
......

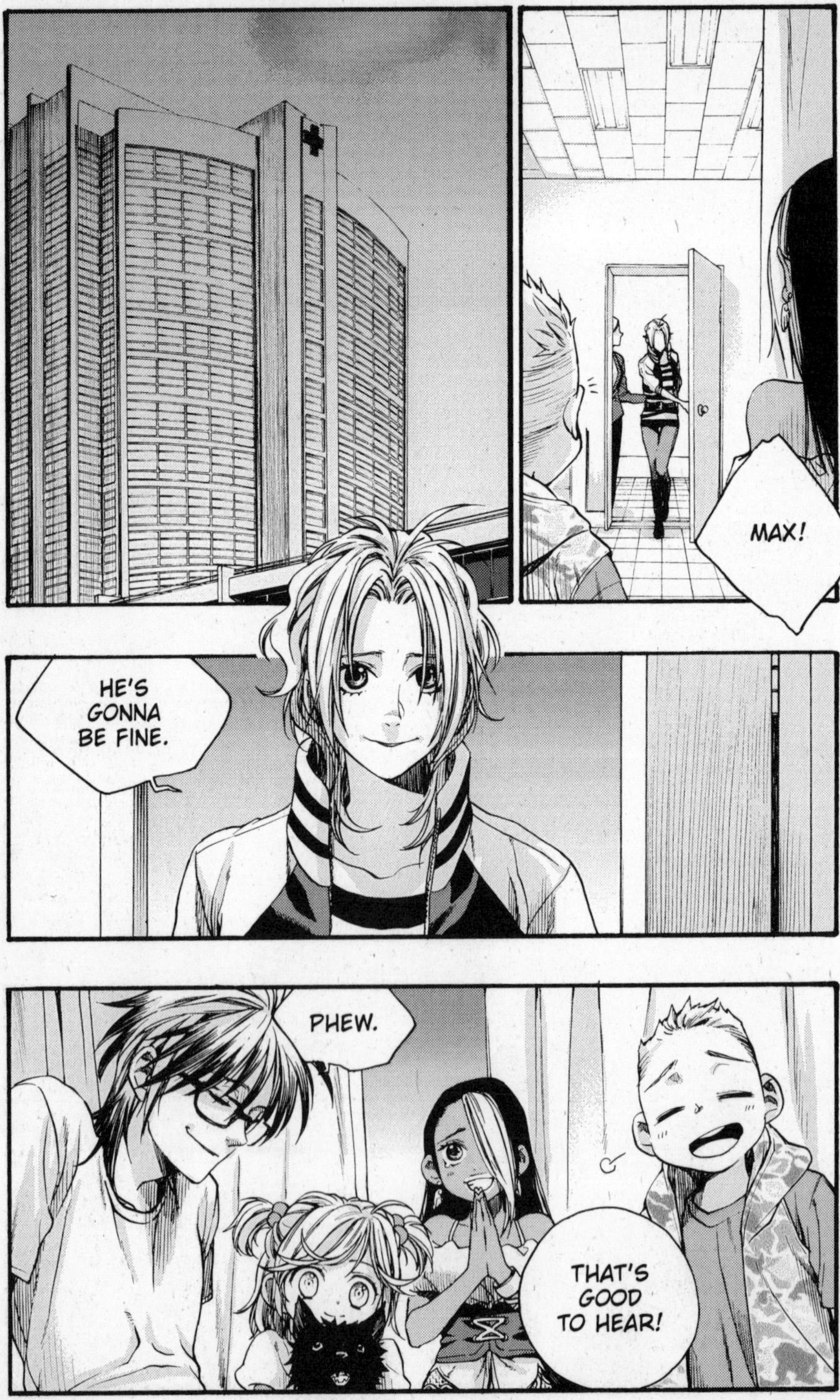
MAX!
HE'S GONNA BE FINE.
PHEW.
THAT'S GOOD TO HEAR!

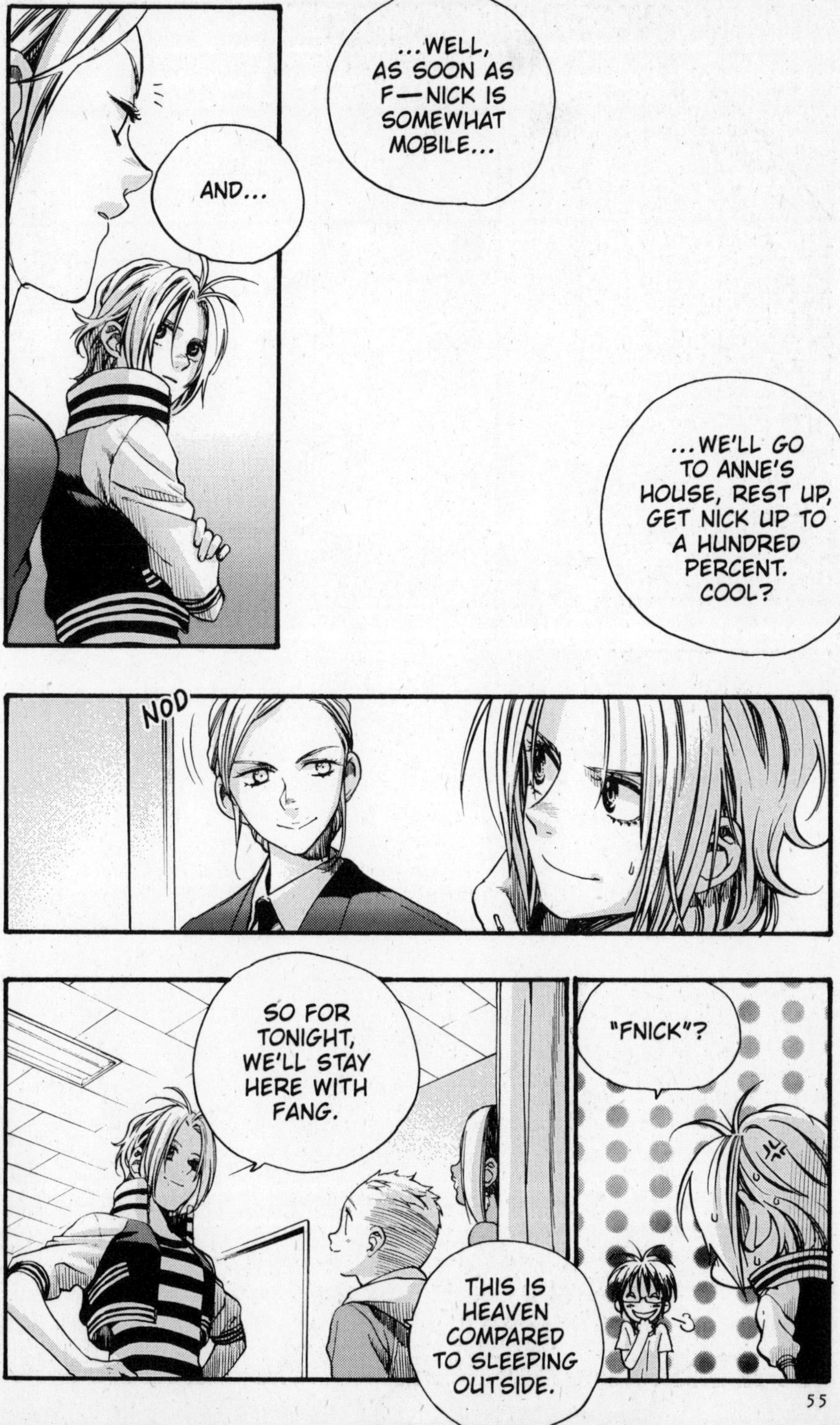

...WELL, AS SOON AS F—NICK IS SOMEWHAT MOBILE...
AND...
...WE'LL GO TO ANNE'S HOUSE, REST UP, GET NICK UP TO A HUNDRED PERCENT. COOL?
NOD
SO FOR TONIGHT, WE'LL STAY HERE WITH FANG.
THIS IS HEAVEN COMPARED TO SLEEPING OUTSIDE.
"FNICK"?

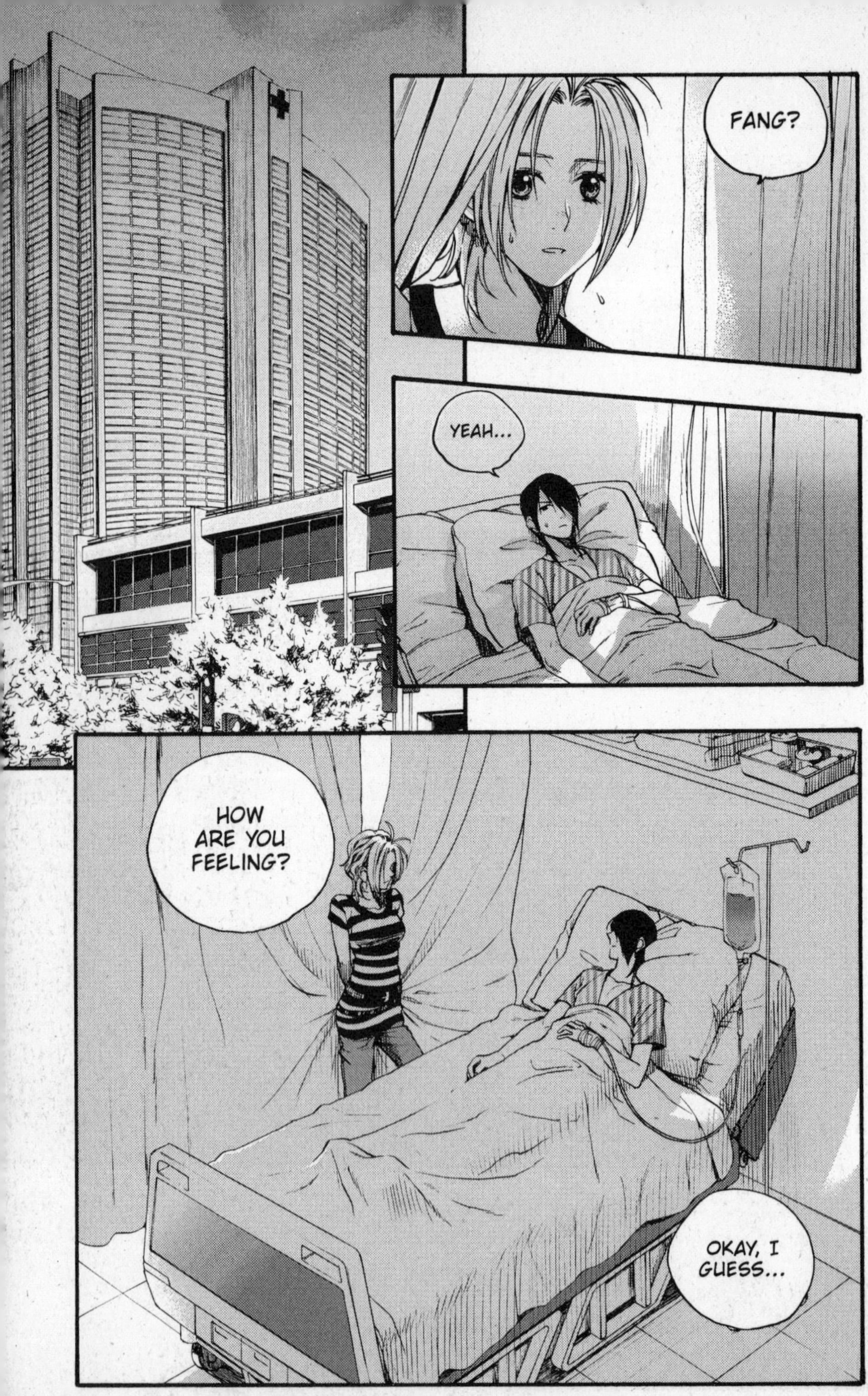
FANG?
YEAH...
HOW ARE YOU FEELING?
OKAY, I GUESS...

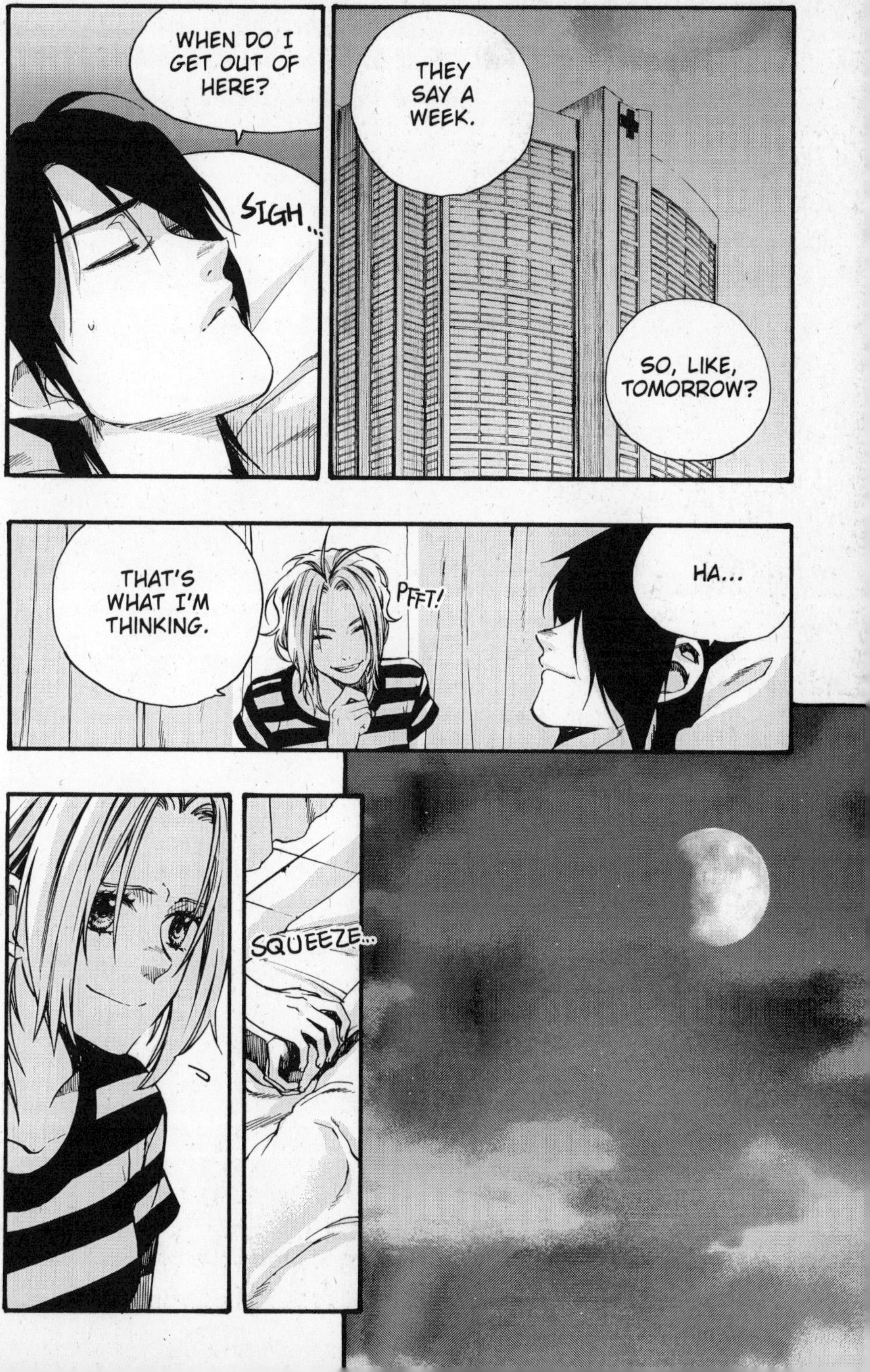
WHEN DO I GET OUT OF HERE?
SIGH...
THEY SAY A WEEK.
SO, LIKE, TOMORROW?
THAT'S WHAT I'M THINKING.
PFFT!
HA...
SQUEEZE...

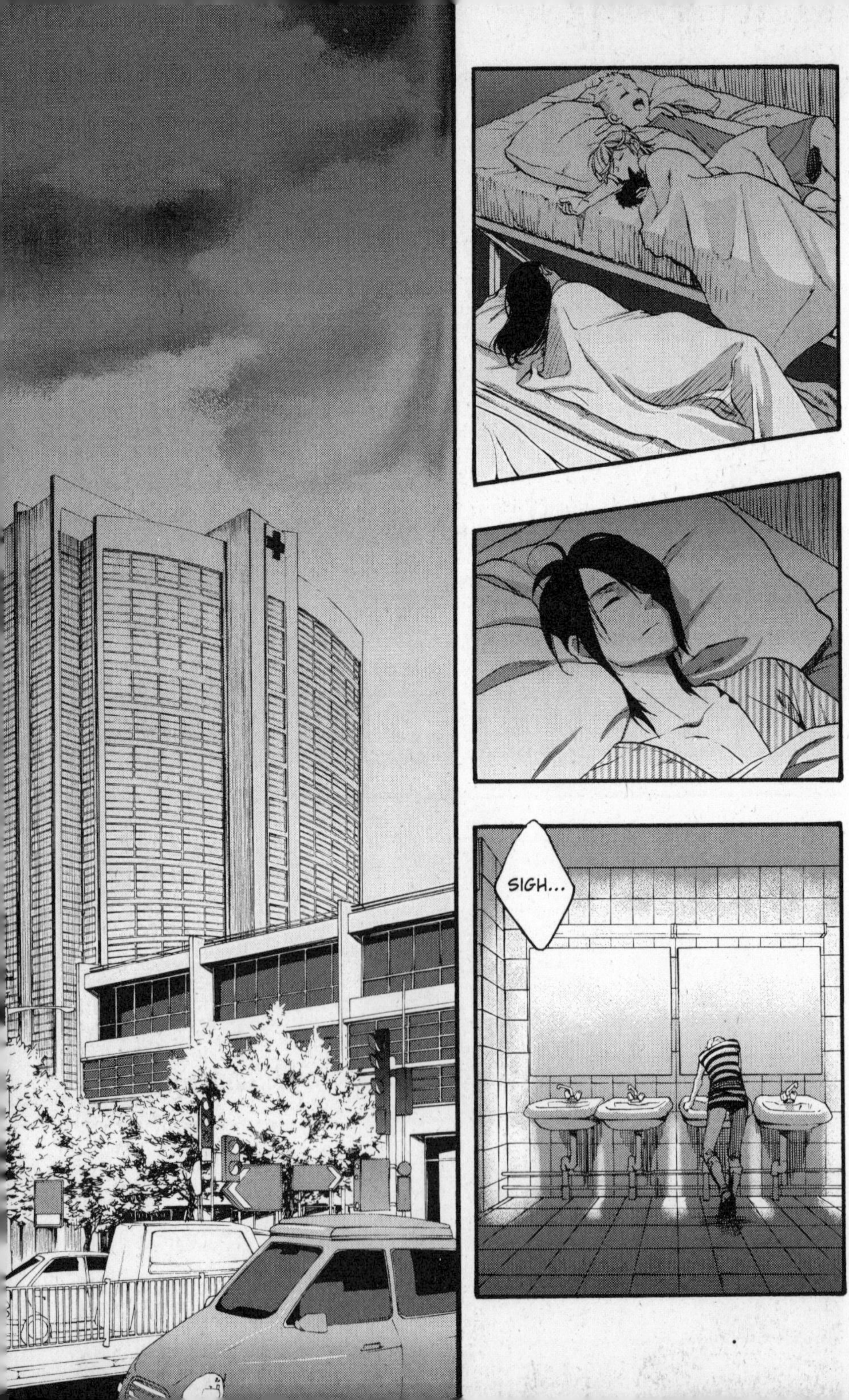
SIGH...

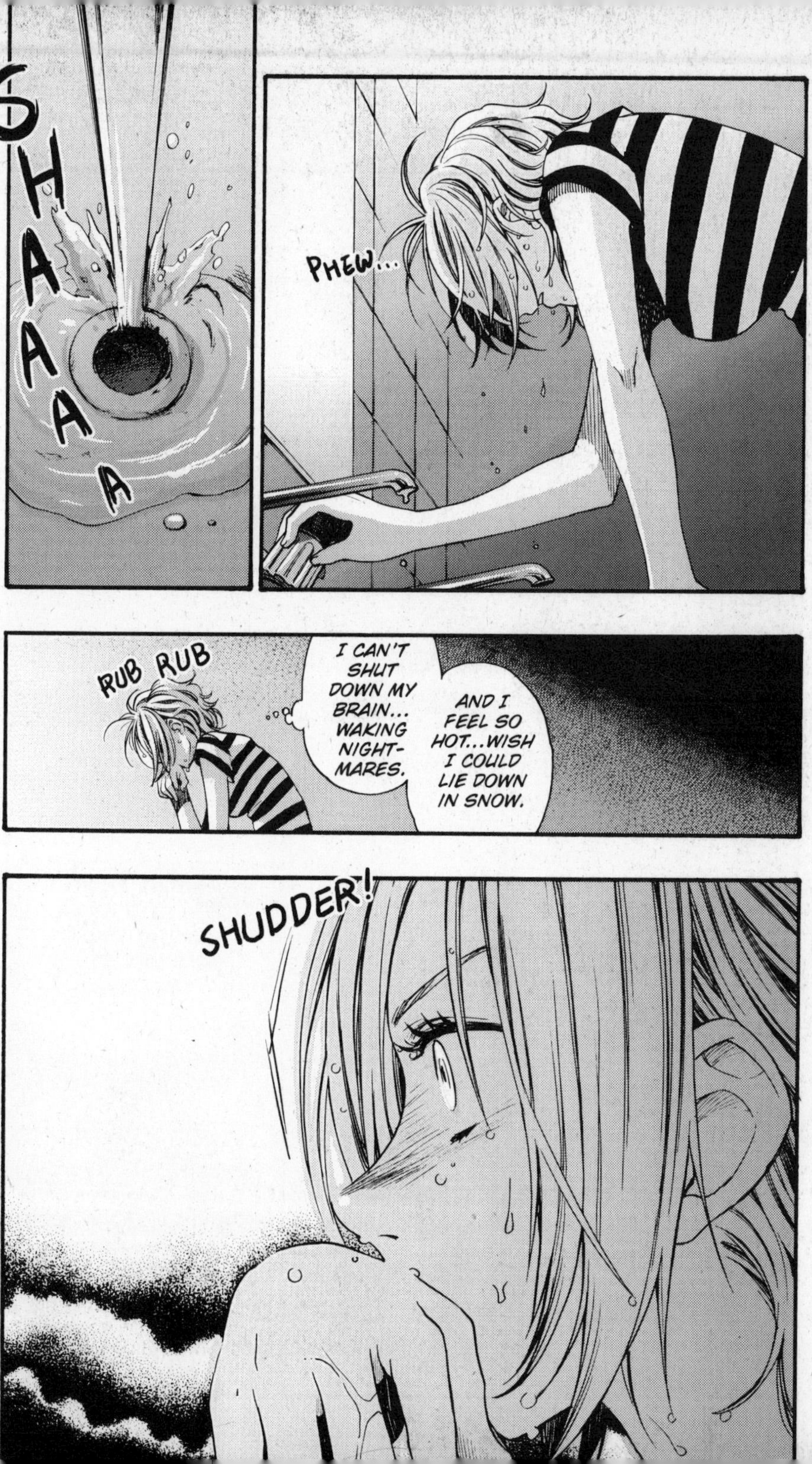
SHAAAAA
PHEW...
RUB RUB
I CAN'T SHUT DOWN MY BRAIN... WAKING NIGHT-MARES.
AND I FEEL SO HOT...WISH I COULD LIE DOWN IN SNOW.
SHUDDER!

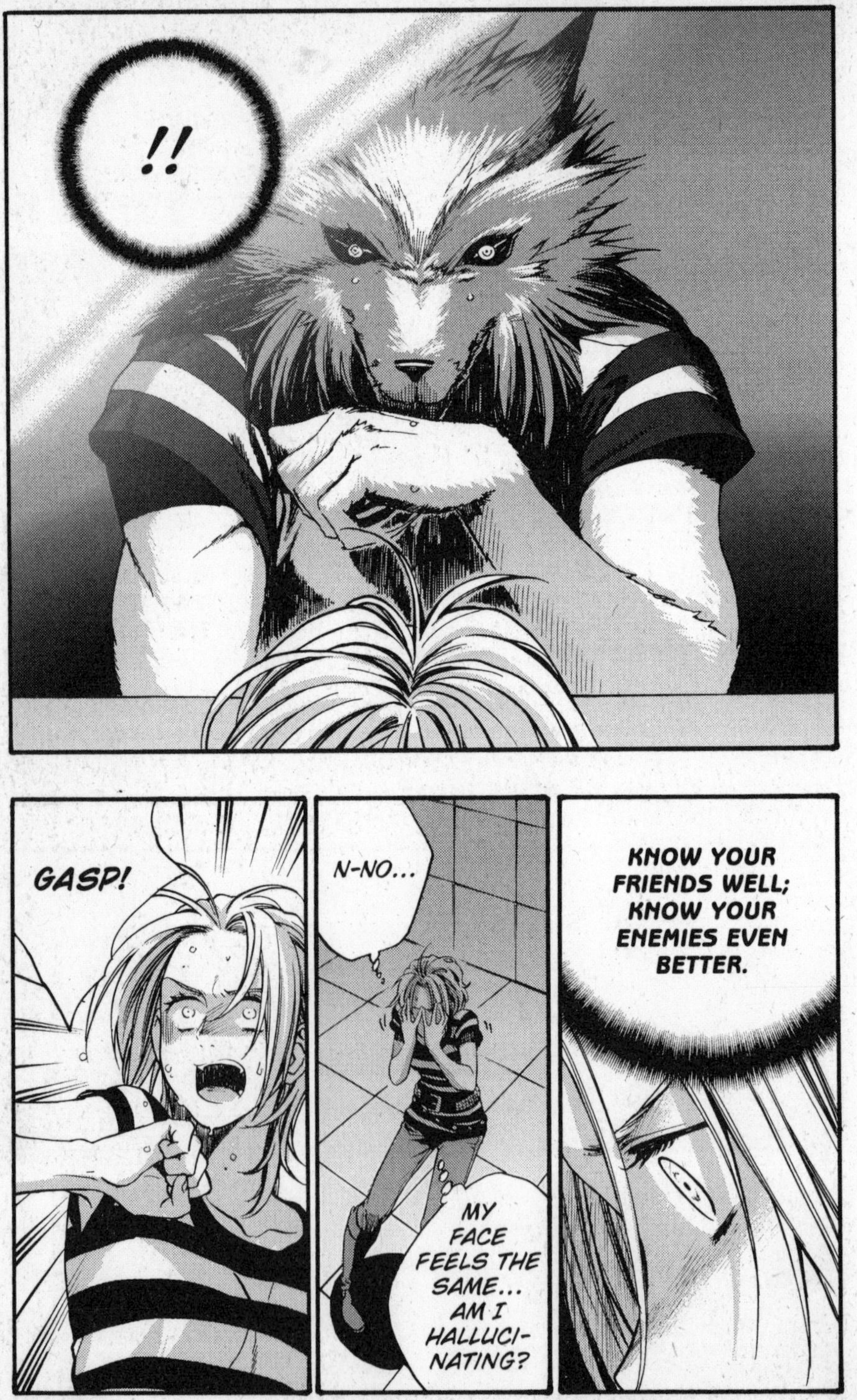
!!
GASP!
N-NO...
MY FACE FEELS THE SAME... AM I HALLUCINATING?
KNOW YOUR FRIENDS WELL; KNOW YOUR ENEMIES EVEN BETTER.

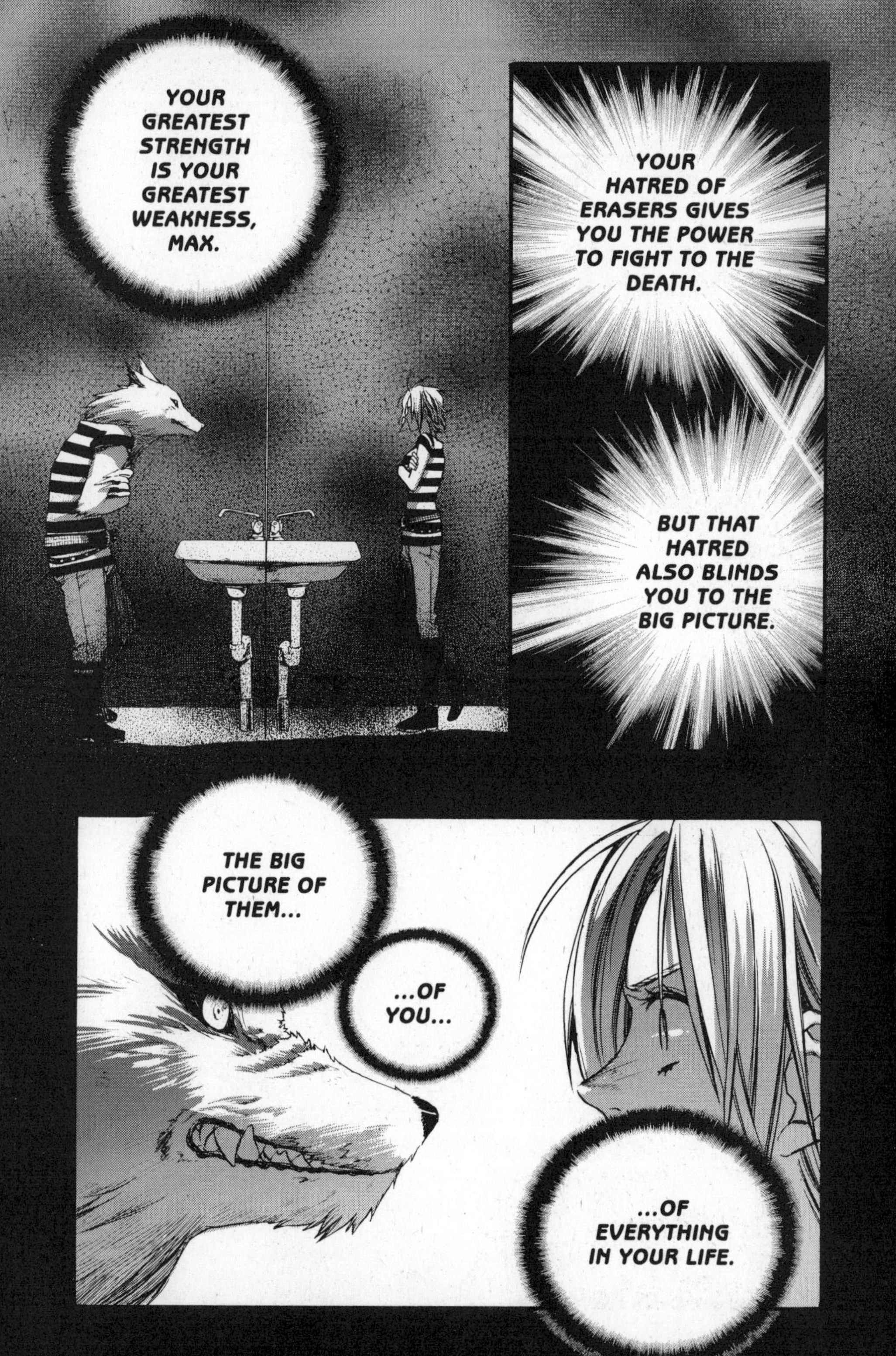
YOUR GREATEST STRENGTH IS YOUR GREATEST WEAKNESS, MAX.
YOUR HATRED OF ERASERS GIVES YOU THE POWER TO FIGHT TO THE DEATH.
BUT THAT HATRED ALSO BLINDS YOU TO THE BIG PICTURE.
THE BIG PICTURE OF THEM...
...OF YOU...
...OF EVERYTHING IN YOUR LIFE.

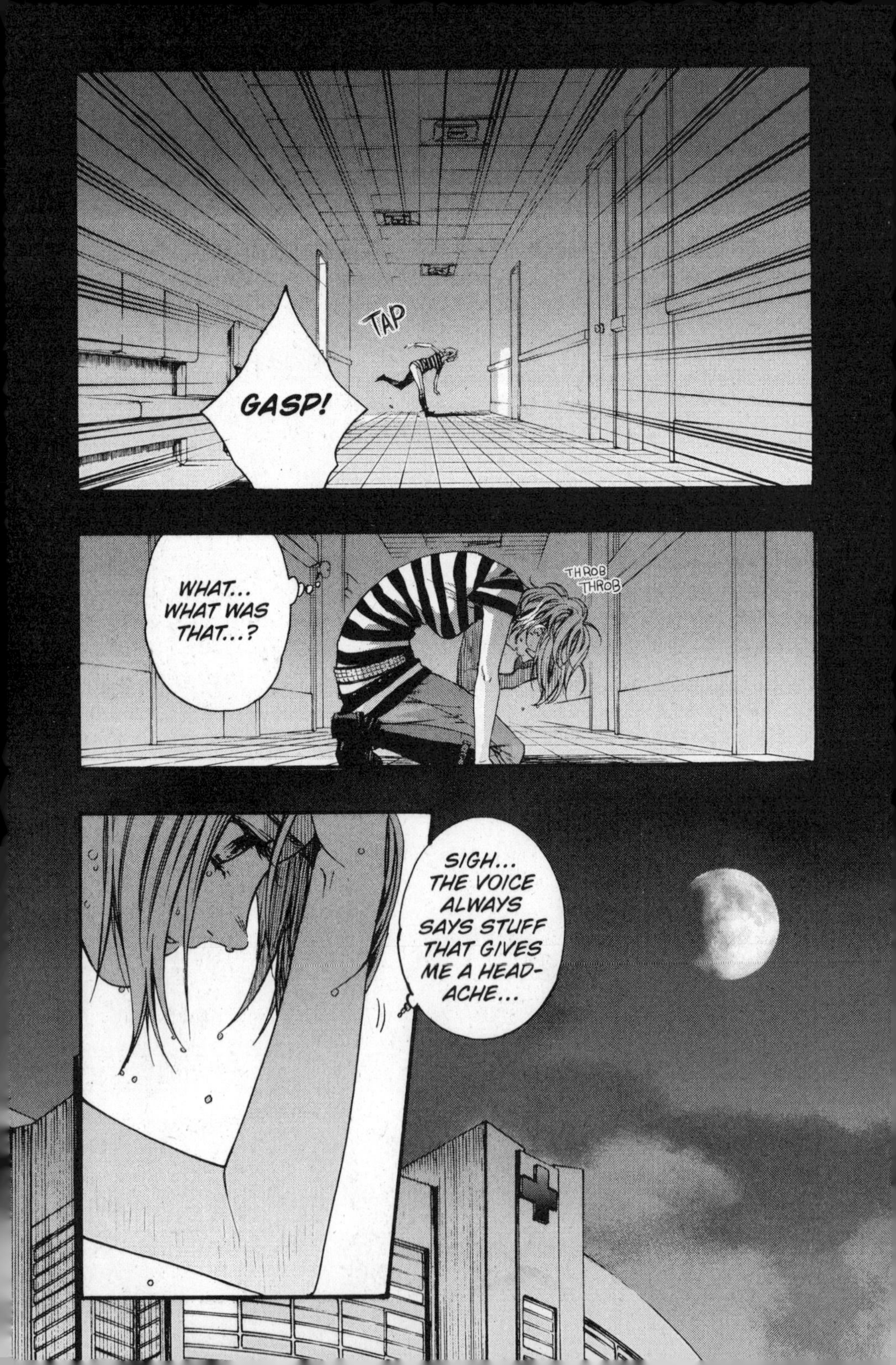
GASP!
TAP
WHAT... WHAT WAS THAT...?
THROB THROB
SIGH... THE VOICE ALWAYS SAYS STUFF THAT GIVES ME A HEAD-ACHE...

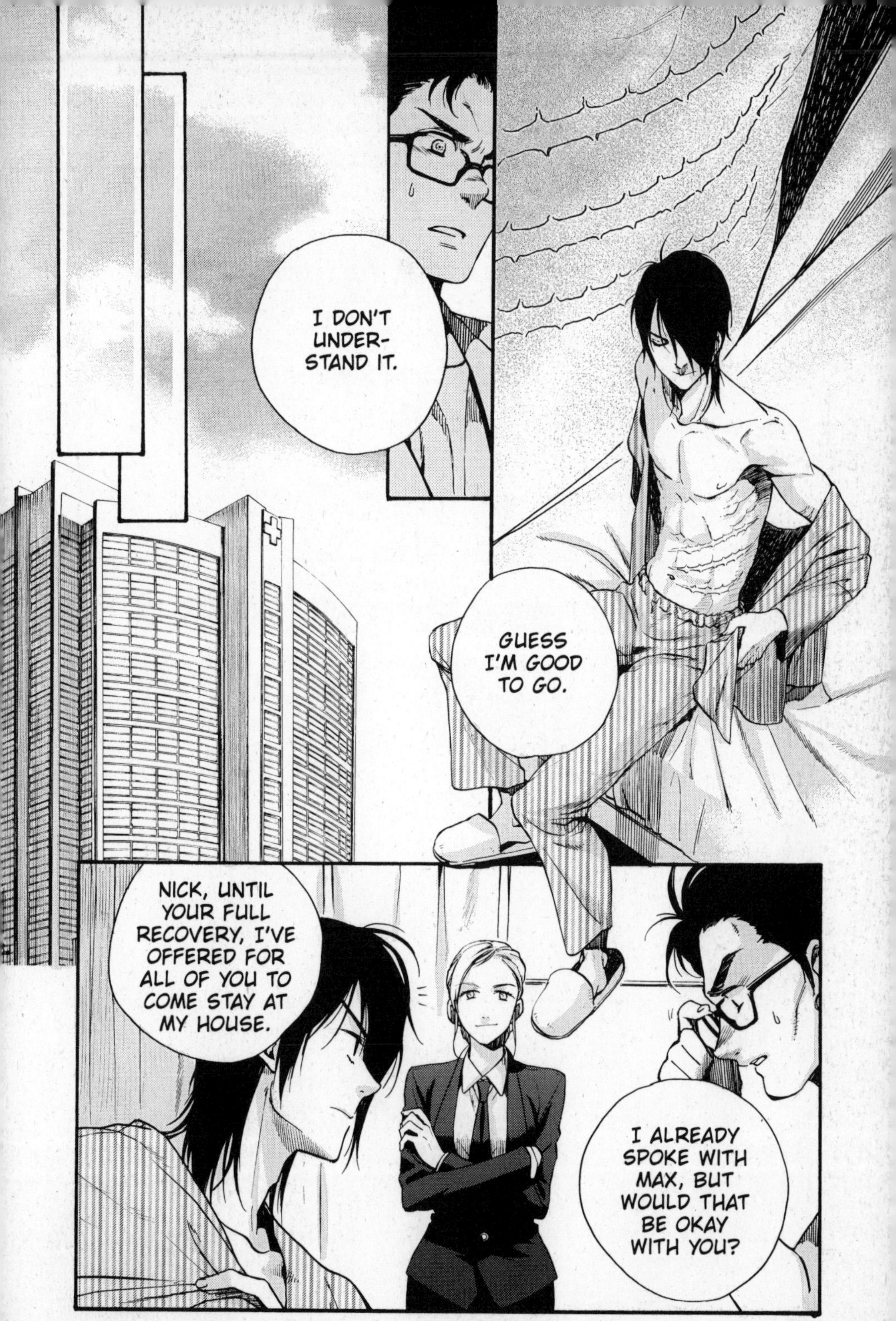
I DON'T UNDER-STAND IT.
GUESS I'M GOOD TO GO.
NICK, UNTIL YOUR FULL RECOVERY, I'VE OFFERED FOR ALL OF YOU TO COME STAY AT MY HOUSE.
I ALREADY SPOKE WITH MAX, BUT WOULD THAT BE OKAY WITH YOU?

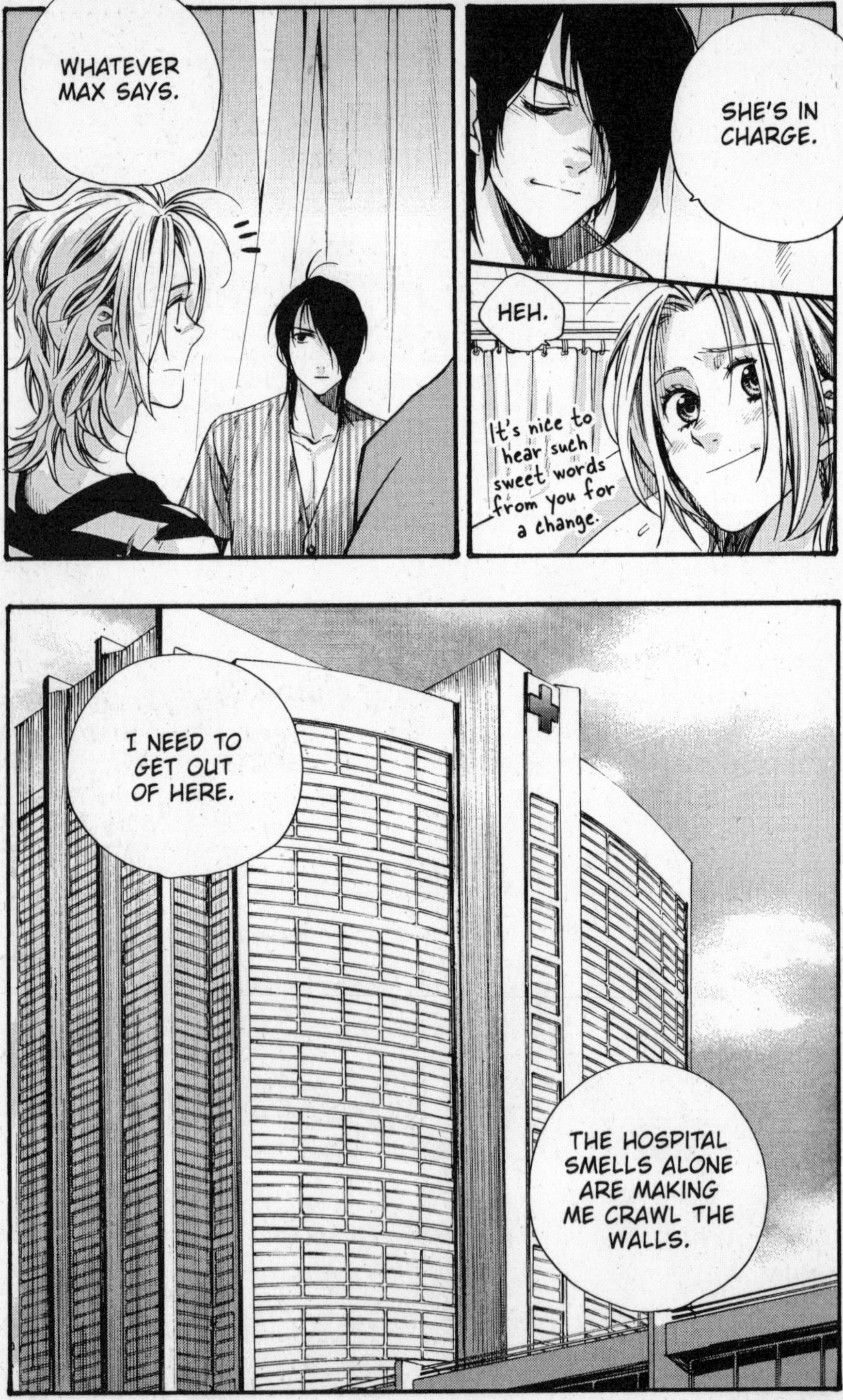
WHATEVER MAX SAYS.
SHE'S IN CHARGE.
HEH.
It's nice to hear such sweet words from you for a change.
I NEED TO GET OUT OF HERE.
THE HOSPITAL SMELLS ALONE ARE MAKING ME CRAWL THE WALLS.

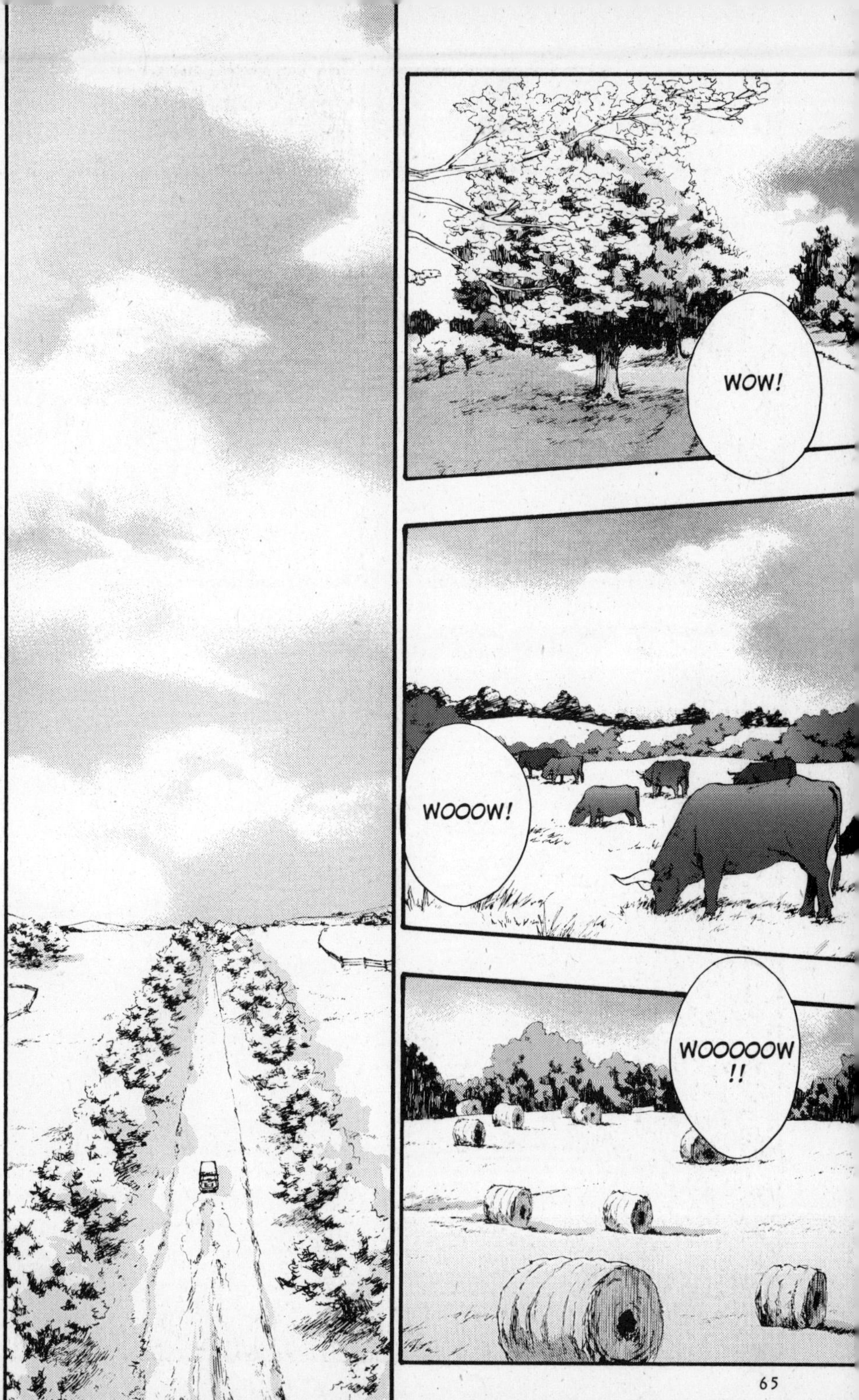
WOW!
WOOOW!
WOOOOOW !!

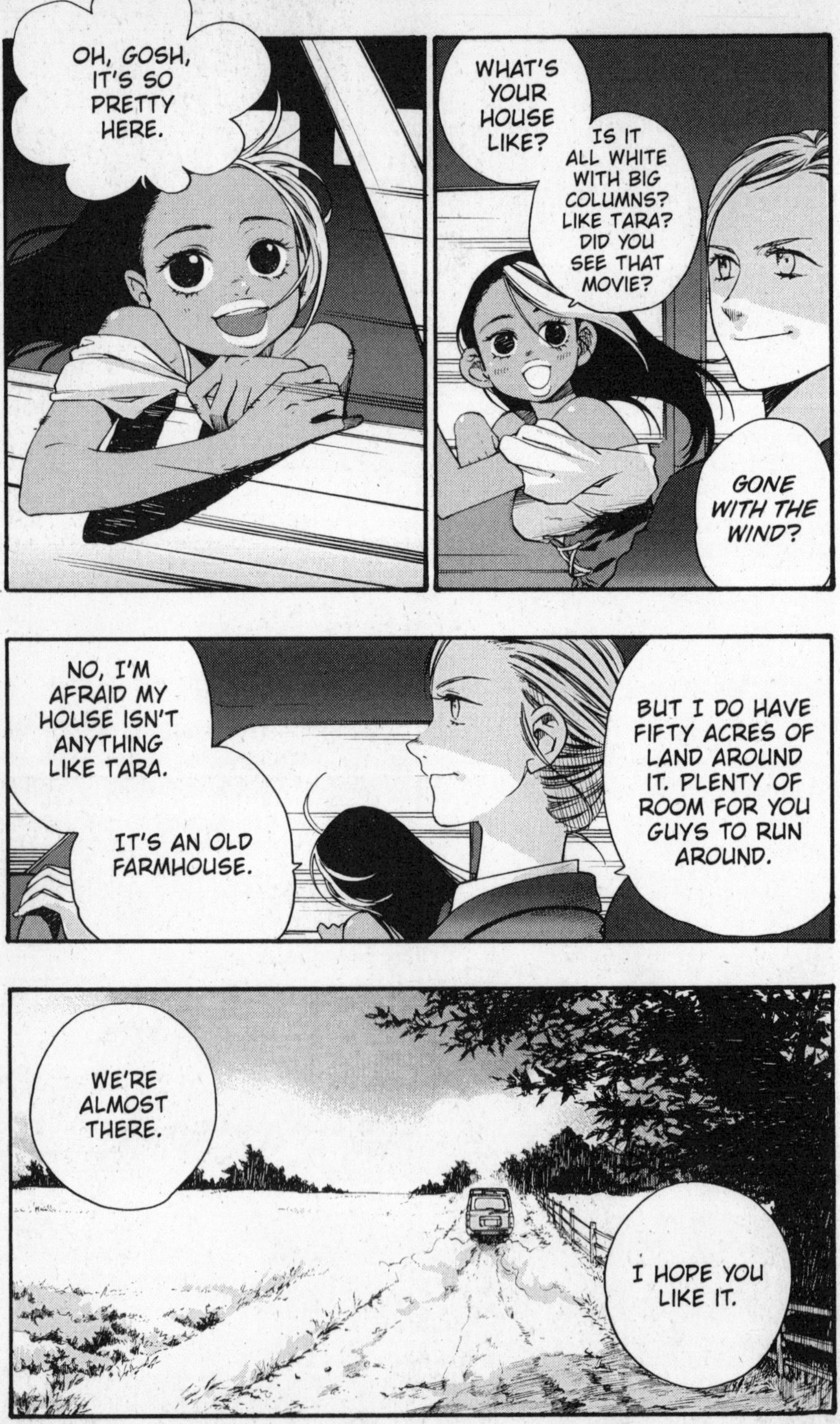
OH, GOSH, IT'S SO PRETTY HERE.
WHAT'S YOUR HOUSE LIKE?
IS IT ALL WHITE WITH BIG COLUMNS? LIKE TARA? DID YOU SEE THAT MOVIE?
GONE WITH THE WIND?
NO, I'M AFRAID MY HOUSE ISN'T ANYTHING LIKE TARA.
IT'S AN OLD FARMHOUSE.
BUT I DO HAVE FIFTY ACRES OF LAND AROUND IT. PLENTY OF ROOM FOR YOU GUYS TO RUN AROUND.
WE'RE ALMOST THERE.
I HOPE YOU LIKE IT.

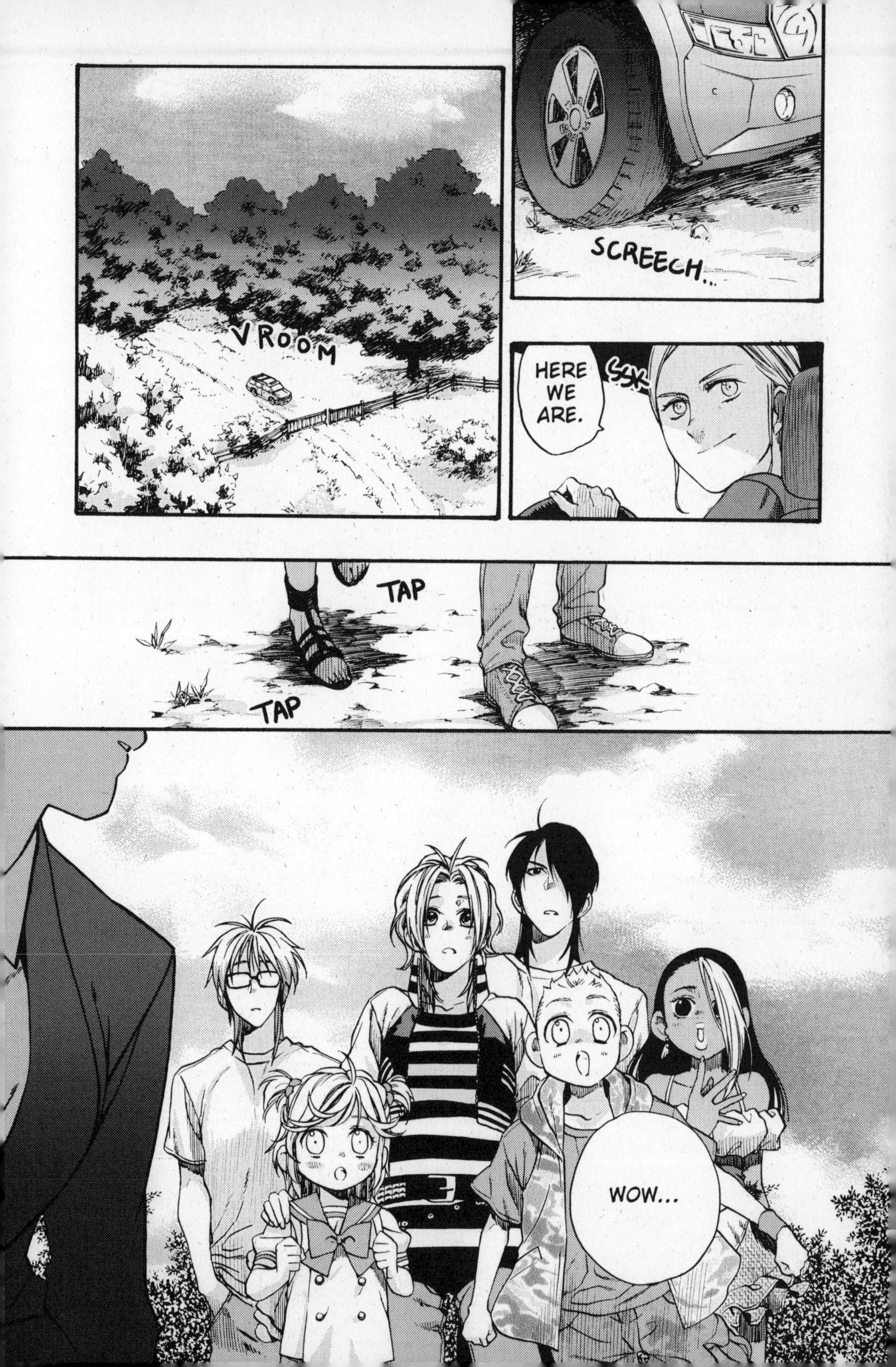

VROOM
SCREECH...
SSK
HERE WE ARE.
TAP
TAP
WOW...

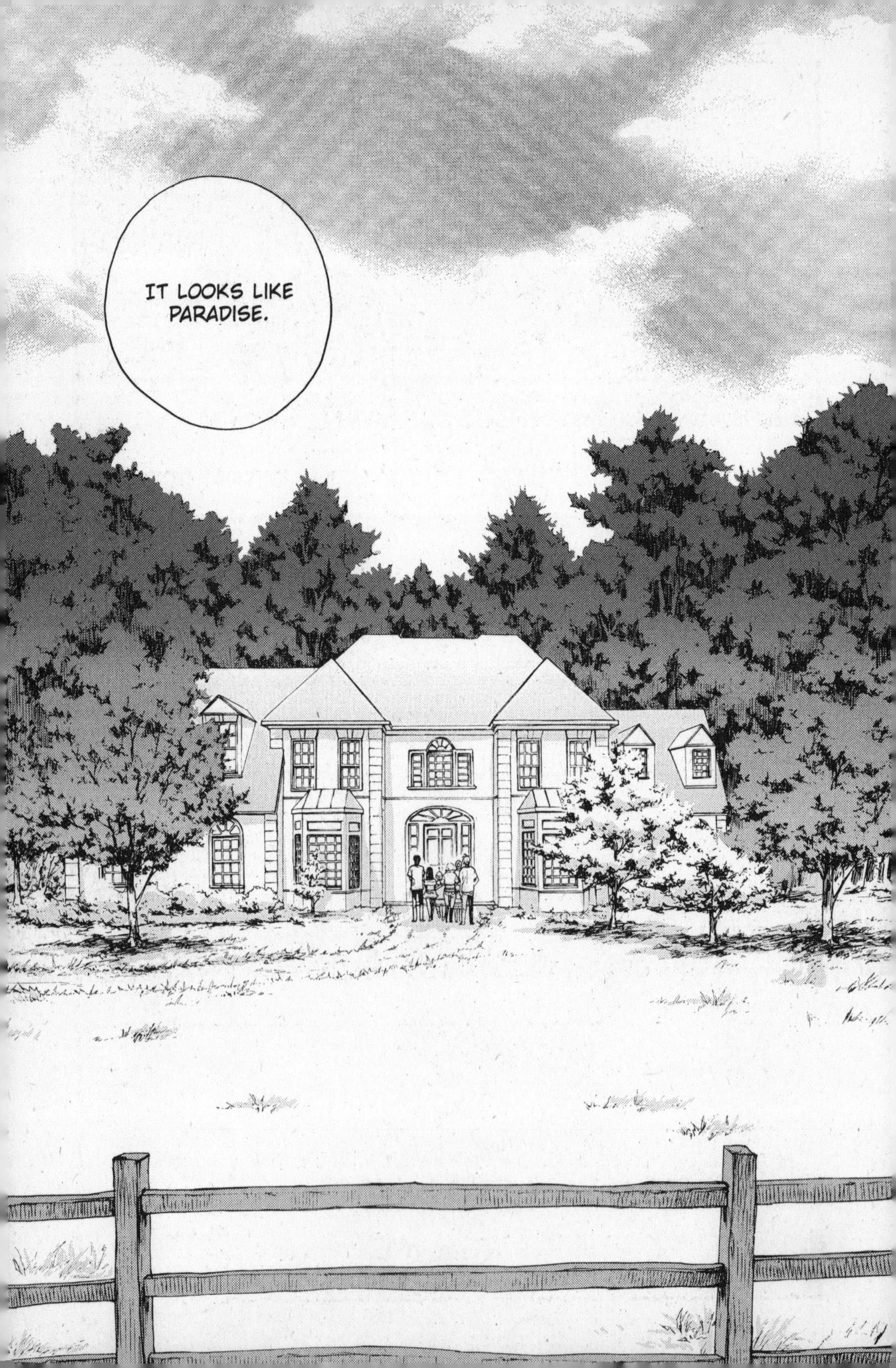
IT LOOKS LIKE PARADISE.

THERE'S A POND OUT BACK. IT'S SHALLOW, SO IT MIGHT STILL BE WARM ENOUGH TO GO SWIMMING IN THE AFTERNOONS.

LET'S GO IN. I'LL SHOW YOU YOUR ROOMS.

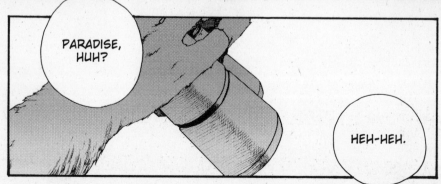

PARADISE, HUH?

HEH-HEH.

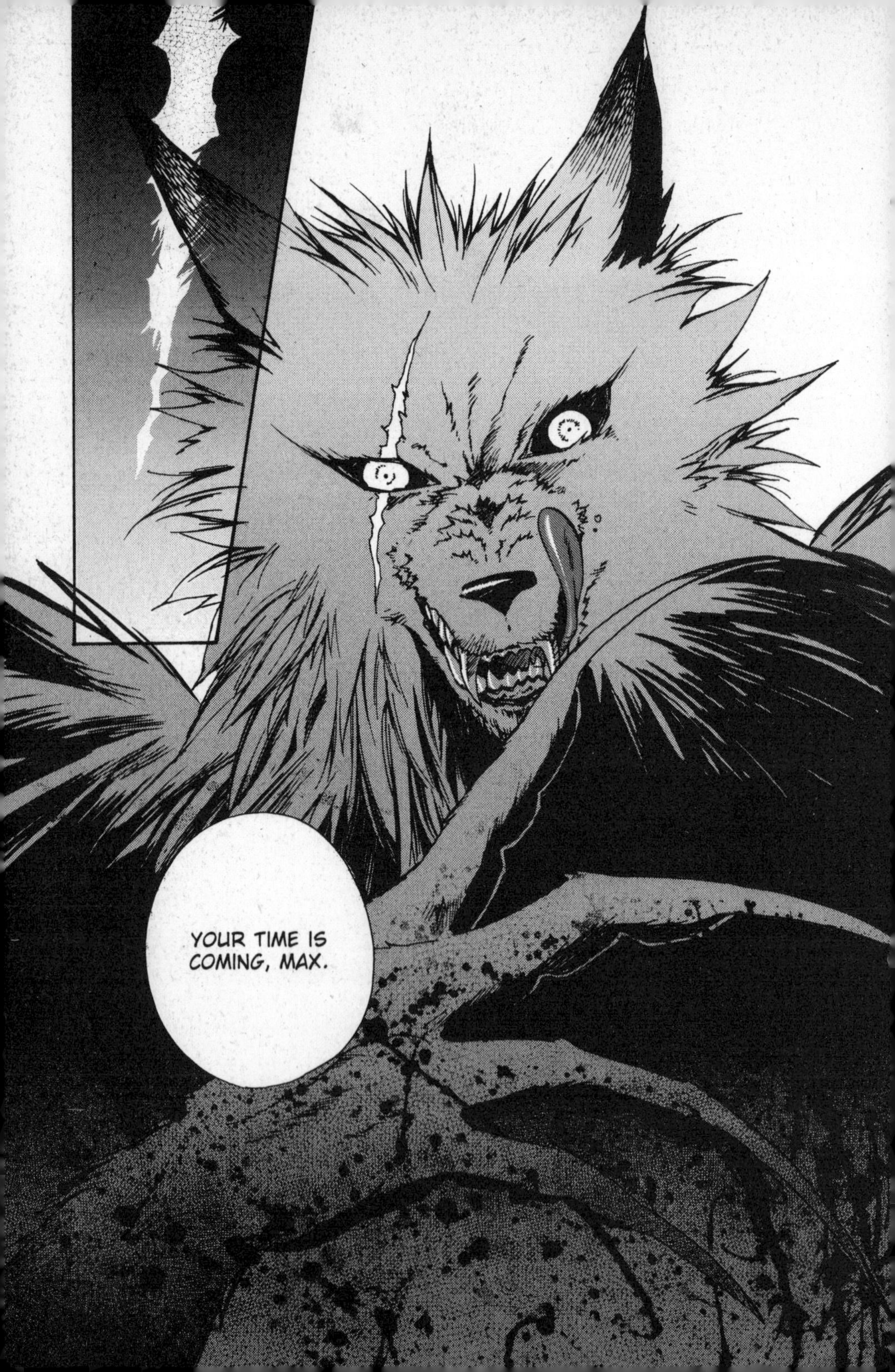
YOUR TIME IS COMING, MAX.

MAXIMUM
RIDE

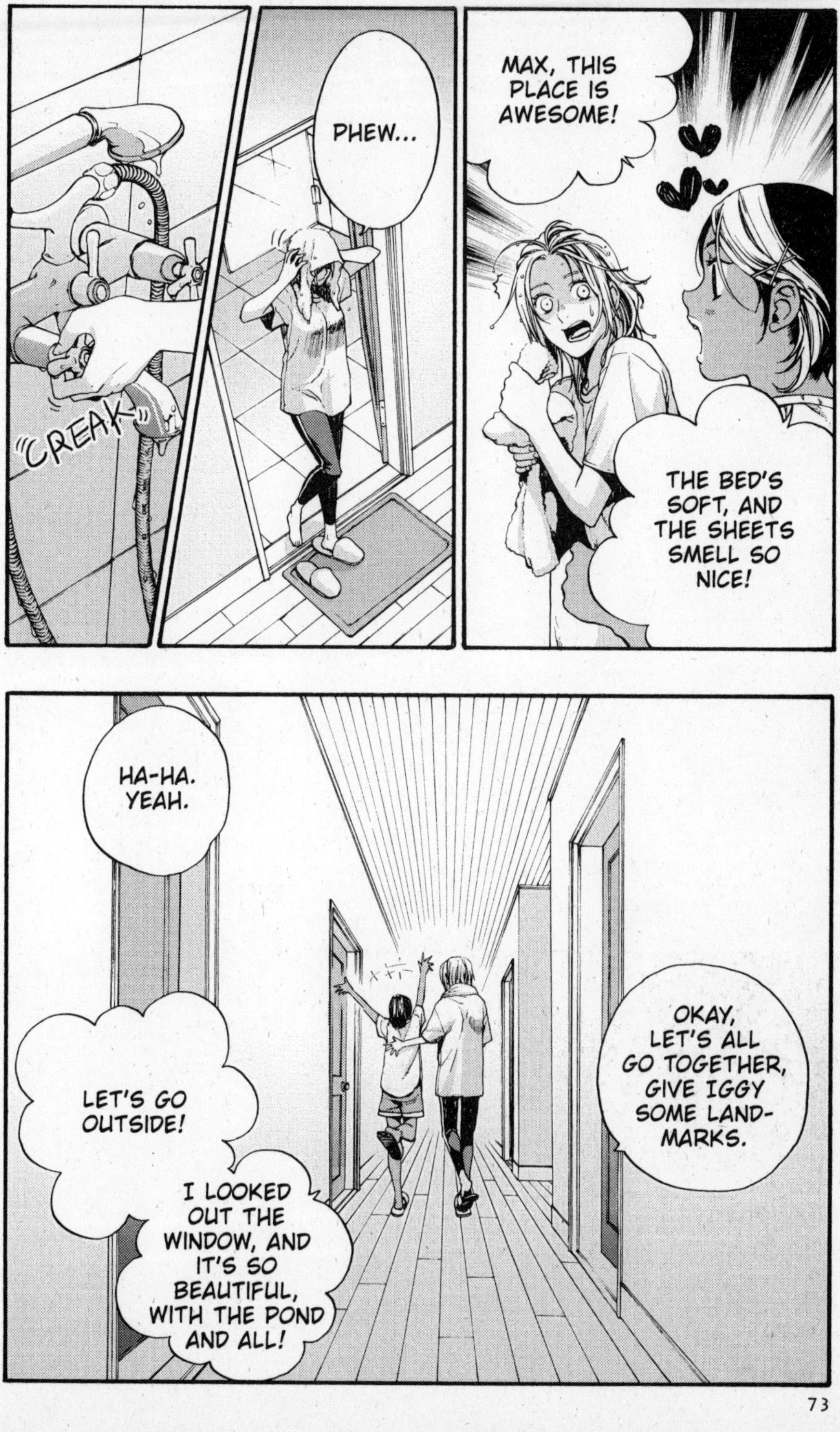
"CREAK"
PHEW...
MAX, THIS PLACE IS AWESOME!
THE BED'S SOFT, AND THE SHEETS SMELL SO NICE!
HA-HA. YEAH.
LET'S GO OUTSIDE!
I LOOKED OUT THE WINDOW, AND IT'S SO BEAUTIFUL, WITH THE POND AND ALL!
OKAY, LET'S ALL GO TOGETHER, GIVE IGGY SOME LAND-MARKS.

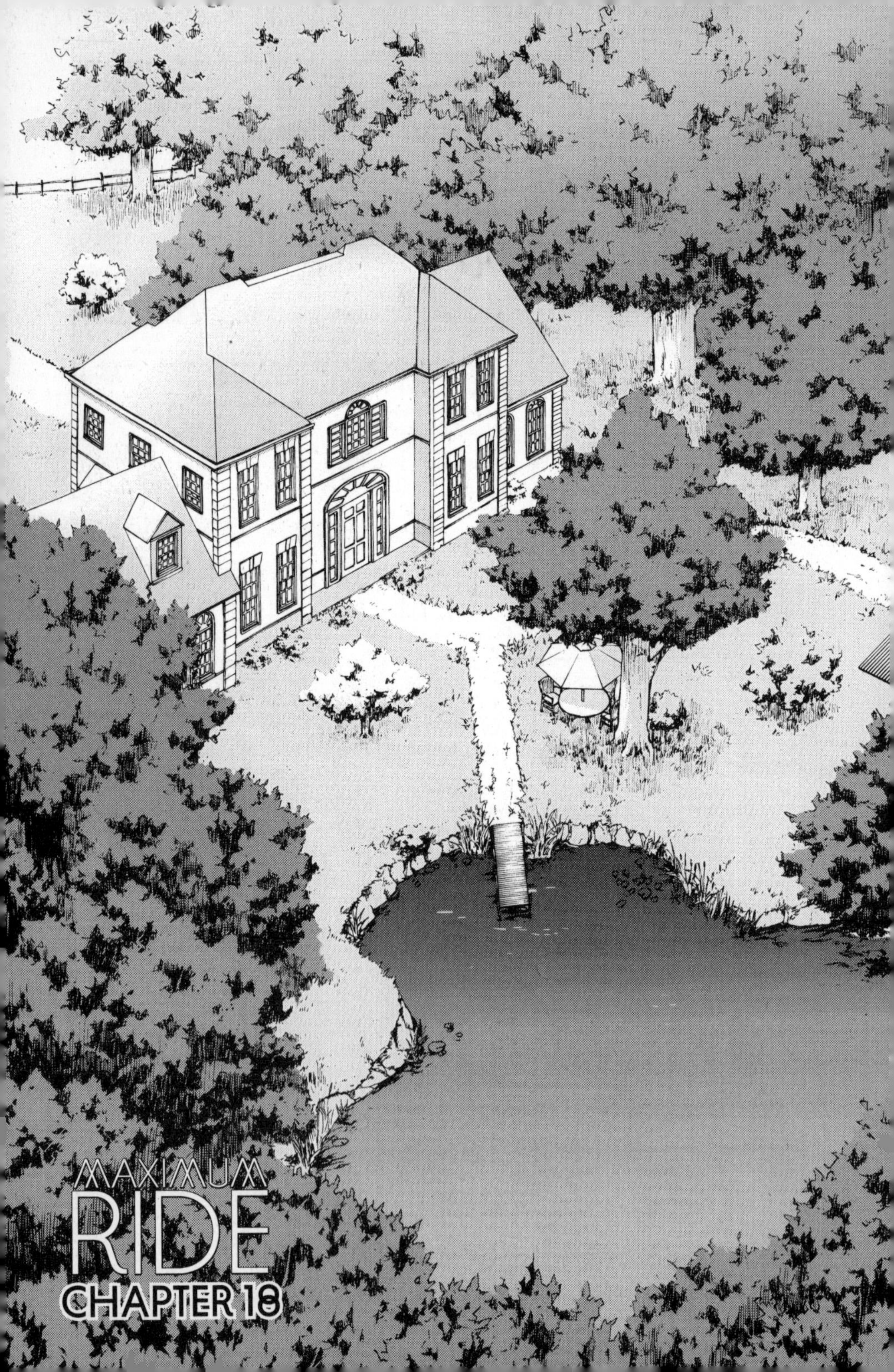
MAXIMUM
RIDE
CHAPTER 18

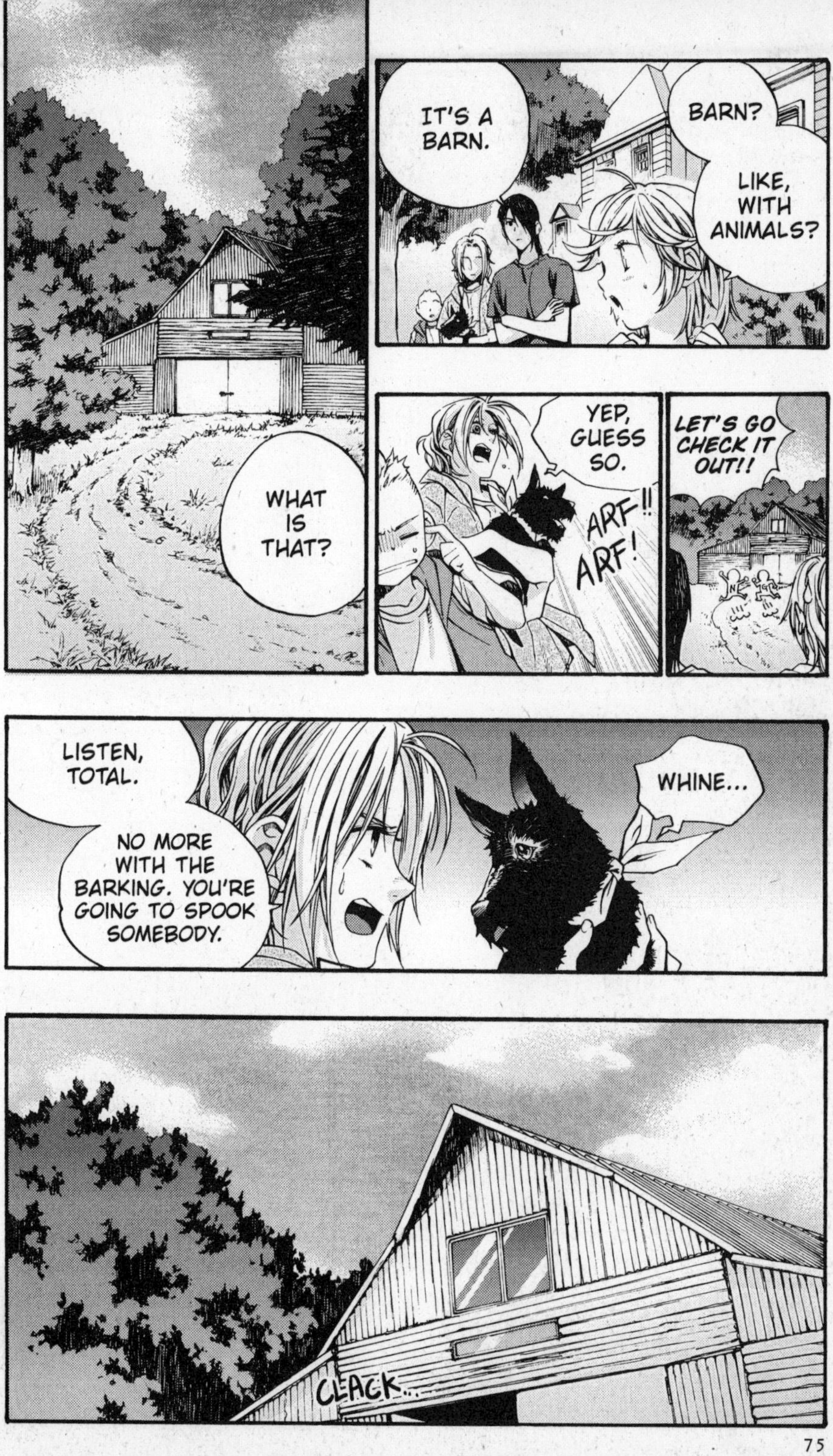
WHAT IS THAT?
IT'S A BARN.
BARN?
LIKE, WITH ANIMALS?
YEP, GUESS SO.
ARF!!
ARF!
LET'S GO CHECK IT OUT!!
LISTEN, TOTAL.
NO MORE WITH THE BARKING. YOU'RE GOING TO SPOOK SOMEBODY.
WHINE...
CLACK...

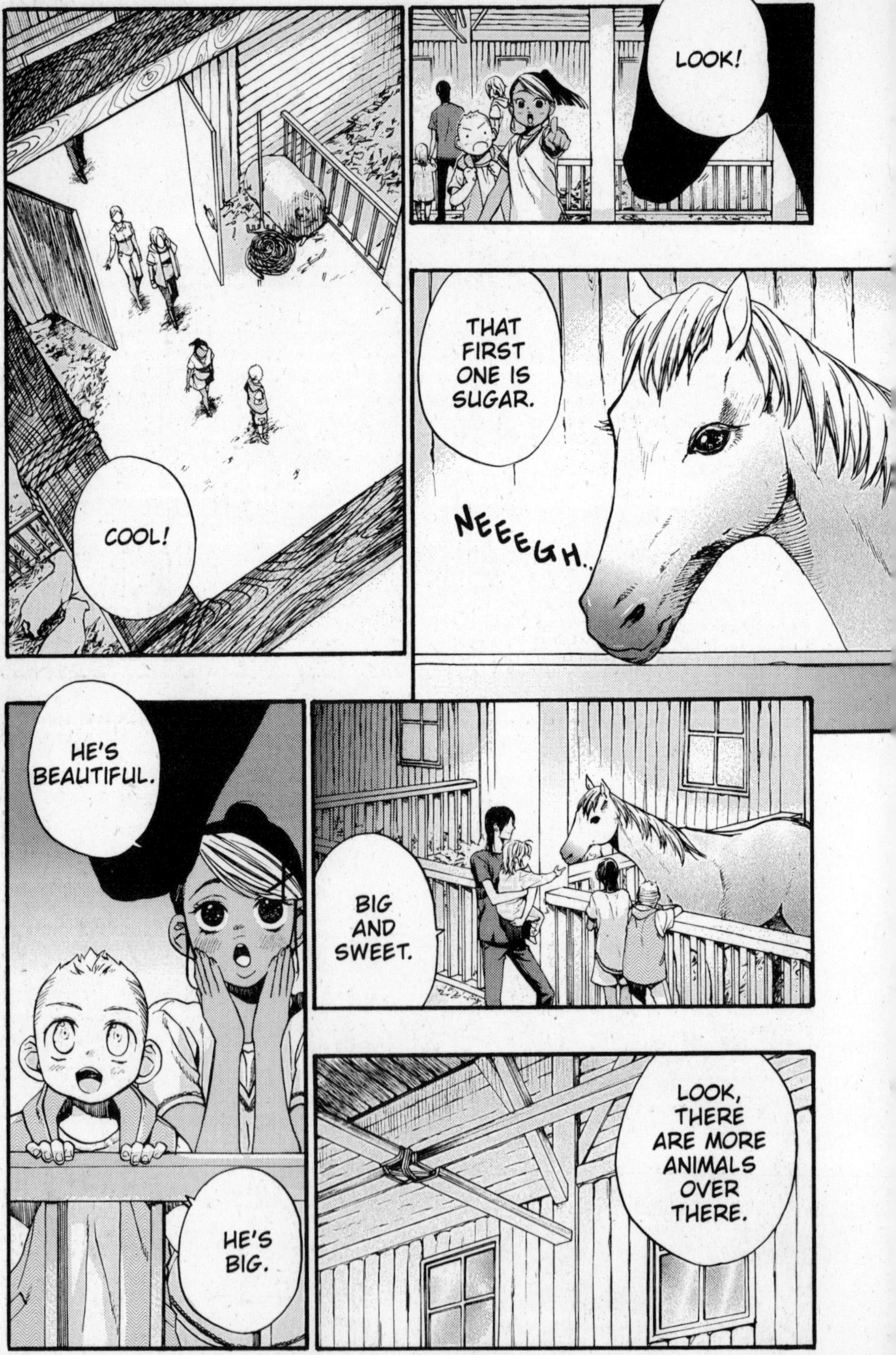
COOL!
LOOK!
THAT FIRST ONE IS SUGAR.
NEEEGH...
HE'S BEAUTIFUL.
HE'S BIG.
BIG AND SWEET.
LOOK, THERE ARE MORE ANIMALS OVER THERE.

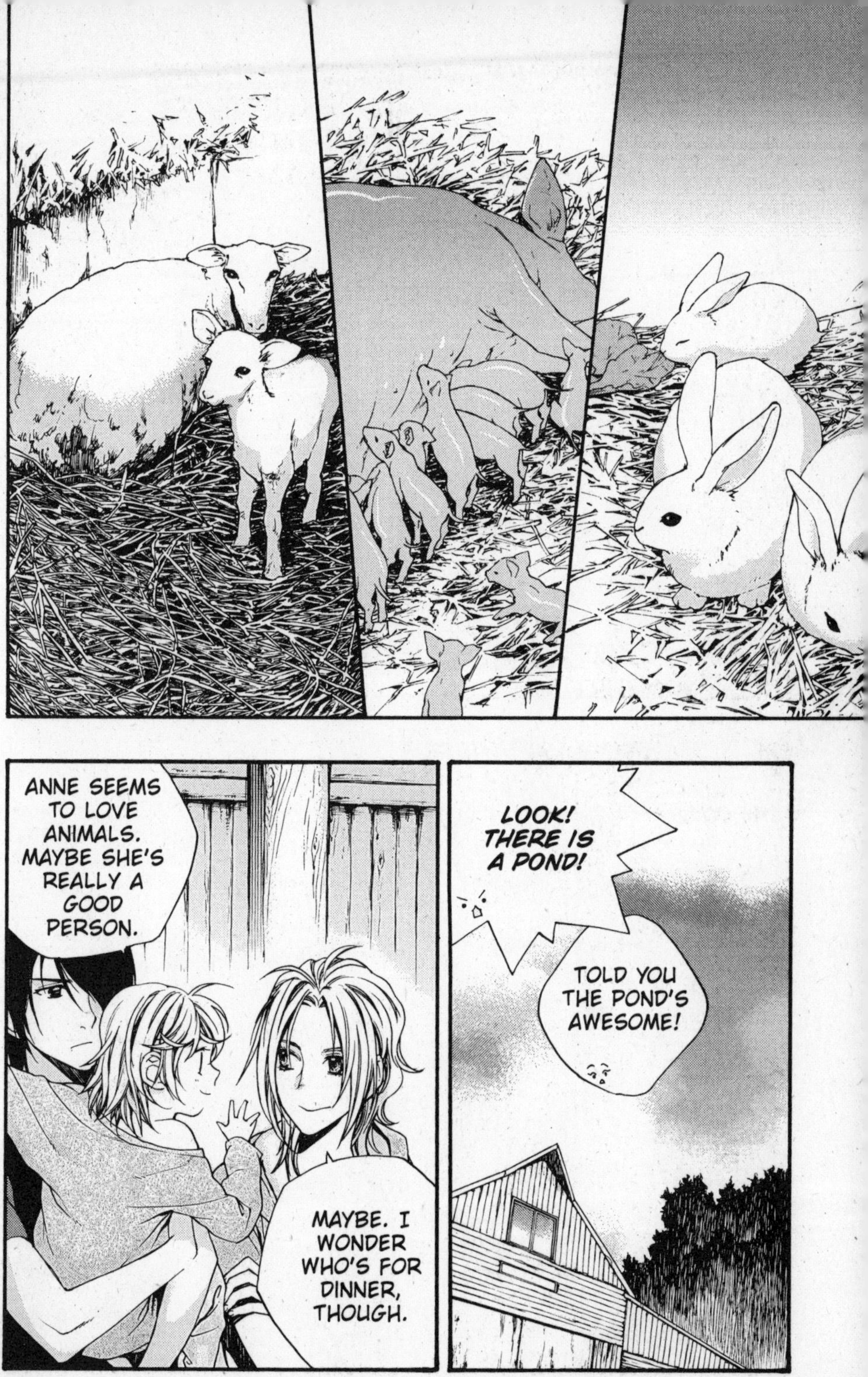
ANNE SEEMS TO LOVE ANIMALS. MAYBE SHE'S REALLY A GOOD PERSON.
MAYBE. I WONDER WHO'S FOR DINNER, THOUGH.
LOOK! THERE IS A POND!
TOLD YOU THE POND'S AWESOME!

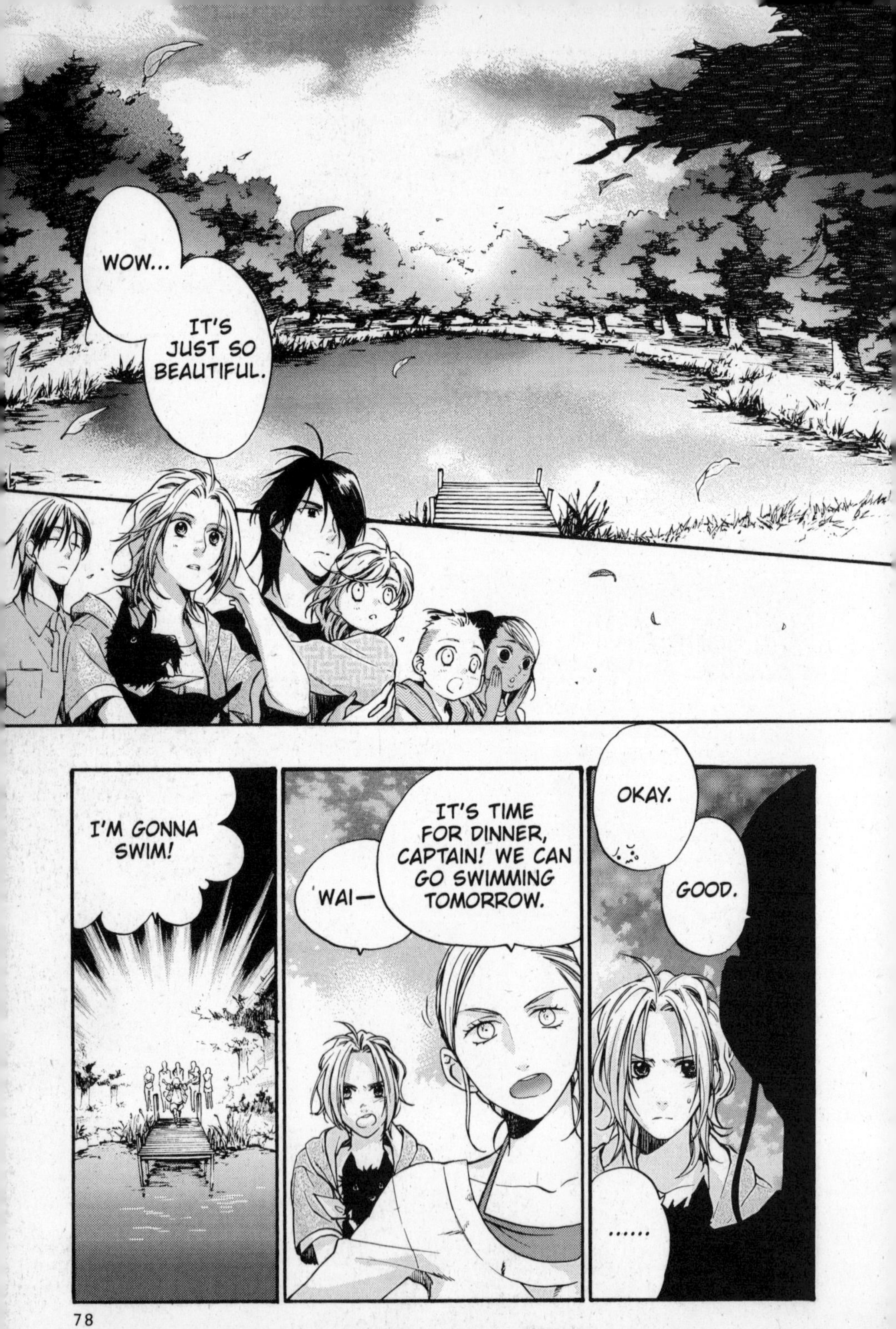
WOW...
IT'S JUST SO BEAUTIFUL.
I'M GONNA SWIM!
WAI—
IT'S TIME FOR DINNER, CAPTAIN! WE CAN GO SWIMMING TOMORROW.
OKAY.
GOOD.
......

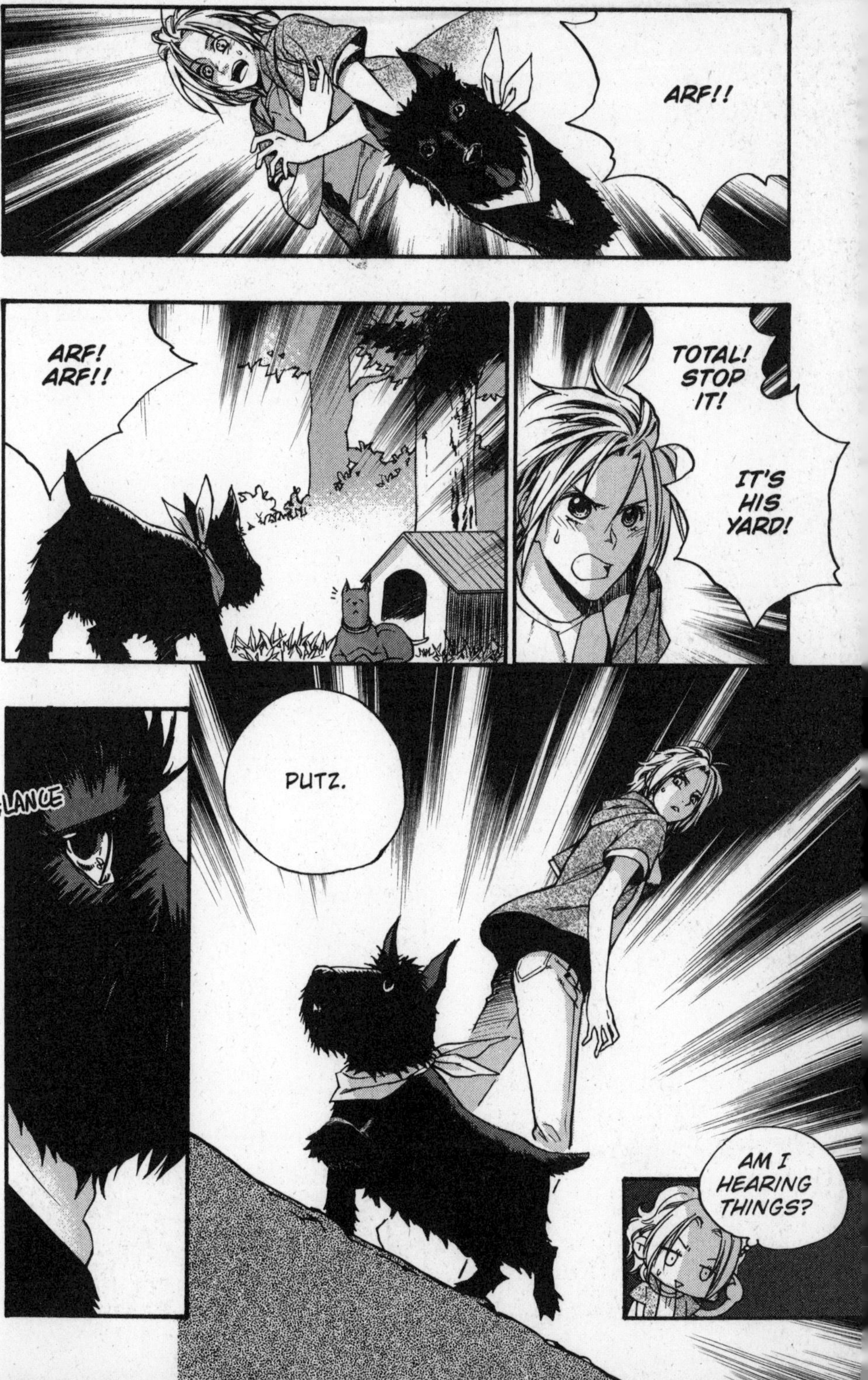
ARF!!
ARF!
ARF!!
TOTAL! STOP IT!
IT'S HIS YARD!
GLANCE
PUTZ.
AM I HEARING THINGS?

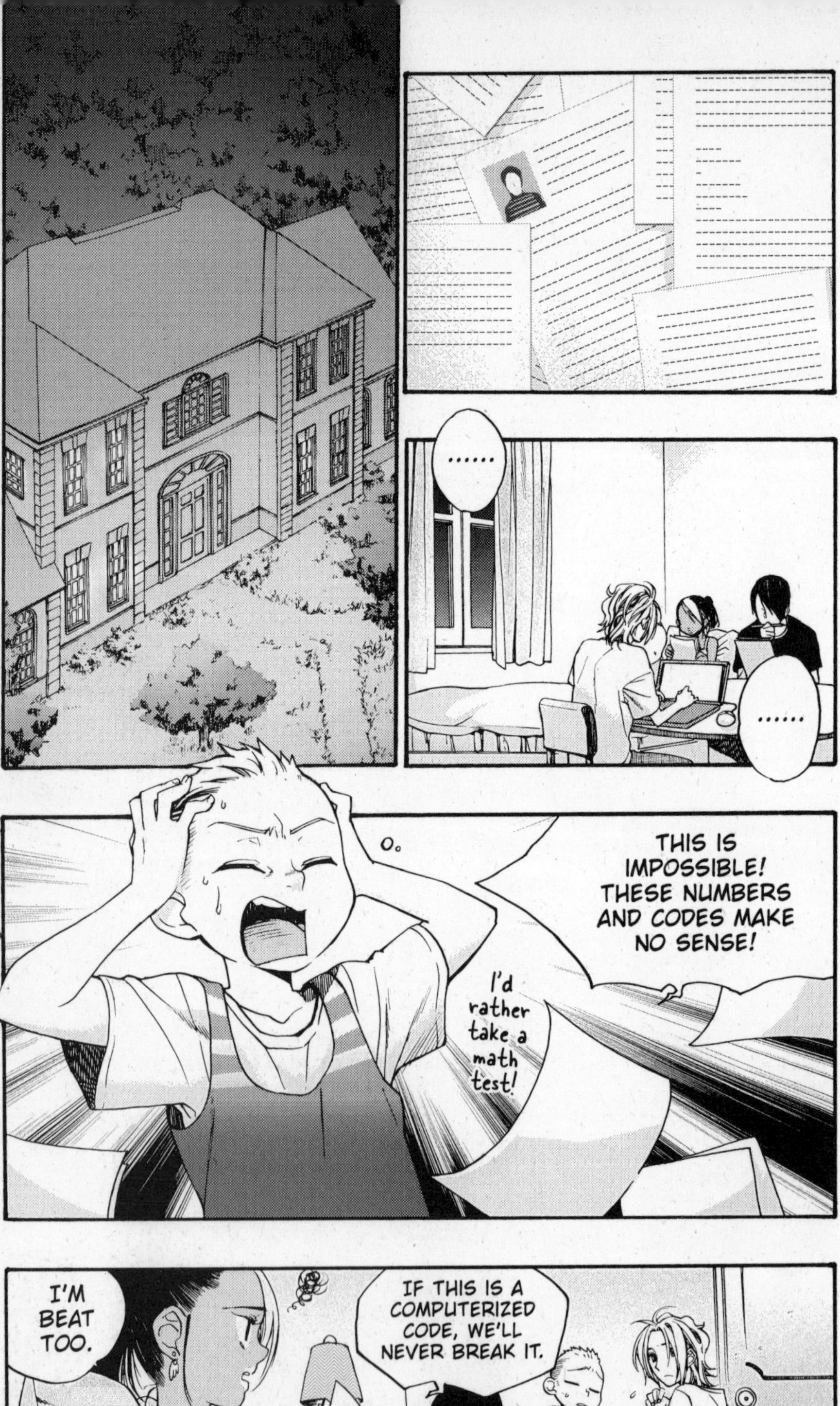
......
......
THIS IS IMPOSSIBLE! THESE NUMBERS AND CODES MAKE NO SENSE!
I'd rather take a math test!
I'M BEAT TOO.
IF THIS IS A COMPUTERIZED CODE, WE'LL NEVER BREAK IT.

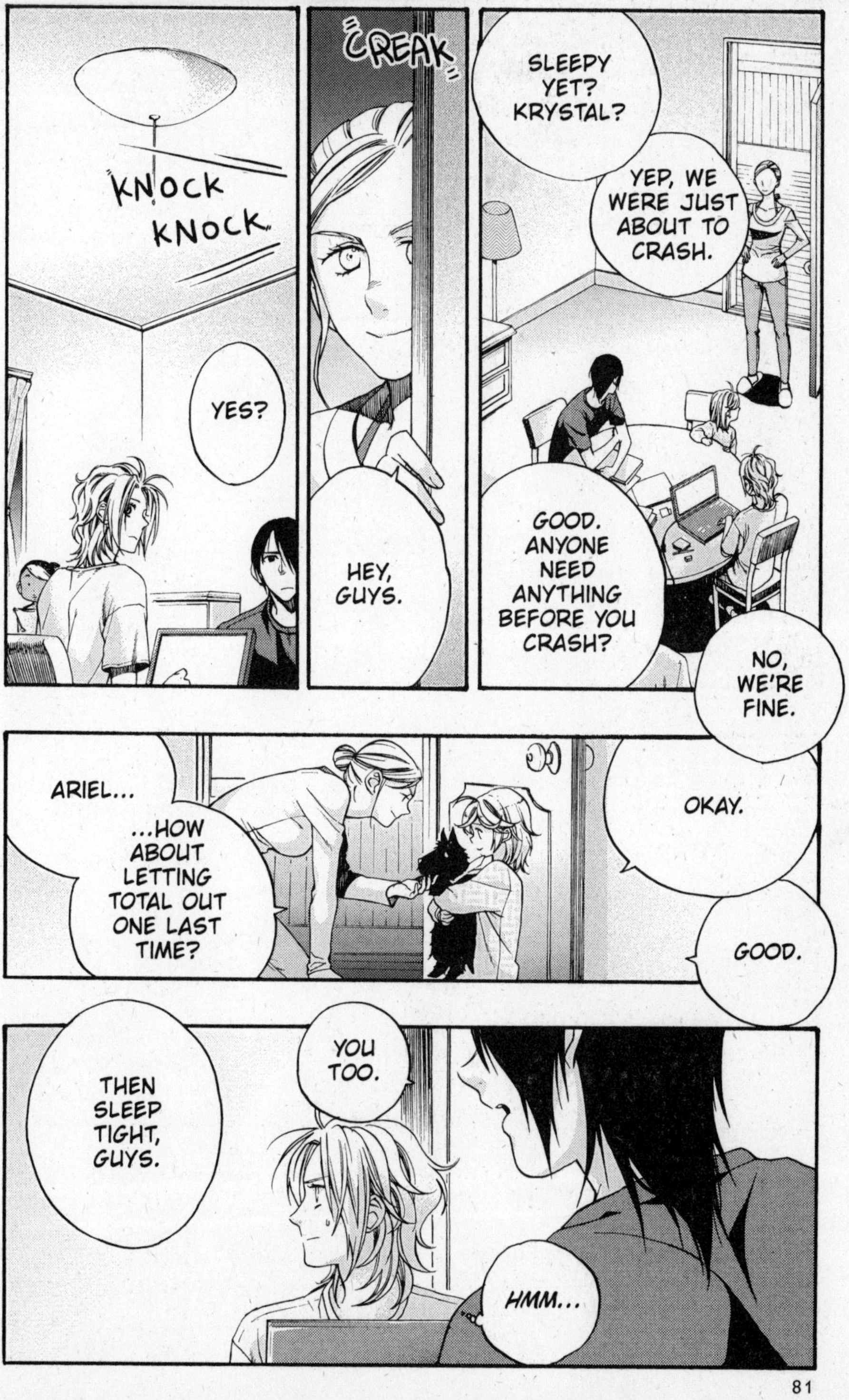
KNOCK KNOCK
YES?
CREAK
HEY, GUYS.
SLEEPY YET? KRYSTAL?
YEP, WE WERE JUST ABOUT TO CRASH.
GOOD. ANYONE NEED ANYTHING BEFORE YOU CRASH?
NO, WE'RE FINE.
ARIEL...
...HOW ABOUT LETTING TOTAL OUT ONE LAST TIME?
OKAY.
GOOD.
THEN SLEEP TIGHT, GUYS.
YOU TOO.
HMM...

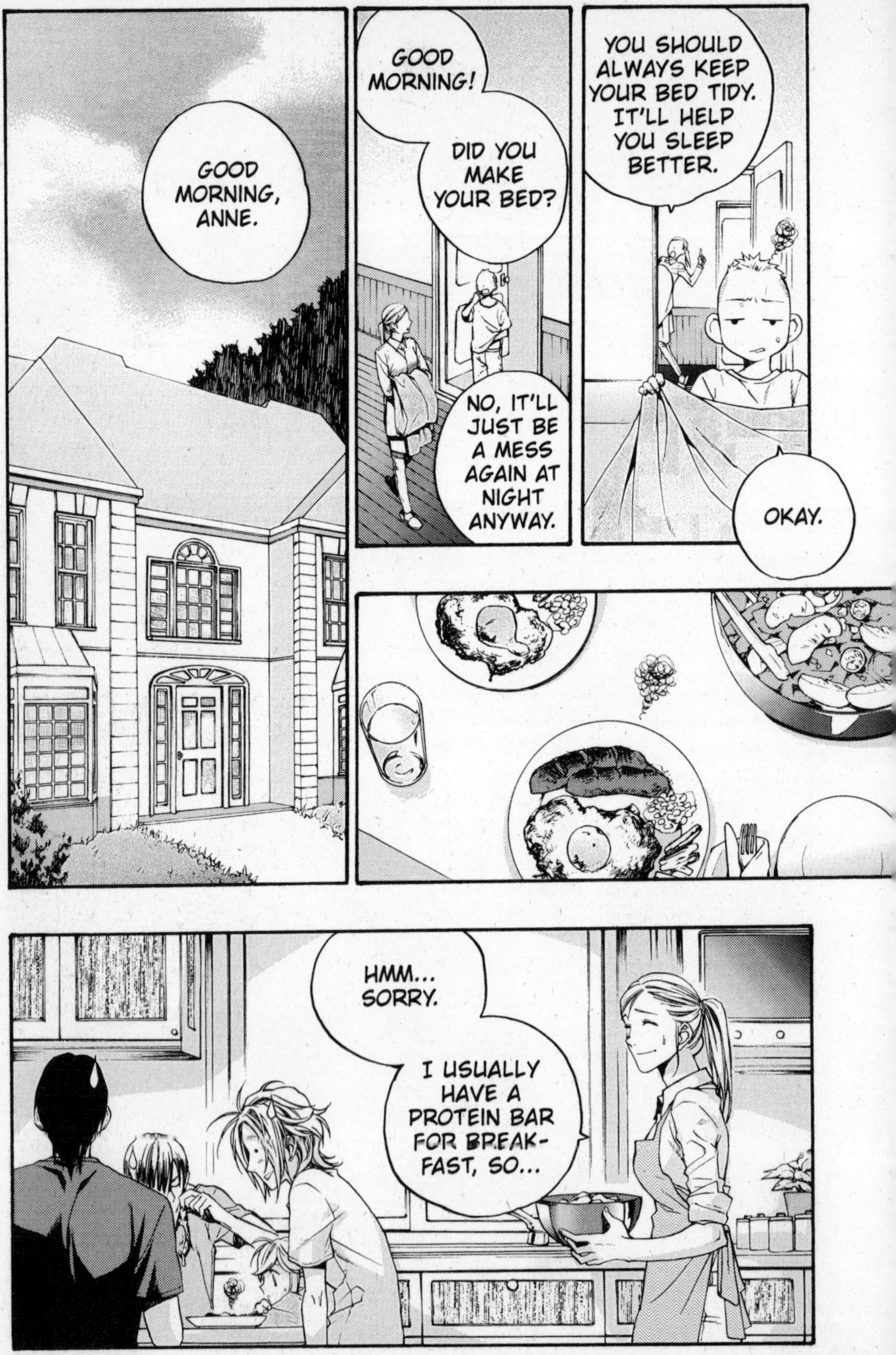
GOOD MORNING, ANNE.
GOOD MORNING!
DID YOU MAKE YOUR BED?
NO, IT'LL JUST BE A MESS AGAIN AT NIGHT ANYWAY.
YOU SHOULD ALWAYS KEEP YOUR BED TIDY. IT'LL HELP YOU SLEEP BETTER.
OKAY.
HMM... SORRY.
I USUALLY HAVE A PROTEIN BAR FOR BREAK-FAST, SO...

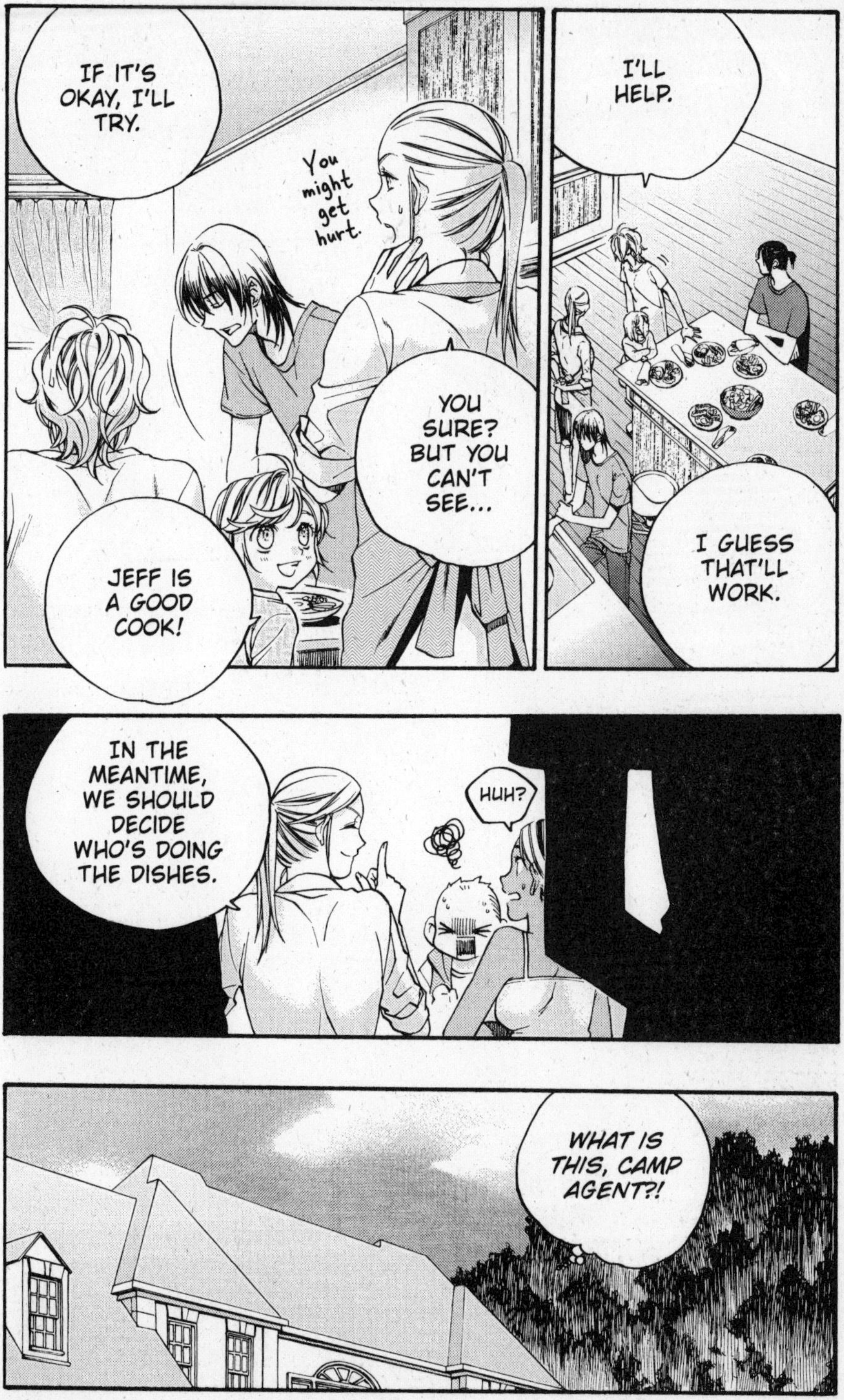
IF IT'S OKAY, I'LL TRY.
You might get hurt.
YOU SURE? BUT YOU CAN'T SEE...
JEFF IS A GOOD COOK!
I'LL HELP.
I GUESS THAT'LL WORK.
IN THE MEANTIME, WE SHOULD DECIDE WHO'S DOING THE DISHES.
HUH?
WHAT IS THIS, CAMP AGENT?!

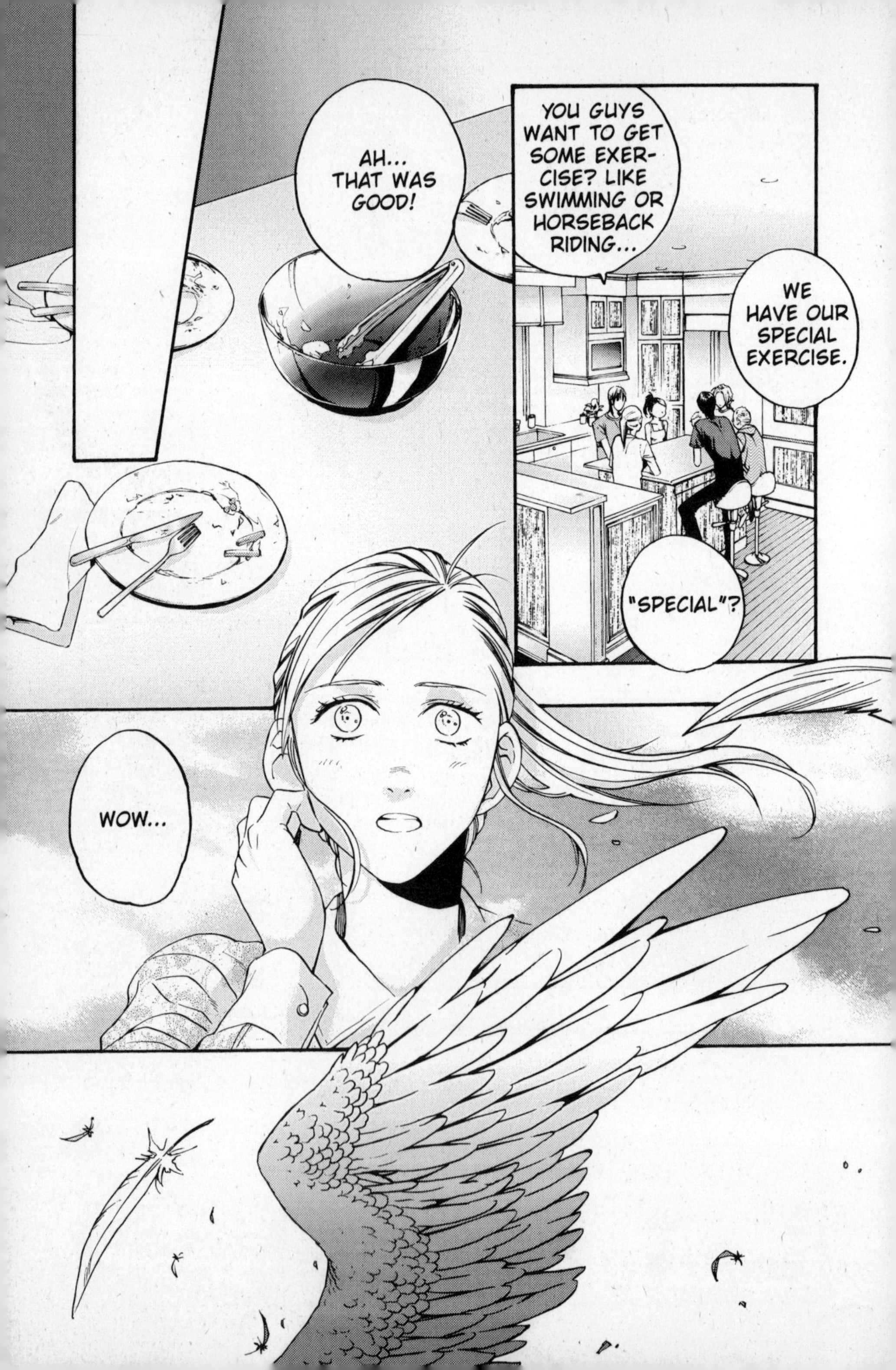
AH... THAT WAS GOOD!
YOU GUYS WANT TO GET SOME EXER-CISE? LIKE SWIMMING OR HORSEBACK RIDING...
WE HAVE OUR SPECIAL EXERCISE.
"SPECIAL"?
WOW...

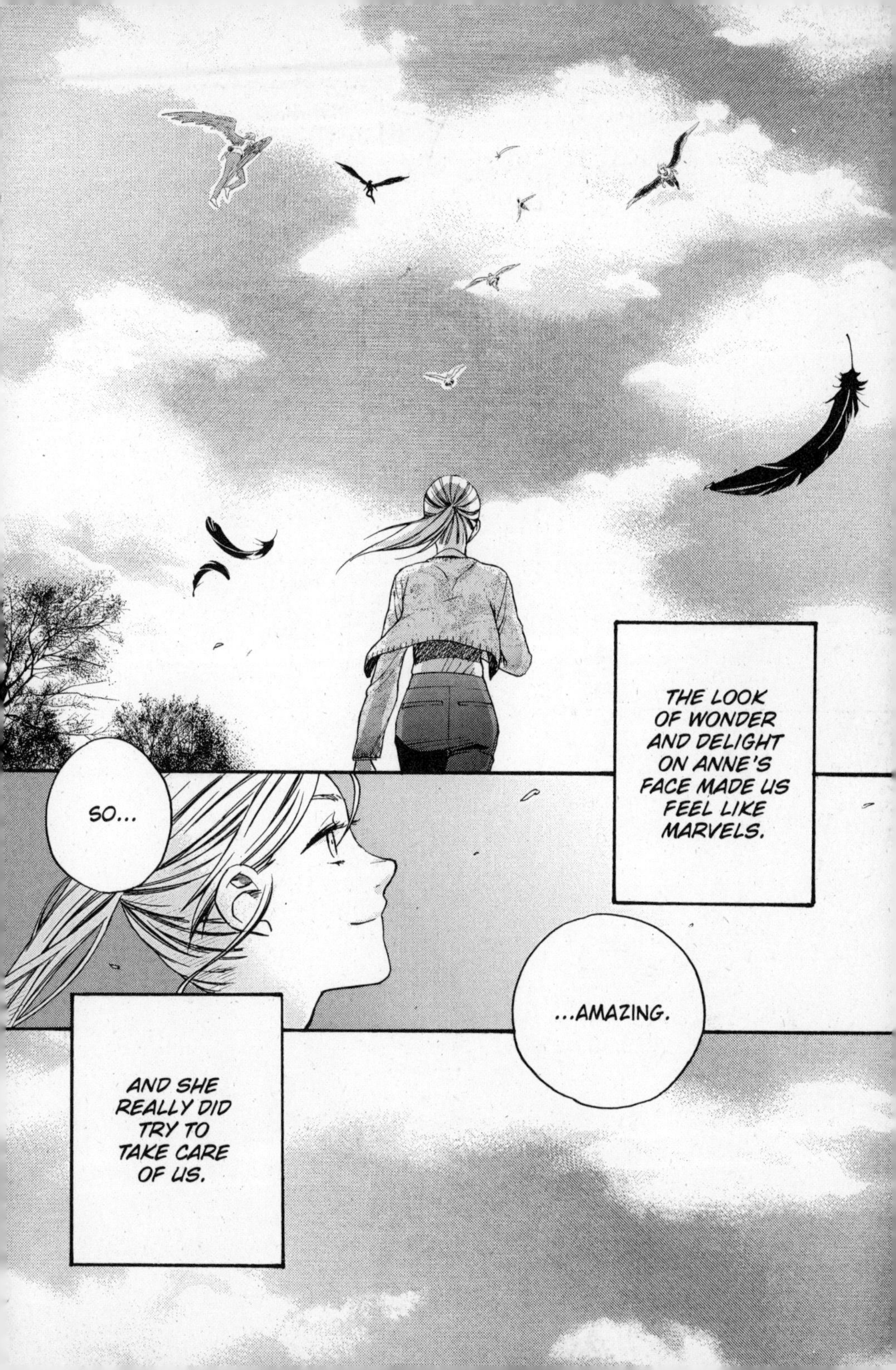
THE LOOK OF WONDER AND DELIGHT ON ANNE'S FACE MADE US FEEL LIKE MARVELS.
SO...
...AMAZING.
AND SHE REALLY DID TRY TO TAKE CARE OF US.

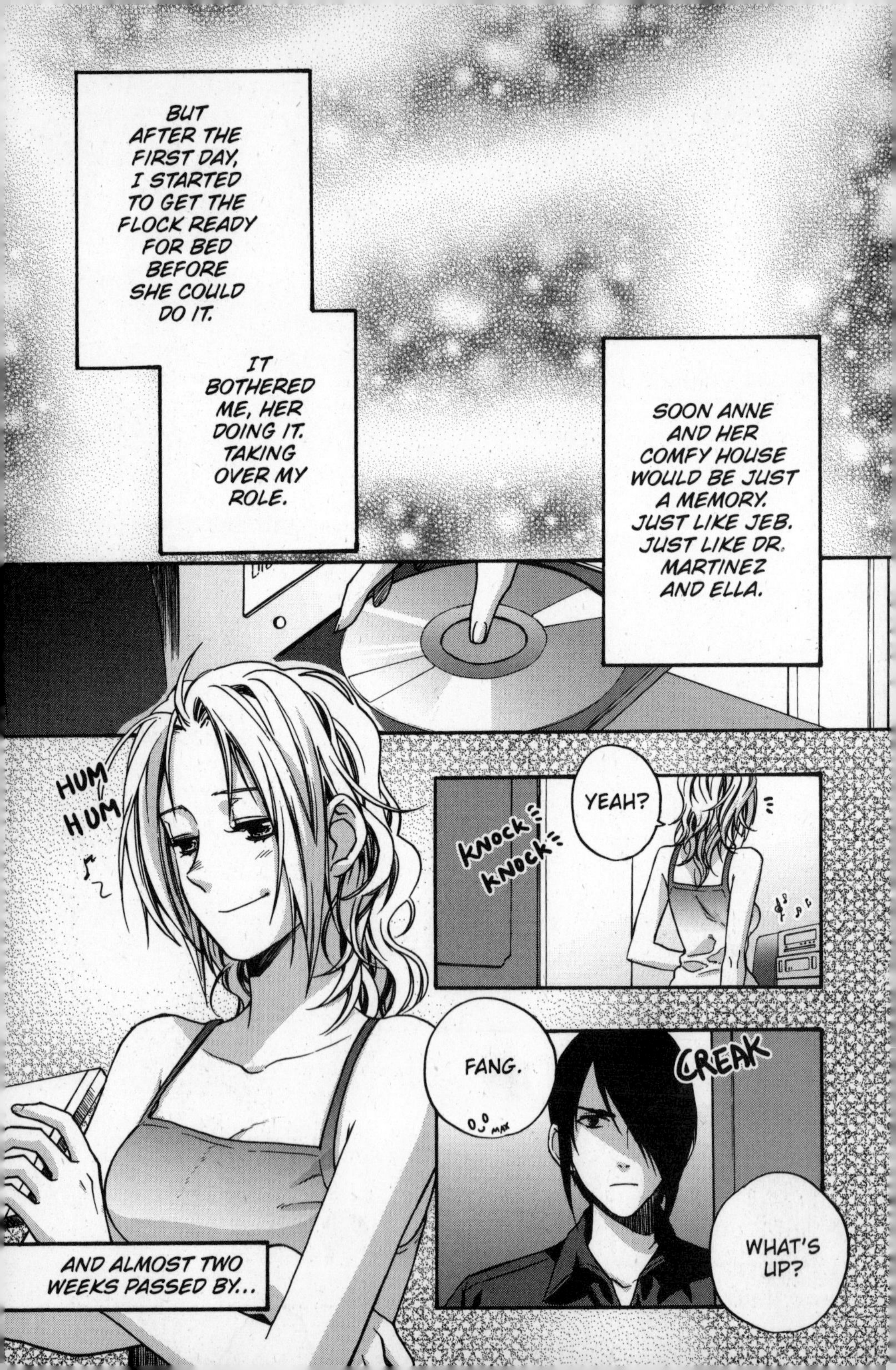
BUT AFTER THE FIRST DAY, I STARTED TO GET THE FLOCK READY FOR BED BEFORE SHE COULD DO IT.
IT BOTHERED ME, HER DOING IT. TAKING OVER MY ROLE.
SOON ANNE AND HER COMFY HOUSE WOULD BE JUST A MEMORY. JUST LIKE JEB. JUST LIKE DR. MARTINEZ AND ELLA.
HUM HUM
AND ALMOST TWO WEEKS PASSED BY...
KNOCK KNOCK
YEAH?
FANG.
CREAK
WHAT'S UP?

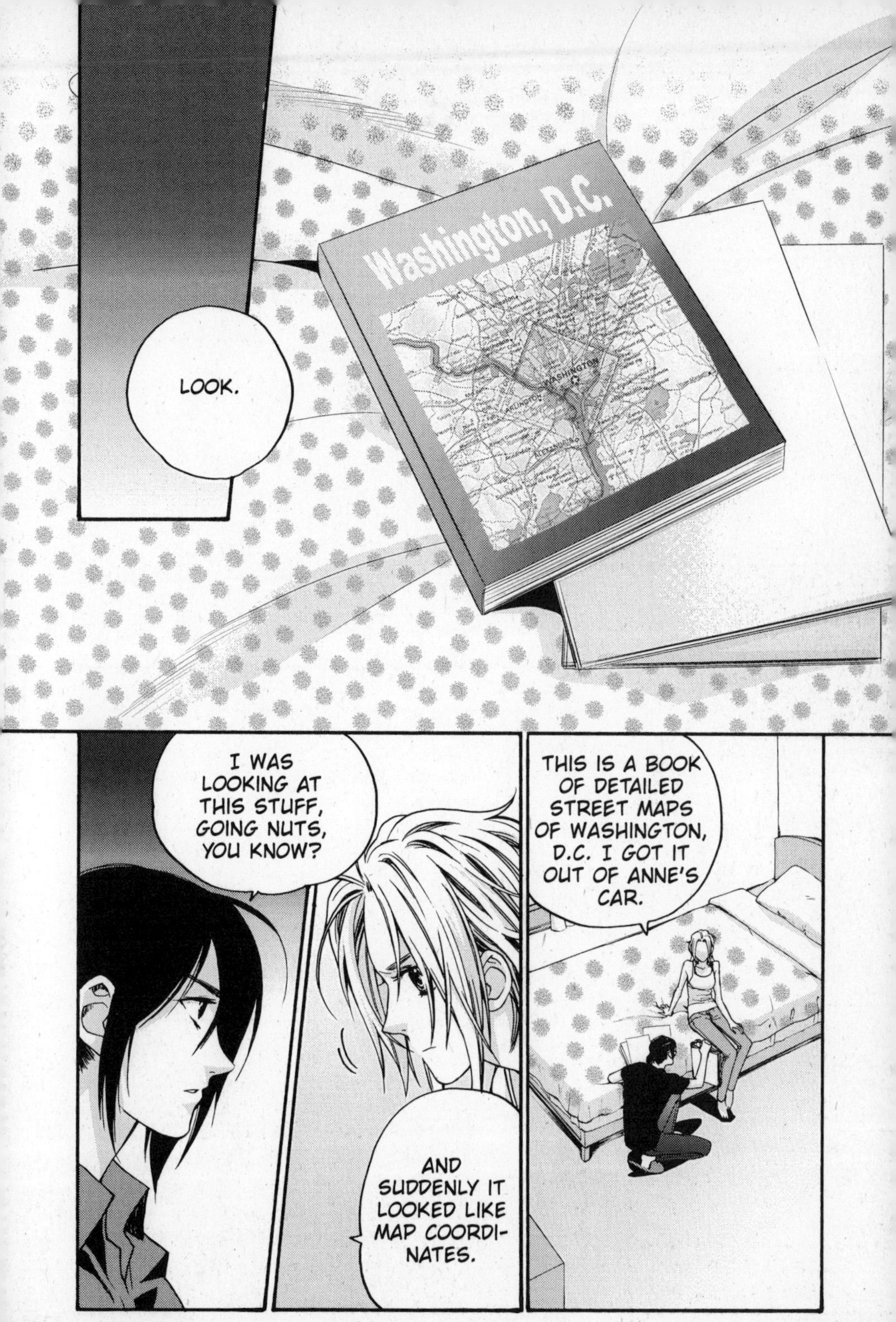
LOOK.
Washington, D.C.
WASHINGTON
I WAS LOOKING AT THIS STUFF, GOING NUTS, YOU KNOW?
AND SUDDENLY IT LOOKED LIKE MAP COORDI-NATES.
THIS IS A BOOK OF DETAILED STREET MAPS OF WASHINGTON, D.C. I GOT IT OUT OF ANNE'S CAR.

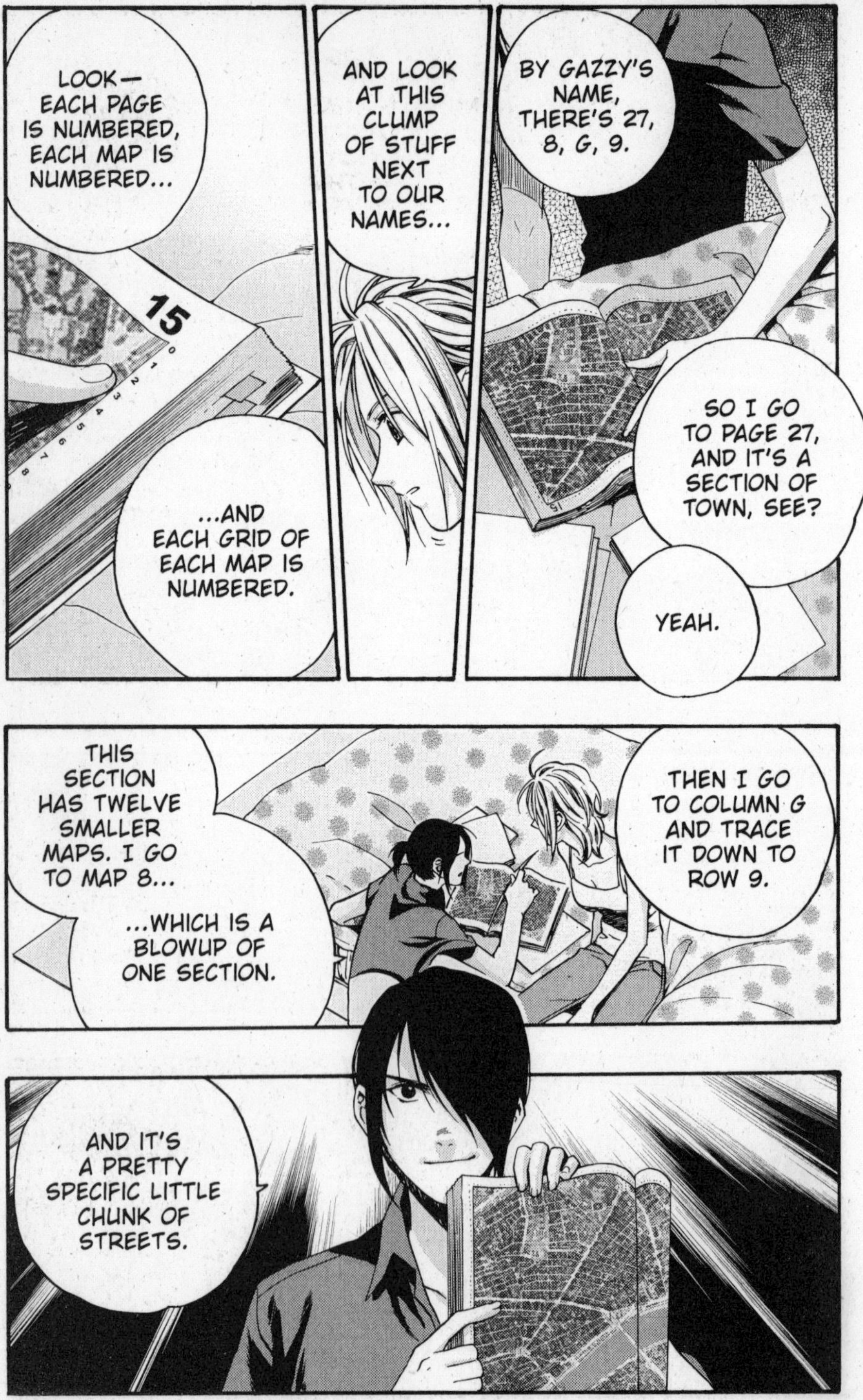
LOOK— EACH PAGE IS NUMBERED, EACH MAP IS NUMBERED...
15
...AND EACH GRID OF EACH MAP IS NUMBERED.
AND LOOK AT THIS CLUMP OF STUFF NEXT TO OUR NAMES...
BY GAZZY'S NAME, THERE'S 27, 8, G, 9.
SO I GO TO PAGE 27, AND IT'S A SECTION OF TOWN, SEE?
YEAH.
THIS SECTION HAS TWELVE SMALLER MAPS. I GO TO MAP 8...
...WHICH IS A BLOWUP OF ONE SECTION.
THEN I GO TO COLUMN G AND TRACE IT DOWN TO ROW 9.
AND IT'S A PRETTY SPECIFIC LITTLE CHUNK OF STREETS.

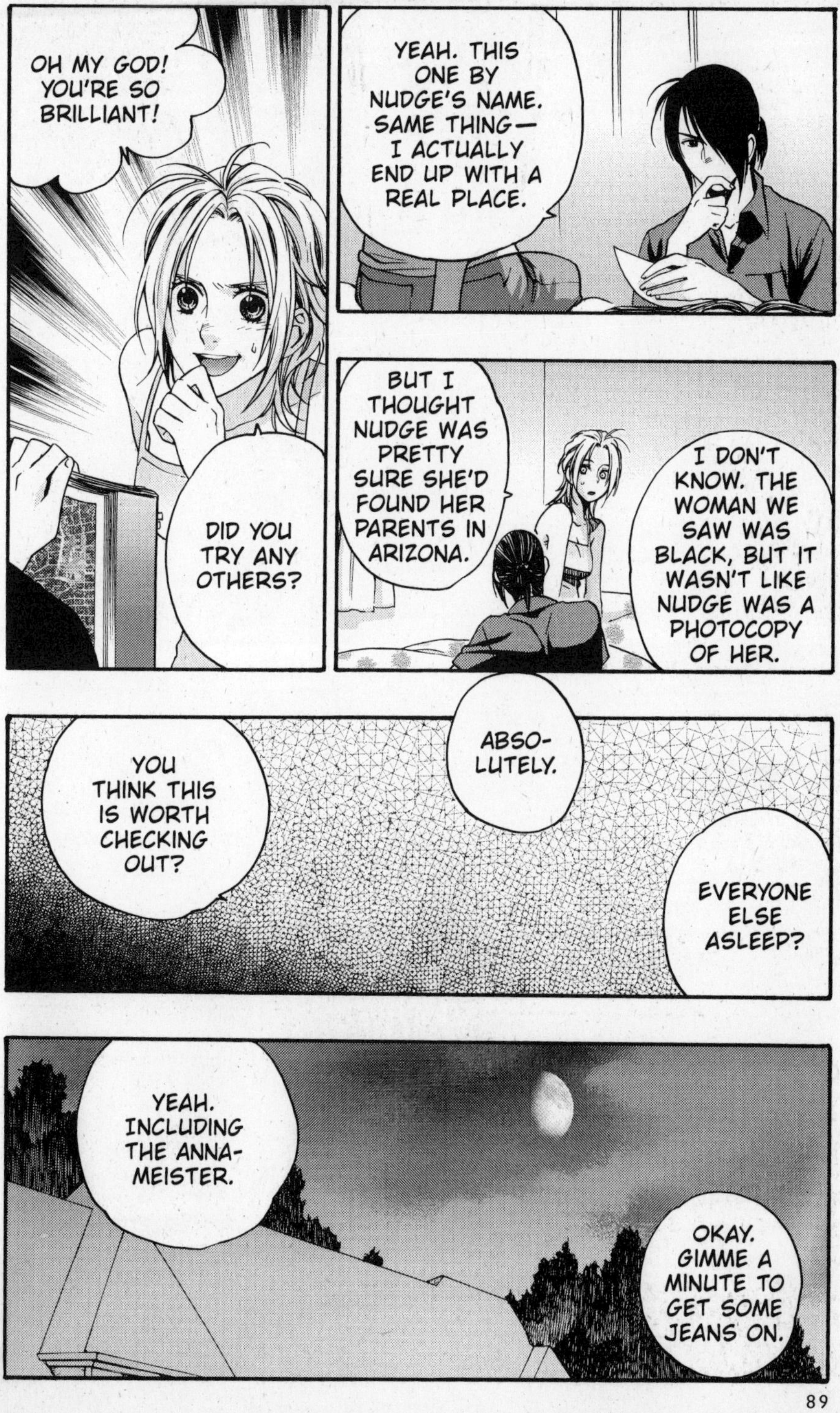
OH MY GOD! YOU'RE SO BRILLIANT!
DID YOU TRY ANY OTHERS?
YEAH. THIS ONE BY NUDGE'S NAME. SAME THING— I ACTUALLY END UP WITH A REAL PLACE.
BUT I THOUGHT NUDGE WAS PRETTY SURE SHE'D FOUND HER PARENTS IN ARIZONA.
I DON'T KNOW. THE WOMAN WE SAW WAS BLACK, BUT IT WASN'T LIKE NUDGE WAS A PHOTOCOPY OF HER.
YOU THINK THIS IS WORTH CHECKING OUT?
ABSO-LUTELY.
EVERYONE ELSE ASLEEP?
YEAH. INCLUDING THE ANNA-MEISTER.
OKAY. GIMME A MINUTE TO GET SOME JEANS ON.

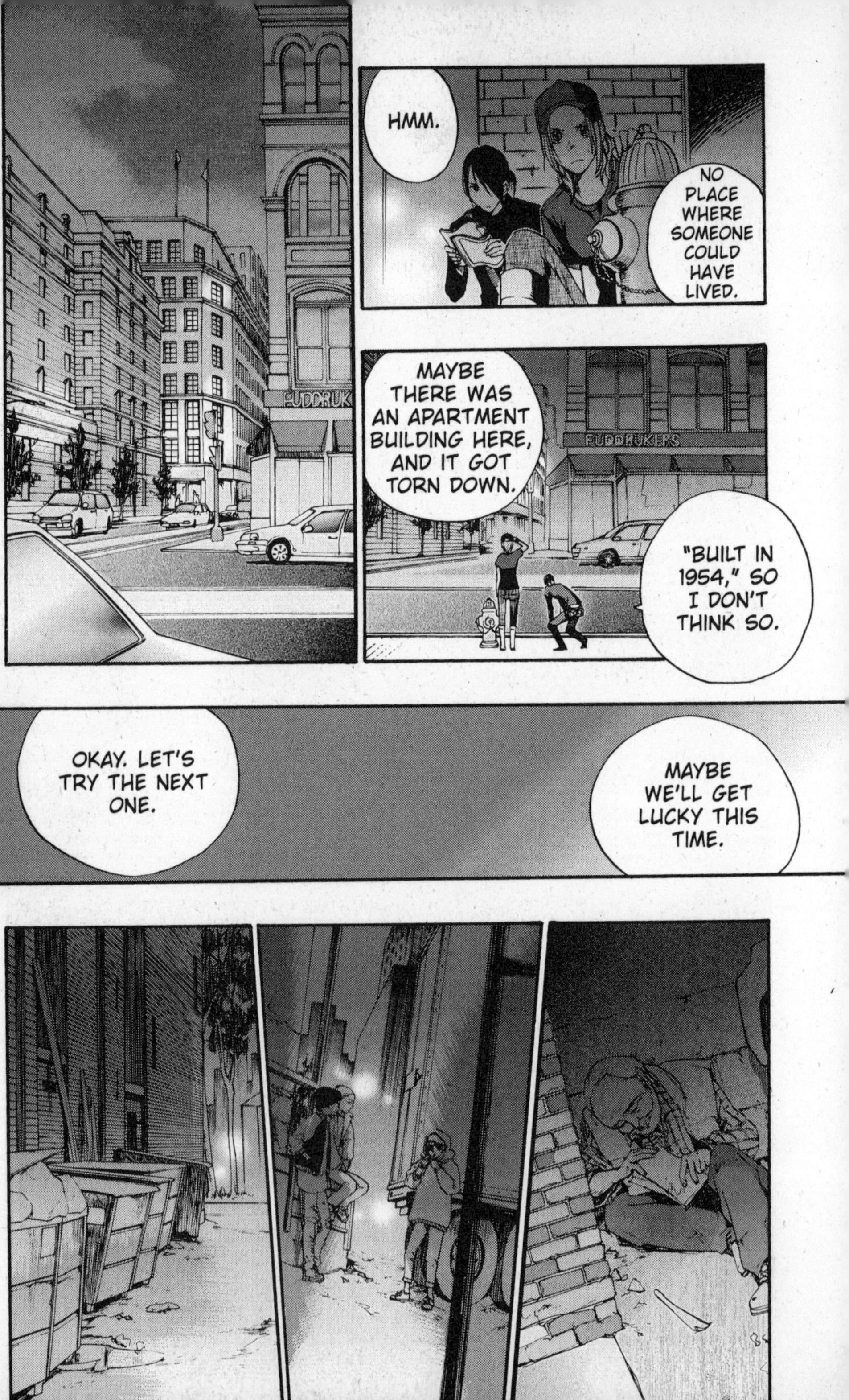
HMM.
NO PLACE WHERE SOMEONE COULD HAVE LIVED.
MAYBE THERE WAS AN APARTMENT BUILDING HERE, AND IT GOT TORN DOWN.
FUDDRUKERS
"BUILT IN 1954," SO I DON'T THINK SO.
OKAY. LET'S TRY THE NEXT ONE.
MAYBE WE'LL GET LUCKY THIS TIME.

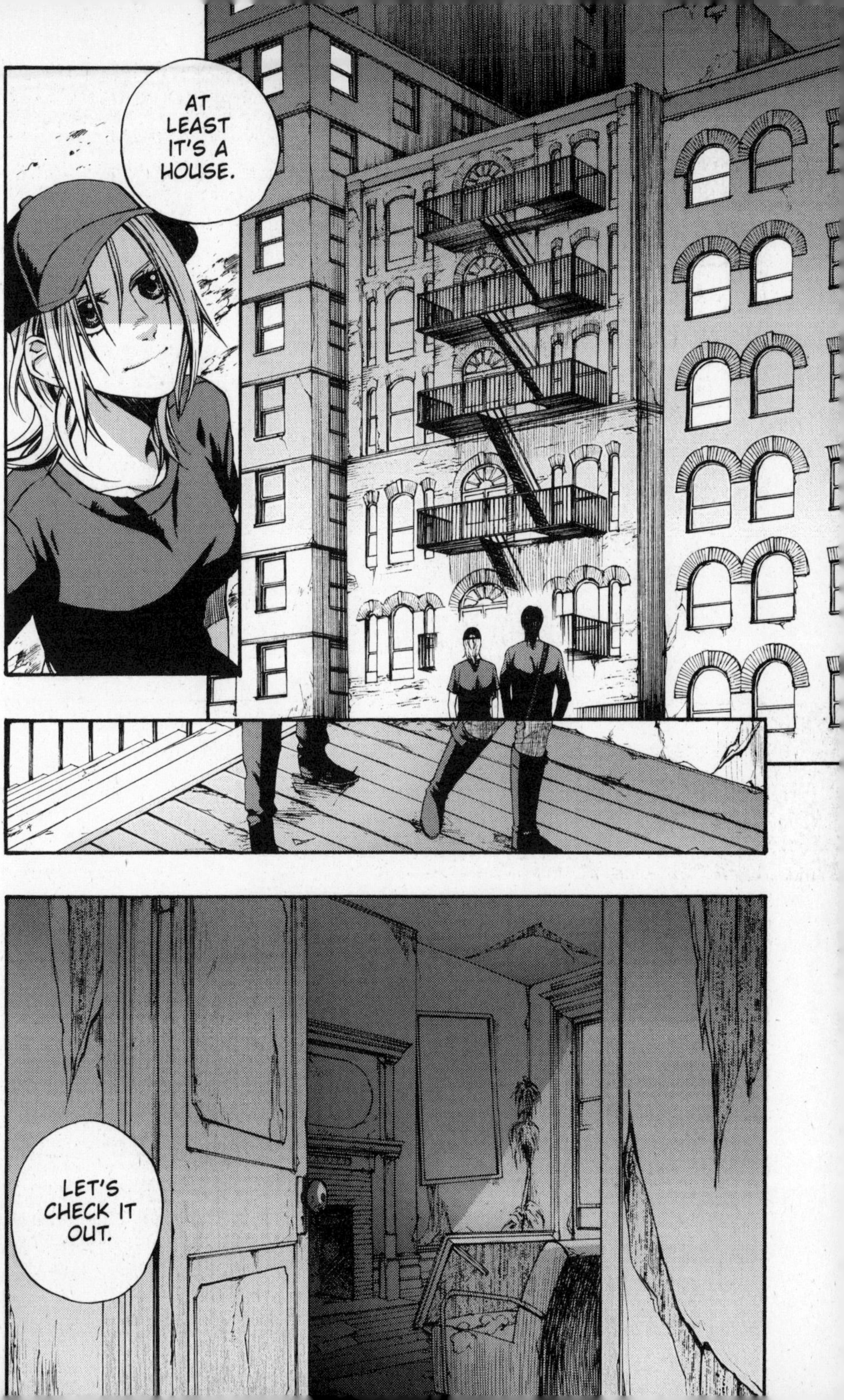
AT LEAST IT'S A HOUSE.
LET'S CHECK IT OUT.

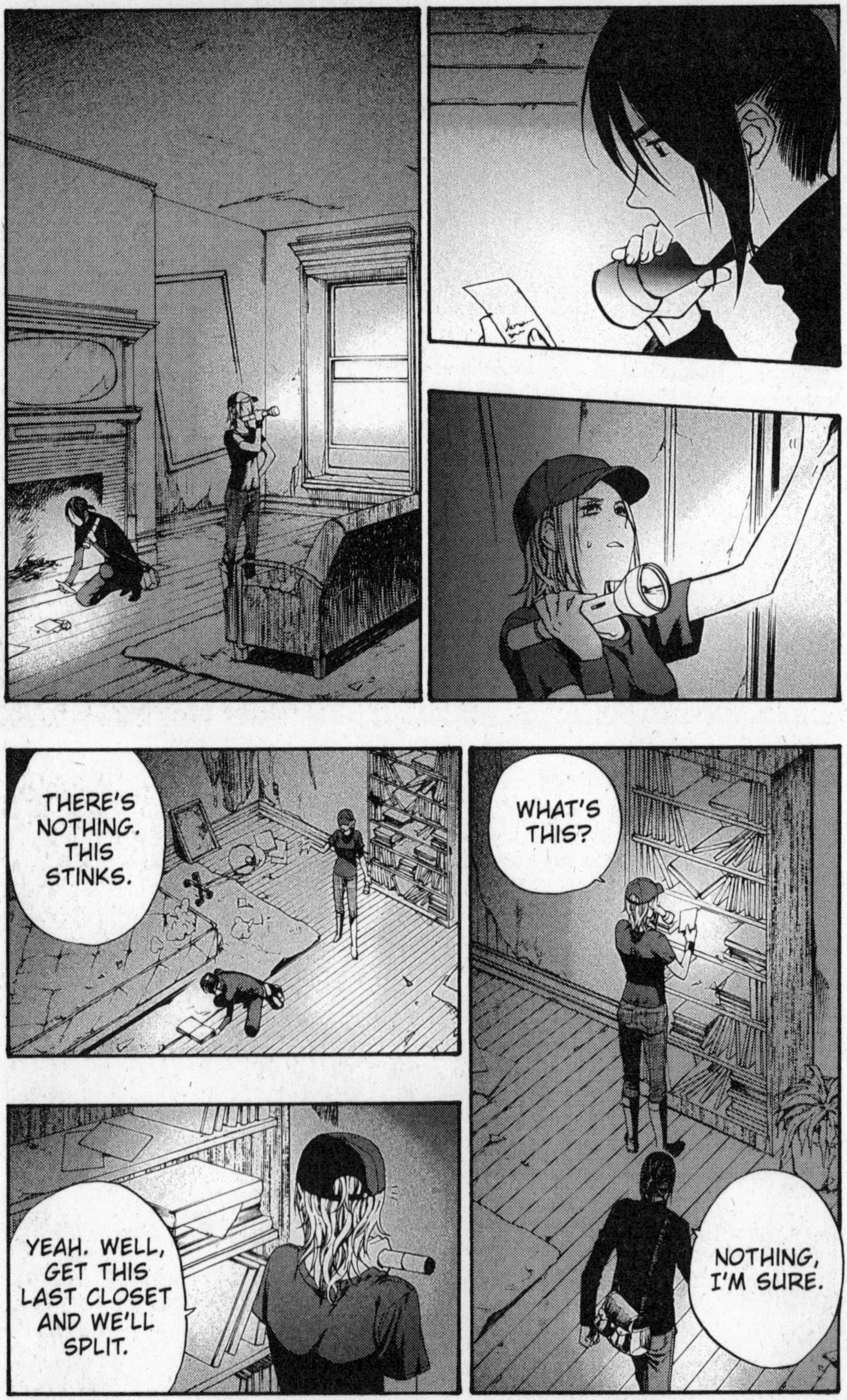
THERE'S NOTHING. THIS STINKS.
YEAH. WELL, GET THIS LAST CLOSET AND WE'LL SPLIT.
WHAT'S THIS?
NOTHING, I'M SURE.

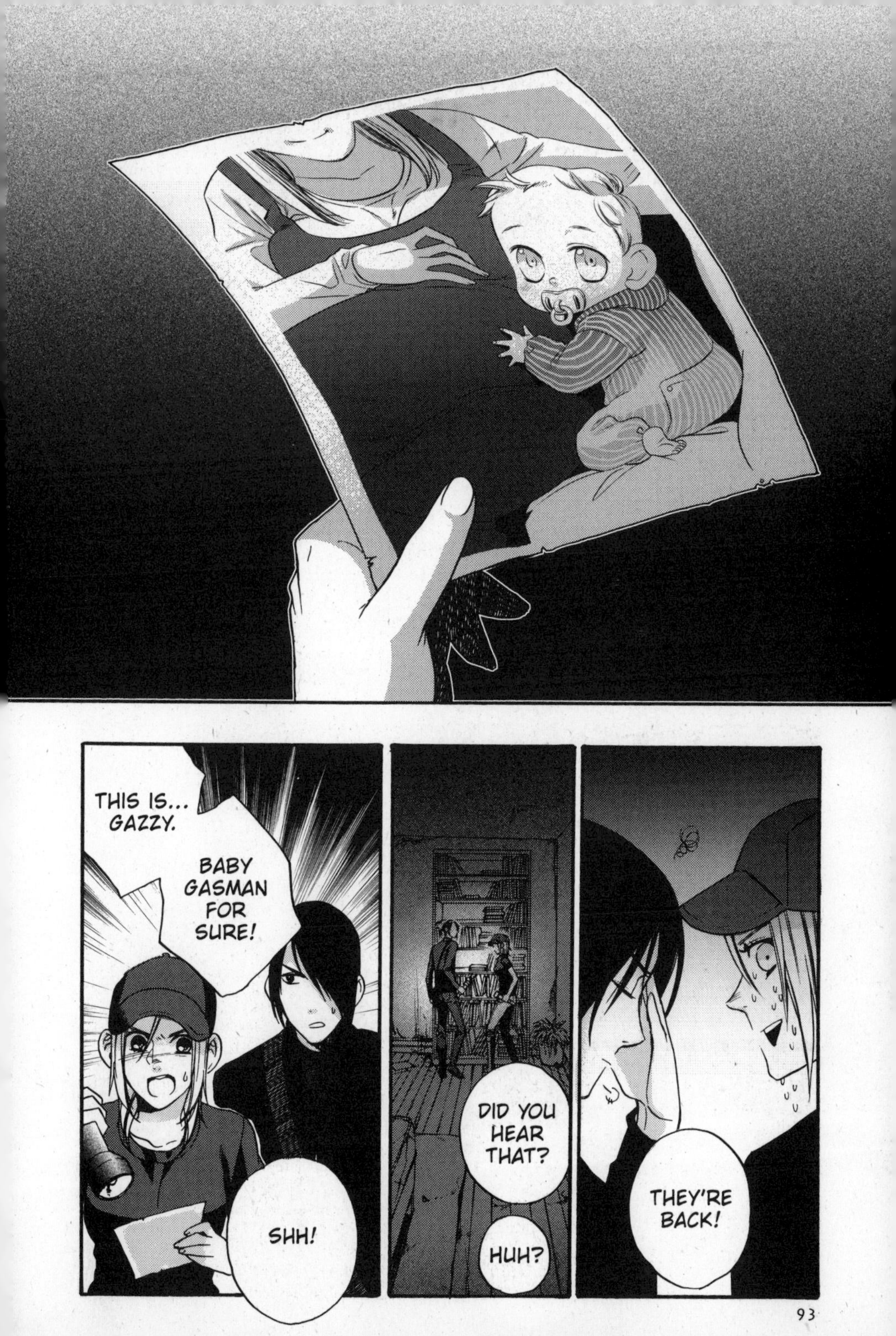
THIS IS... GAZZY.
BABY GASMAN FOR SURE!
SHH!
DID YOU HEAR THAT?
HUH?
THEY'RE BACK!

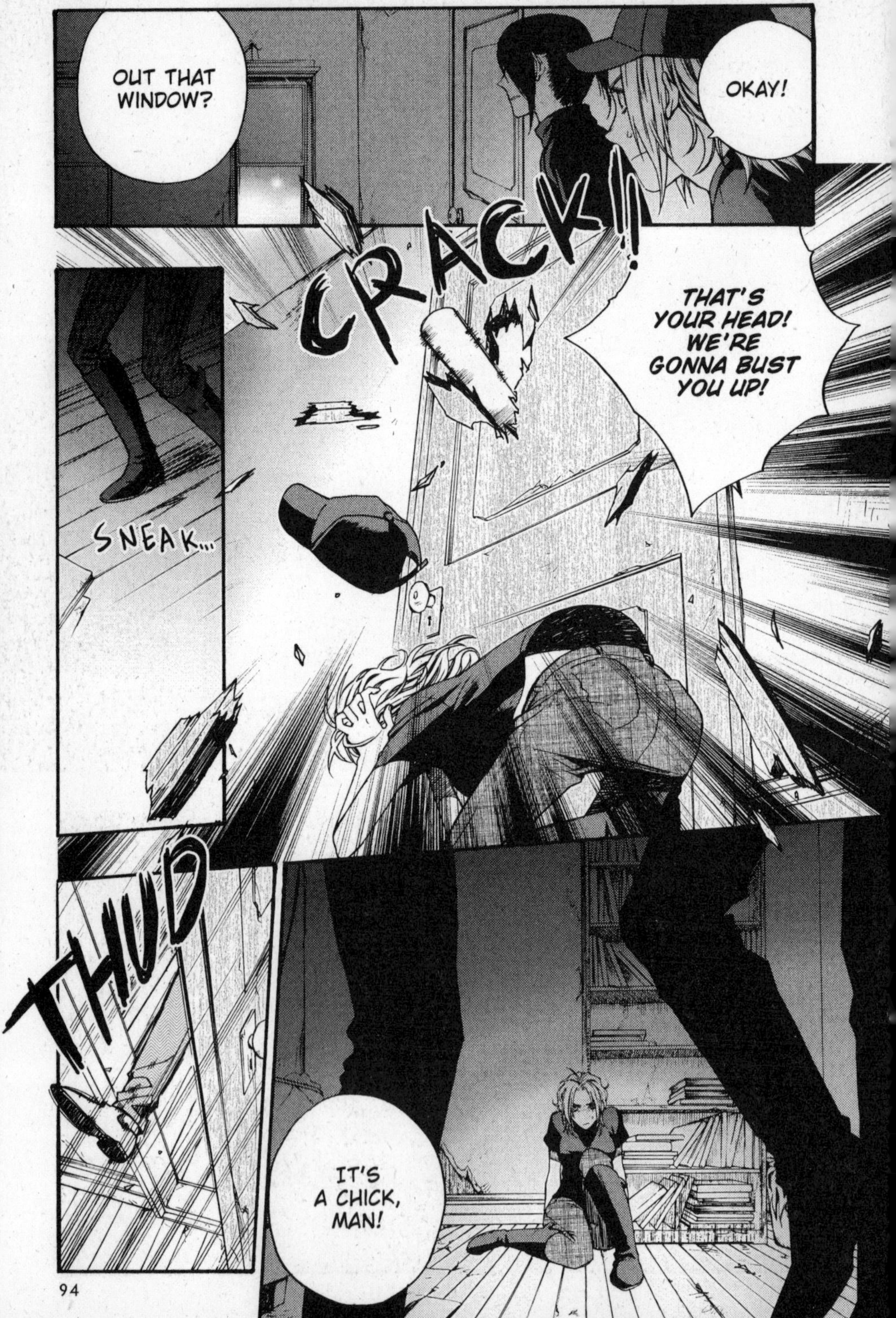
OUT THAT WINDOW?
OKAY!
CRACK!!
THAT'S YOUR HEAD! WE'RE GONNA BUST YOU UP!
SNEAK...
THUD
IT'S A CHICK, MAN!

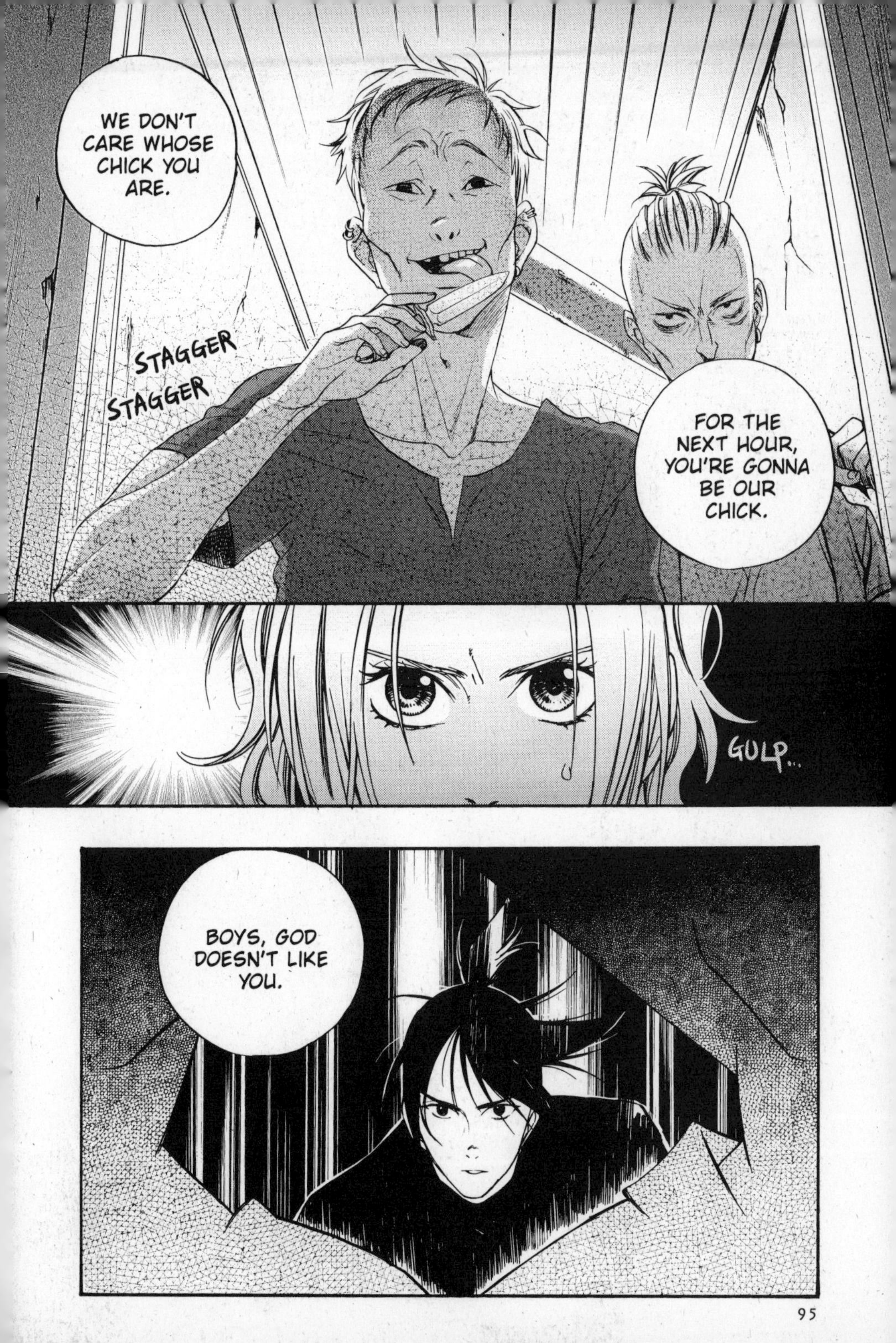
WE DON'T CARE WHOSE CHICK YOU ARE.
STAGGER STAGGER
FOR THE NEXT HOUR, YOU'RE GONNA BE OUR CHICK.
GULP...
BOYS, GOD DOESN'T LIKE YOU.

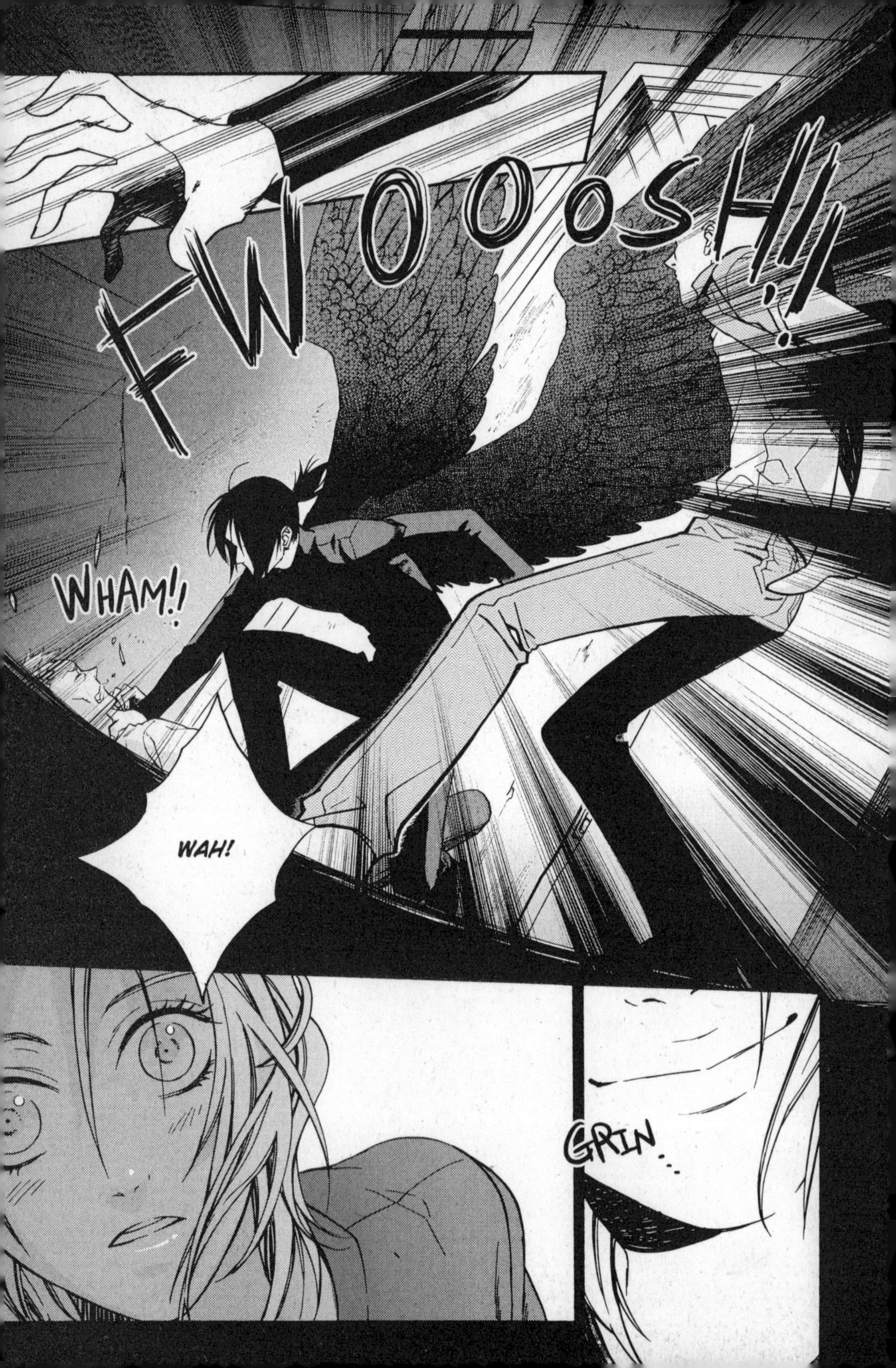
FWOOOSH!!
WHAM!!
WAH!
GRIN...

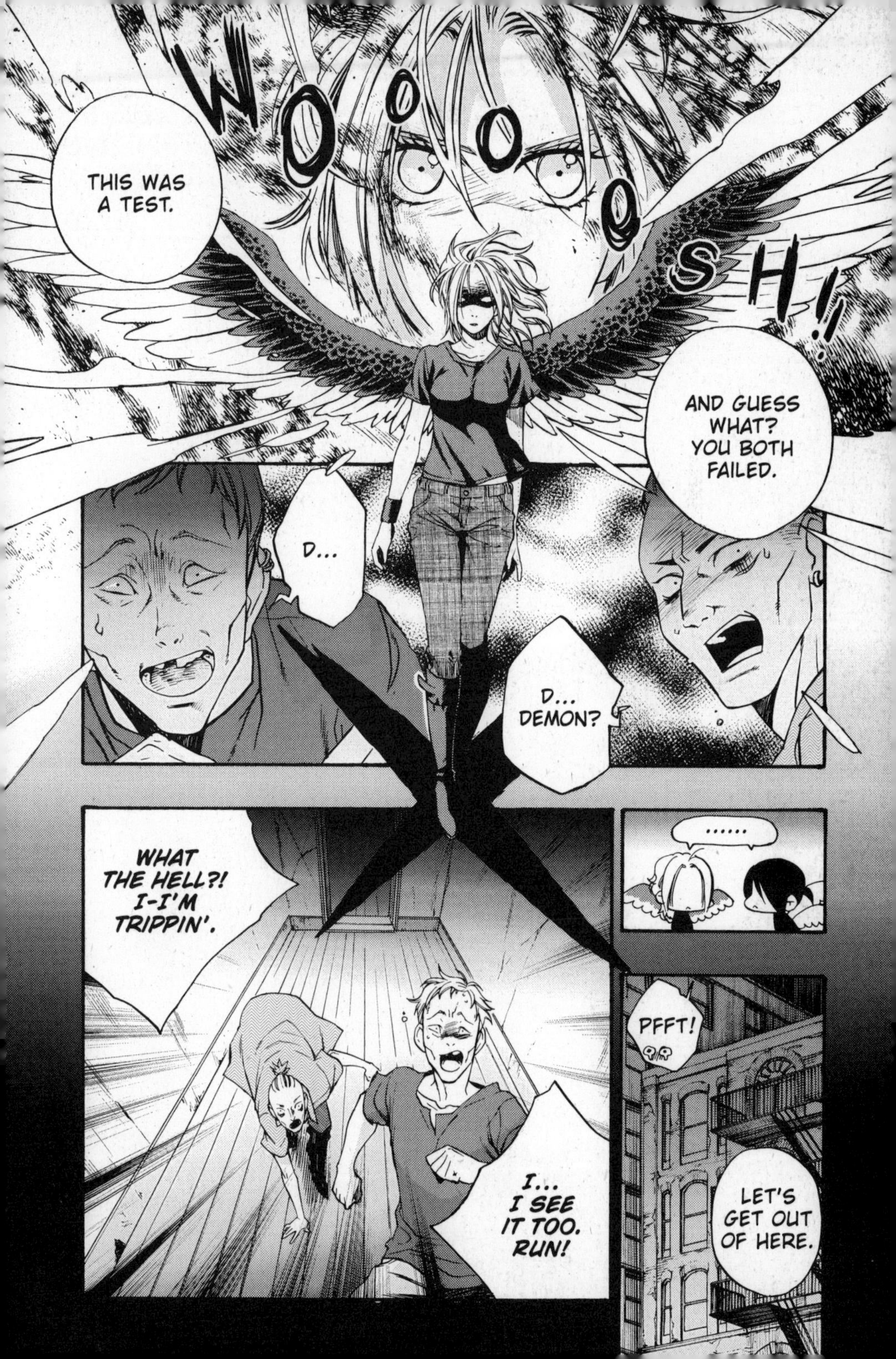
THIS WAS A TEST.
WOOOOOOSH!!
AND GUESS WHAT? YOU BOTH FAILED.
D...
D... DEMON?
WHAT THE HELL?! I-I'M TRIPPIN'.
I... I SEE IT TOO. RUN!
......
PFFT!
LET'S GET OUT OF HERE.

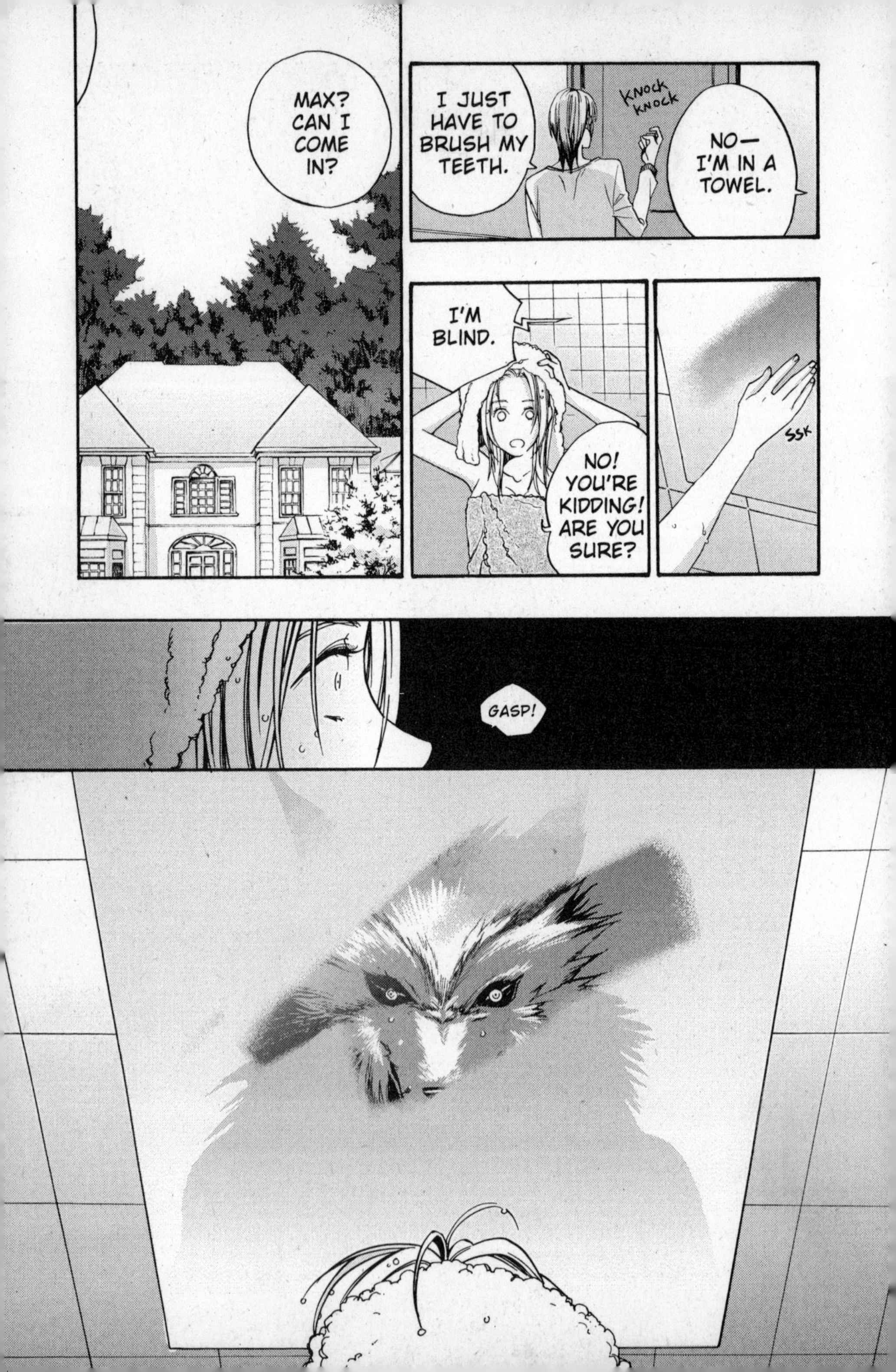
MAX? CAN I COME IN?
I JUST HAVE TO BRUSH MY TEETH.
KNOCK KNOCK
NO— I'M IN A TOWEL.
I'M BLIND.
NO! YOU'RE KIDDING! ARE YOU SURE?
SSK
GASP!

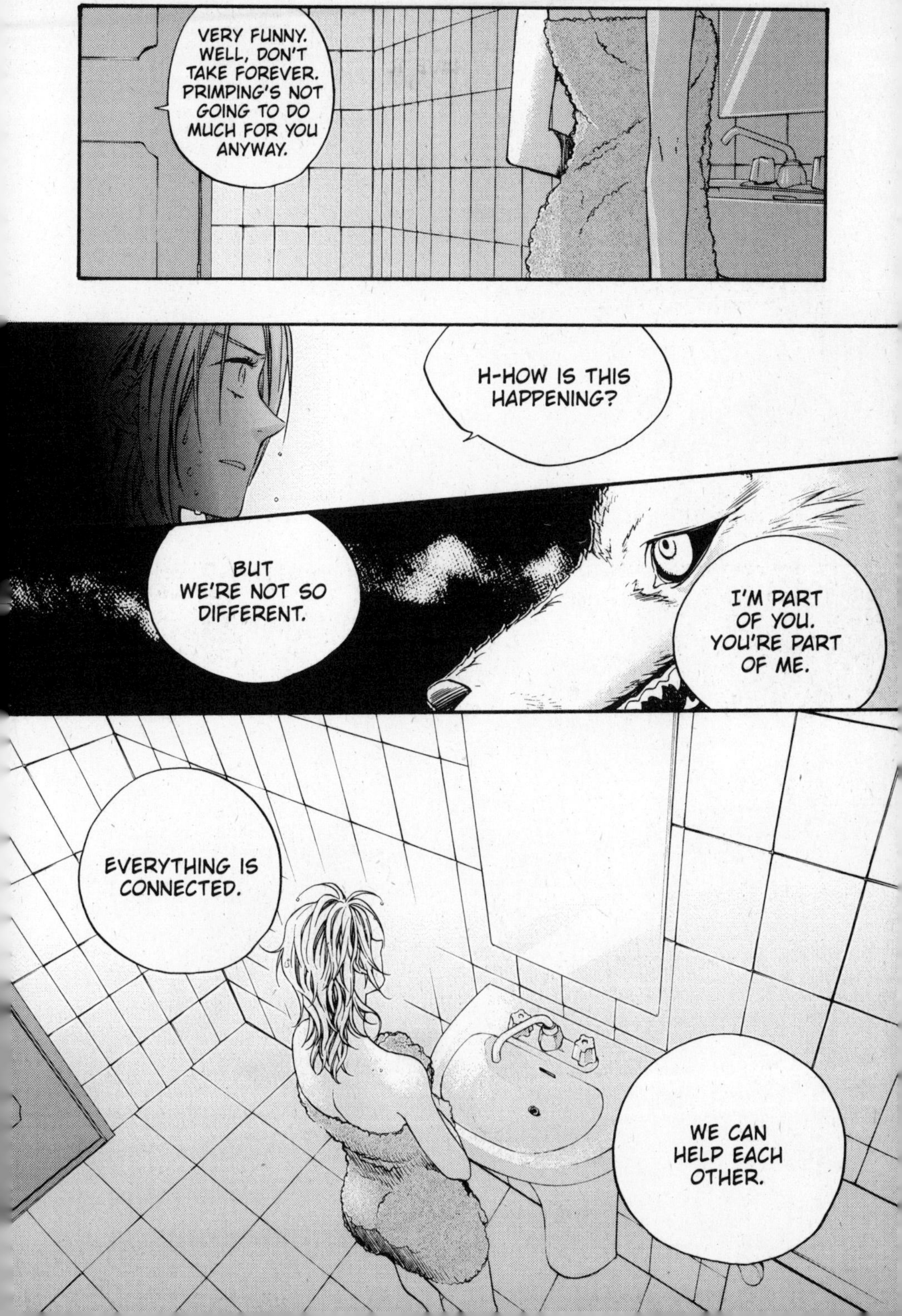
VERY FUNNY. WELL, DON'T TAKE FOREVER. PRIMPING'S NOT GOING TO DO MUCH FOR YOU ANYWAY.
H-HOW IS THIS HAPPENING?
BUT WE'RE NOT SO DIFFERENT.
I'M PART OF YOU. YOU'RE PART OF ME.
EVERYTHING IS CONNECTED.
WE CAN HELP EACH OTHER.

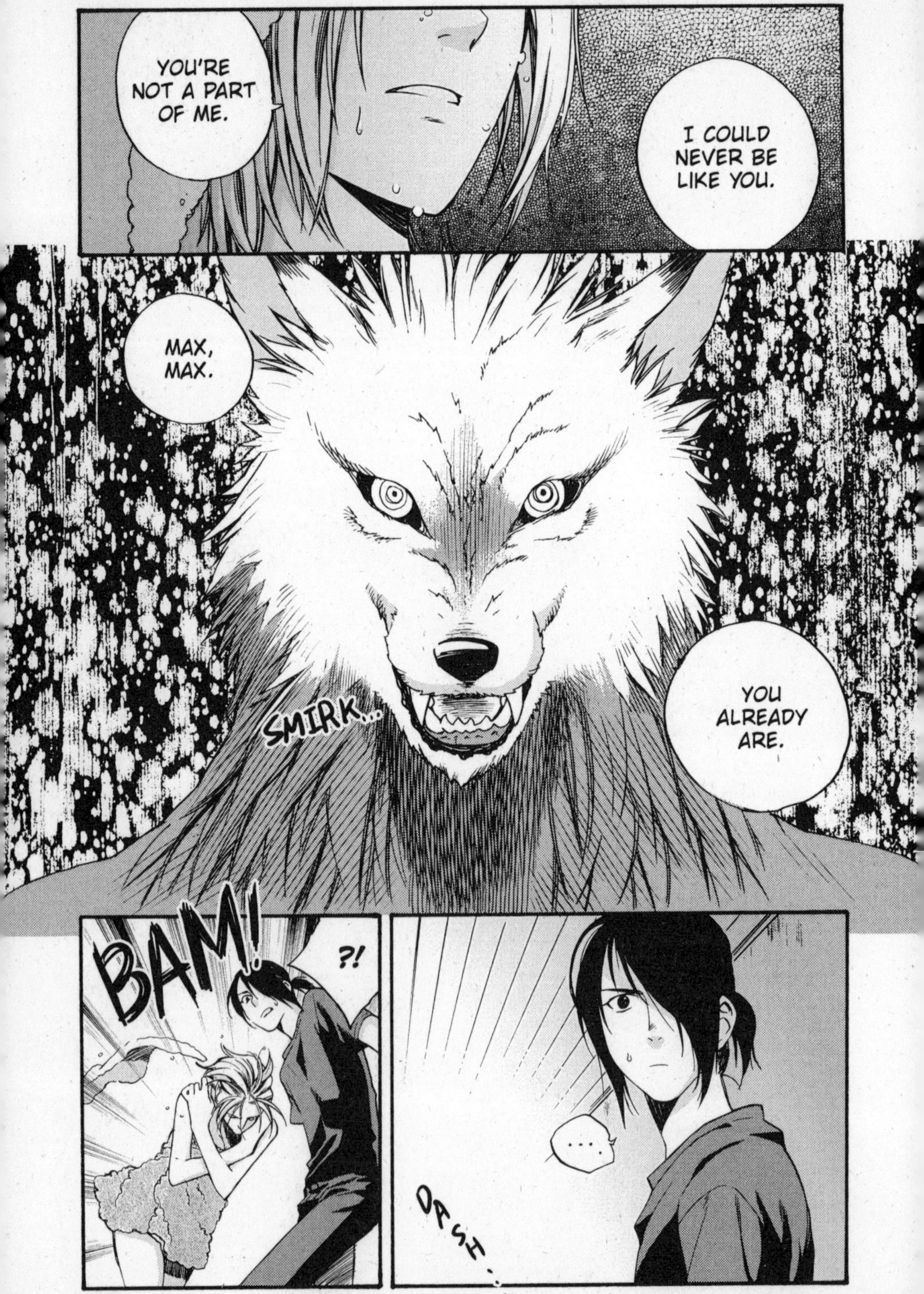
YOU'RE NOT A PART OF ME.
I COULD NEVER BE LIKE YOU.
MAX, MAX.
SMIRK...
YOU ALREADY ARE.
BAM!
?!
....
DASH...

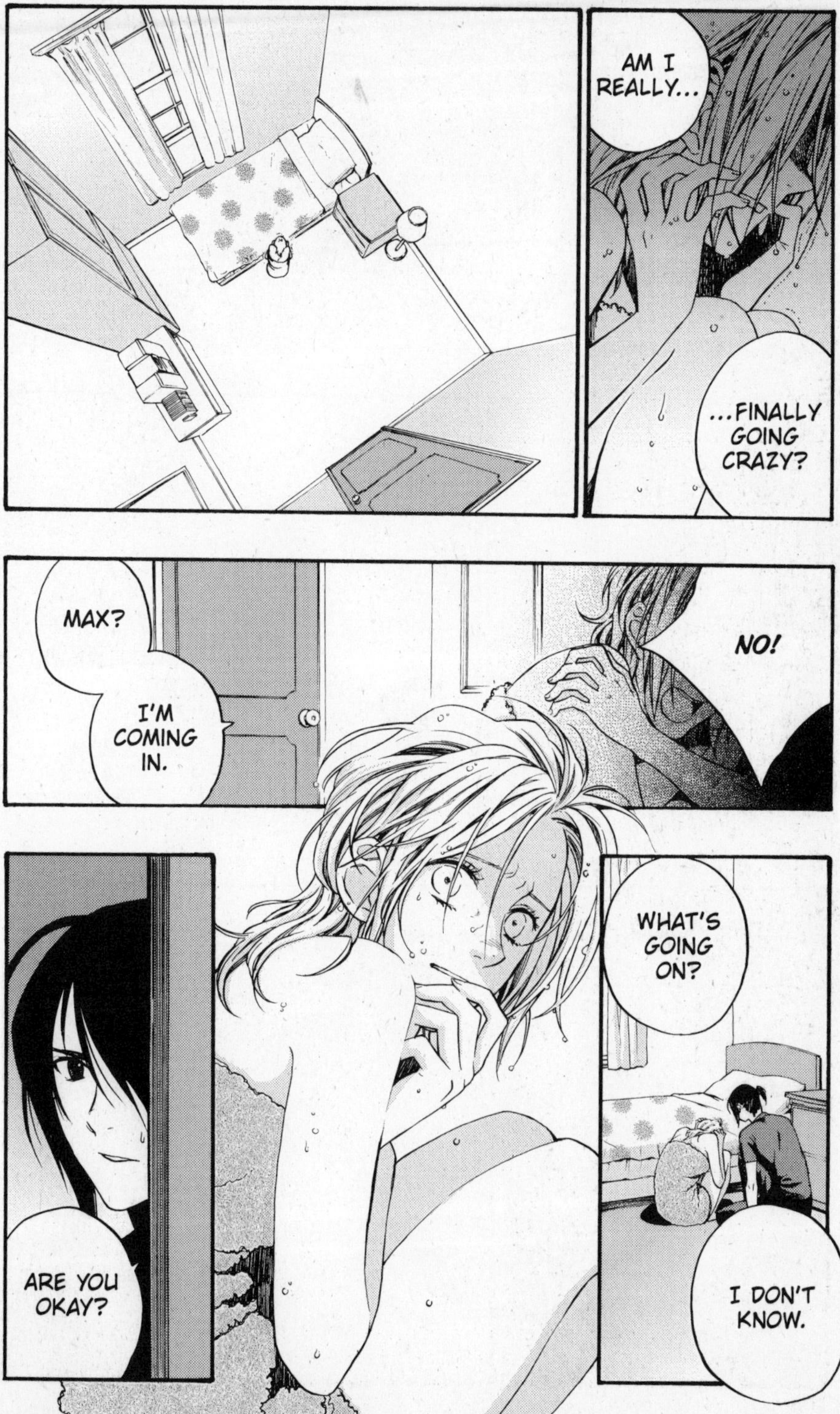
AM I REALLY...
...FINALLY GOING CRAZY?
MAX?
I'M COMING IN.
NO!
ARE YOU OKAY?
WHAT'S GOING ON?
I DON'T KNOW.

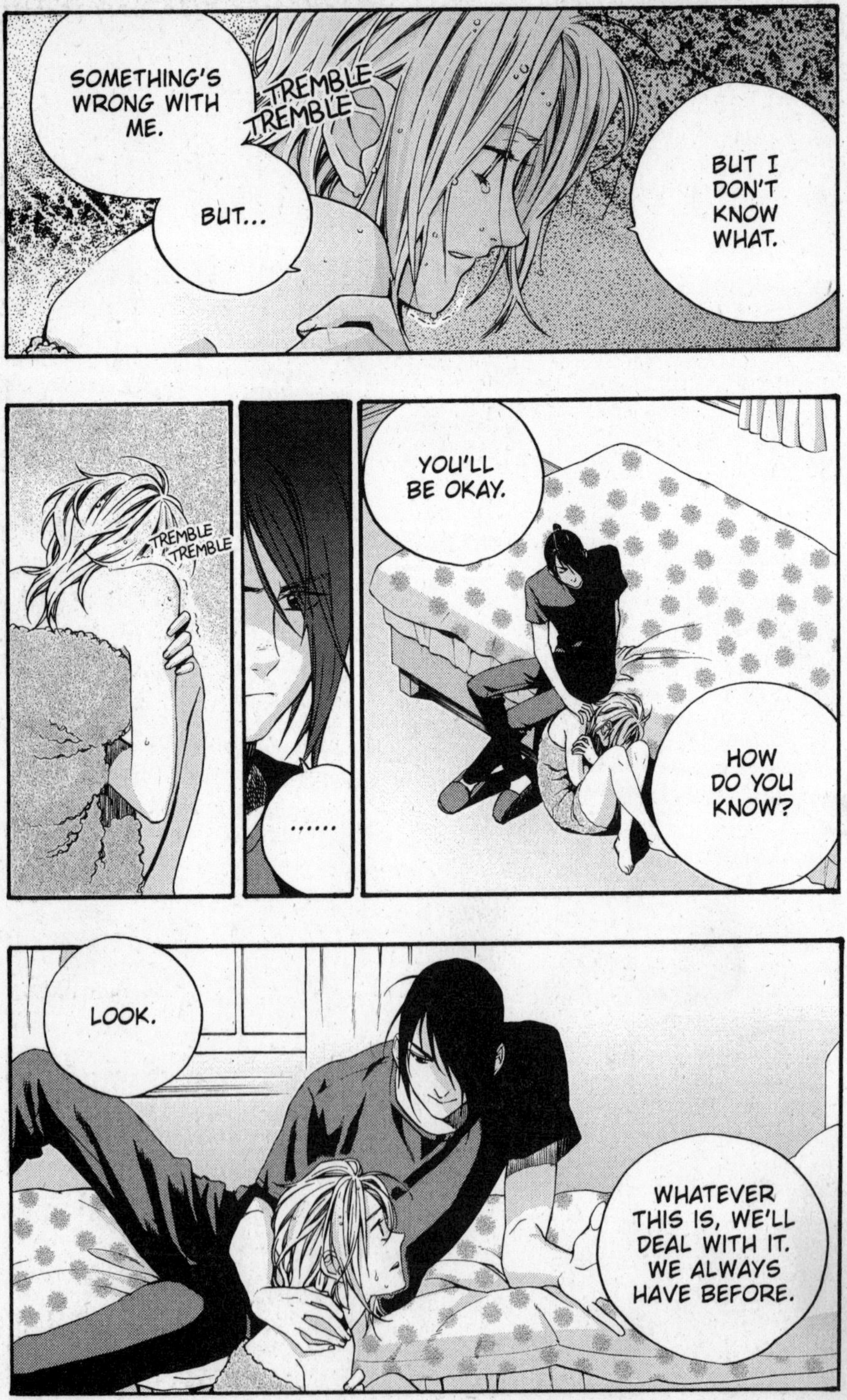
SOMETHING'S WRONG WITH ME.
TREMBLE TREMBLE
BUT...
BUT I DON'T KNOW WHAT.
TREMBLE TREMBLE
......
YOU'LL BE OKAY.
HOW DO YOU KNOW?
LOOK.
WHATEVER THIS IS, WE'LL DEAL WITH IT. WE ALWAYS HAVE BEFORE.

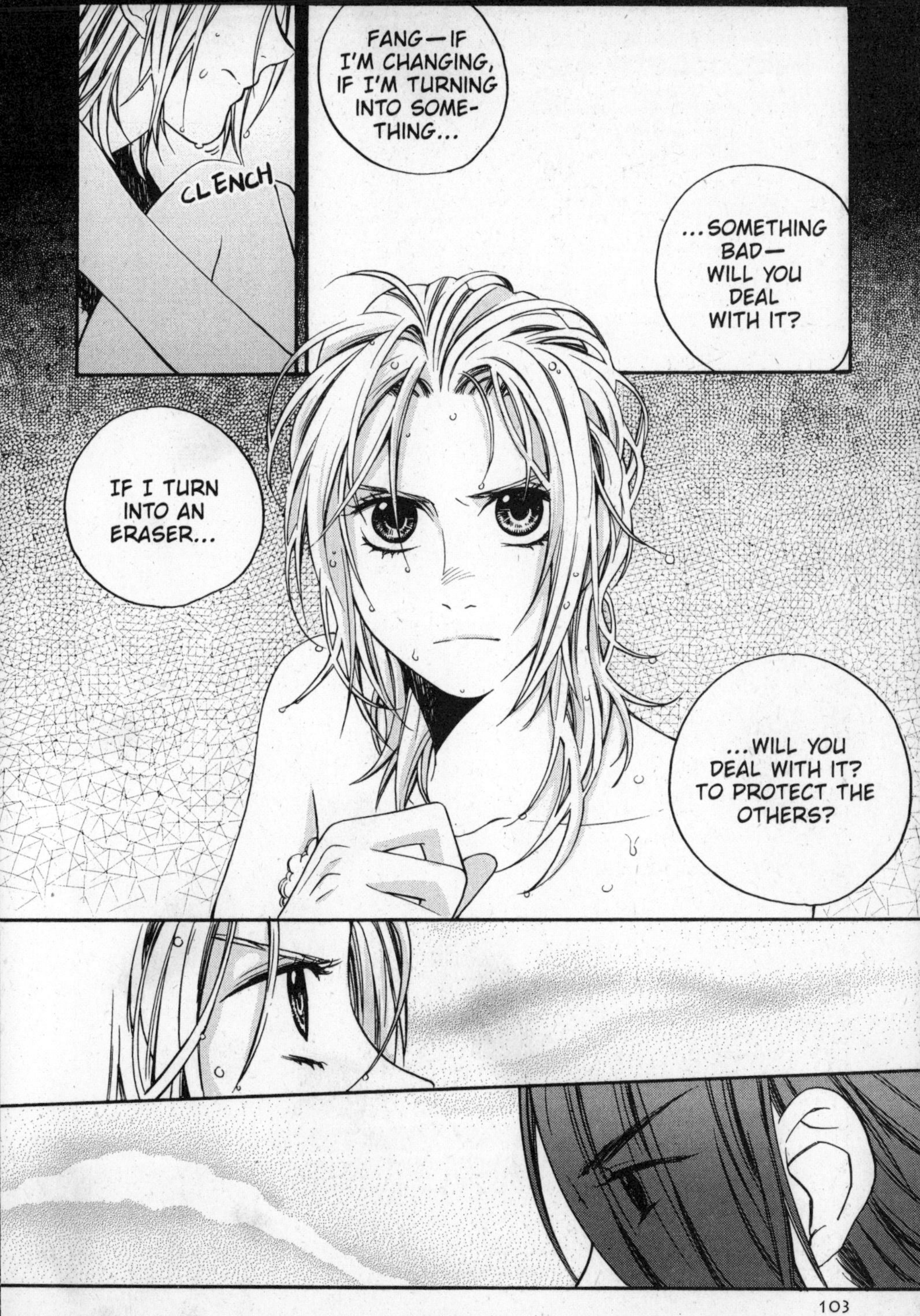
CLENCH
FANG—IF I'M CHANGING, IF I'M TURNING INTO SOME-THING...
...SOMETHING BAD—WILL YOU DEAL WITH IT?
IF I TURN INTO AN ERASER...
...WILL YOU DEAL WITH IT? TO PROTECT THE OTHERS?

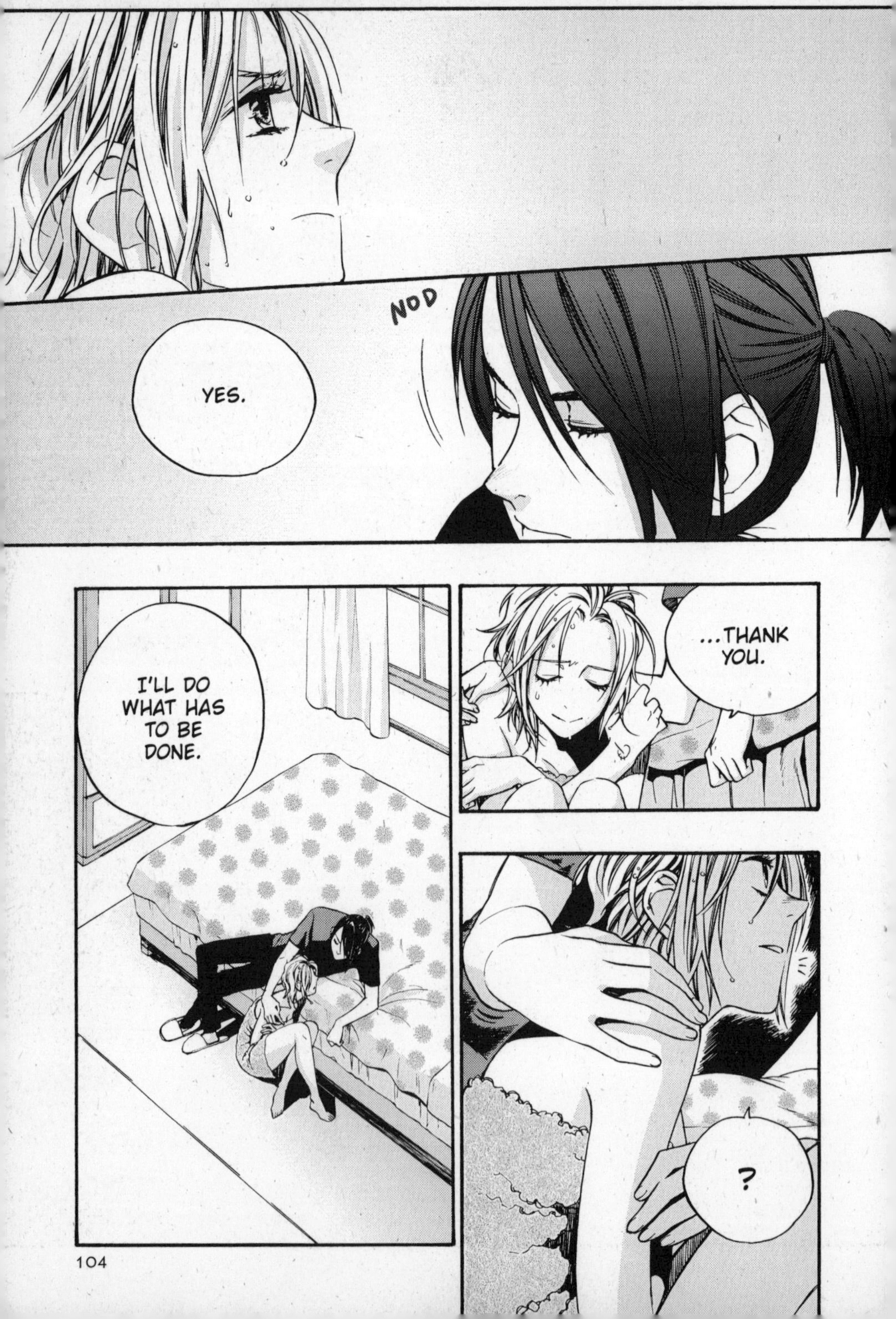
NOD
YES.
I'LL DO WHAT HAS TO BE DONE.
...THANK YOU.
?

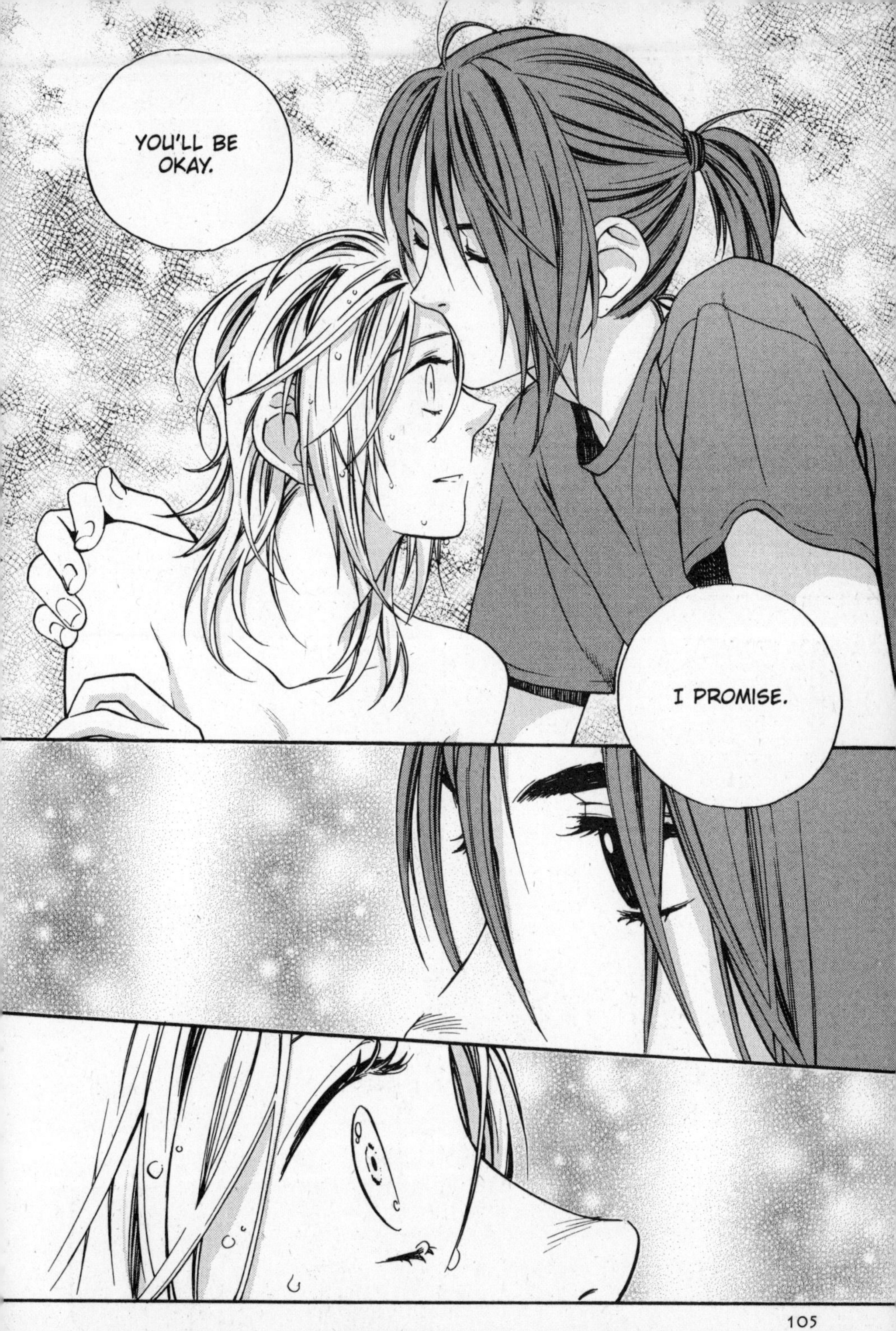
YOU'LL BE OKAY.
I PROMISE.

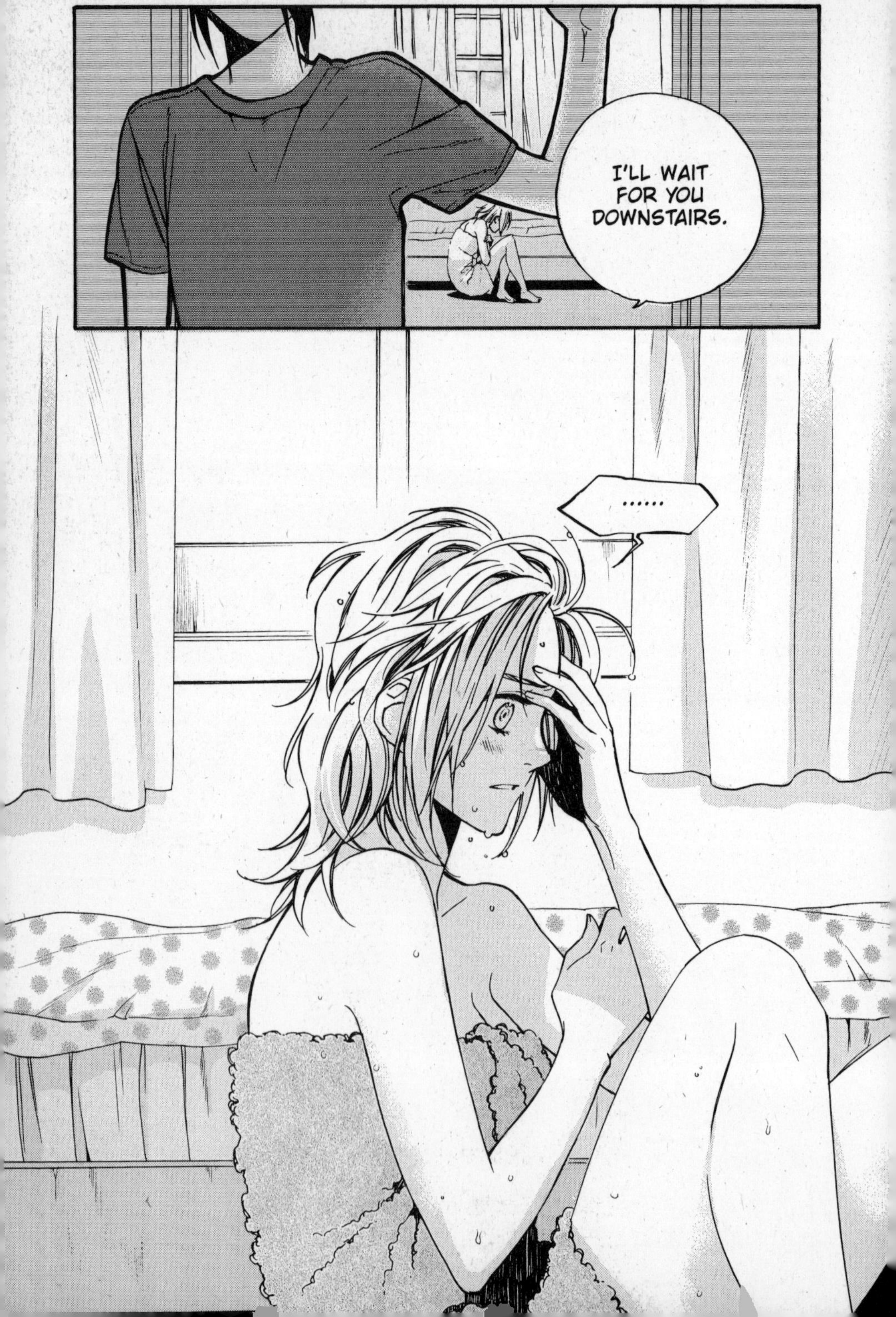
I'LL WAIT FOR YOU DOWNSTAIRS.
......

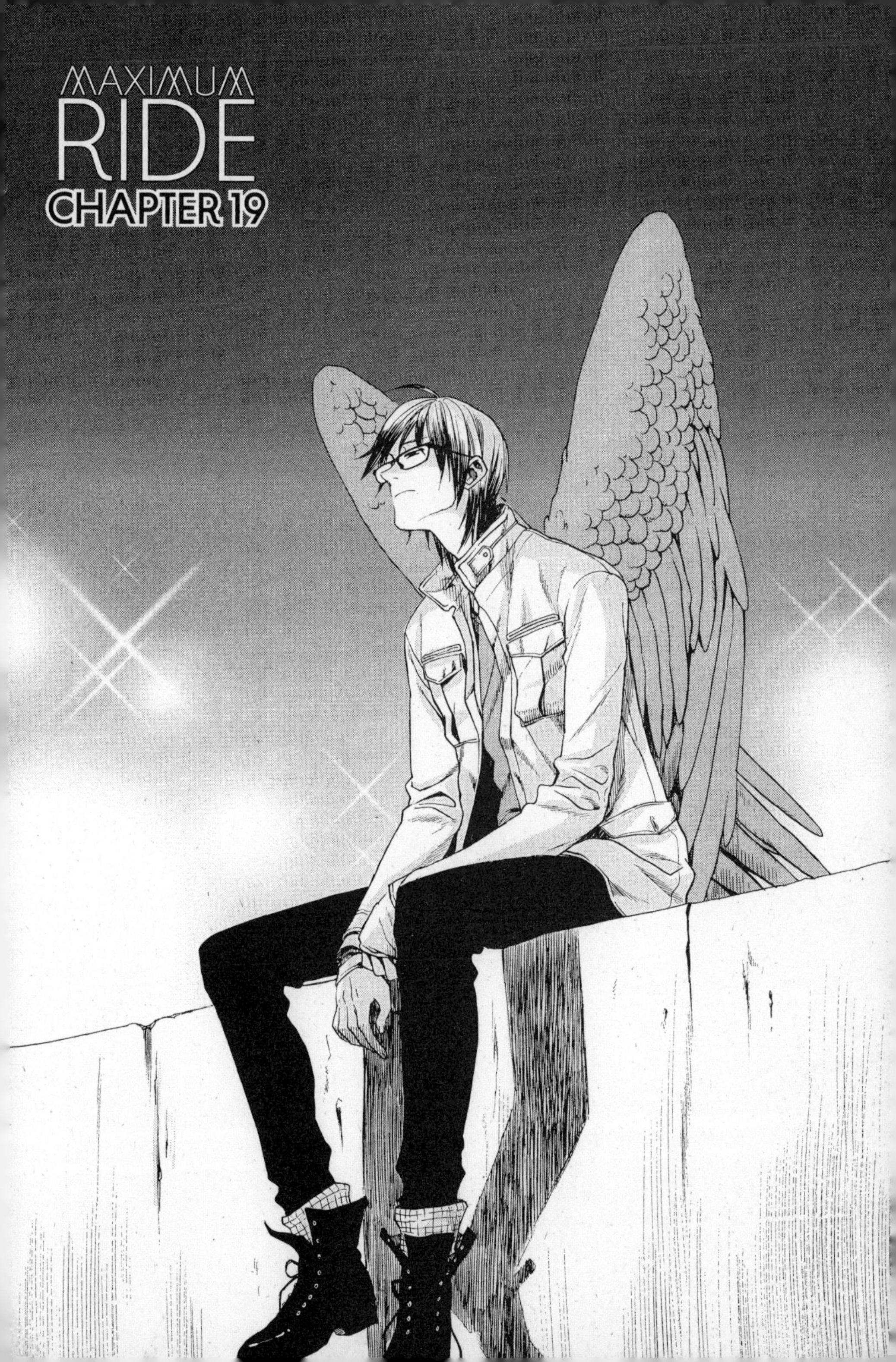
MAXIMUM
RIDE
CHAPTER 19

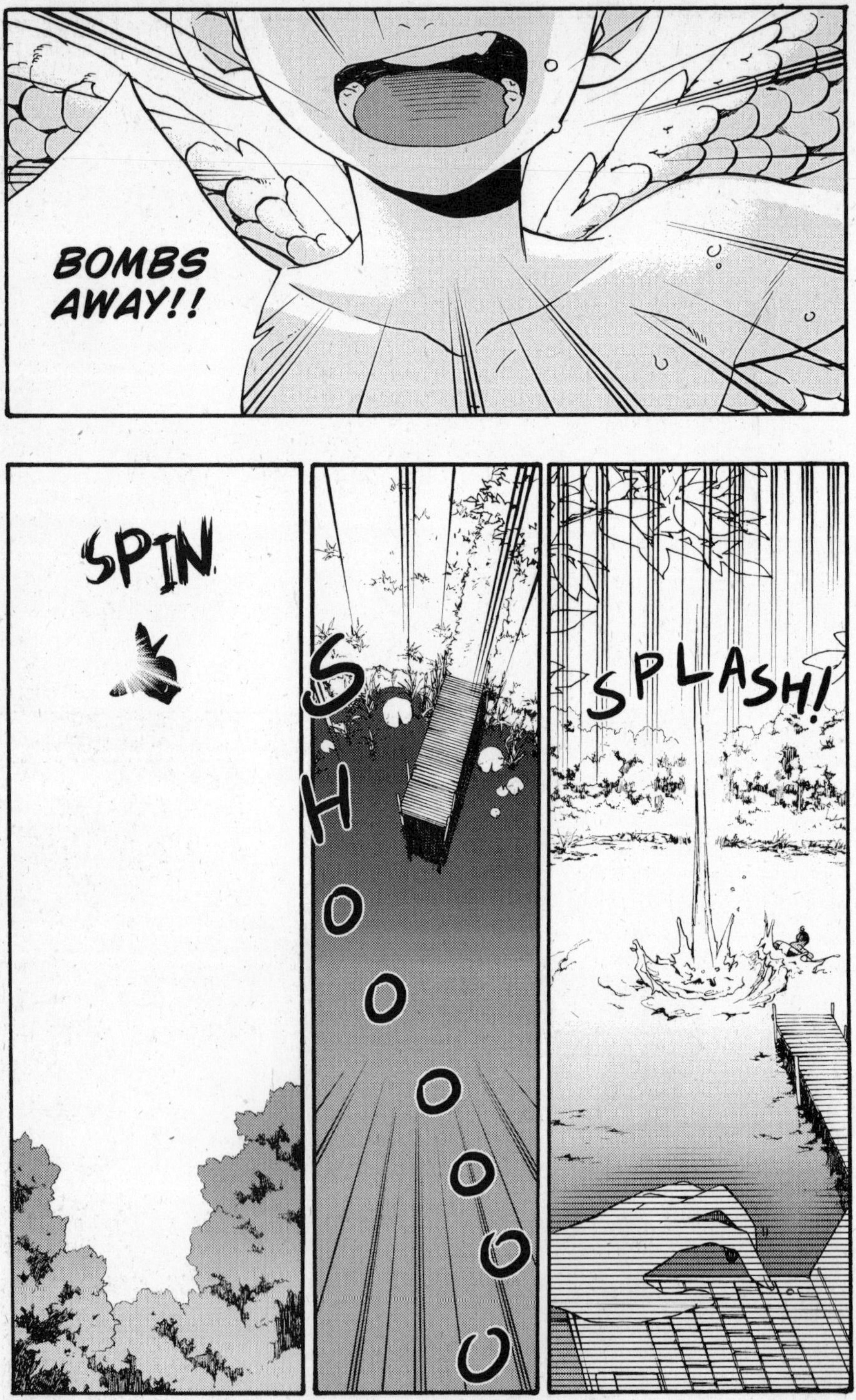
BOMBS AWAY!!
SPIN
SHOOOOOO
SPLASH!

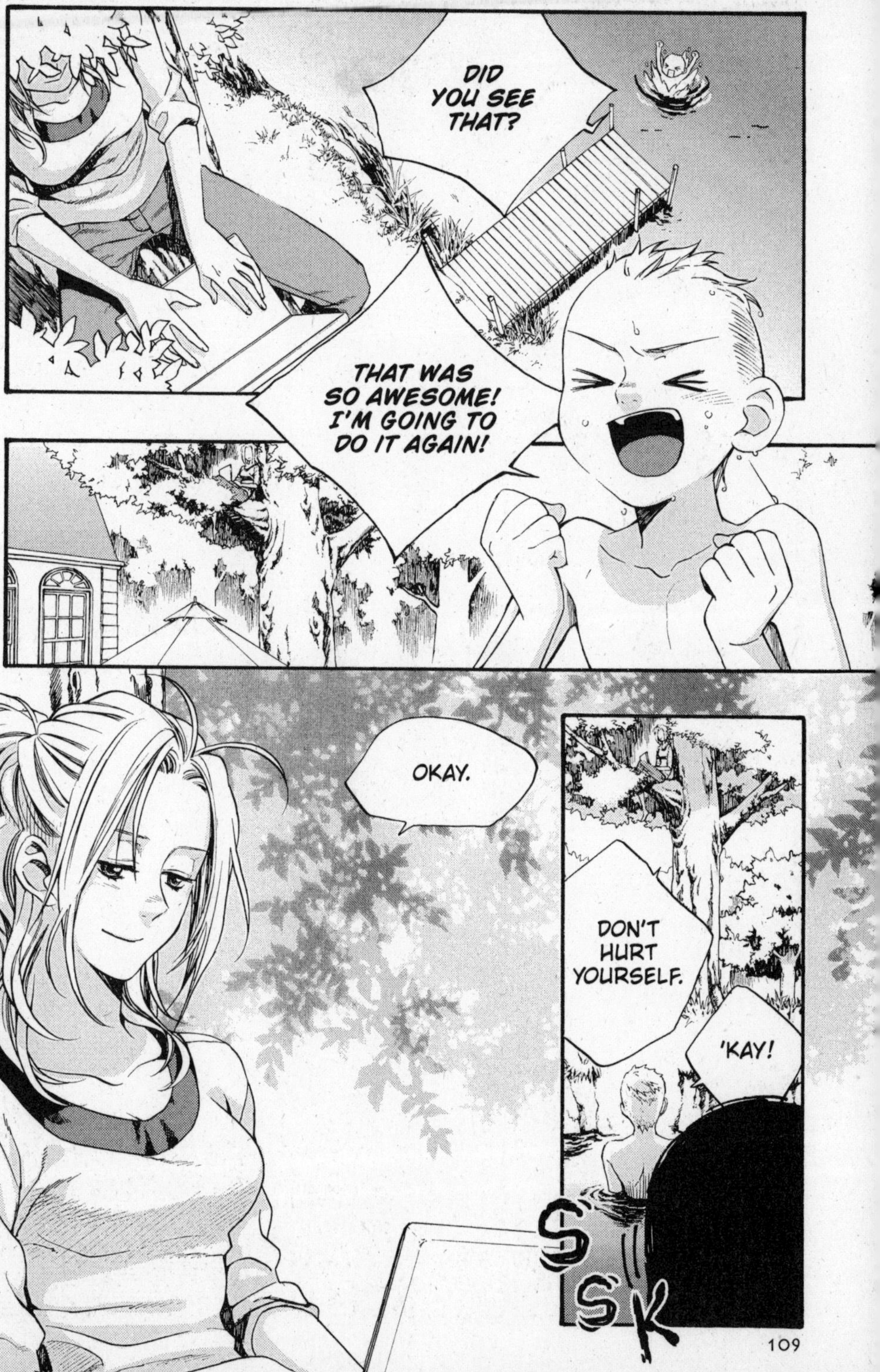

DID YOU SEE THAT?
THAT WAS SO AWESOME! I'M GOING TO DO IT AGAIN!
OKAY.
DON'T HURT YOURSELF.
'KAY!
SSK

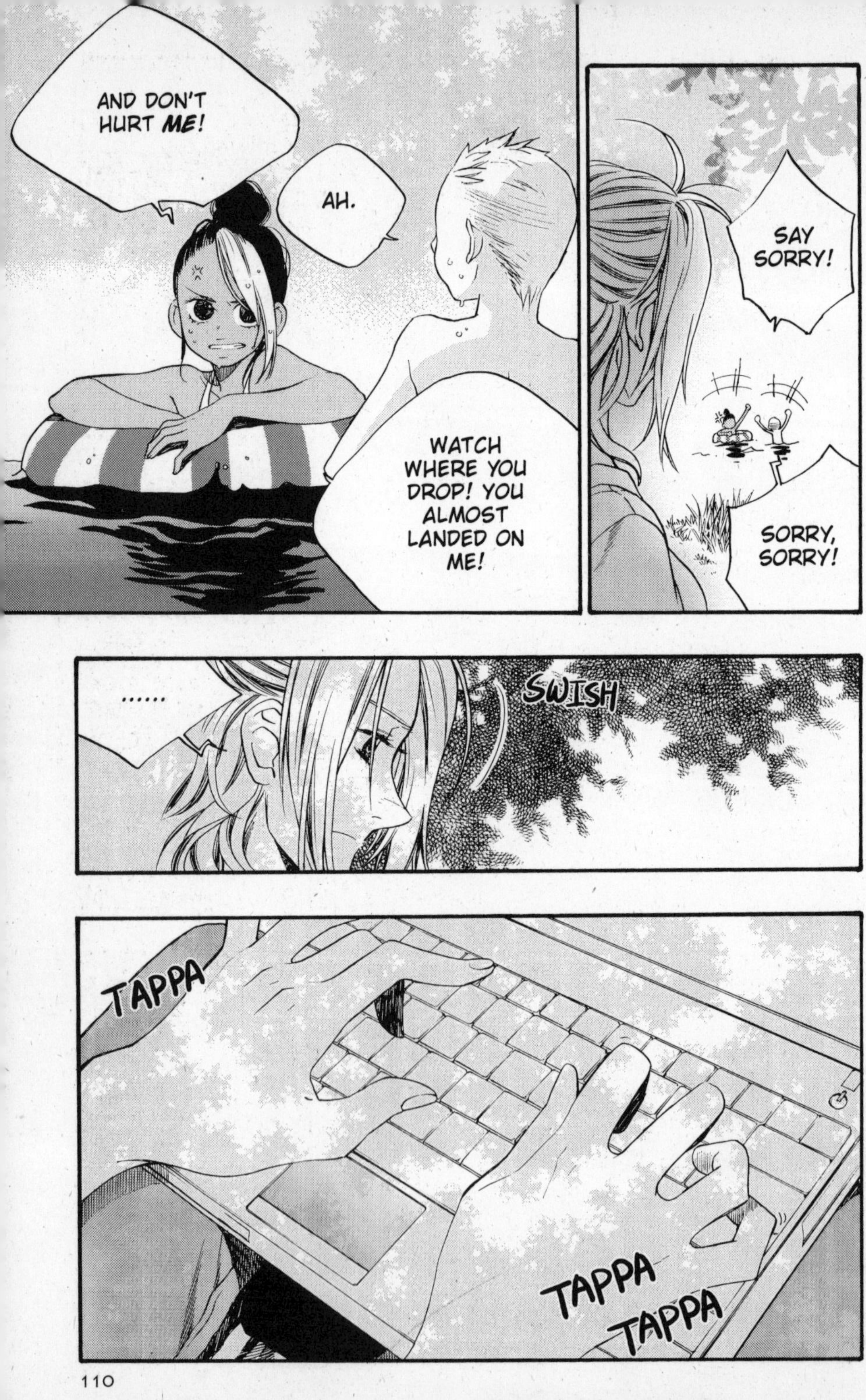
AND DON'T HURT ME!
AH.
WATCH WHERE YOU DROP! YOU ALMOST LANDED ON ME!
SAY SORRY!
SORRY, SORRY!
......
SWISH
TAPPA
TAPPA TAPPA

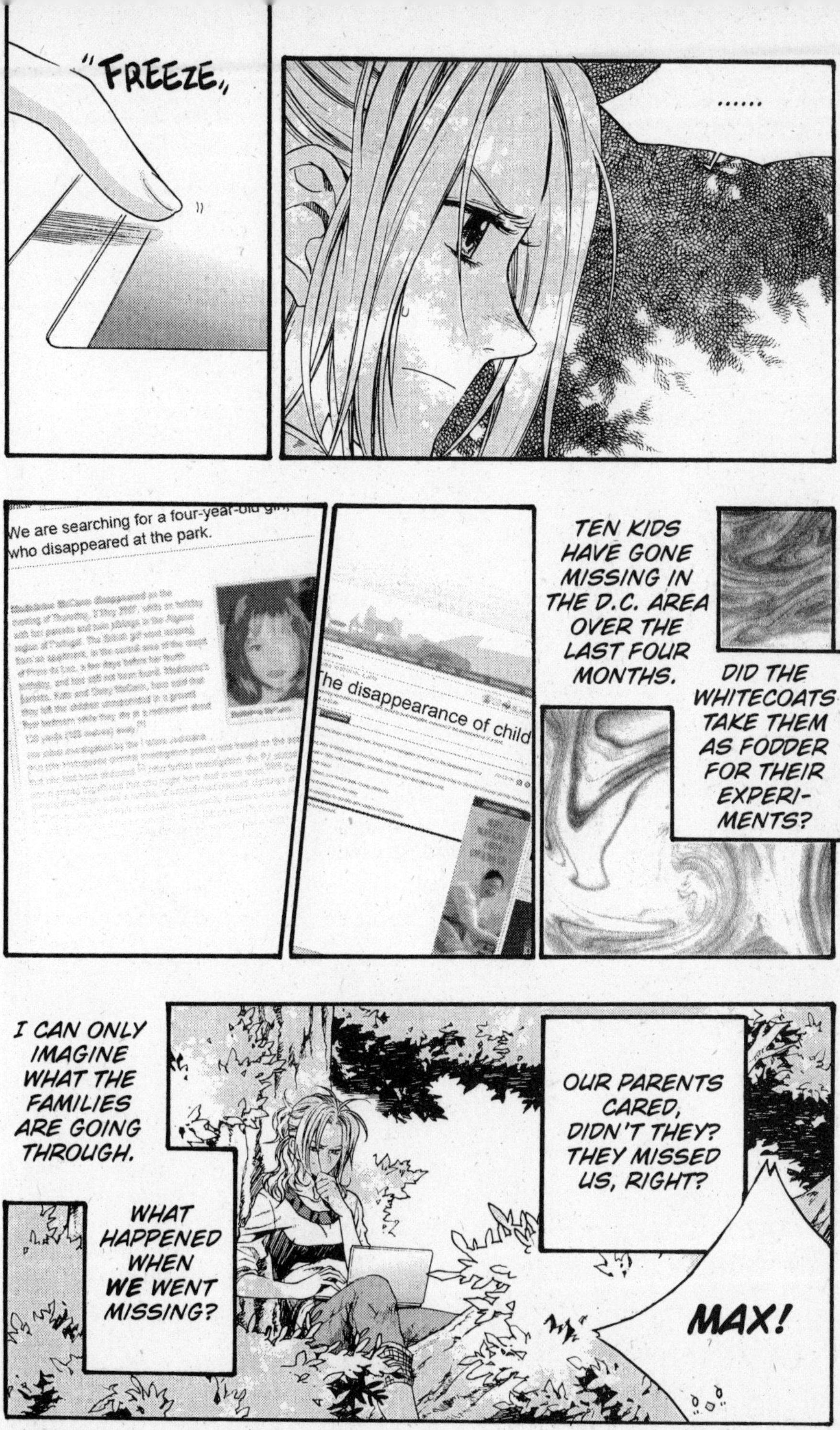
"FREEZE"
......
We are searching for a four-year-old gir
who disappeared at the park.
The disappearance of child
TEN KIDS HAVE GONE MISSING IN THE D.C. AREA OVER THE LAST FOUR MONTHS.
DID THE WHITECOATS TAKE THEM AS FODDER FOR THEIR EXPERI-MENTS?
I CAN ONLY IMAGINE WHAT THE FAMILIES ARE GOING THROUGH.
WHAT HAPPENED WHEN WE WENT MISSING?
OUR PARENTS CARED, DIDN'T THEY? THEY MISSED US, RIGHT?
MAX!

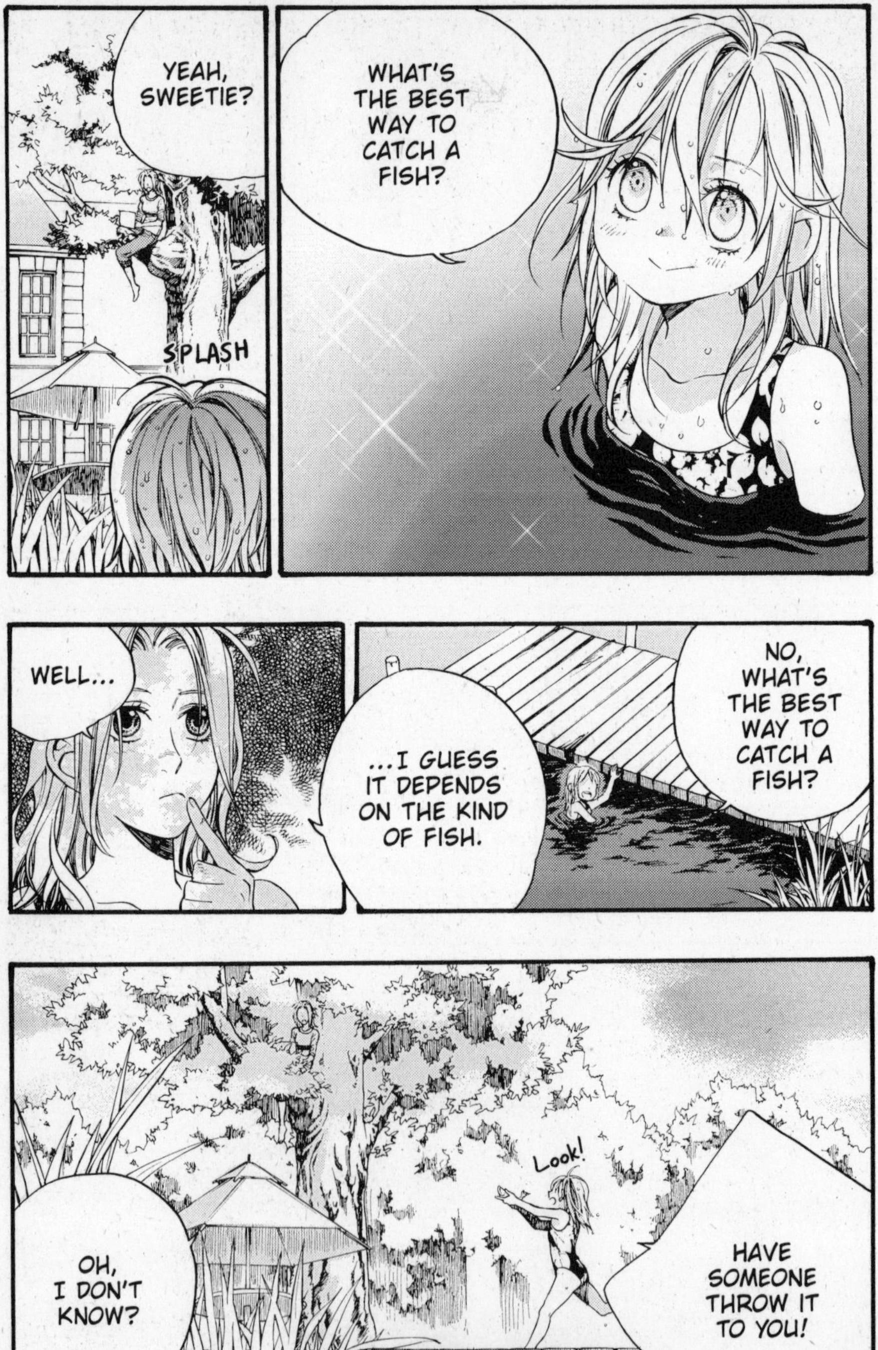
YEAH, SWEETIE?
SPLASH
WHAT'S THE BEST WAY TO CATCH A FISH?
WELL...
...I GUESS IT DEPENDS ON THE KIND OF FISH.
NO, WHAT'S THE BEST WAY TO CATCH A FISH?
OH, I DON'T KNOW?
Look!
HAVE SOMEONE THROW IT TO YOU!

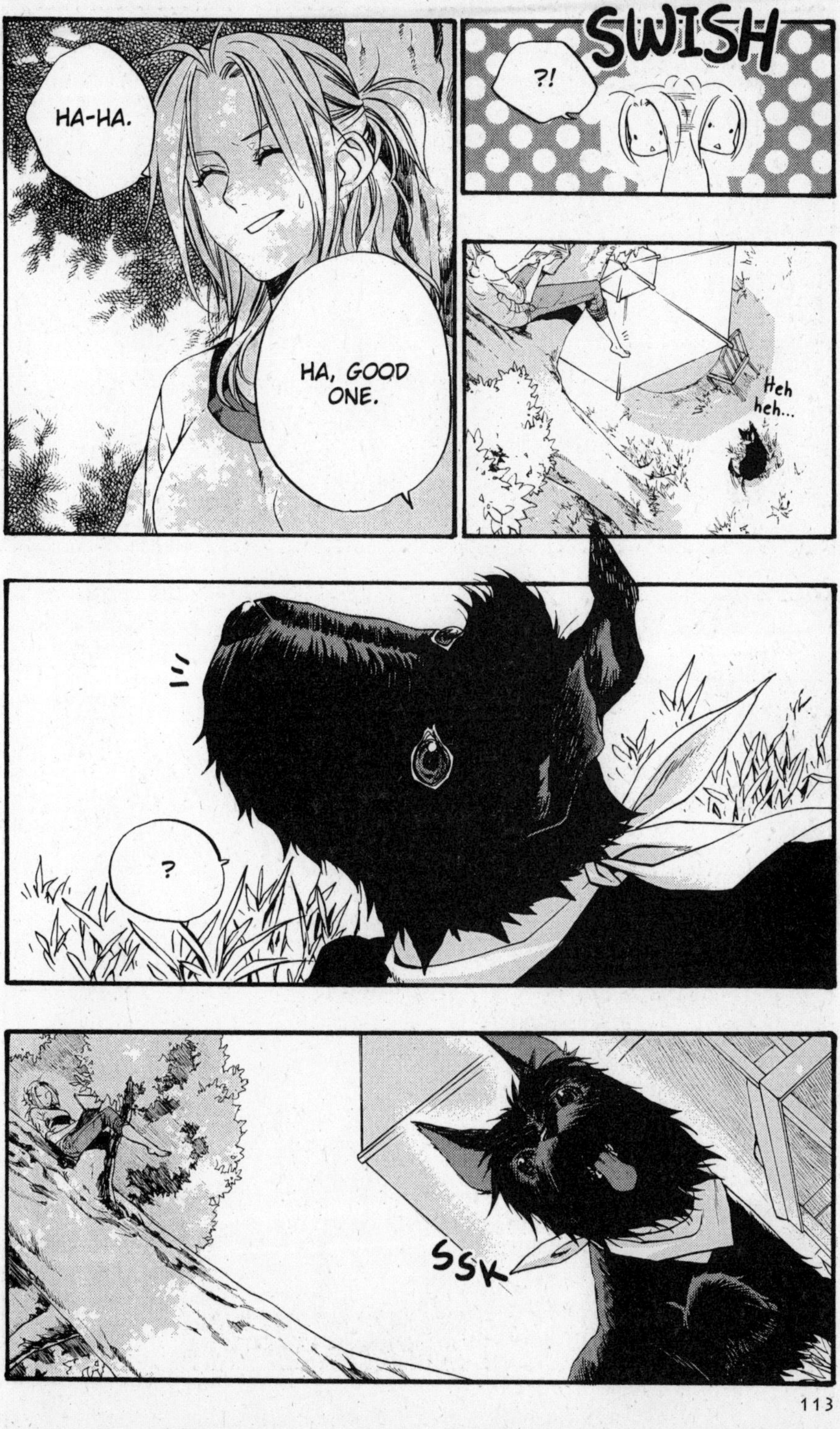
HA-HA.
HA, GOOD ONE.
?!
SWISH
Heh heh...
?
SSK

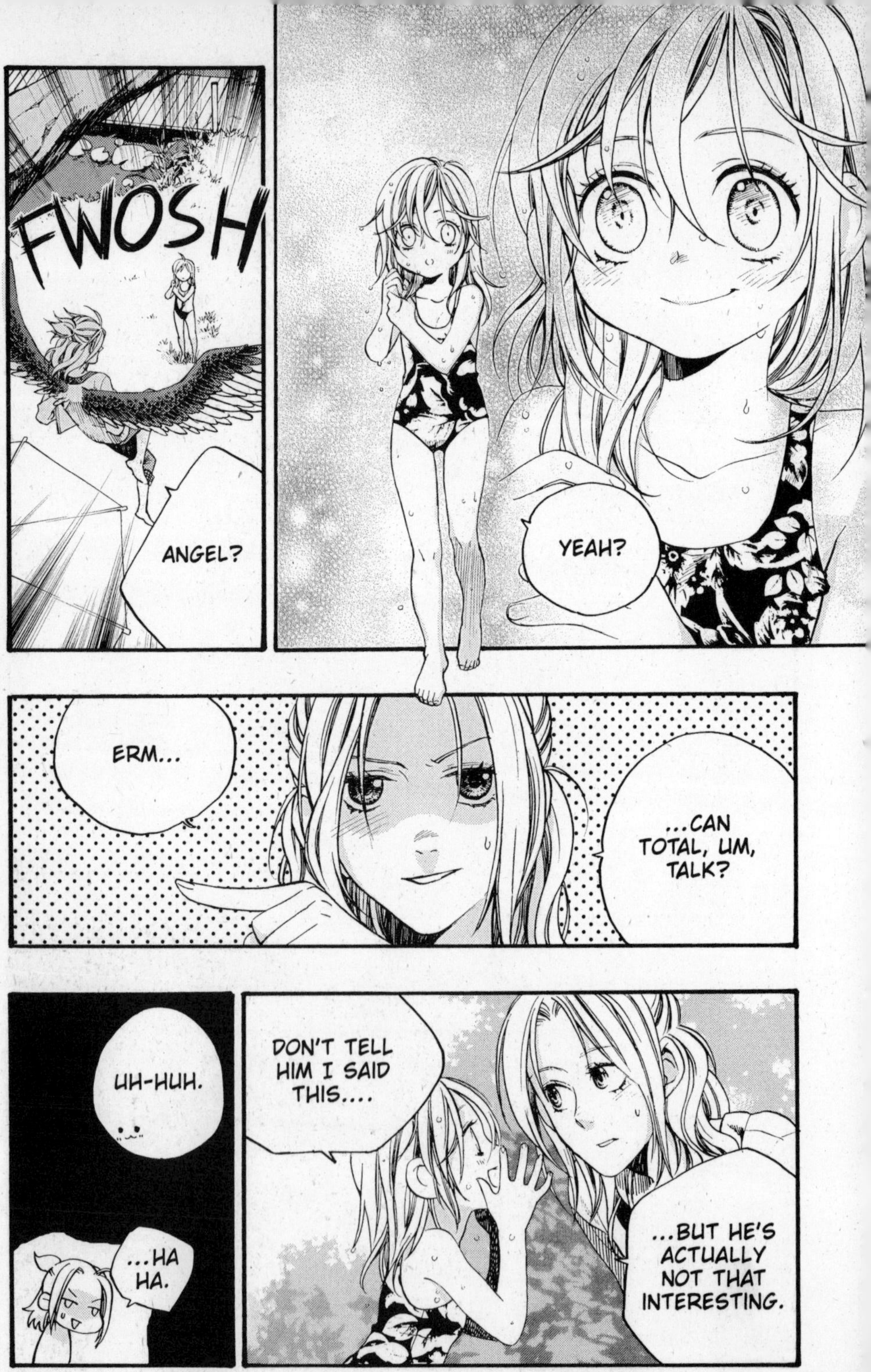
FWOSH
ANGEL?
YEAH?
ERM...
...CAN TOTAL, UM, TALK?
UH-HUH.
...HA HA.
DON'T TELL HIM I SAID THIS....
...BUT HE'S ACTUALLY NOT THAT INTERESTING.

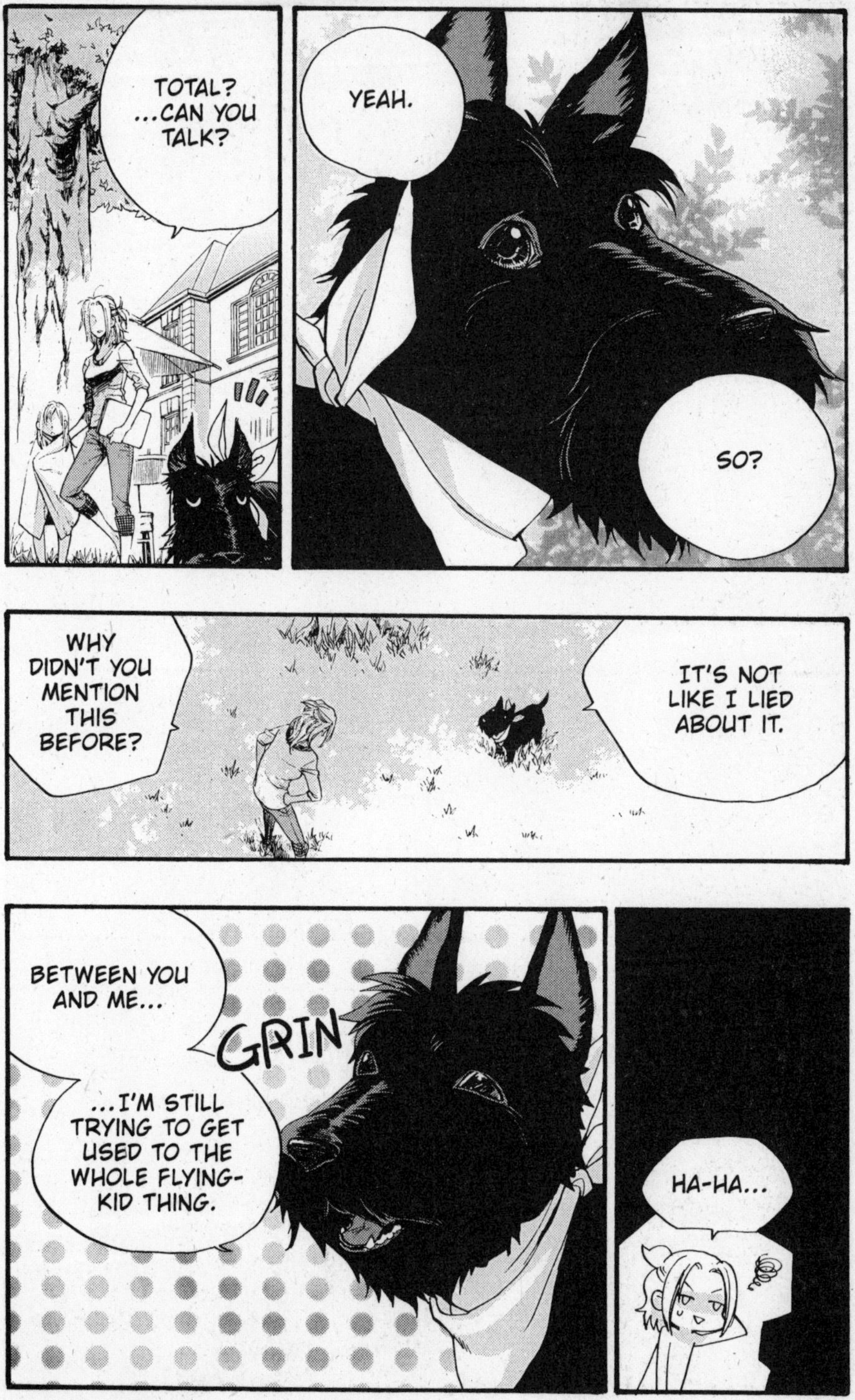

TOTAL? ...CAN YOU TALK?
YEAH.
SO?
WHY DIDN'T YOU MENTION THIS BEFORE?
IT'S NOT LIKE I LIED ABOUT IT.
BETWEEN YOU AND ME...
GRIN
...I'M STILL TRYING TO GET USED TO THE WHOLE FLYING-KID THING.
HA-HA...

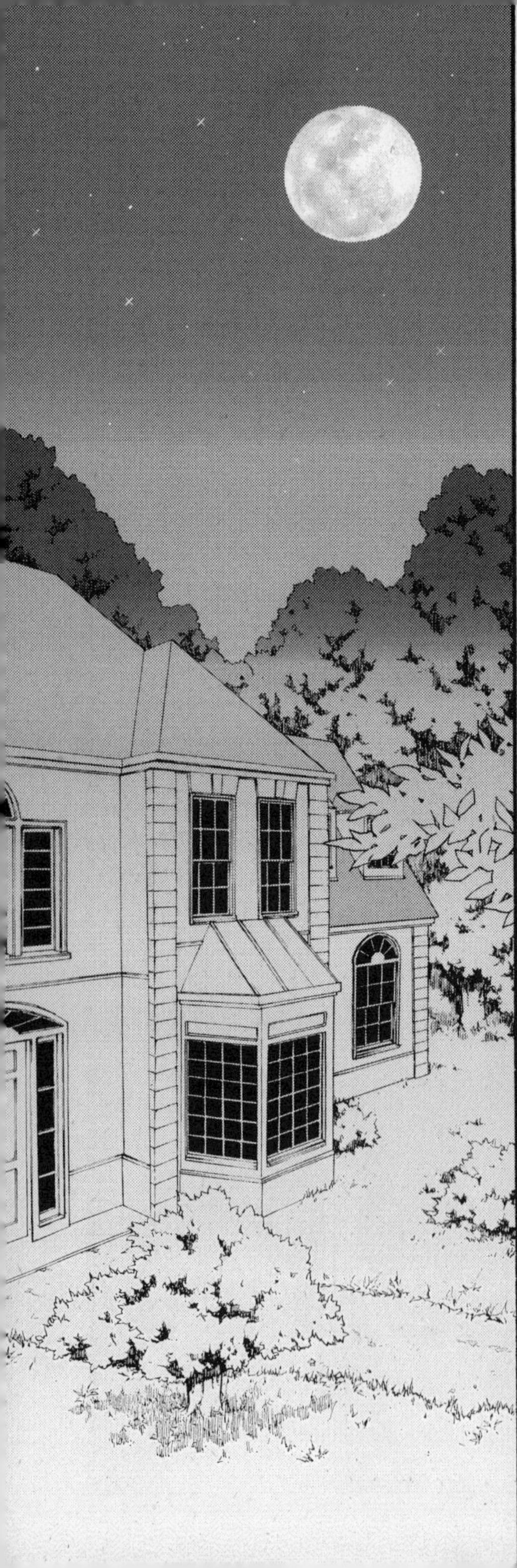

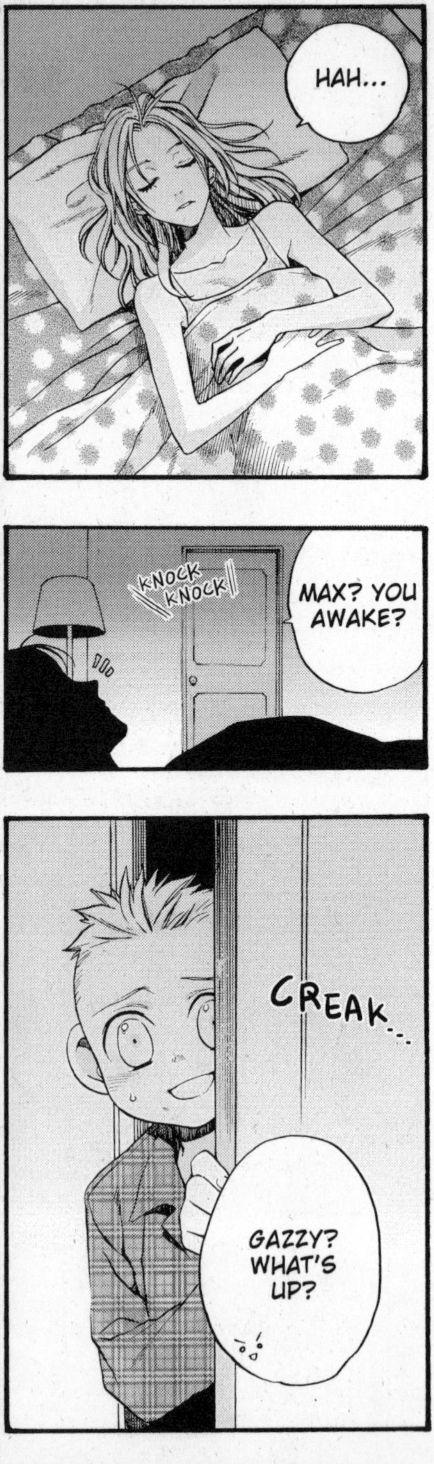
HAH...
KNOCK KNOCK
MAX? YOU AWAKE?
CREAK...
GAZZY? WHAT'S UP?

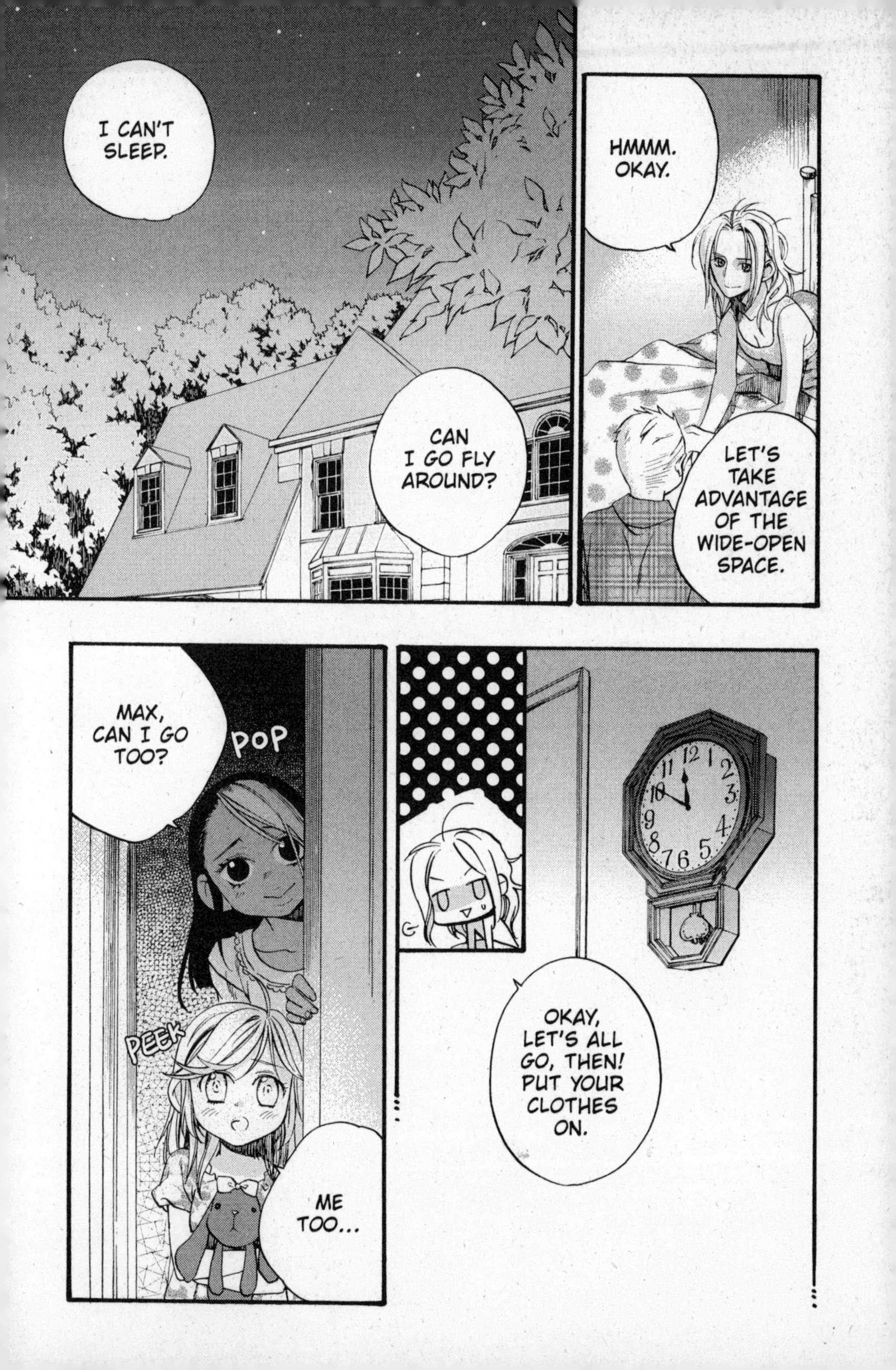
I CAN'T SLEEP.
CAN I GO FLY AROUND?
HMMM. OKAY.
LET'S TAKE ADVANTAGE OF THE WIDE-OPEN SPACE.
MAX, CAN I GO TOO?
POP
PEEK
ME TOO...
OKAY, LET'S ALL GO, THEN! PUT YOUR CLOTHES ON.

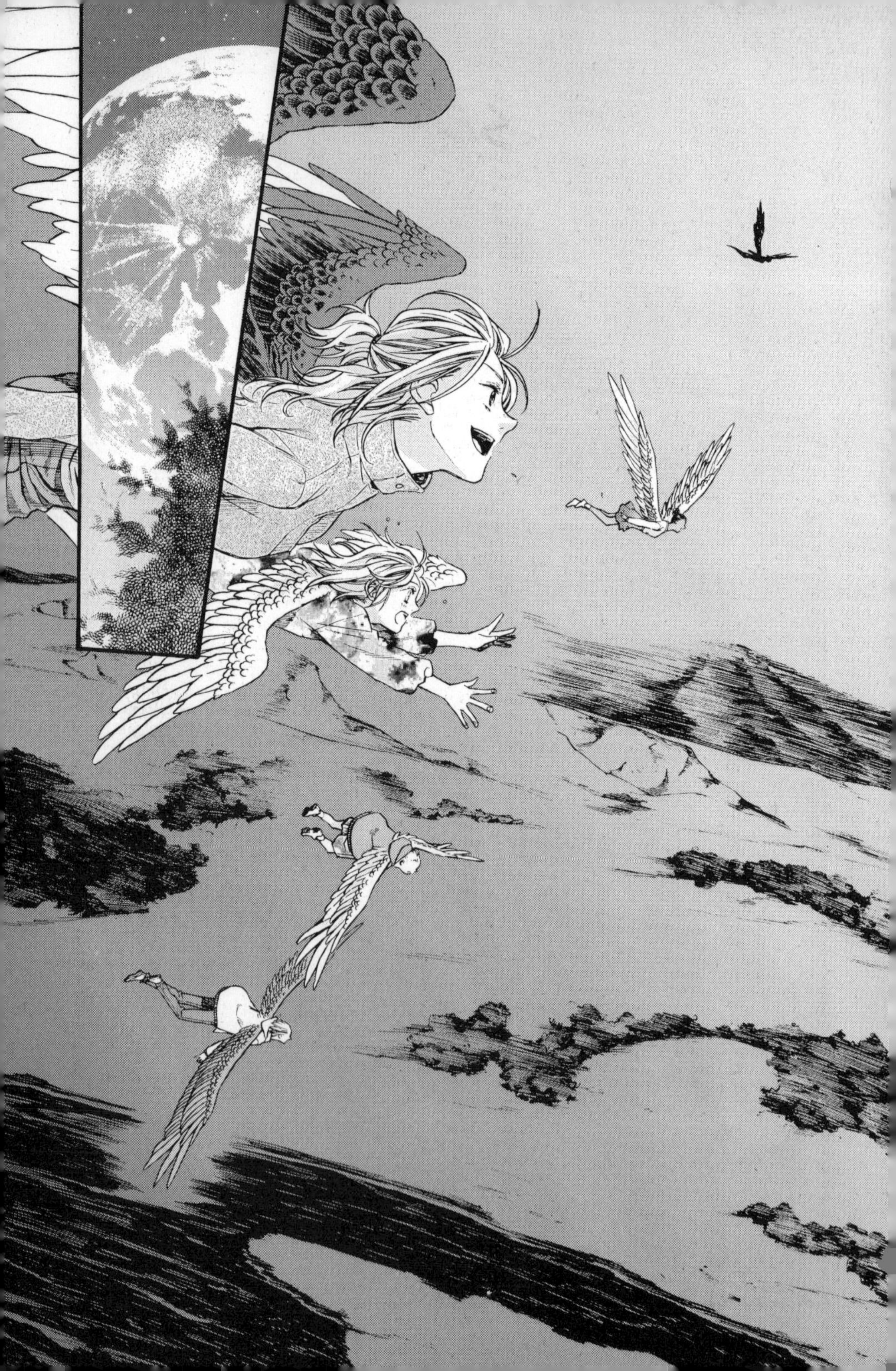

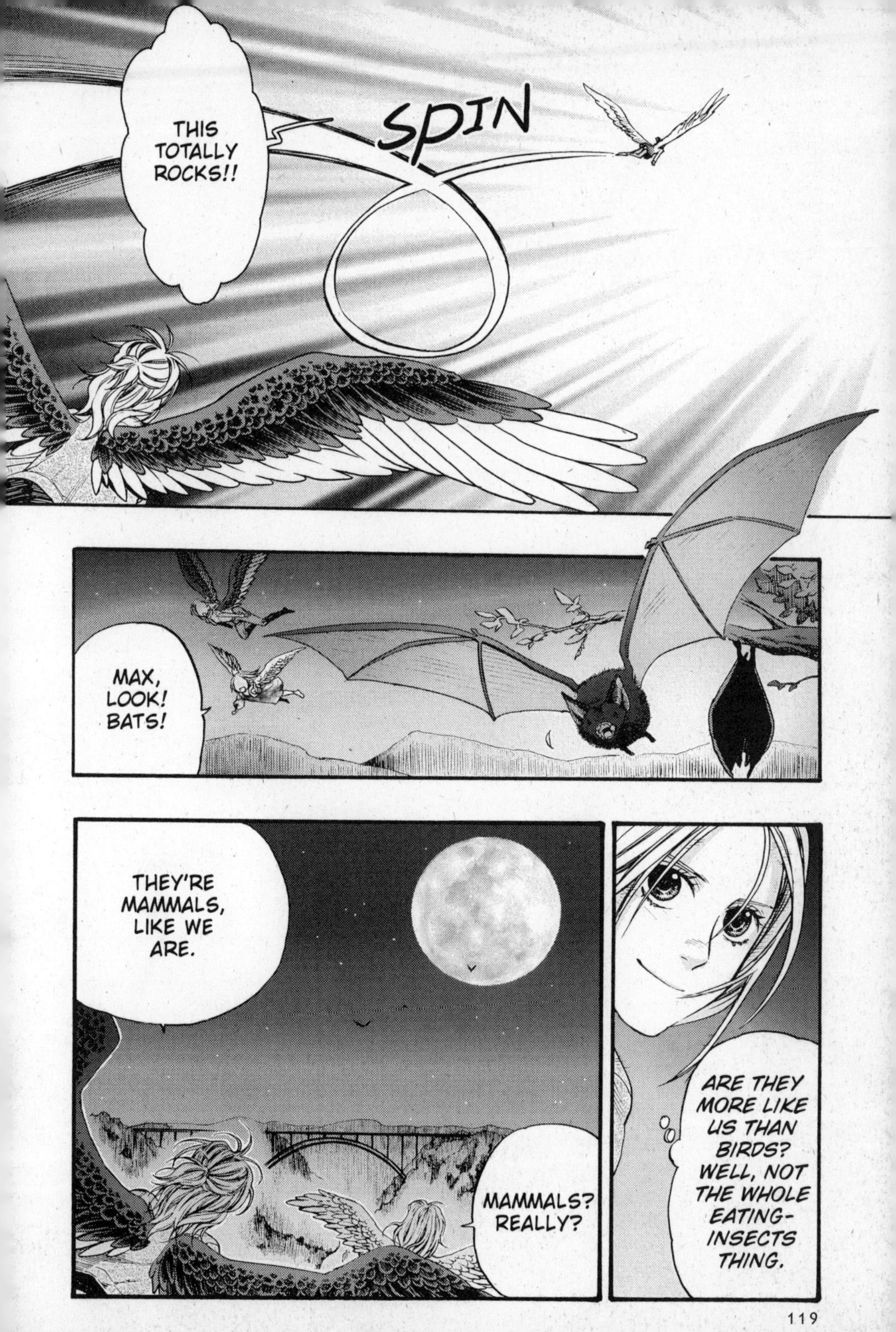
THIS TOTALLY ROCKS!!
SPIN
MAX, LOOK! BATS!
THEY'RE MAMMALS, LIKE WE ARE.
MAMMALS? REALLY?
ARE THEY MORE LIKE US THAN BIRDS? WELL, NOT THE WHOLE EATING-INSECTS THING.

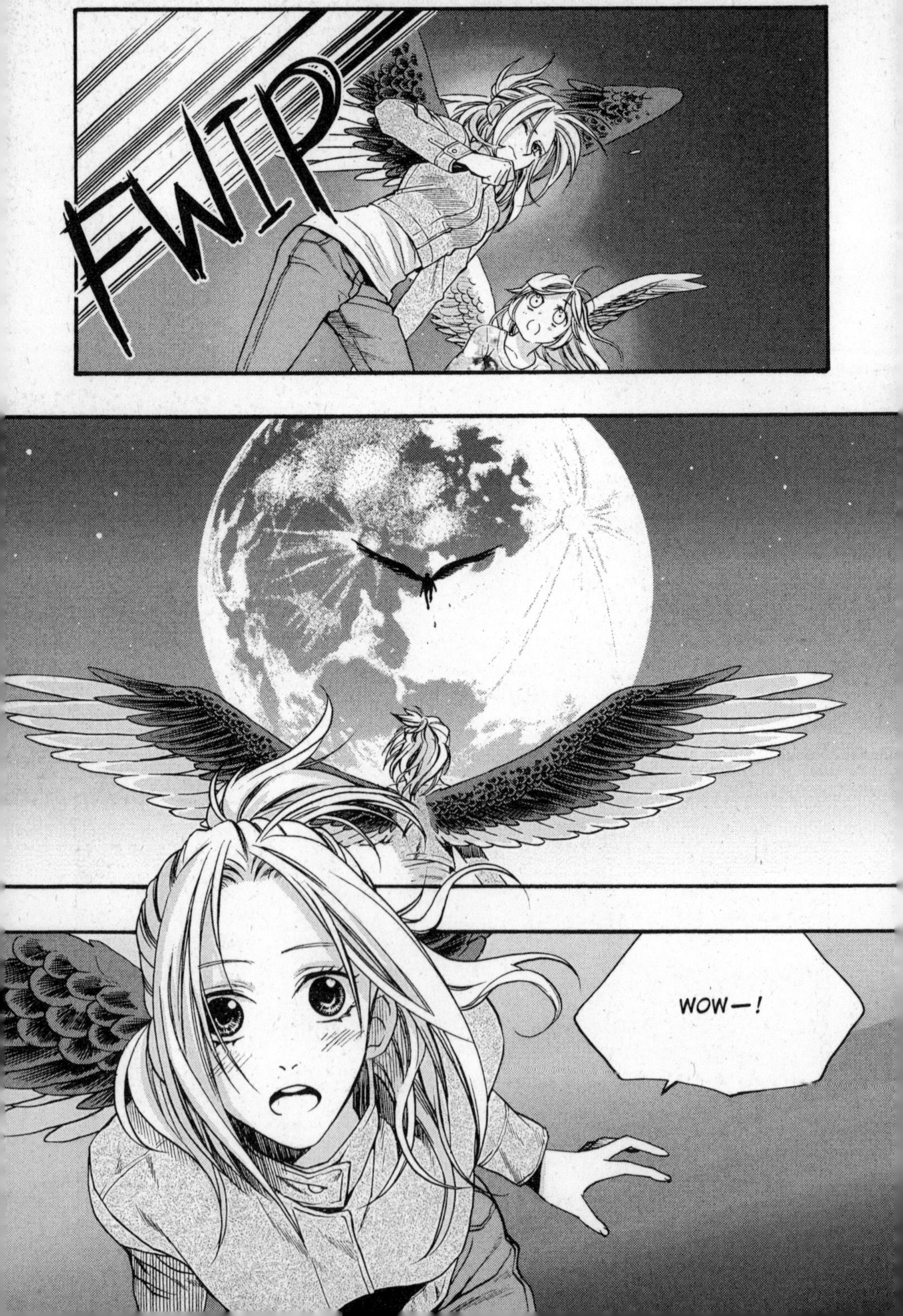
FWIP
WOW—!

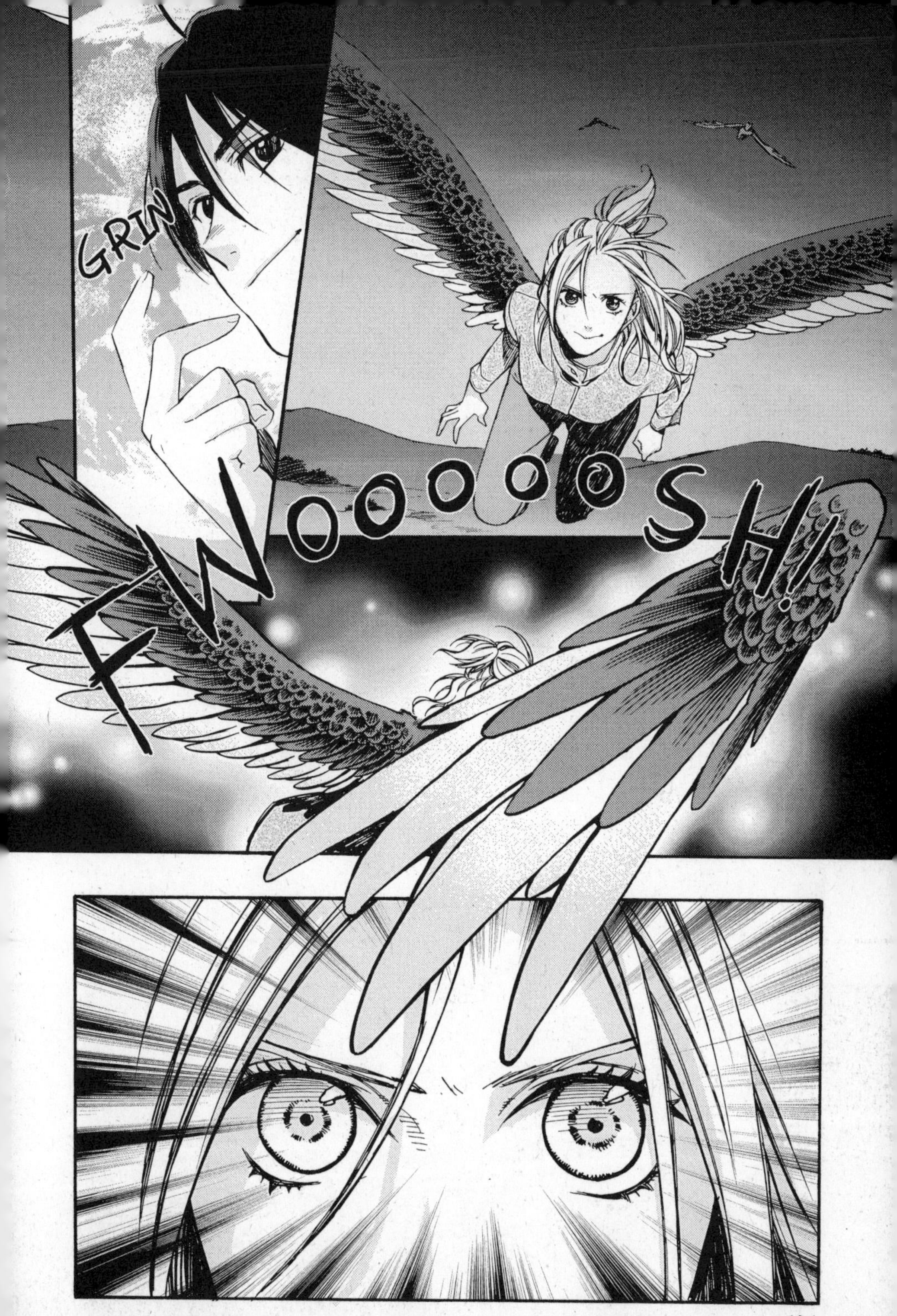
GRIN
FWOOOOOSH!!

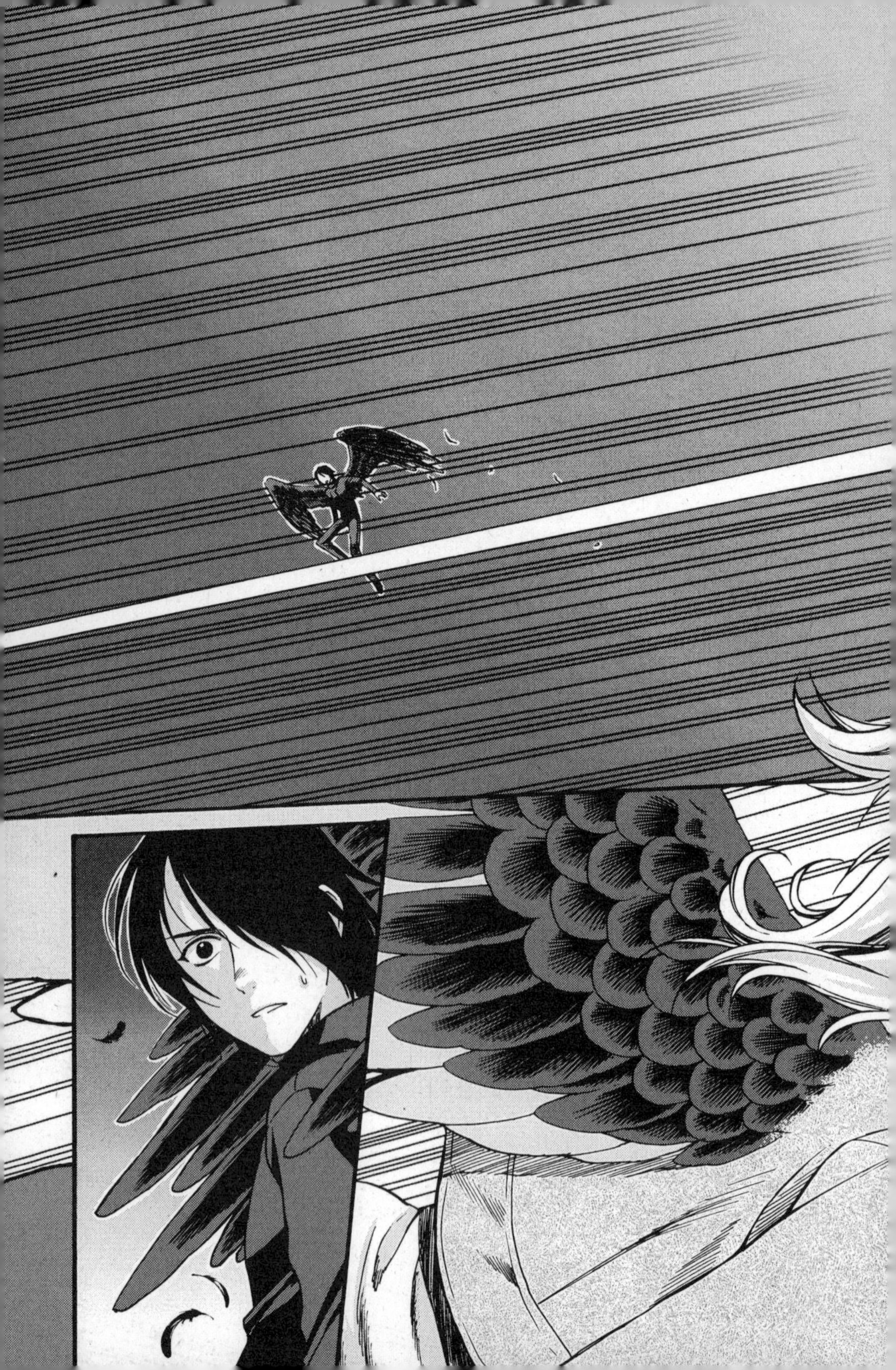

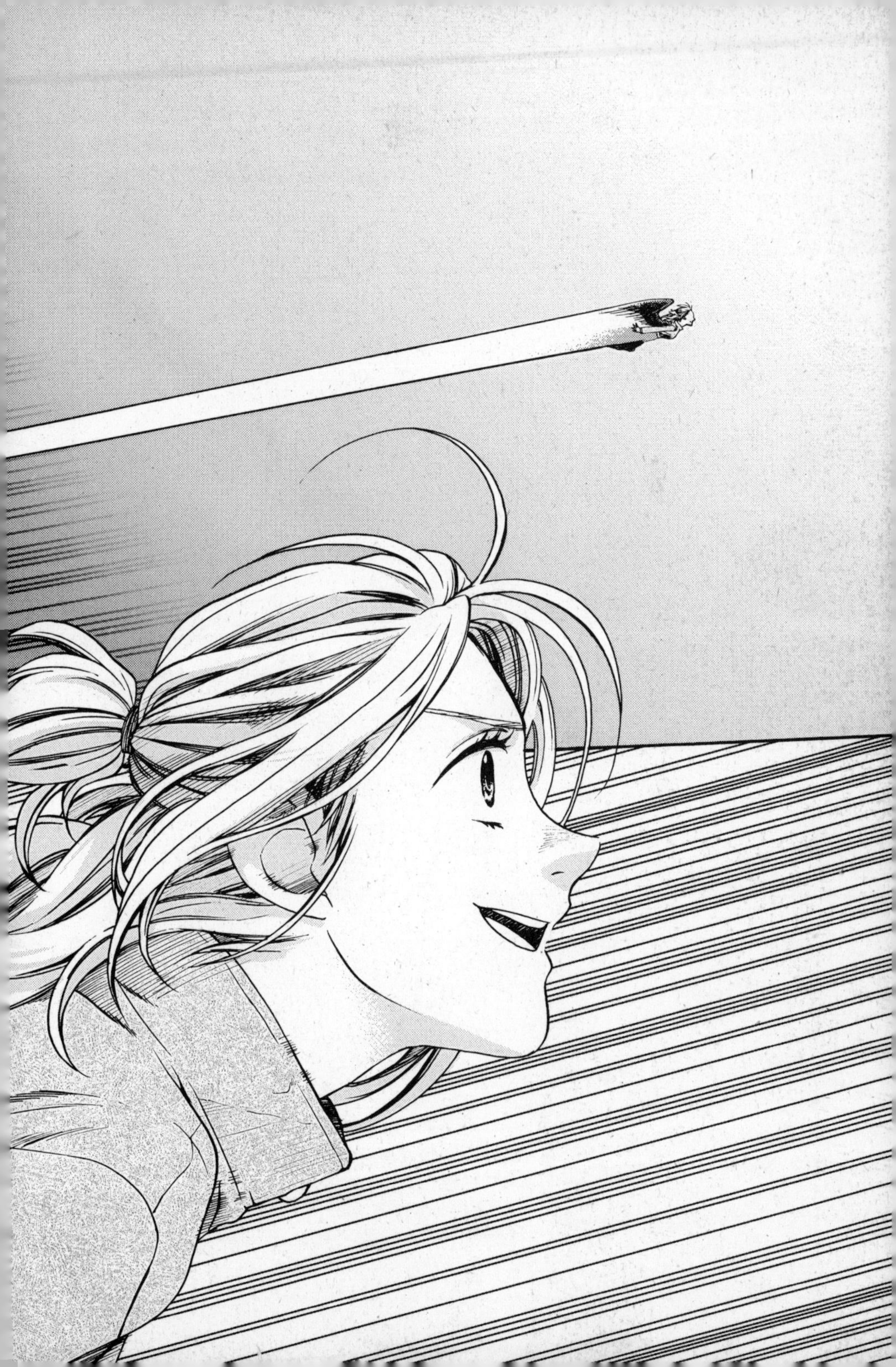

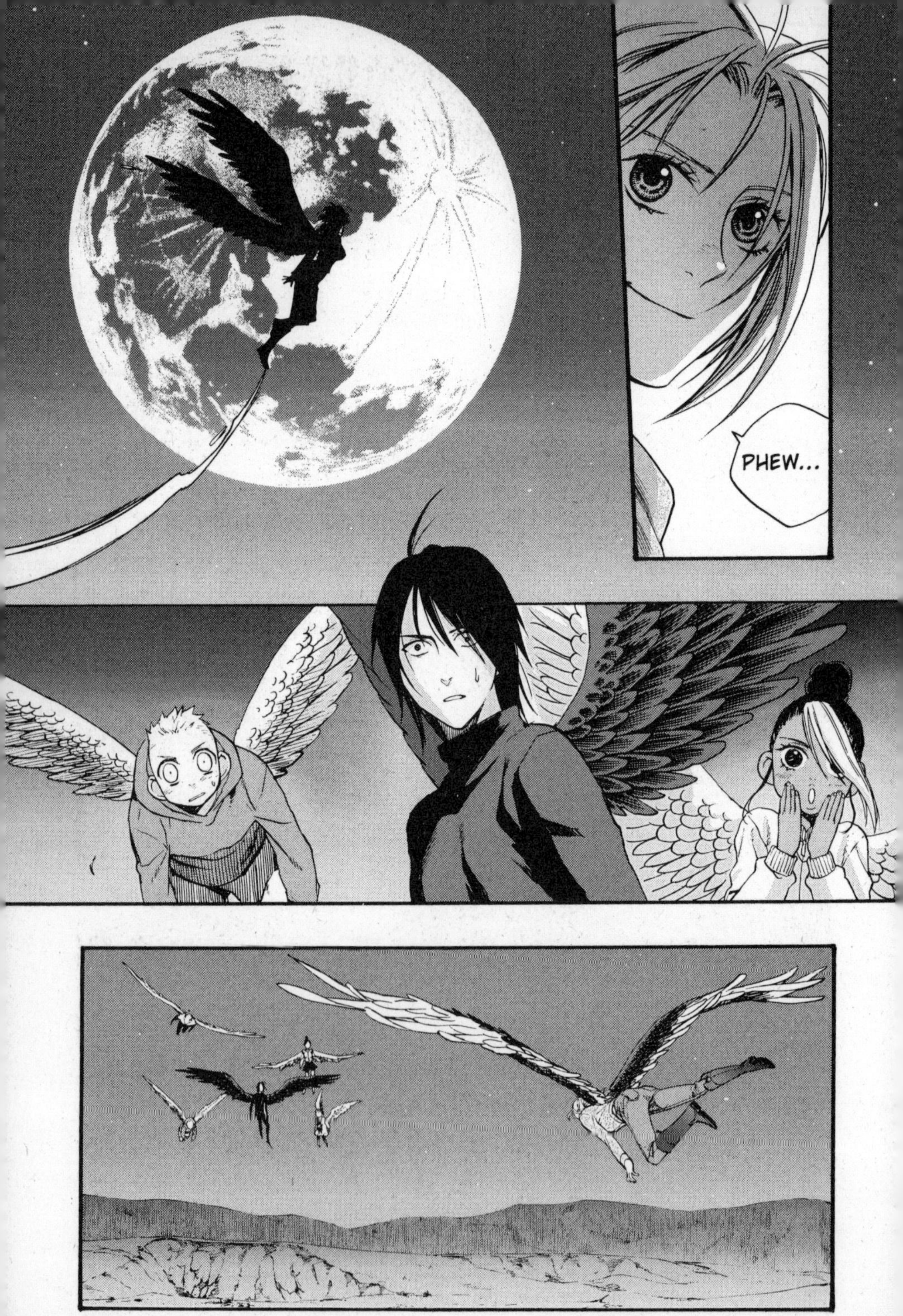
PHEW...

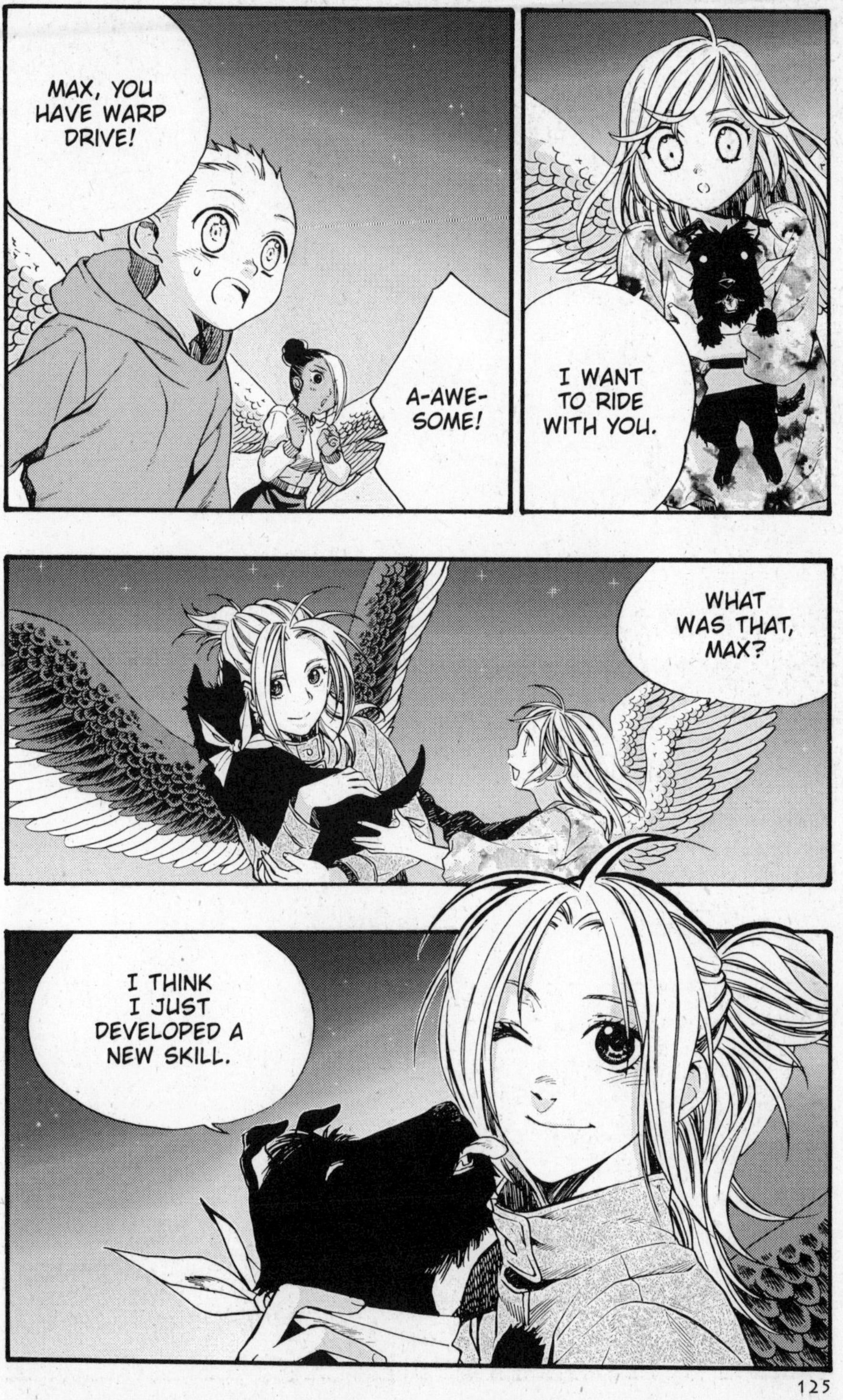
MAX, YOU HAVE WARP DRIVE!
A-AWE-SOME!
I WANT TO RIDE WITH YOU.
WHAT WAS THAT, MAX?
I THINK I JUST DEVELOPED A NEW SKILL.

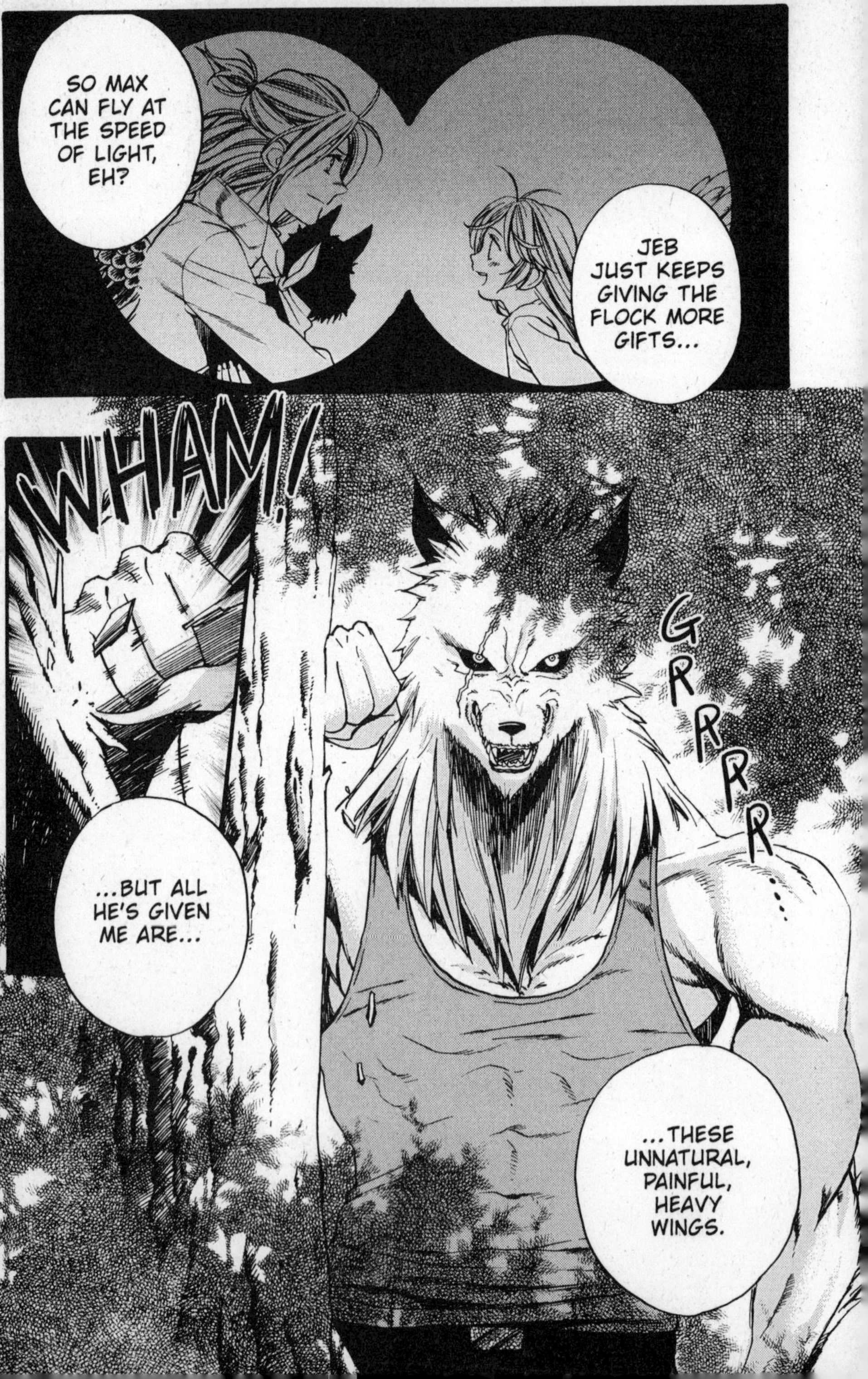
SO MAX CAN FLY AT THE SPEED OF LIGHT, EH?
JEB JUST KEEPS GIVING THE FLOCK MORE GIFTS...
WHAM!
GRRRRR...
...BUT ALL HE'S GIVEN ME ARE...
...THESE UNNATURAL, PAINFUL, HEAVY WINGS.

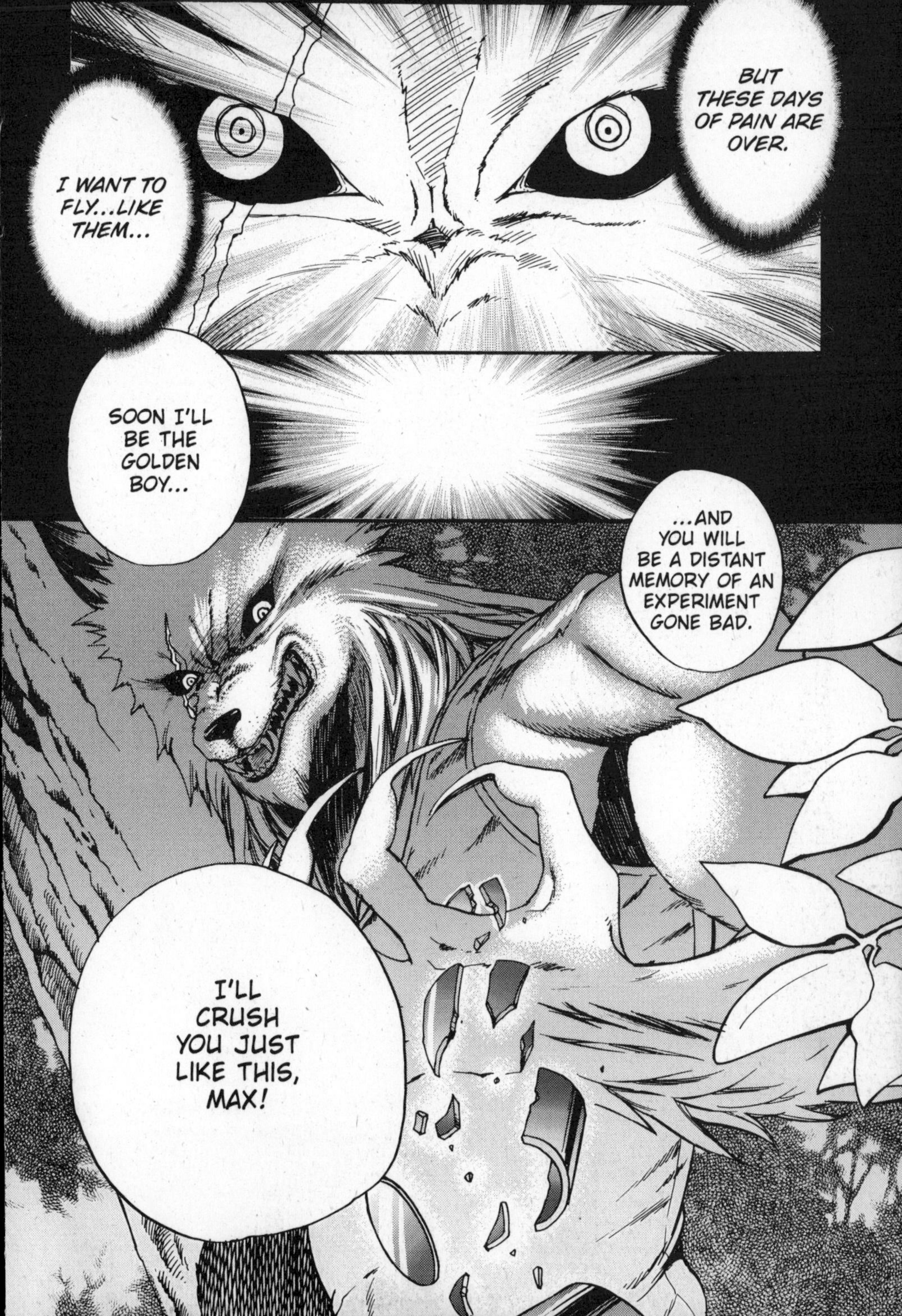
BUT THESE DAYS OF PAIN ARE OVER.
I WANT TO FLY...LIKE THEM...
SOON I'LL BE THE GOLDEN BOY...
...AND YOU WILL BE A DISTANT MEMORY OF AN EXPERIMENT GONE BAD.
I'LL CRUSH YOU JUST LIKE THIS, MAX!

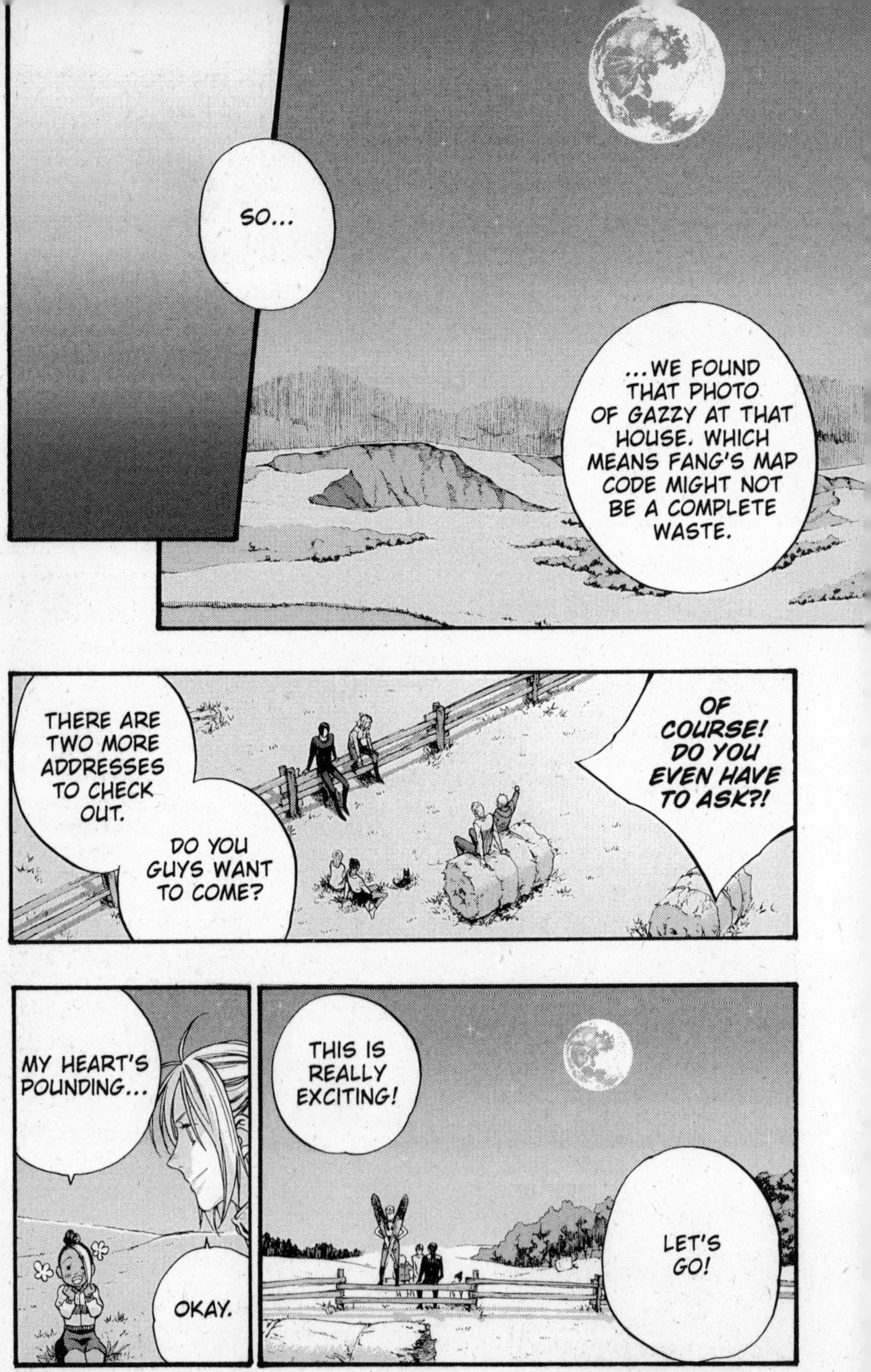
SO...
...WE FOUND THAT PHOTO OF GAZZY AT THAT HOUSE. WHICH MEANS FANG'S MAP CODE MIGHT NOT BE A COMPLETE WASTE.
THERE ARE TWO MORE ADDRESSES TO CHECK OUT.
DO YOU GUYS WANT TO COME?
OF COURSE! DO YOU EVEN HAVE TO ASK?!
MY HEART'S POUNDING...
OKAY.
THIS IS REALLY EXCITING!
LET'S GO!

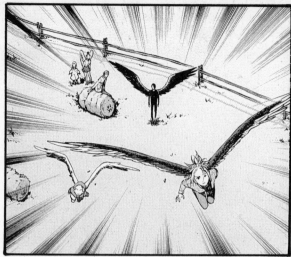

SO, ANGEL?

HUH?

HAVE YOU PICKED UP ANYTHING FROM ANNE, ABOUT ANYTHING? ANYTHING OFF?

NOT REALLY. FROM WHAT I CAN TELL, SHE DOES WORK FOR THE FBI. SHE DOES CARE ABOUT US...

...AND WANTS US TO BE HAPPY. SHE THINKS THE BOYS ARE SLOBS.

I'M BLIND. HOW AM I SUPPOSED TO MAKE EVERYTHING ALL TIDY?

YEAH, BECAUSE YOU'RE SO HANDICAPPED.

LIKE...

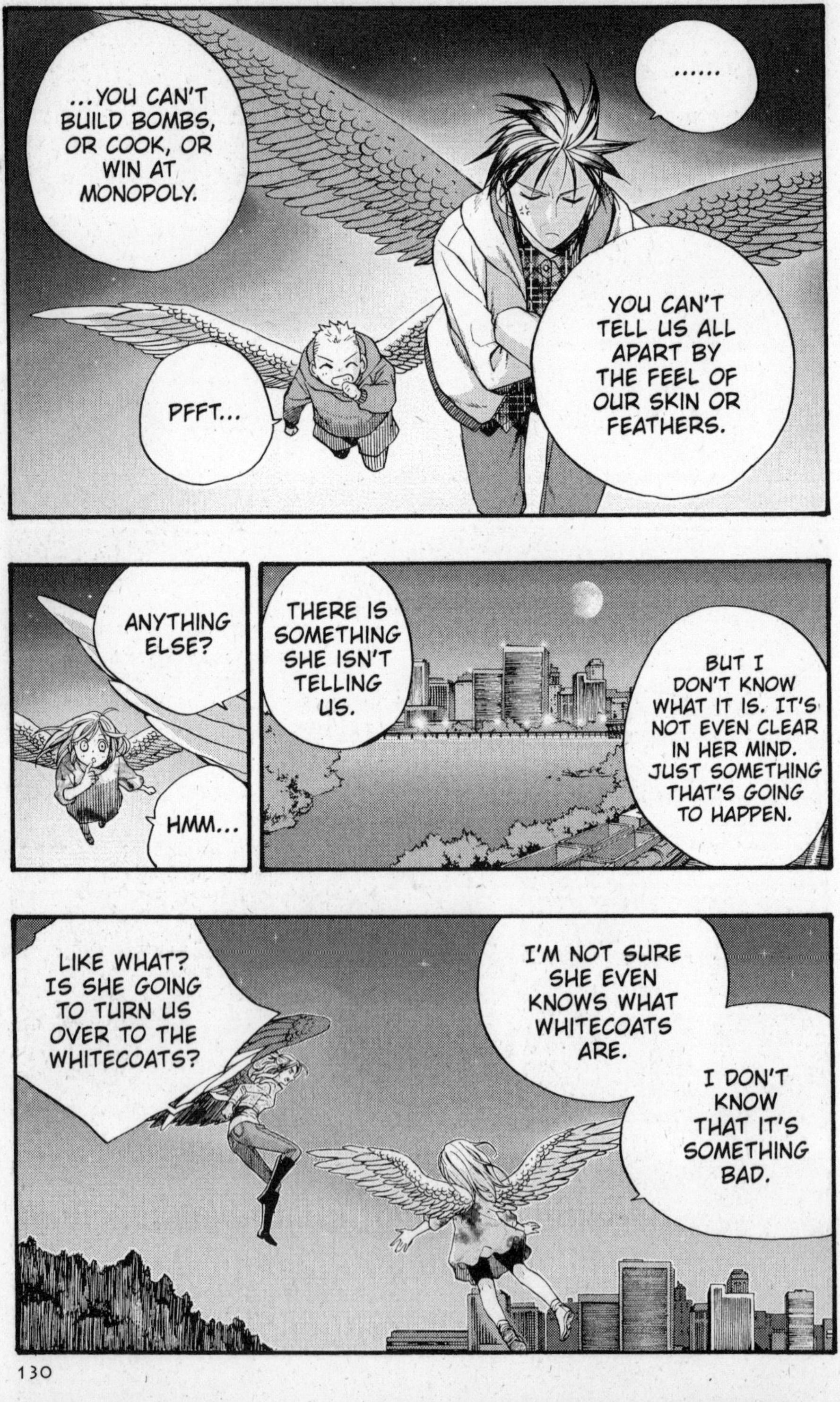

...YOU CAN'T BUILD BOMBS, OR COOK, OR WIN AT MONOPOLY.
......
YOU CAN'T TELL US ALL APART BY THE FEEL OF OUR SKIN OR FEATHERS.
PFFT...
ANYTHING ELSE?
HMM...
THERE IS SOMETHING SHE ISN'T TELLING US.
BUT I DON'T KNOW WHAT IT IS. IT'S NOT EVEN CLEAR IN HER MIND. JUST SOMETHING THAT'S GOING TO HAPPEN.
LIKE WHAT? IS SHE GOING TO TURN US OVER TO THE WHITECOATS?
I'M NOT SURE SHE EVEN KNOWS WHAT WHITECOATS ARE.
I DON'T KNOW THAT IT'S SOMETHING BAD.

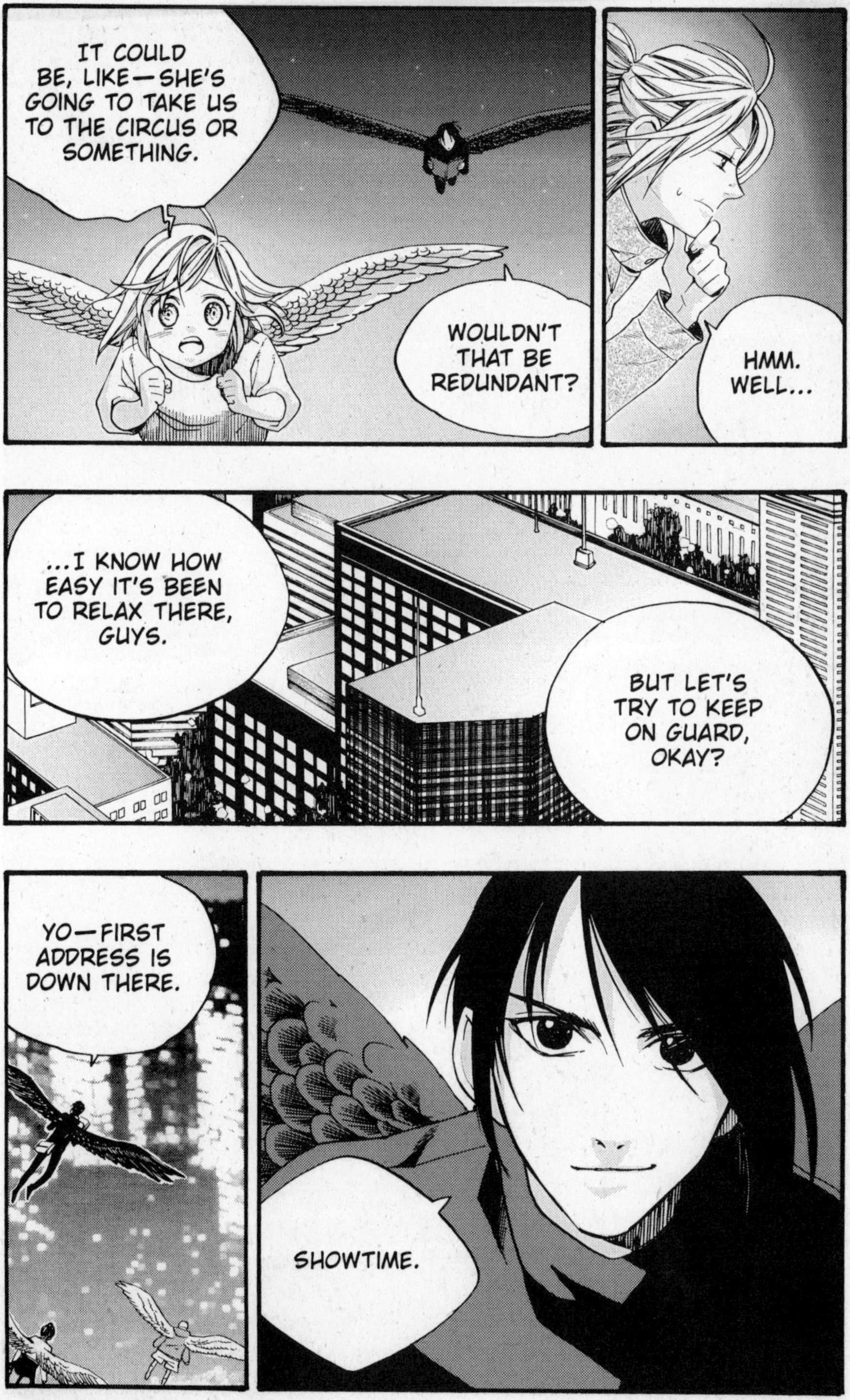
IT COULD BE, LIKE—SHE'S GOING TO TAKE US TO THE CIRCUS OR SOMETHING.
WOULDN'T THAT BE REDUNDANT?
HMM. WELL...
...I KNOW HOW EASY IT'S BEEN TO RELAX THERE, GUYS.
BUT LET'S TRY TO KEEP ON GUARD, OKAY?
YO—FIRST ADDRESS IS DOWN THERE.
SHOWTIME.

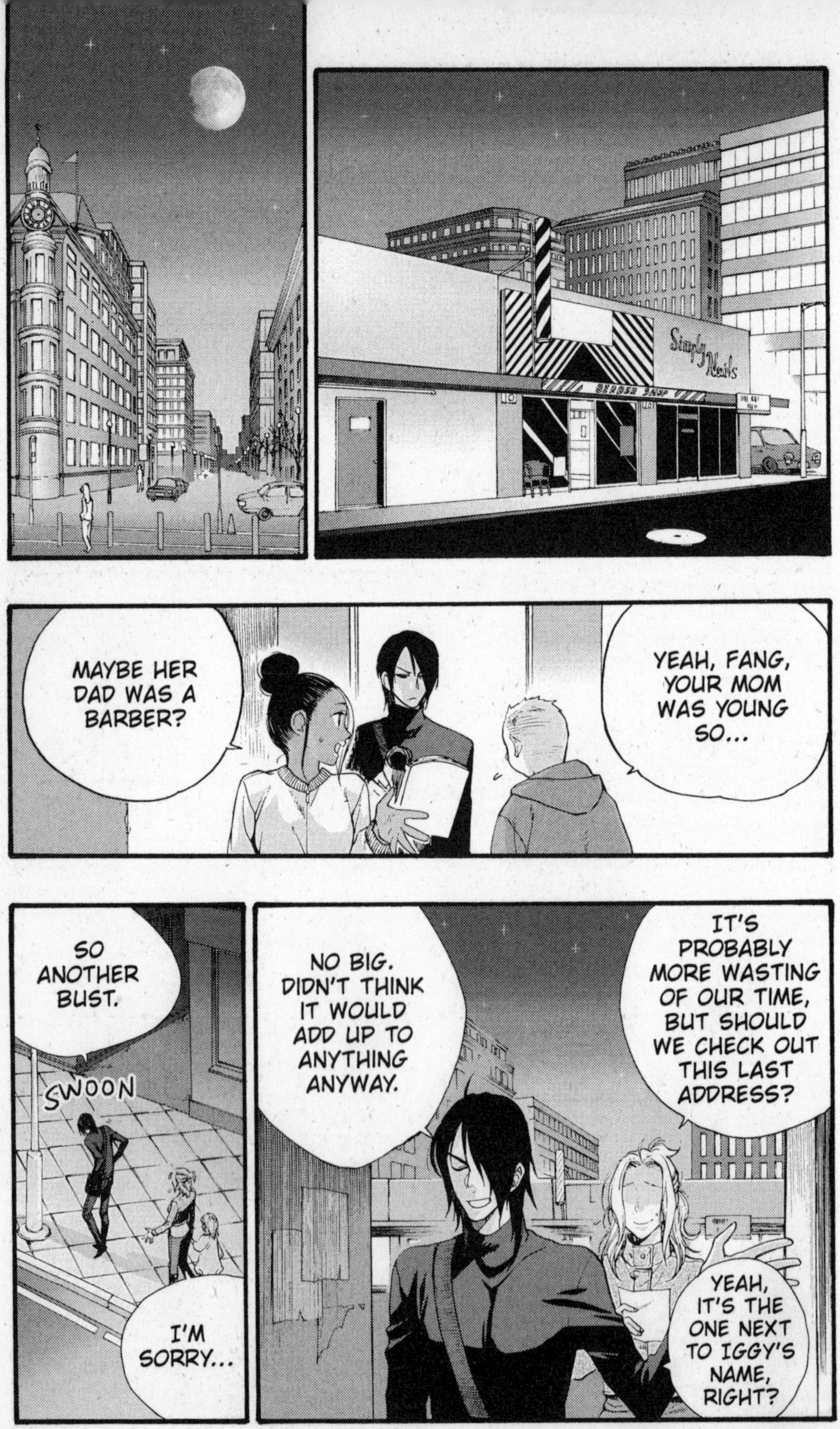
Simply Nails
MAYBE HER DAD WAS A BARBER?
YEAH, FANG, YOUR MOM WAS YOUNG SO...
SO ANOTHER BUST.
SWOON
I'M SORRY...
NO BIG. DIDN'T THINK IT WOULD ADD UP TO ANYTHING ANYWAY.
IT'S PROBABLY MORE WASTING OF OUR TIME, BUT SHOULD WE CHECK OUT THIS LAST ADDRESS?
YEAH, IT'S THE ONE NEXT TO IGGY'S NAME, RIGHT?

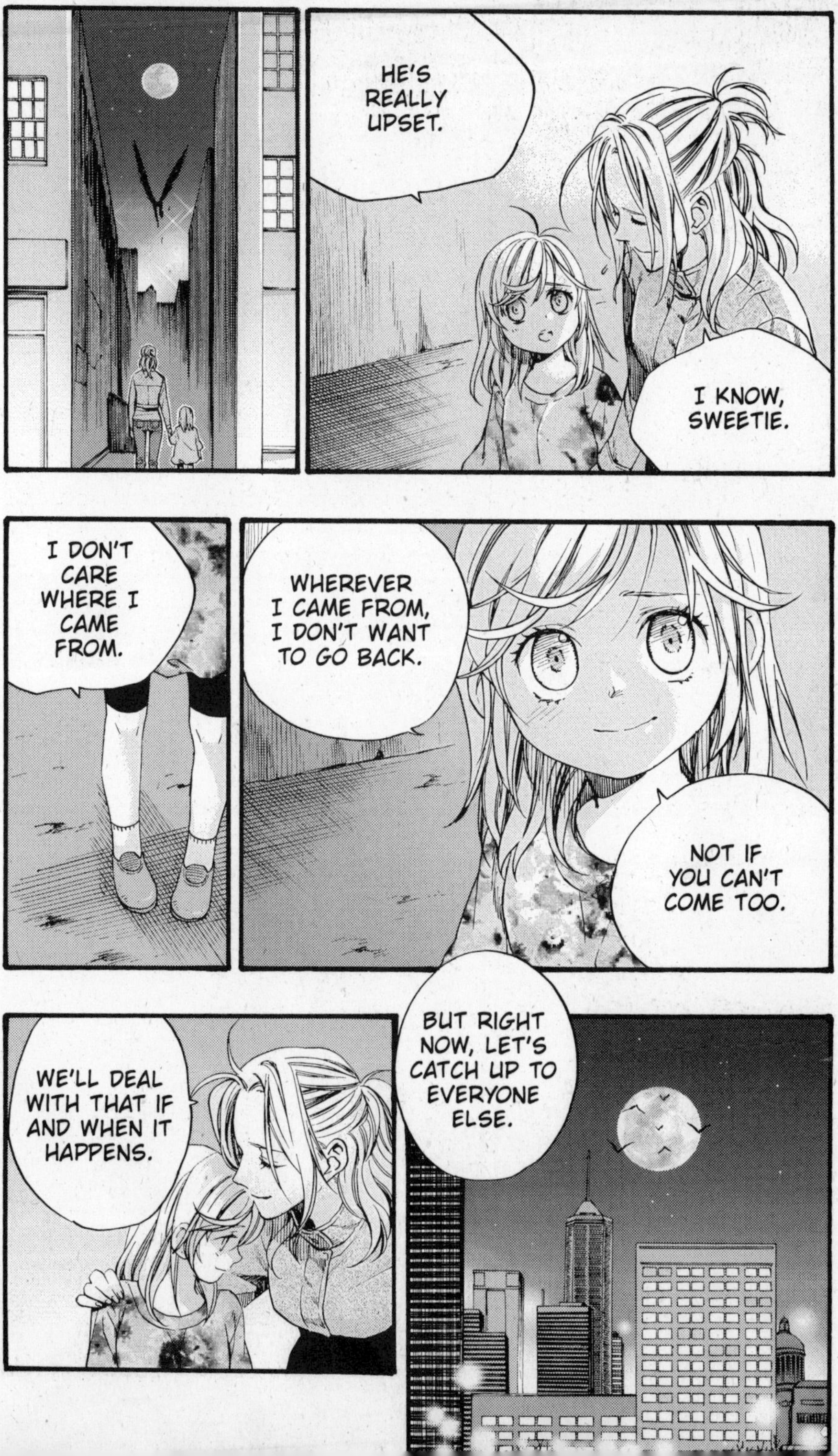
HE'S REALLY UPSET.
I KNOW, SWEETIE.
I DON'T CARE WHERE I CAME FROM.
WHEREVER I CAME FROM, I DON'T WANT TO GO BACK.
NOT IF YOU CAN'T COME TOO.
WE'LL DEAL WITH THAT IF AND WHEN IT HAPPENS.
BUT RIGHT NOW, LET'S CATCH UP TO EVERYONE ELSE.

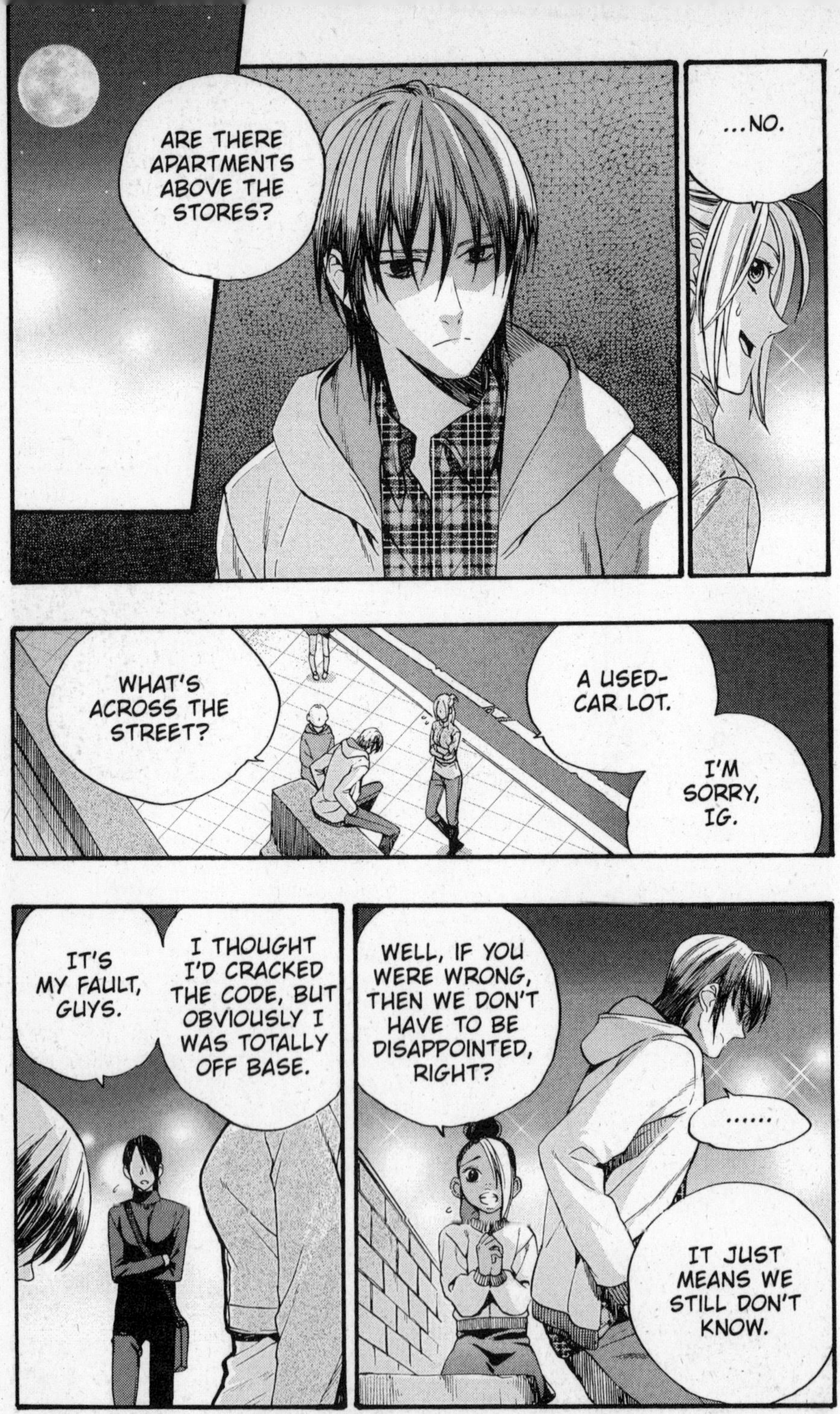
ARE THERE APARTMENTS ABOVE THE STORES?
...NO.
WHAT'S ACROSS THE STREET?
A USED-CAR LOT.
I'M SORRY, IG.
IT'S MY FAULT, GUYS.
I THOUGHT I'D CRACKED THE CODE, BUT OBVIOUSLY I WAS TOTALLY OFF BASE.
WELL, IF YOU WERE WRONG, THEN WE DON'T HAVE TO BE DISAPPOINTED, RIGHT?
......
IT JUST MEANS WE STILL DON'T KNOW.

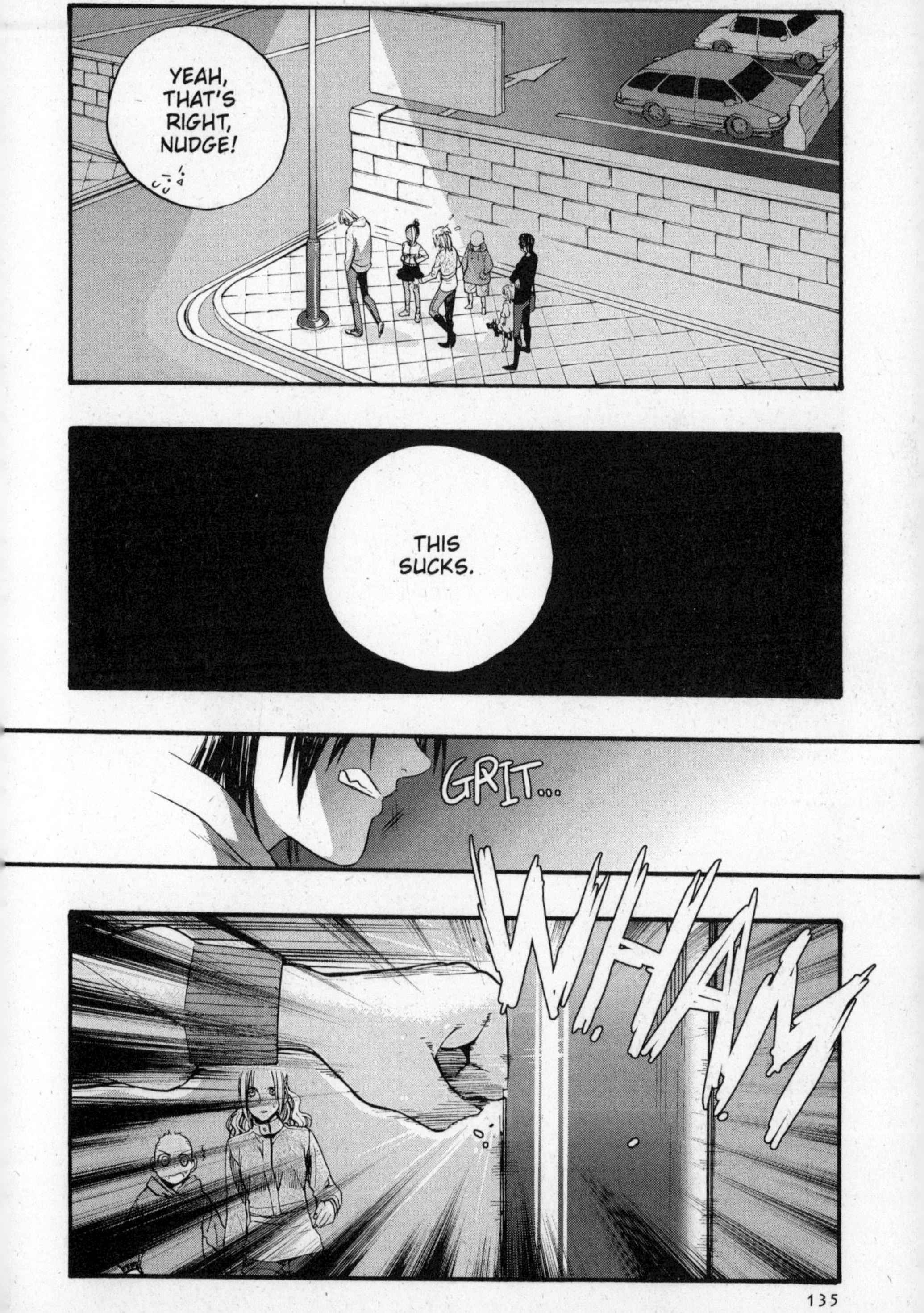
YEAH, THAT'S RIGHT, NUDGE!
THIS SUCKS.
GRIT...
WHAM

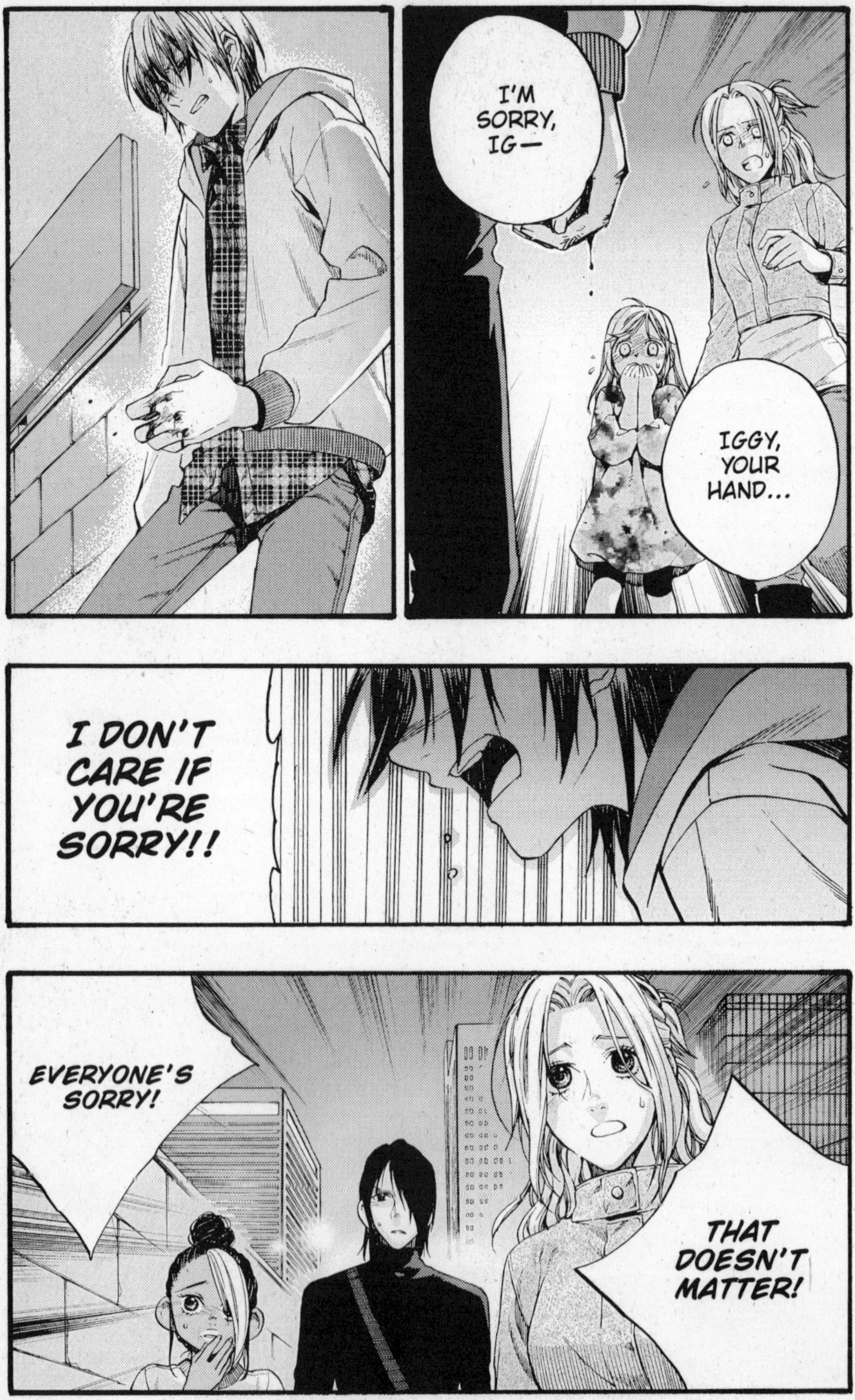
I'M SORRY, IG—
IGGY, YOUR HAND...
I DON'T CARE IF YOU'RE SORRY!!
EVERYONE'S SORRY!
THAT DOESN'T MATTER!

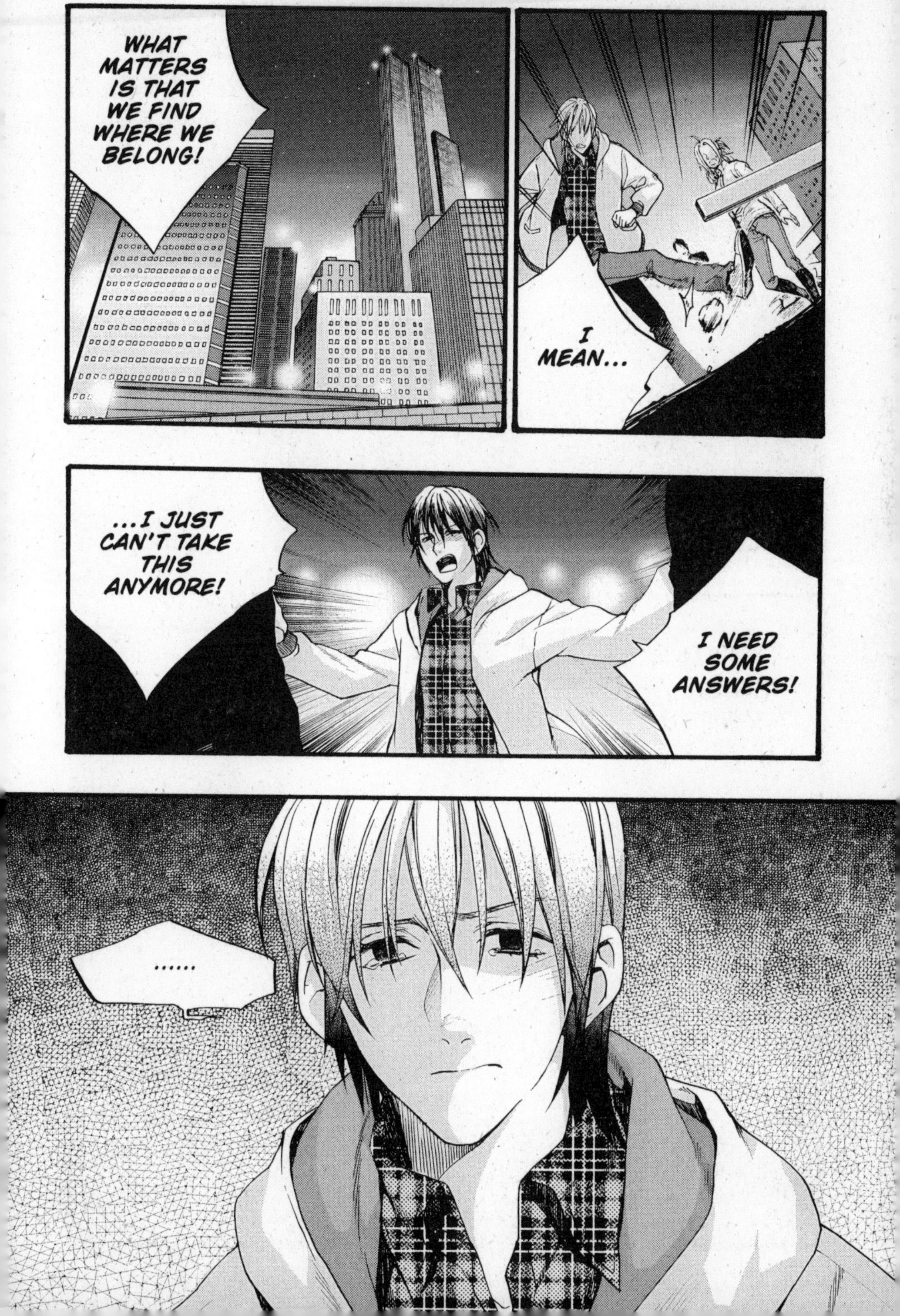
WHAT MATTERS IS THAT WE FIND WHERE WE BELONG!
I MEAN...
...I JUST CAN'T TAKE THIS ANYMORE!
I NEED SOME ANSWERS!
......

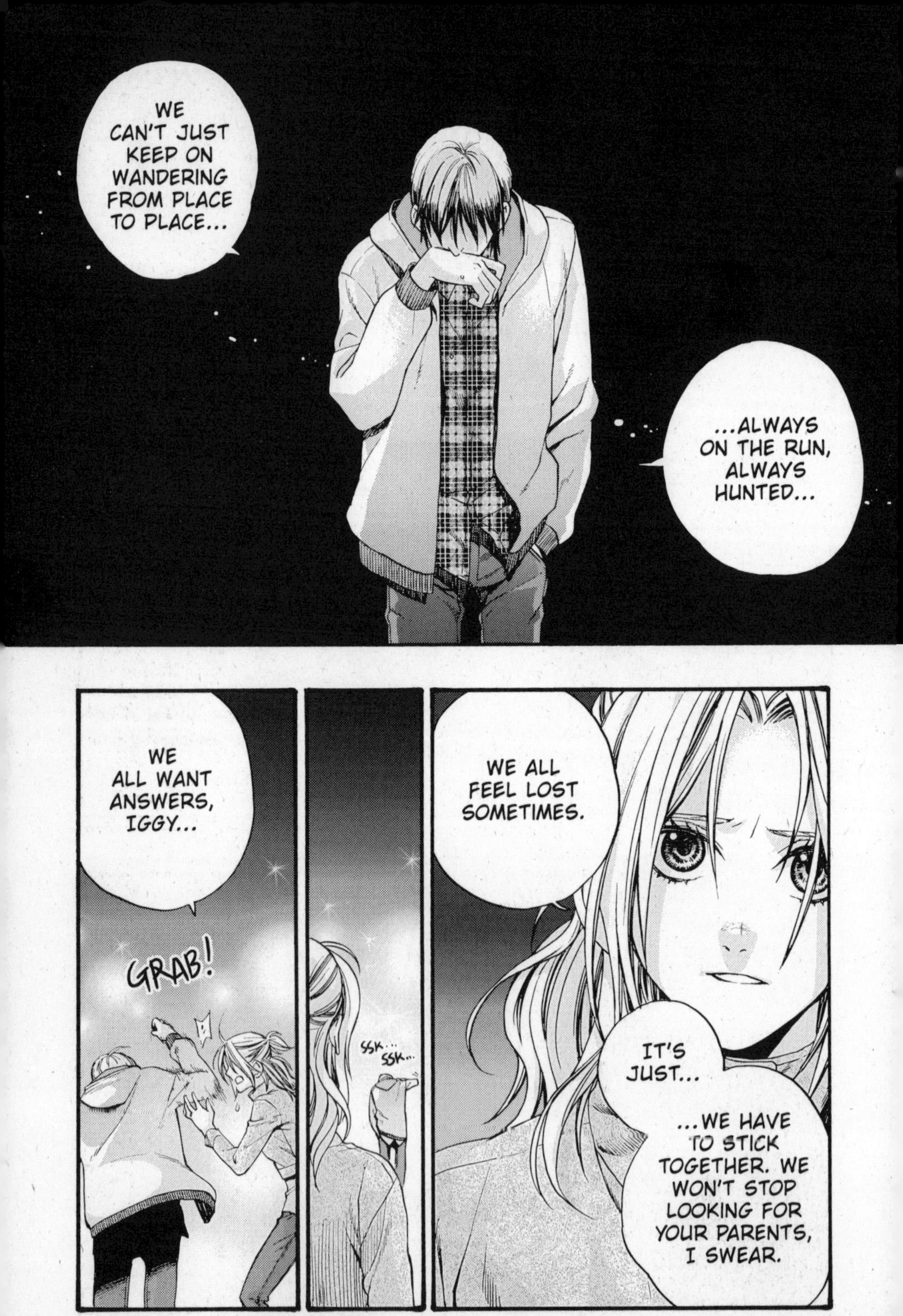
WE CAN'T JUST KEEP ON WANDERING FROM PLACE TO PLACE...
...ALWAYS ON THE RUN, ALWAYS HUNTED...
WE ALL WANT ANSWERS, IGGY...
GRAB!
SSK... SSK...
WE ALL FEEL LOST SOMETIMES.
IT'S JUST...
...WE HAVE TO STICK TOGETHER. WE WON'T STOP LOOKING FOR YOUR PARENTS, I SWEAR.

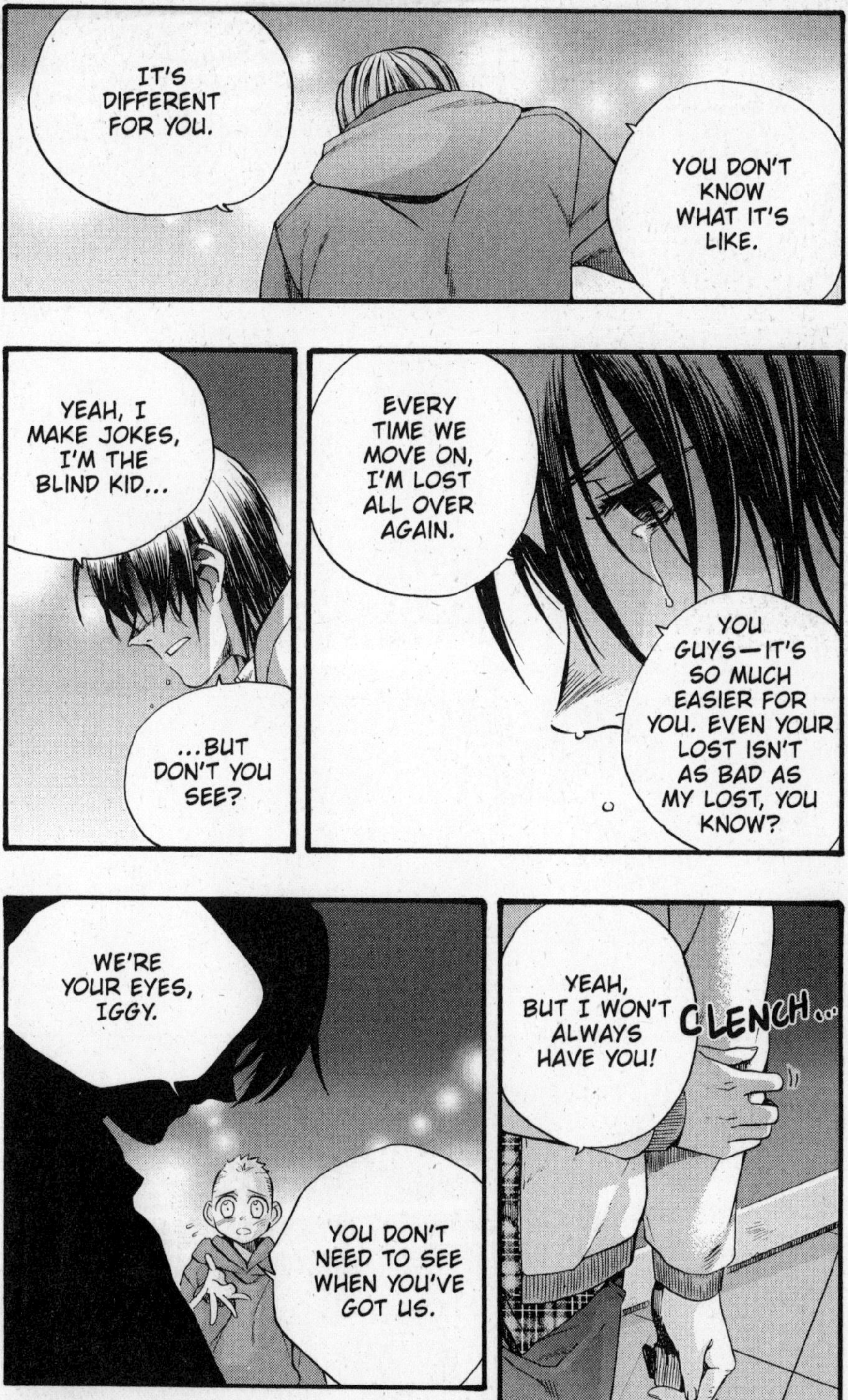
IT'S DIFFERENT FOR YOU.
YOU DON'T KNOW WHAT IT'S LIKE.
YEAH, I MAKE JOKES, I'M THE BLIND KID...
...BUT DON'T YOU SEE?
EVERY TIME WE MOVE ON, I'M LOST ALL OVER AGAIN.
YOU GUYS—IT'S SO MUCH EASIER FOR YOU. EVEN YOUR LOST ISN'T AS BAD AS MY LOST, YOU KNOW?
WE'RE YOUR EYES, IGGY.
YOU DON'T NEED TO SEE WHEN YOU'VE GOT US.
YEAH, BUT I WON'T ALWAYS HAVE YOU!
CLENCH...

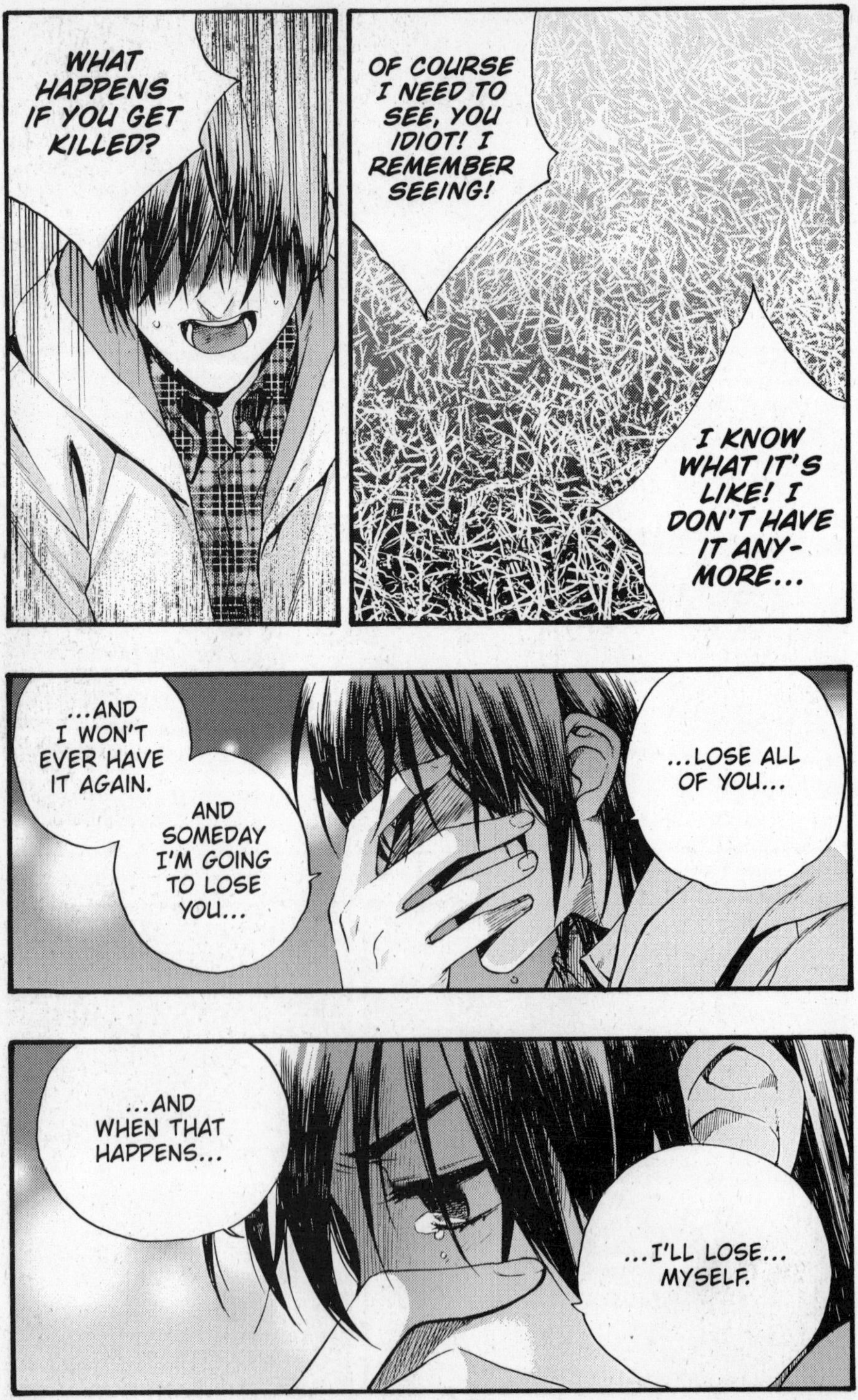
WHAT HAPPENS IF YOU GET KILLED?
OF COURSE I NEED TO SEE, YOU IDIOT! I REMEMBER SEEING!
I KNOW WHAT IT'S LIKE! I DON'T HAVE IT ANY-MORE...
...AND I WON'T EVER HAVE IT AGAIN.
AND SOMEDAY I'M GOING TO LOSE YOU...
...LOSE ALL OF YOU...
...AND WHEN THAT HAPPENS...
...I'LL LOSE... MYSELF.

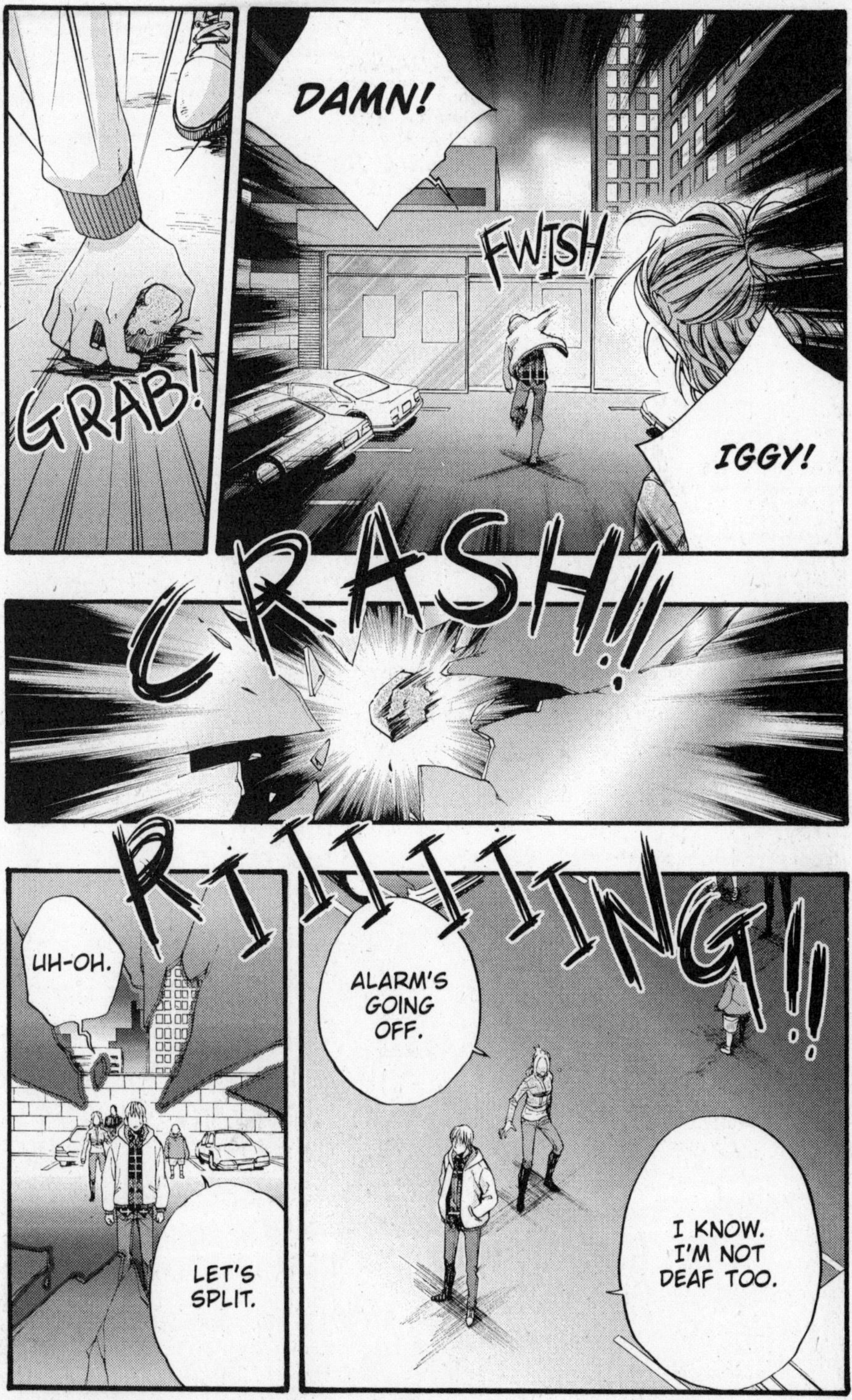

GRAB!
DAMN!
FWISH
IGGY!
CRASH!!
RIIIIING!!
UH-OH.
LET'S SPLIT.
ALARM'S GOING OFF.
I KNOW. I'M NOT DEAF TOO.

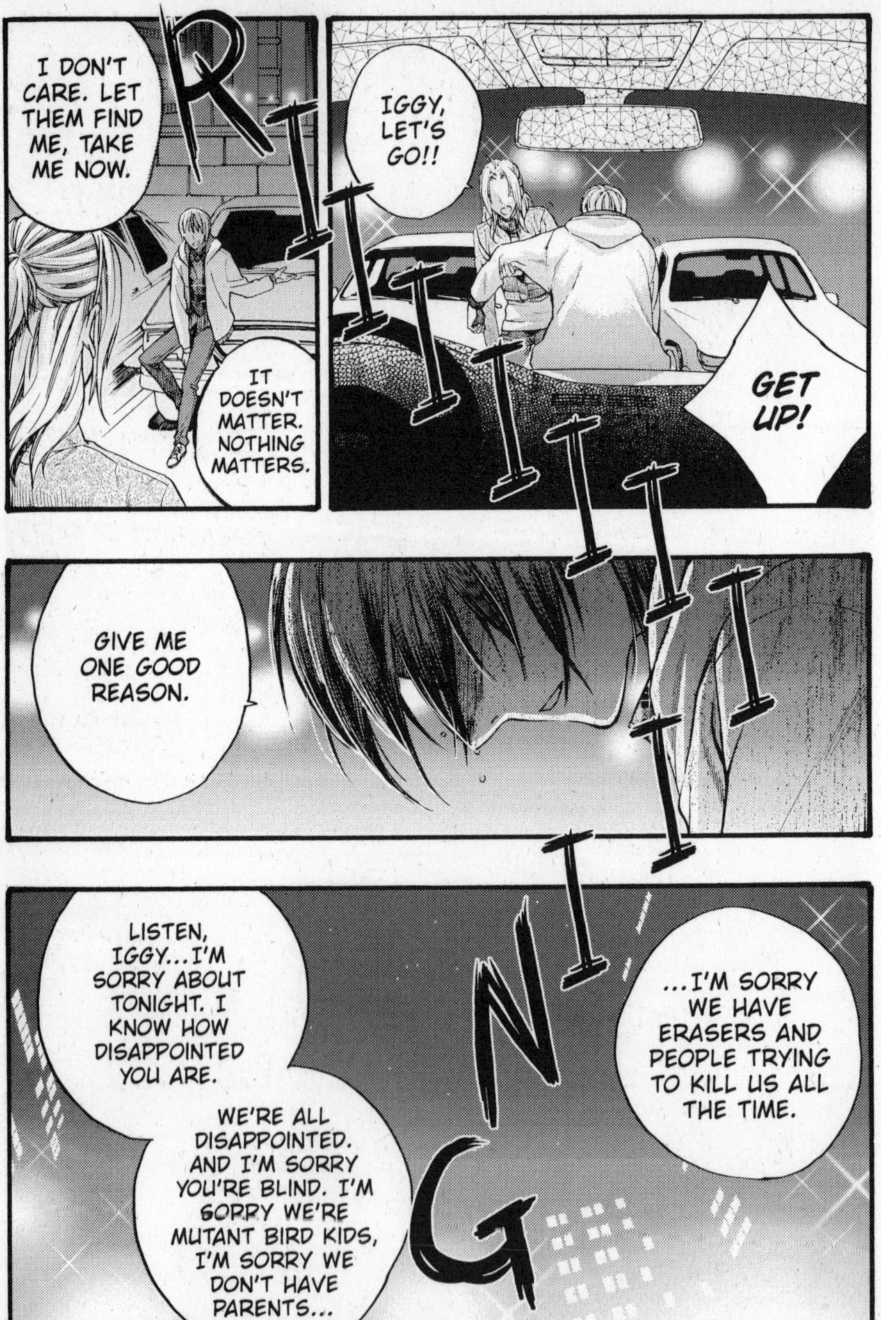
I DON'T CARE. LET THEM FIND ME, TAKE ME NOW.
IT DOESN'T MATTER. NOTHING MATTERS.
RIIIIIIIIING
IGGY, LET'S GO!!
GET UP!
GIVE ME ONE GOOD REASON.
LISTEN, IGGY...I'M SORRY ABOUT TONIGHT. I KNOW HOW DISAPPOINTED YOU ARE.
WE'RE ALL DISAPPOINTED. AND I'M SORRY YOU'RE BLIND. I'M SORRY WE'RE MUTANT BIRD KIDS, I'M SORRY WE DON'T HAVE PARENTS...
...I'M SORRY WE HAVE ERASERS AND PEOPLE TRYING TO KILL US ALL THE TIME.

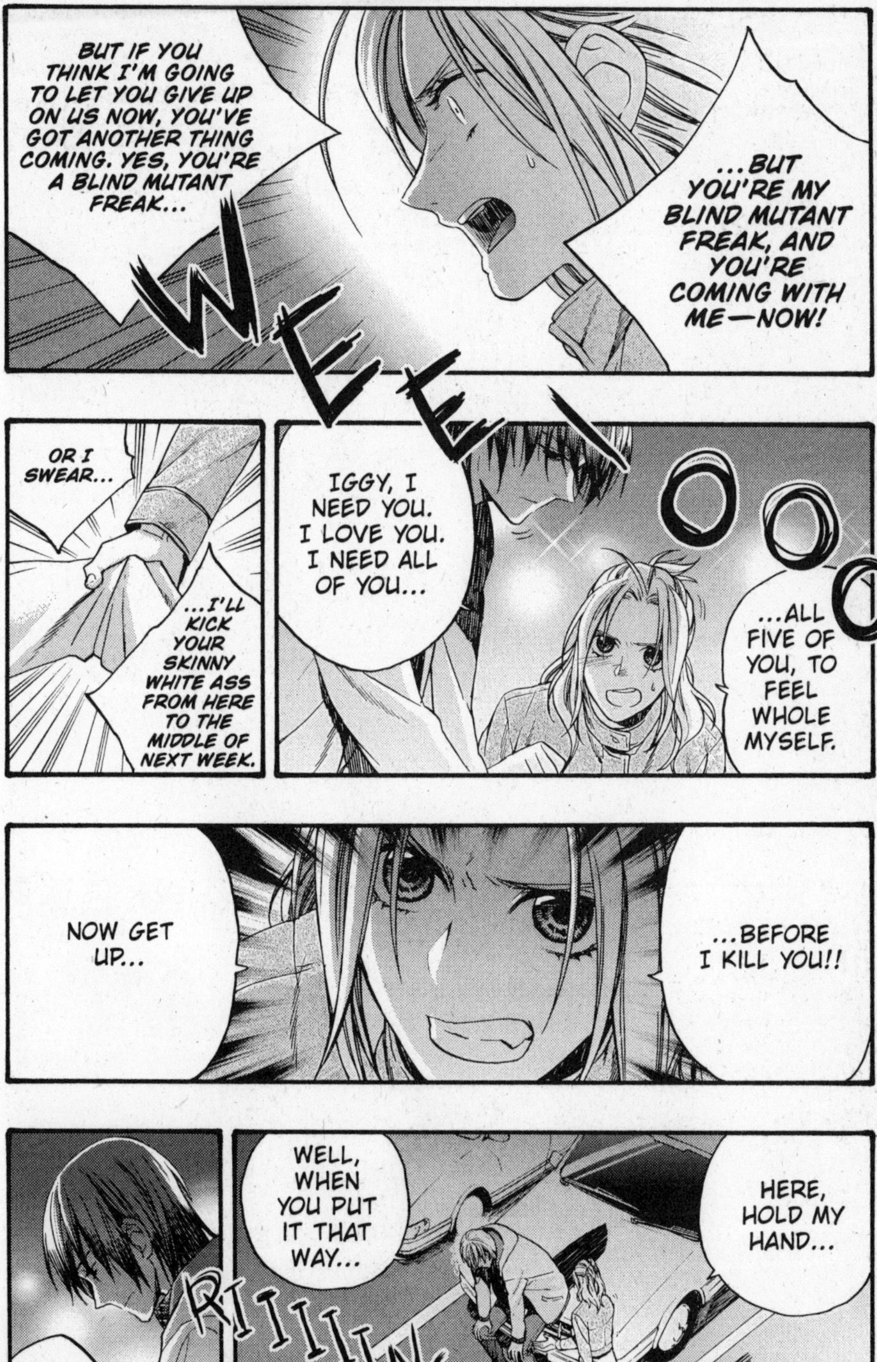
BUT IF YOU THINK I'M GOING TO LET YOU GIVE UP ON US NOW, YOU'VE GOT ANOTHER THING COMING. YES, YOU'RE A BLIND MUTANT FREAK...
...BUT YOU'RE MY BLIND MUTANT FREAK, AND YOU'RE COMING WITH ME—NOW!
WEEIOOO
OR I SWEAR...
...I'LL KICK YOUR SKINNY WHITE ASS FROM HERE TO THE MIDDLE OF NEXT WEEK.
IGGY, I NEED YOU. I LOVE YOU. I NEED ALL OF YOU...
...ALL FIVE OF YOU, TO FEEL WHOLE MYSELF.
NOW GET UP...
...BEFORE I KILL YOU!!
......
WELL, WHEN YOU PUT IT THAT WAY...
HERE, HOLD MY HAND...
RIIIING

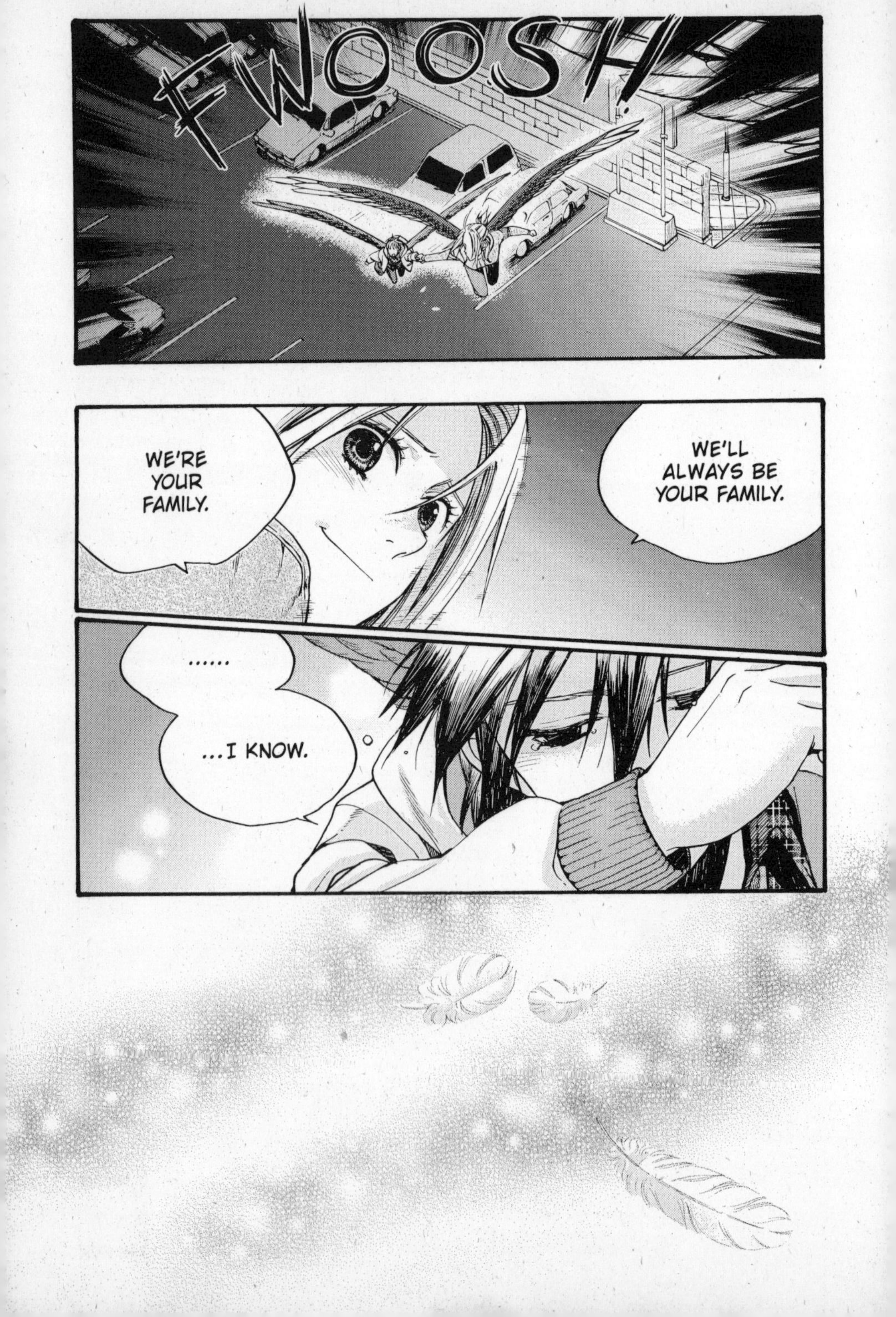
FWOOSH!
WE'RE YOUR FAMILY.
WE'LL ALWAYS BE YOUR FAMILY.
......
...I KNOW.

MAXIMUM
RIDE

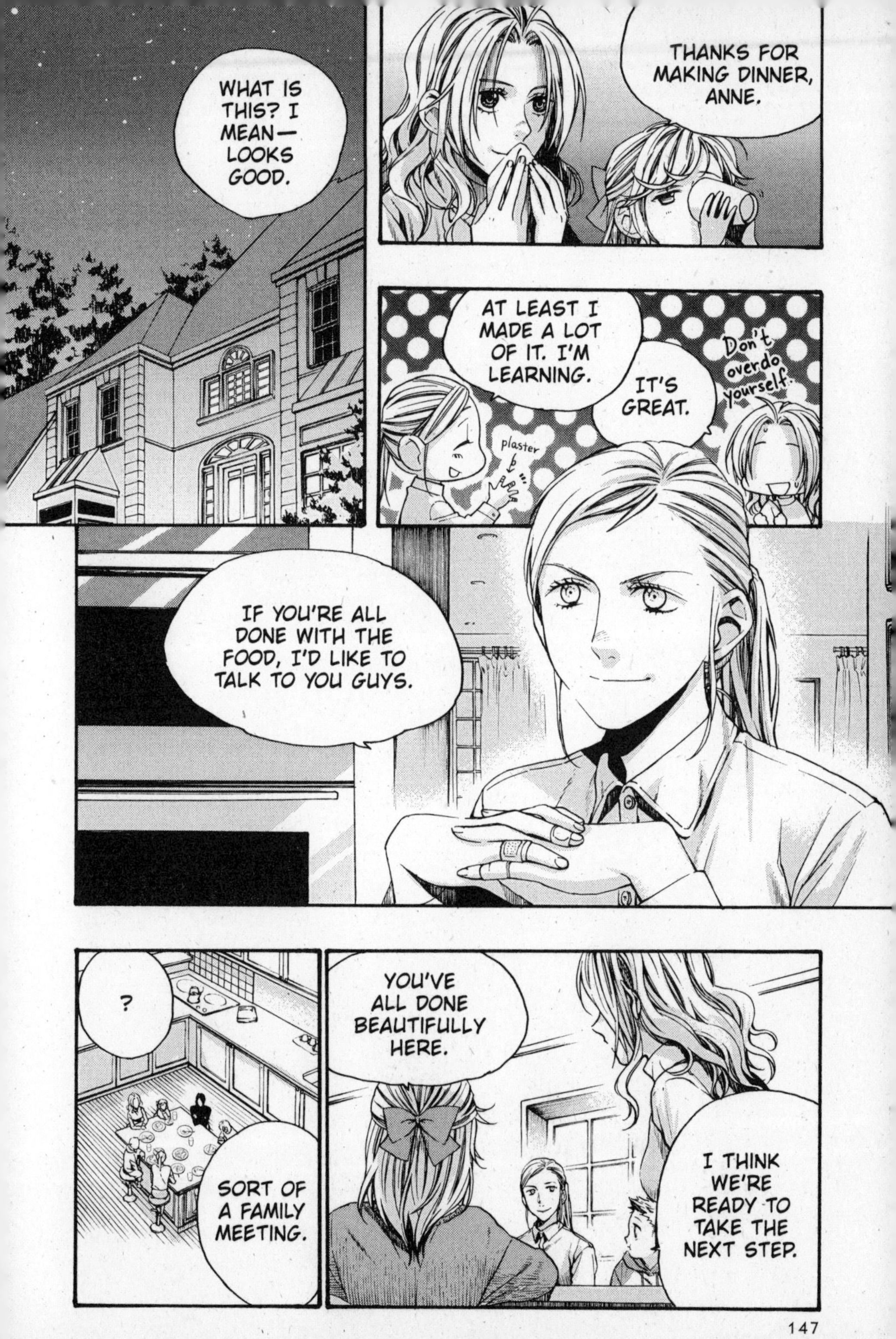
WHAT IS THIS? I MEAN— LOOKS GOOD.
THANKS FOR MAKING DINNER, ANNE.
AT LEAST I MADE A LOT OF IT. I'M LEARNING.
plaster
IT'S GREAT.
Don't overdo yourself.
IF YOU'RE ALL DONE WITH THE FOOD, I'D LIKE TO TALK TO YOU GUYS.
?
SORT OF A FAMILY MEETING.
YOU'VE ALL DONE BEAUTIFULLY HERE.
I THINK WE'RE READY TO TAKE THE NEXT STEP.

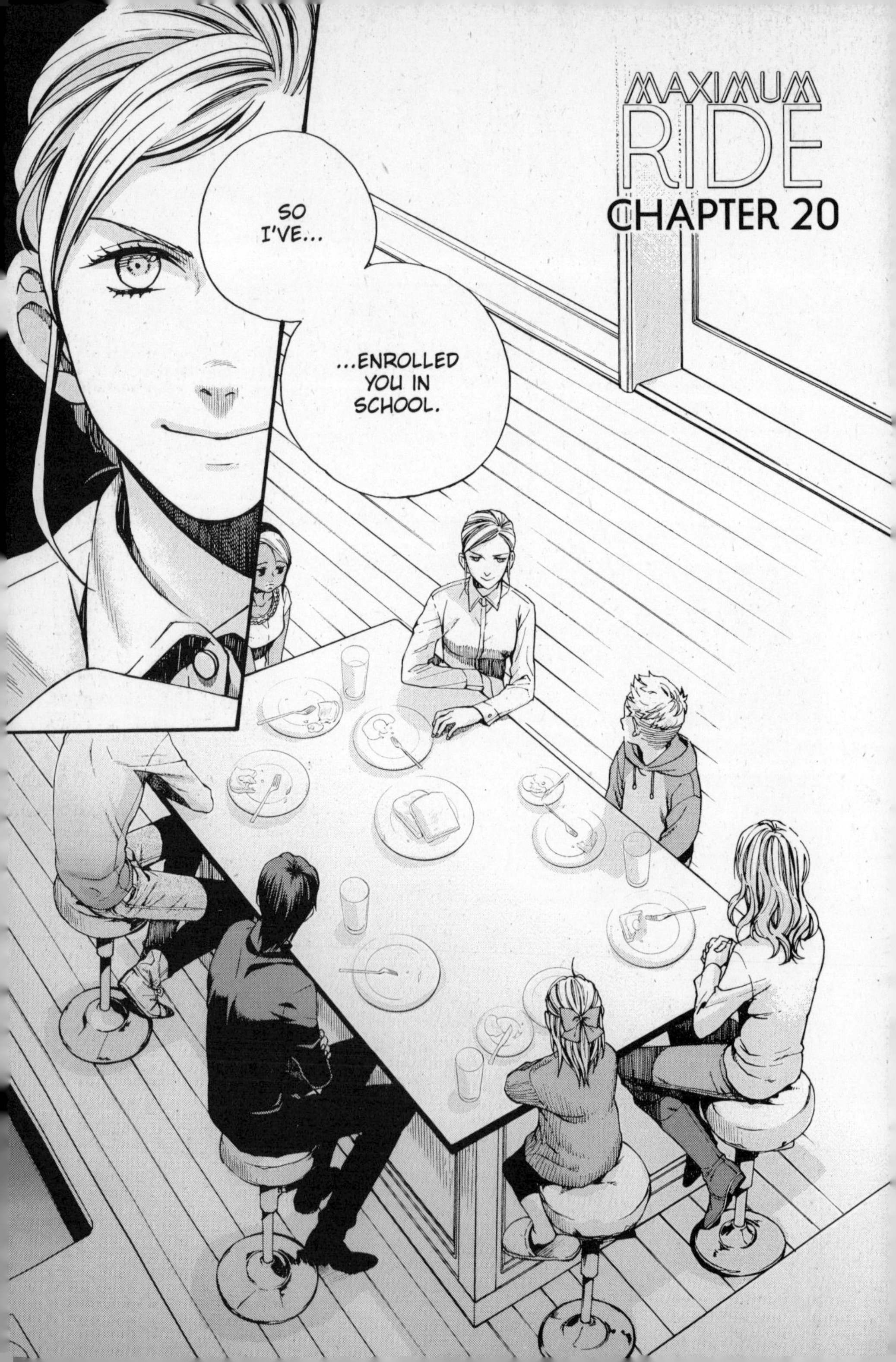
MAXIMUM RIDE
CHAPTER 20
SO I'VE...
...ENROLLED YOU IN SCHOOL.

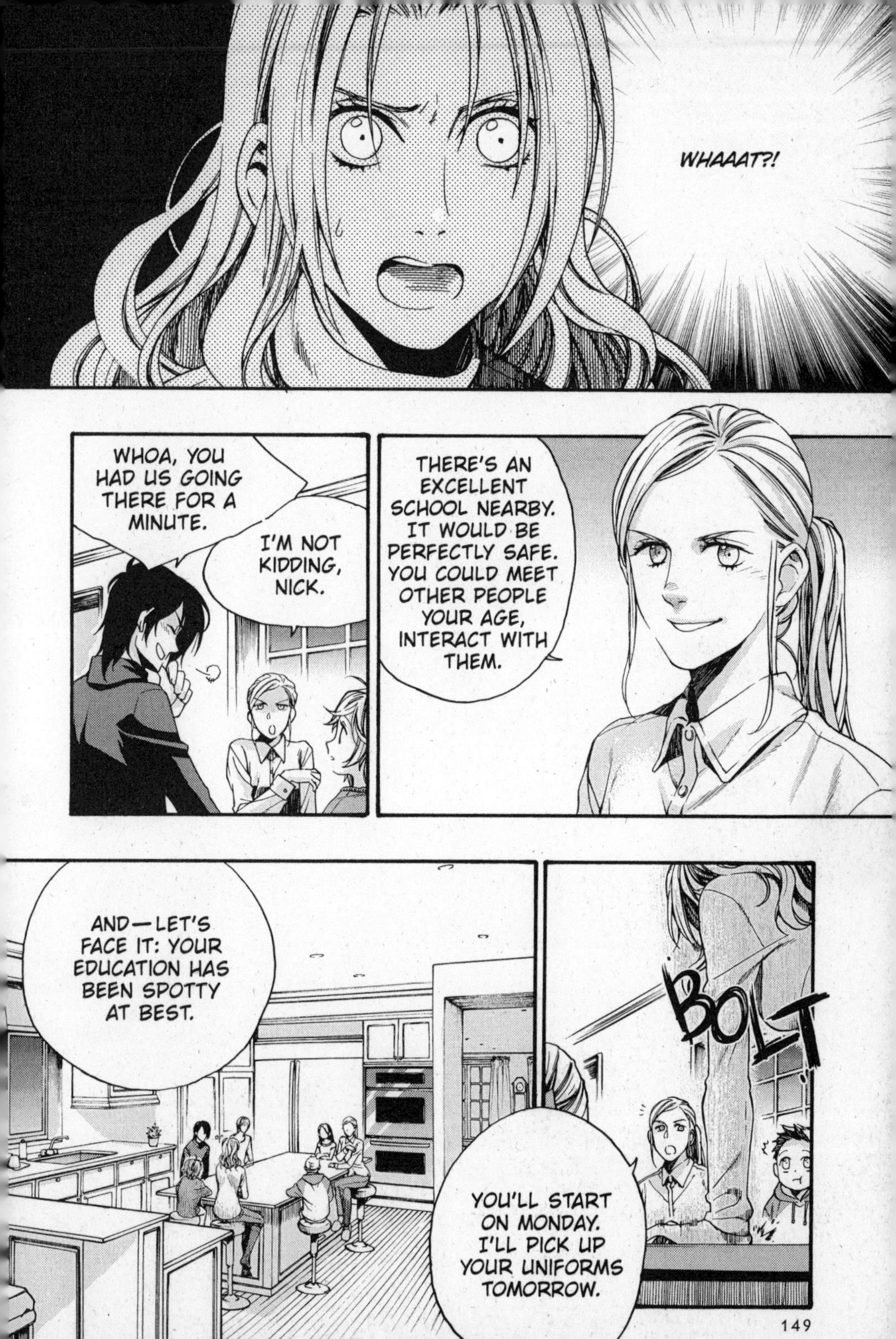
WHAAAT?!
WHOA, YOU HAD US GOING THERE FOR A MINUTE.
I'M NOT KIDDING, NICK.
THERE'S AN EXCELLENT SCHOOL NEARBY. IT WOULD BE PERFECTLY SAFE. YOU COULD MEET OTHER PEOPLE YOUR AGE, INTERACT WITH THEM.
AND—LET'S FACE IT: YOUR EDUCATION HAS BEEN SPOTTY AT BEST.
BOLT
YOU'LL START ON MONDAY. I'LL PICK UP YOUR UNIFORMS TOMORROW.

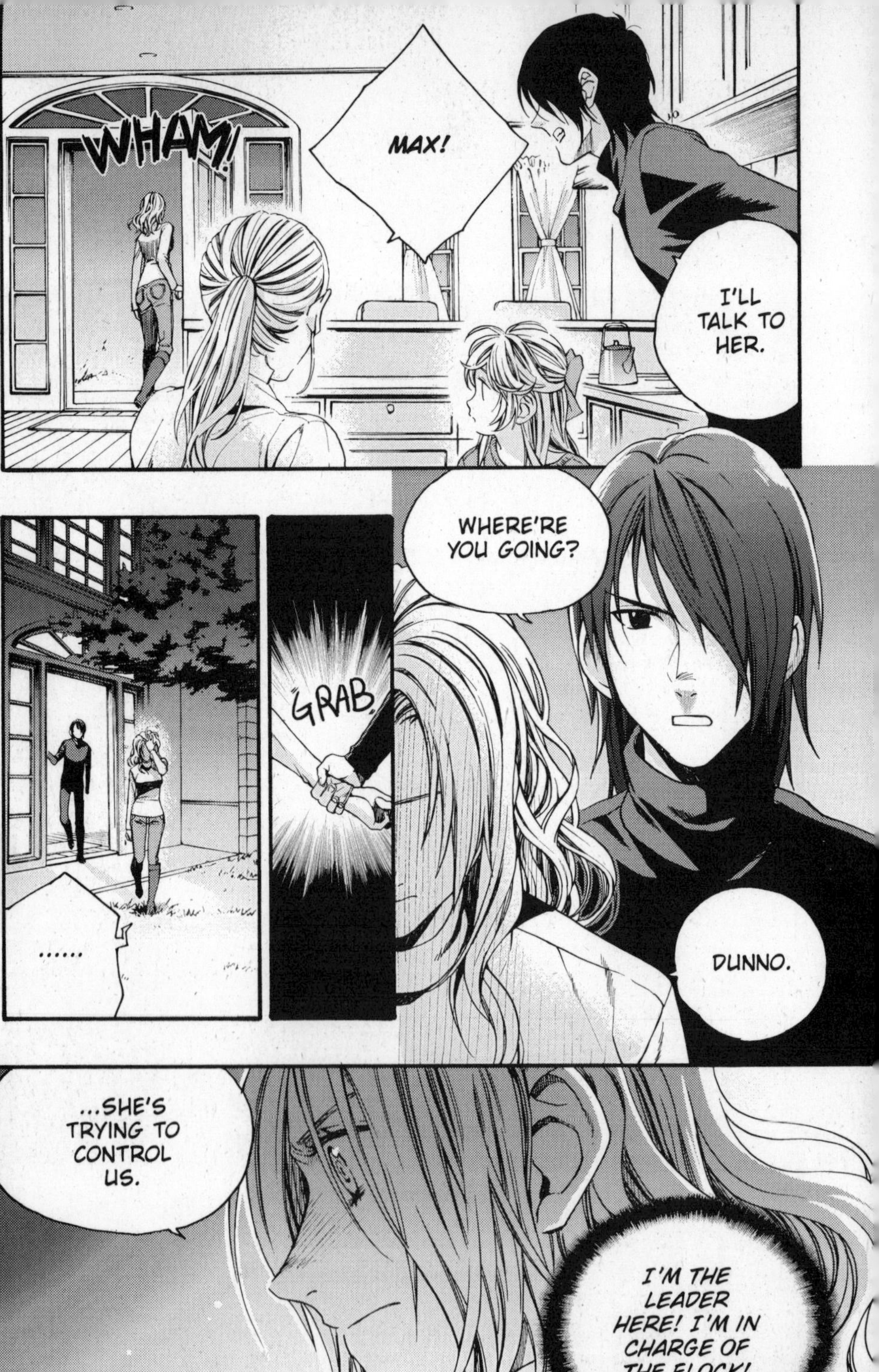
WHAM!
MAX!
I'LL TALK TO HER.
......
GRAB
WHERE'RE YOU GOING?
DUNNO.
...SHE'S TRYING TO CONTROL US.
I'M THE LEADER HERE! I'M IN CHARGE OF THE FLOCK!

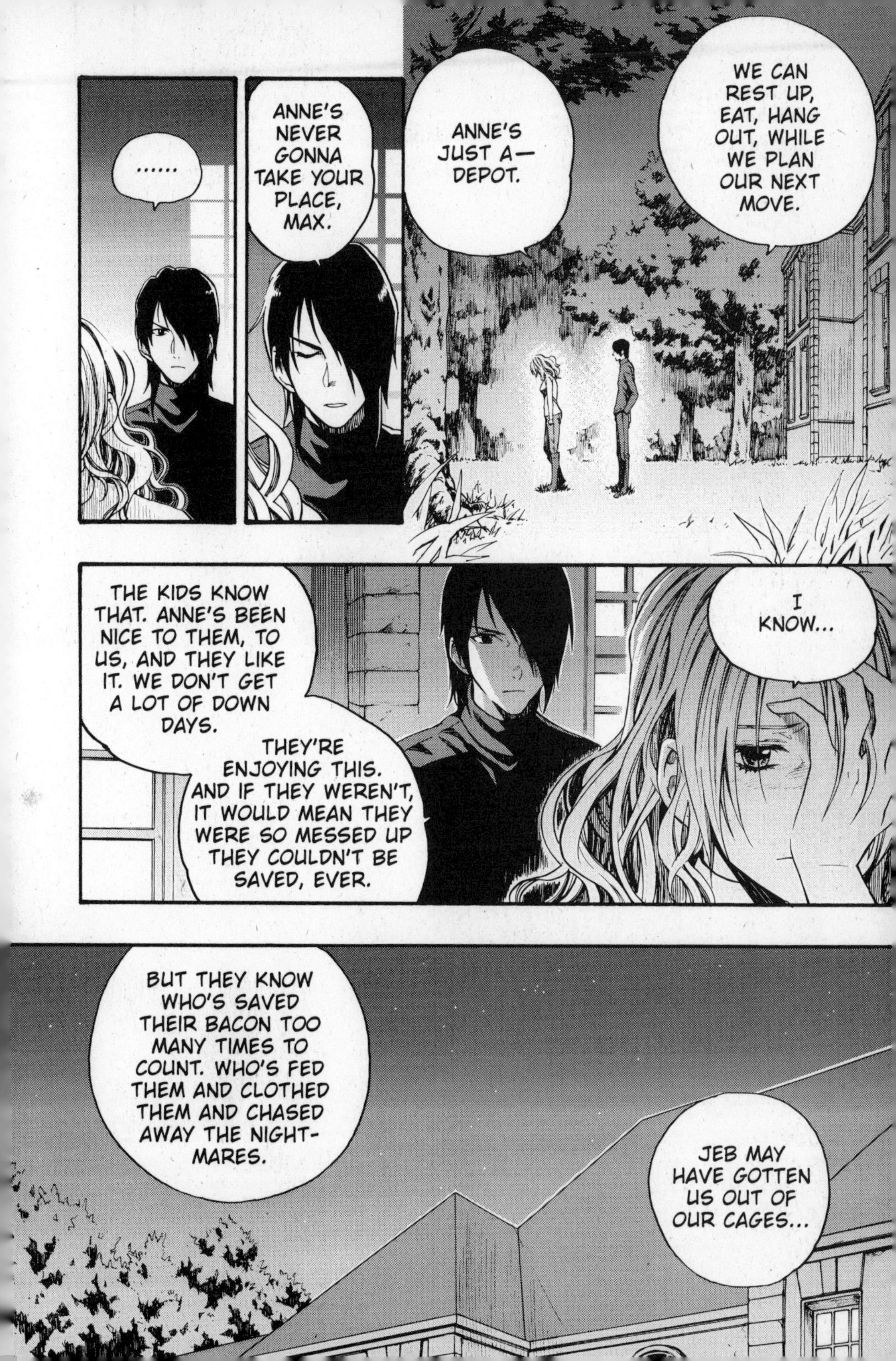
......
ANNE'S NEVER GONNA TAKE YOUR PLACE, MAX.
ANNE'S JUST A—DEPOT.
WE CAN REST UP, EAT, HANG OUT, WHILE WE PLAN OUR NEXT MOVE.
THE KIDS KNOW THAT. ANNE'S BEEN NICE TO THEM, TO US, AND THEY LIKE IT. WE DON'T GET A LOT OF DOWN DAYS.
THEY'RE ENJOYING THIS. AND IF THEY WEREN'T, IT WOULD MEAN THEY WERE SO MESSED UP THEY COULDN'T BE SAVED, EVER.
I KNOW...
BUT THEY KNOW WHO'S SAVED THEIR BACON TOO MANY TIMES TO COUNT. WHO'S FED THEM AND CLOTHED THEM AND CHASED AWAY THE NIGHT-MARES.
JEB MAY HAVE GOTTEN US OUT OF OUR CAGES...

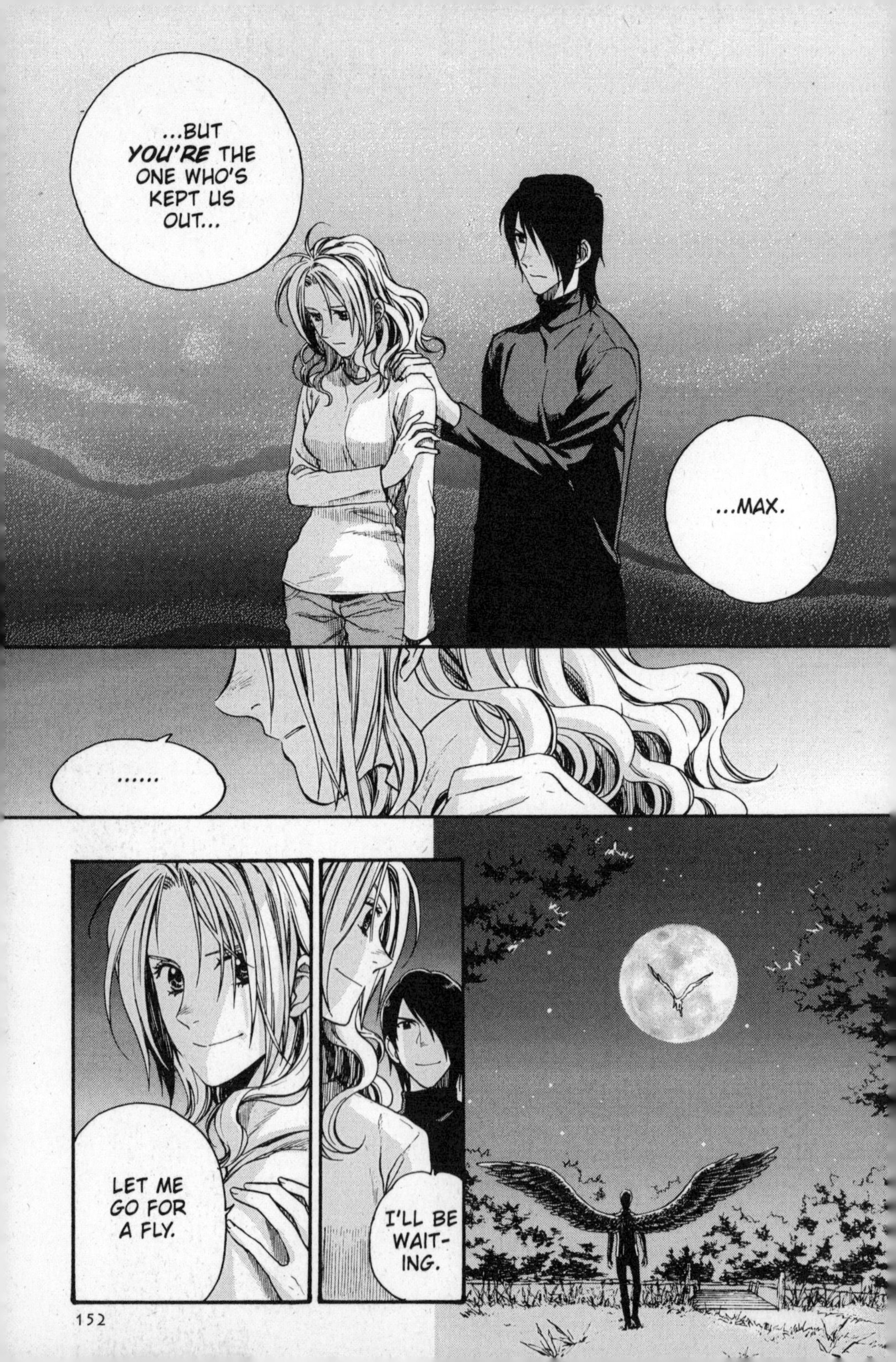
...BUT YOU'RE THE ONE WHO'S KEPT US OUT...
...MAX.
......
LET ME GO FOR A FLY.
I'LL BE WAIT-ING.

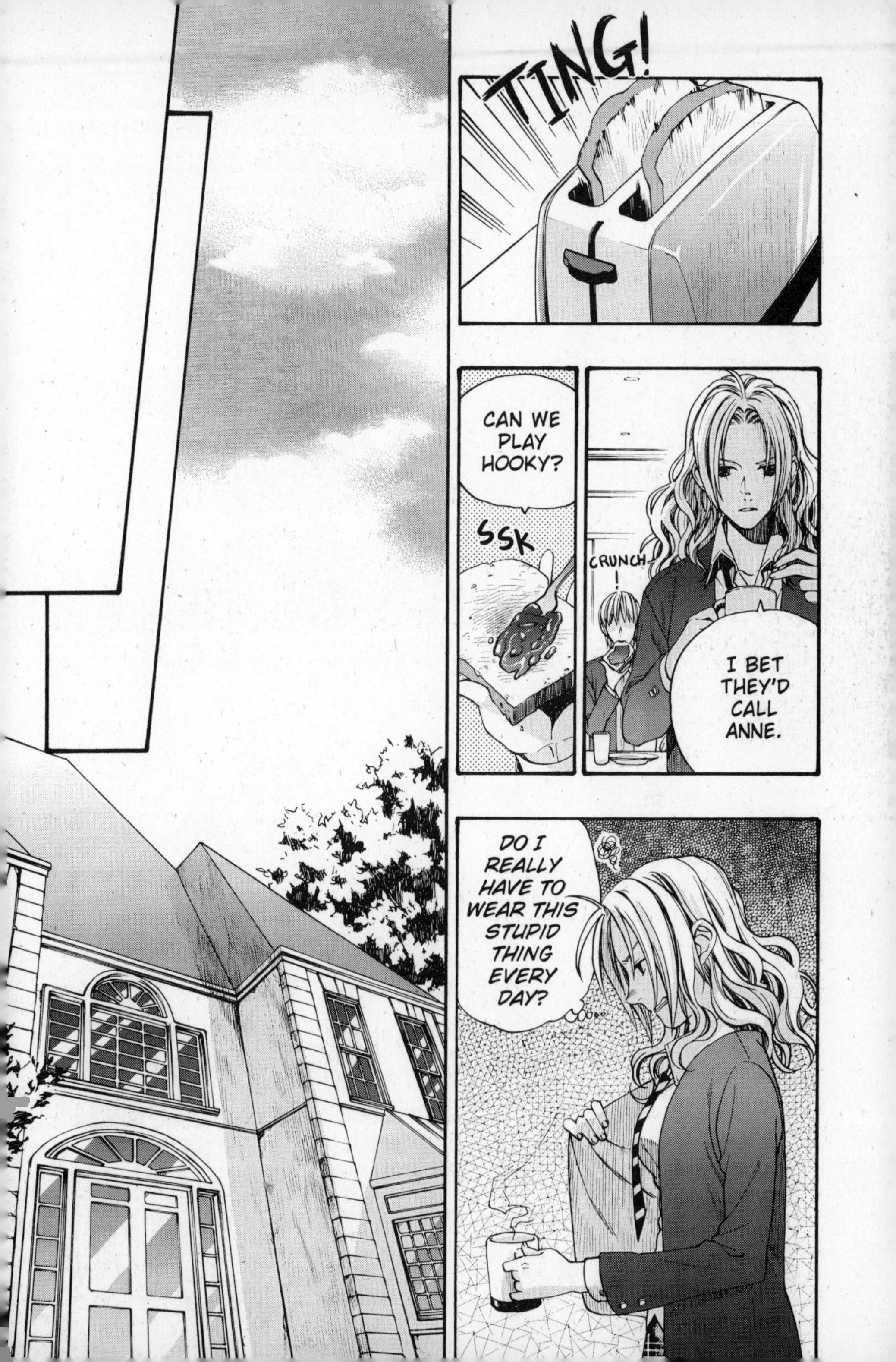
TING!
CAN WE PLAY HOOKY?
SSK
CRUNCH!
I BET THEY'D CALL ANNE.
DO I REALLY HAVE TO WEAR THIS STUPID THING EVERY DAY?

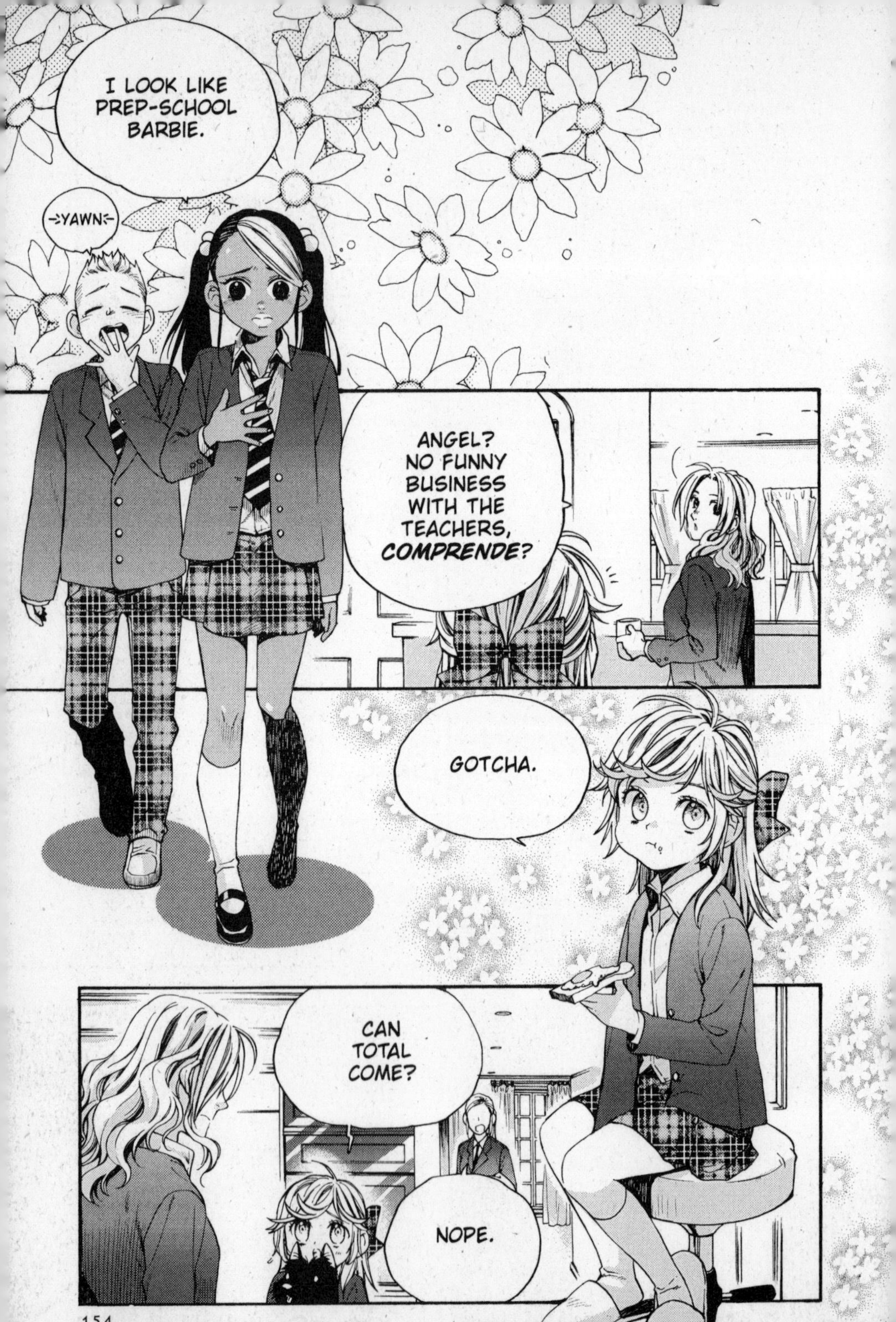
I LOOK LIKE PREP-SCHOOL BARBIE.
~YAWN~
ANGEL? NO FUNNY BUSINESS WITH THE TEACHERS, *COMPRENDE*?
GOTCHA.
CAN TOTAL COME?
NOPE.

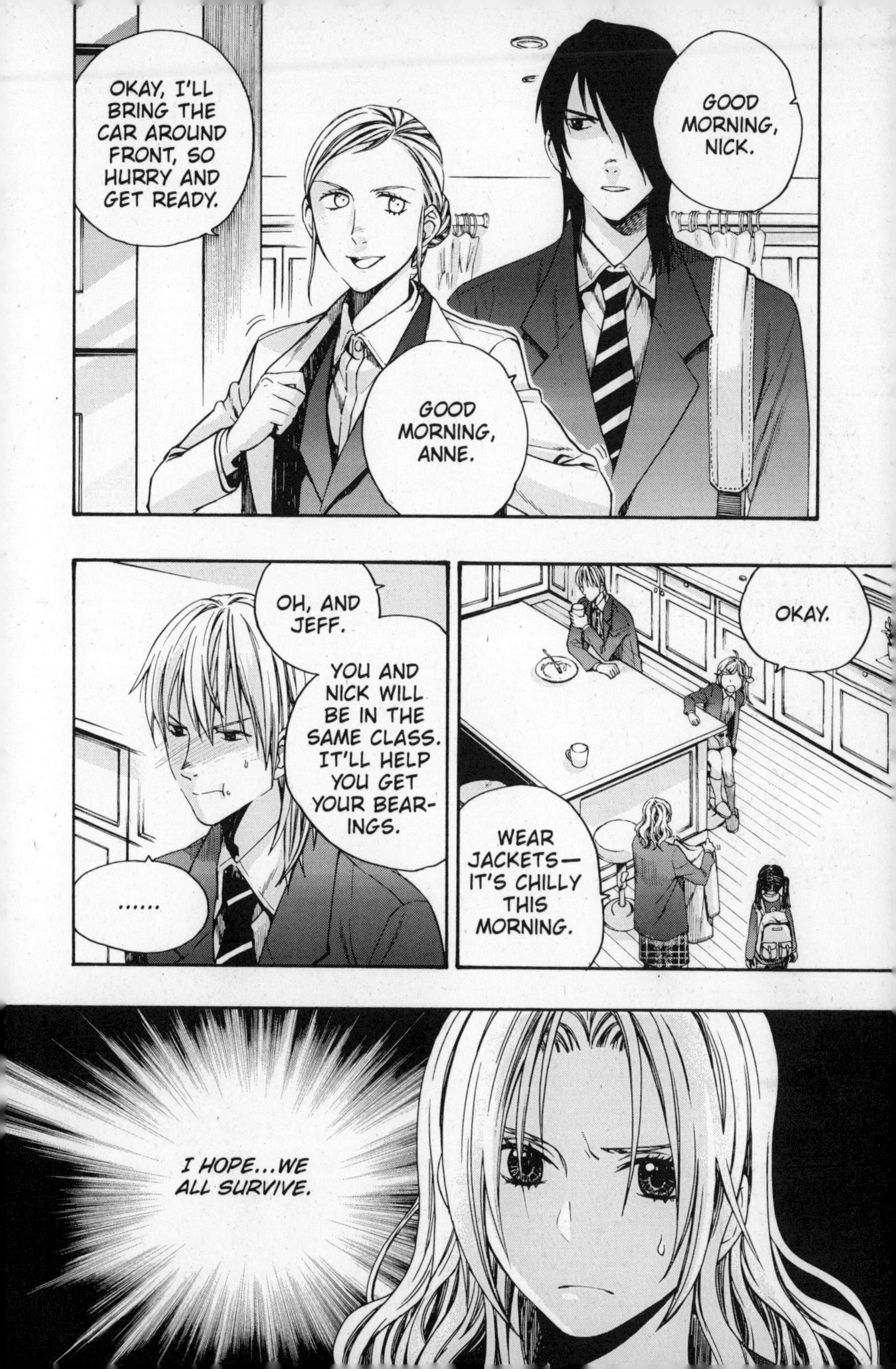
OKAY, I'LL BRING THE CAR AROUND FRONT, SO HURRY AND GET READY.
GOOD MORNING, NICK.
GOOD MORNING, ANNE.
OH, AND JEFF.
YOU AND NICK WILL BE IN THE SAME CLASS. IT'LL HELP YOU GET YOUR BEAR-INGS.
......
OKAY.
WEAR JACKETS—IT'S CHILLY THIS MORNING.
I HOPE...WE ALL SURVIVE.

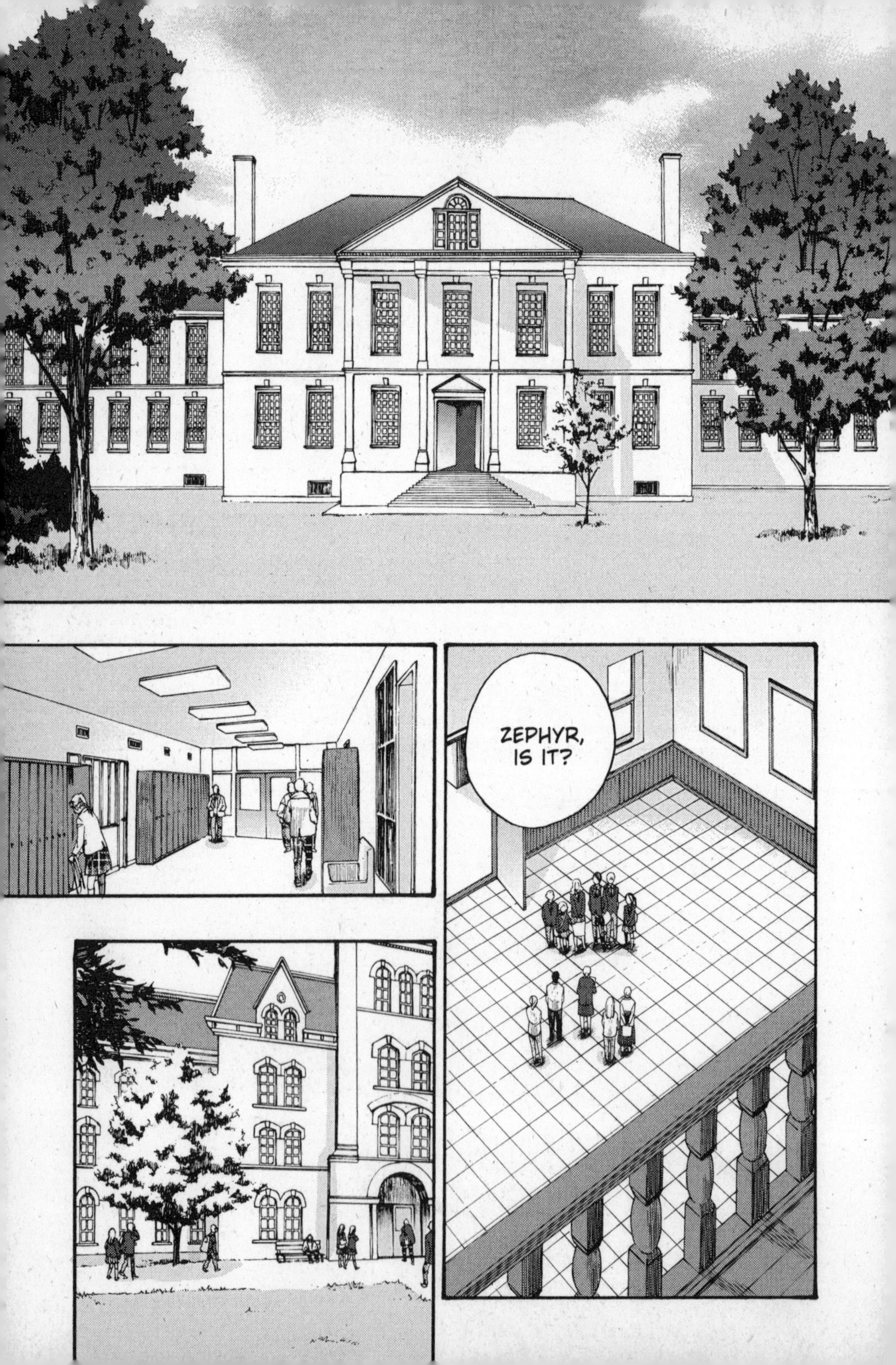
ZEPHYR, IS IT?

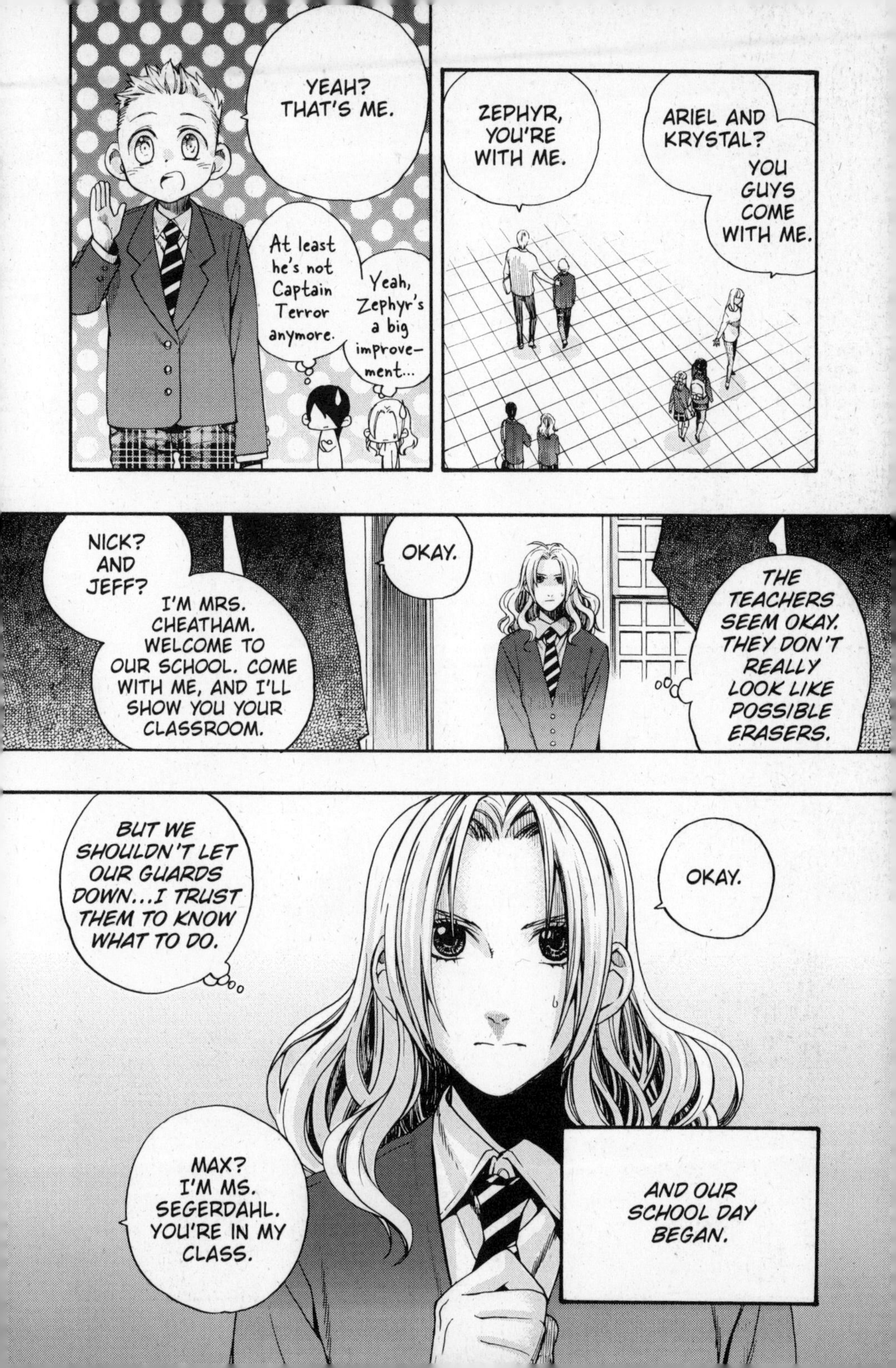
YEAH? THAT'S ME.
At least he's not Captain Terror anymore.
Yeah, Zephyr's a big improvement...
ZEPHYR, YOU'RE WITH ME.
ARIEL AND KRYSTAL?
YOU GUYS COME WITH ME.
NICK? AND JEFF?
I'M MRS. CHEATHAM. WELCOME TO OUR SCHOOL. COME WITH ME, AND I'LL SHOW YOU YOUR CLASSROOM.
OKAY.
THE TEACHERS SEEM OKAY. THEY DON'T REALLY LOOK LIKE POSSIBLE ERASERS.
BUT WE SHOULDN'T LET OUR GUARDS DOWN...I TRUST THEM TO KNOW WHAT TO DO.
OKAY.
MAX? I'M MS. SEGERDAHL. YOU'RE IN MY CLASS.
AND OUR SCHOOL DAY BEGAN.

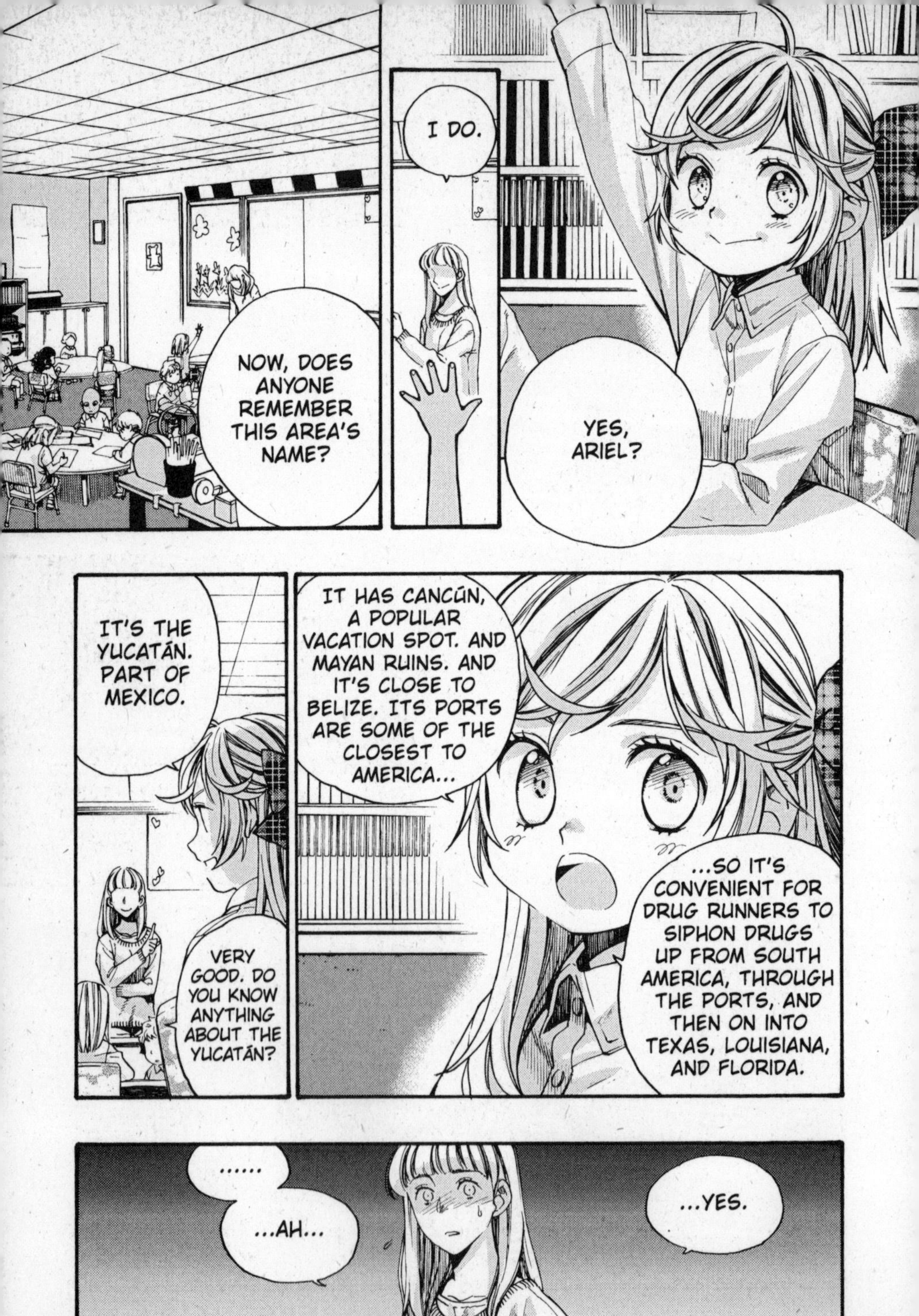
NOW, DOES ANYONE REMEMBER THIS AREA'S NAME?
I DO.
YES, ARIEL?
IT'S THE YUCATÁN. PART OF MEXICO.
VERY GOOD. DO YOU KNOW ANYTHING ABOUT THE YUCATÁN?
IT HAS CANCÚN, A POPULAR VACATION SPOT. AND MAYAN RUINS. AND IT'S CLOSE TO BELIZE. ITS PORTS ARE SOME OF THE CLOSEST TO AMERICA...
...SO IT'S CONVENIENT FOR DRUG RUNNERS TO SIPHON DRUGS UP FROM SOUTH AMERICA, THROUGH THE PORTS, AND THEN ON INTO TEXAS, LOUISIANA, AND FLORIDA.
......
...AH...
...YES.

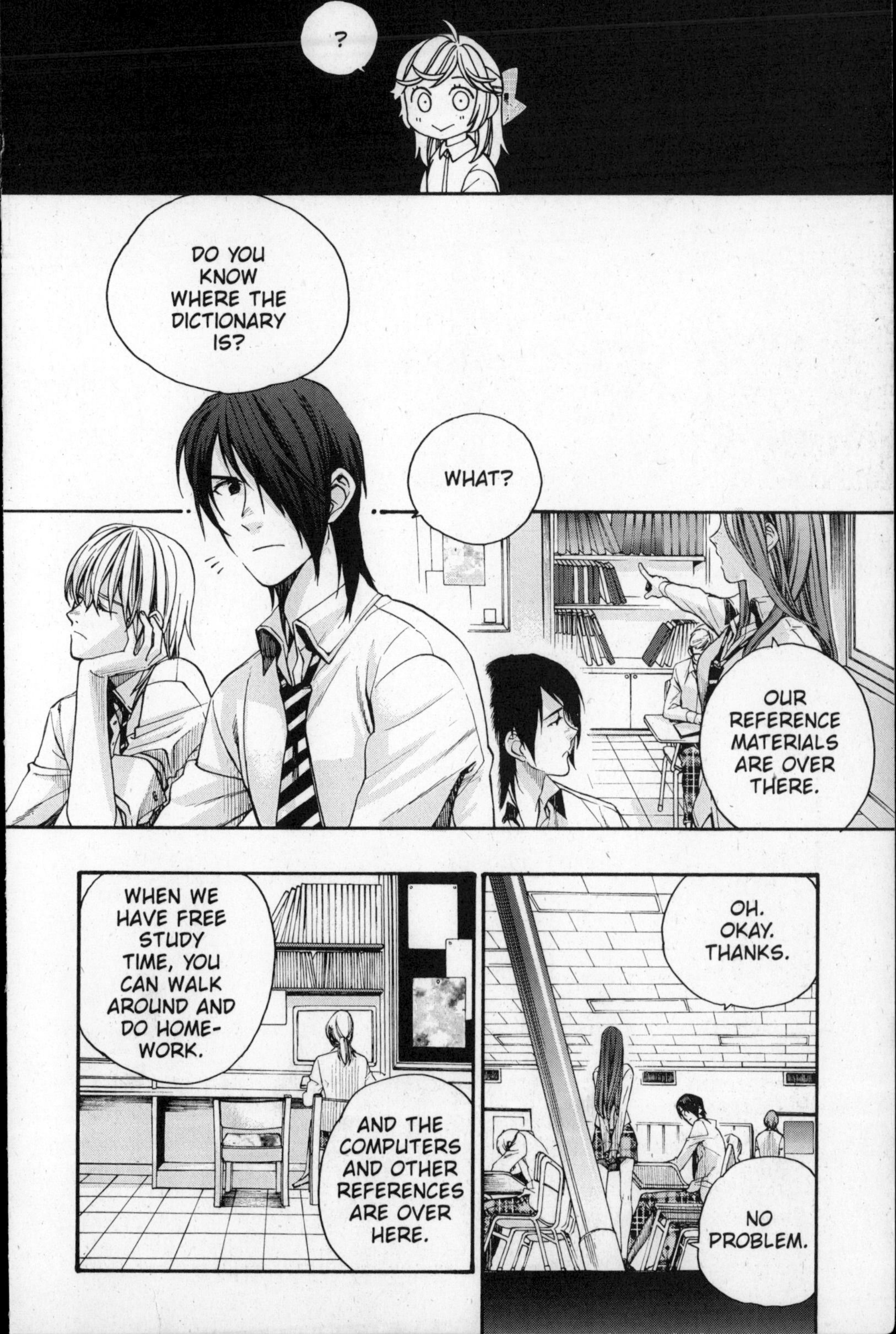
?
DO YOU KNOW WHERE THE DICTIONARY IS?
WHAT?
OUR REFERENCE MATERIALS ARE OVER THERE.
WHEN WE HAVE FREE STUDY TIME, YOU CAN WALK AROUND AND DO HOME-WORK.
AND THE COMPUTERS AND OTHER REFERENCES ARE OVER HERE.
OH. OKAY. THANKS.
NO PROBLEM.

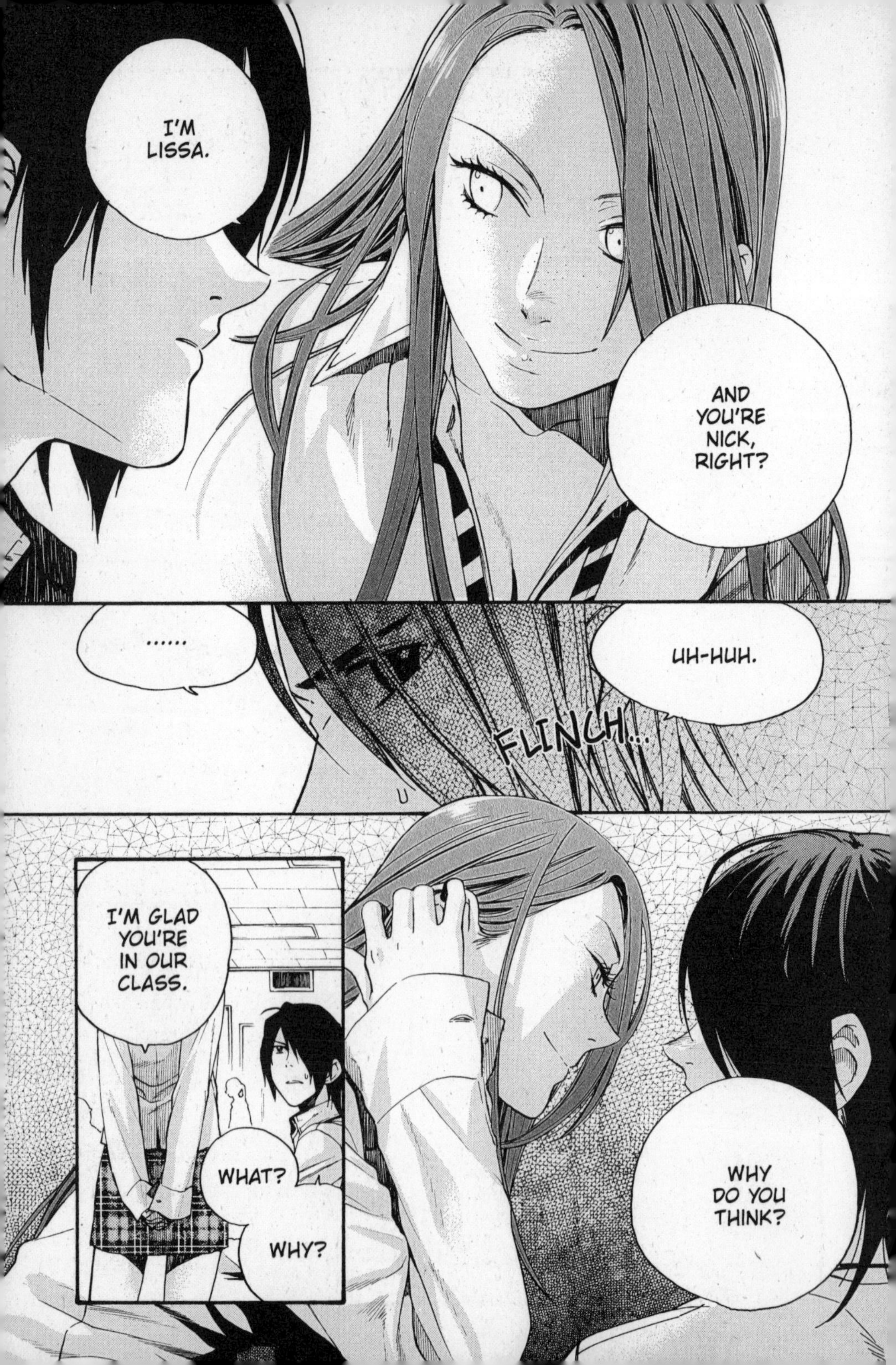
I'M LISSA.
AND YOU'RE NICK, RIGHT?
......
UH-HUH.
FLINCH...
I'M GLAD YOU'RE IN OUR CLASS.
WHAT?
WHY?
WHY DO YOU THINK?

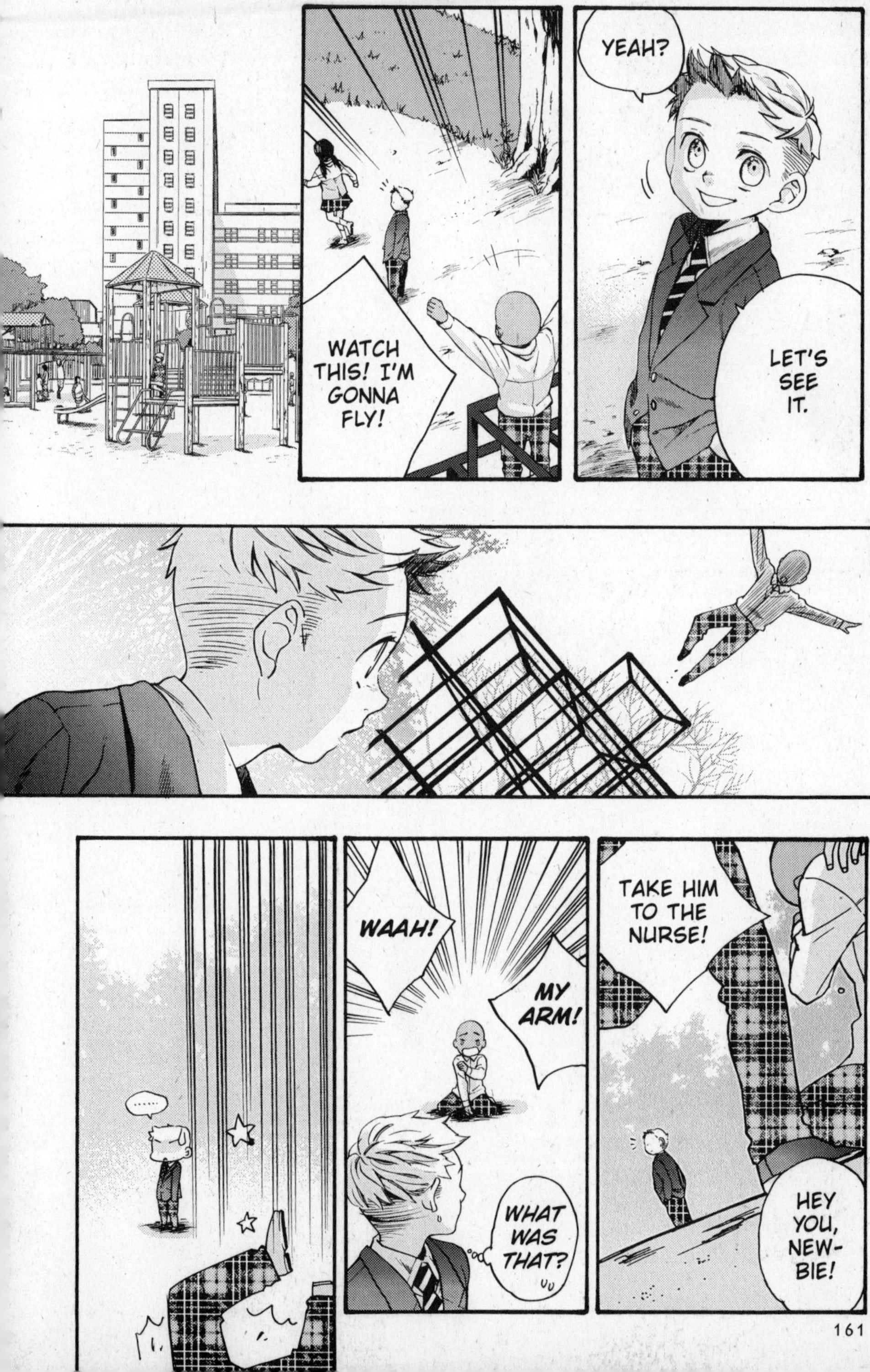
WATCH THIS! I'M GONNA FLY!
YEAH?
LET'S SEE IT.
......
WAAH!
MY ARM!
WHAT WAS THAT?
TAKE HIM TO THE NURSE!
HEY YOU, NEW-BIE!

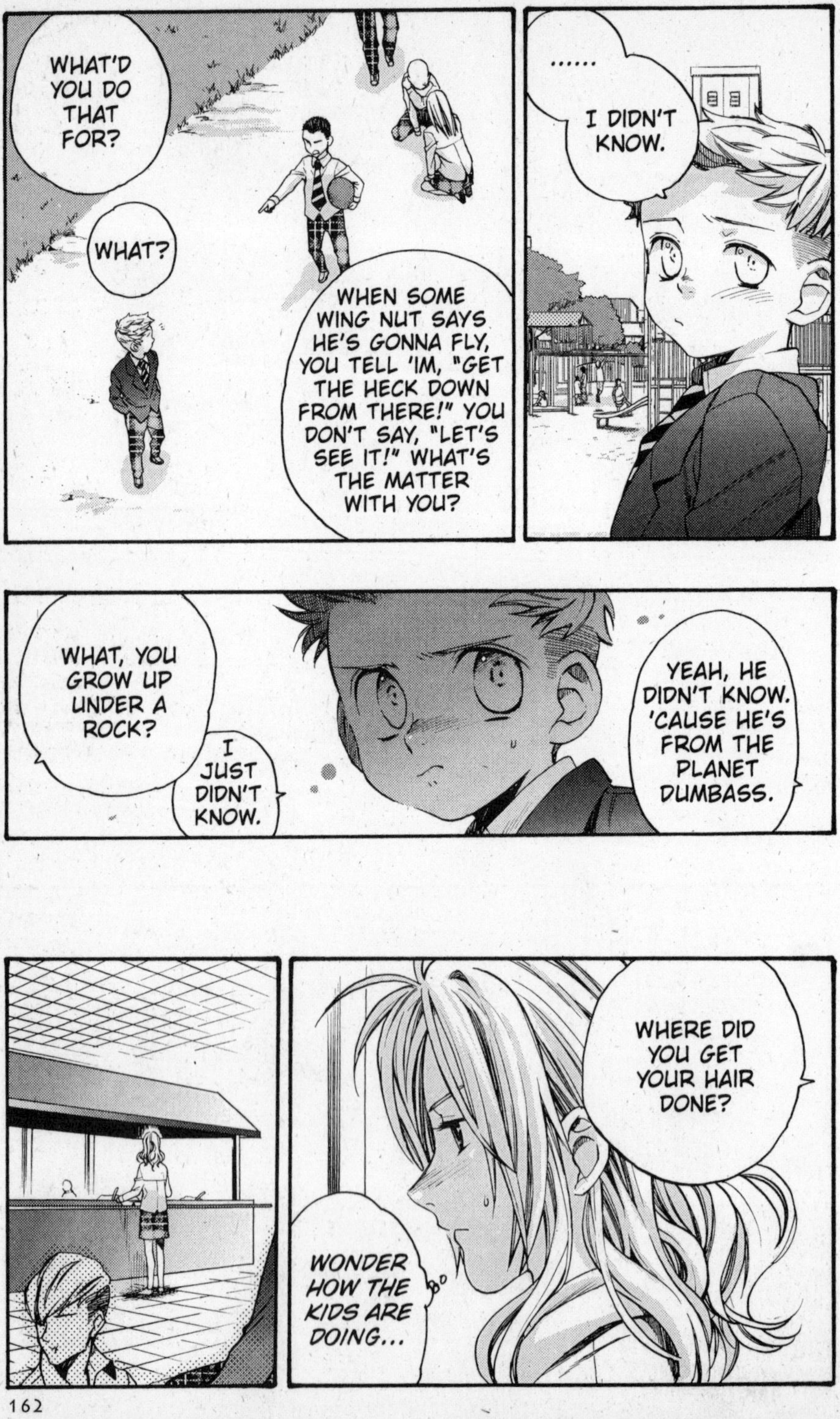
WHAT'D YOU DO THAT FOR?
WHAT?
WHEN SOME WING NUT SAYS HE'S GONNA FLY, YOU TELL 'IM, "GET THE HECK DOWN FROM THERE!" YOU DON'T SAY, "LET'S SEE IT!" WHAT'S THE MATTER WITH YOU?
......
I DIDN'T KNOW.
WHAT, YOU GROW UP UNDER A ROCK?
I JUST DIDN'T KNOW.
YEAH, HE DIDN'T KNOW. 'CAUSE HE'S FROM THE PLANET DUMBASS.
WHERE DID YOU GET YOUR HAIR DONE?
WONDER HOW THE KIDS ARE DOING...

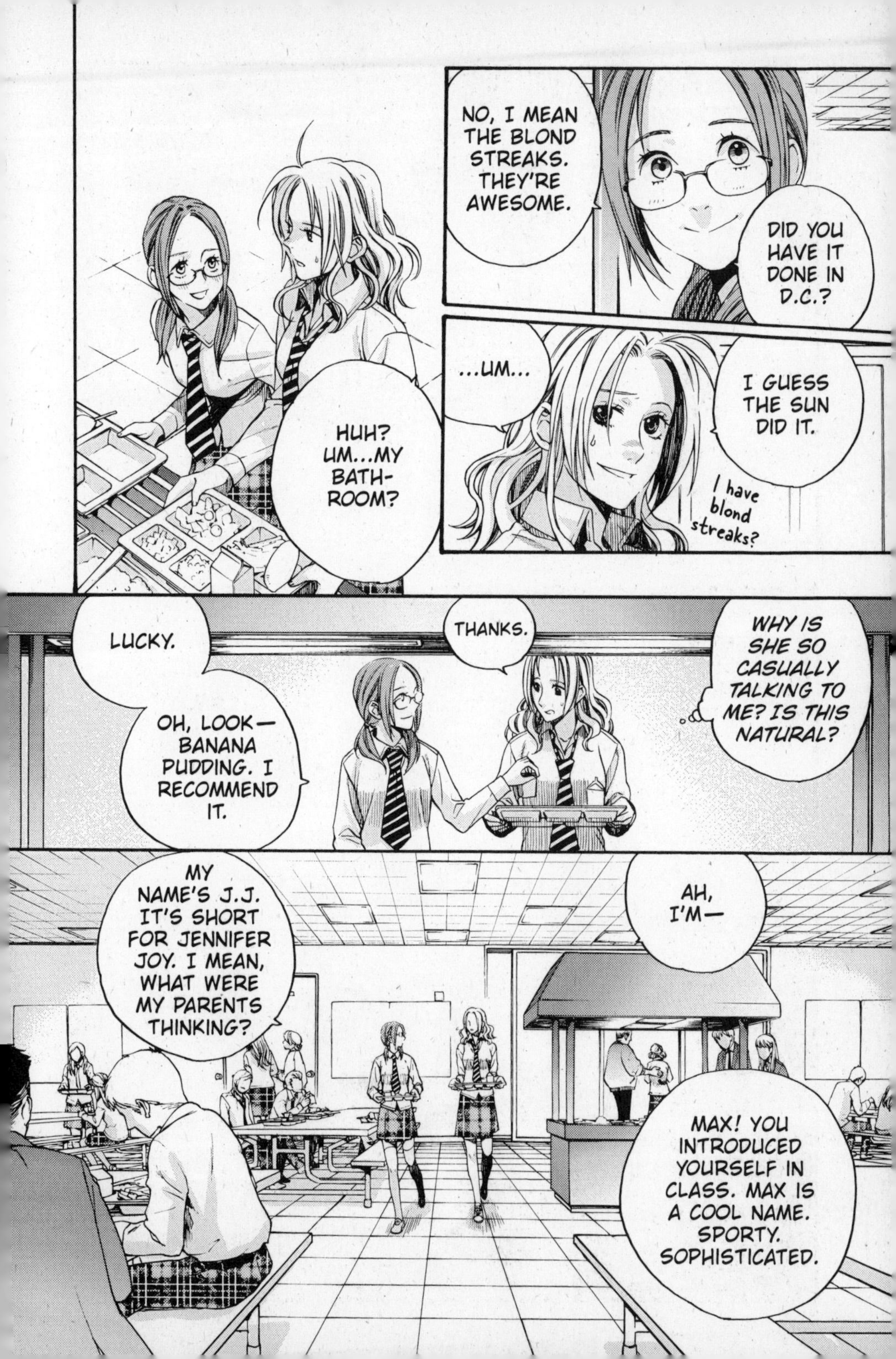
NO, I MEAN THE BLOND STREAKS. THEY'RE AWESOME.
DID YOU HAVE IT DONE IN D.C.?
HUH? UM...MY BATH-ROOM?
...UM...
I GUESS THE SUN DID IT.
I have blond streaks?
LUCKY.
THANKS.
WHY IS SHE SO CASUALLY TALKING TO ME? IS THIS NATURAL?
OH, LOOK—BANANA PUDDING. I RECOMMEND IT.
MY NAME'S J.J. IT'S SHORT FOR JENNIFER JOY. I MEAN, WHAT WERE MY PARENTS THINKING?
AH, I'M—
MAX! YOU INTRODUCED YOURSELF IN CLASS. MAX IS A COOL NAME. SPORTY. SOPHISTICATED.

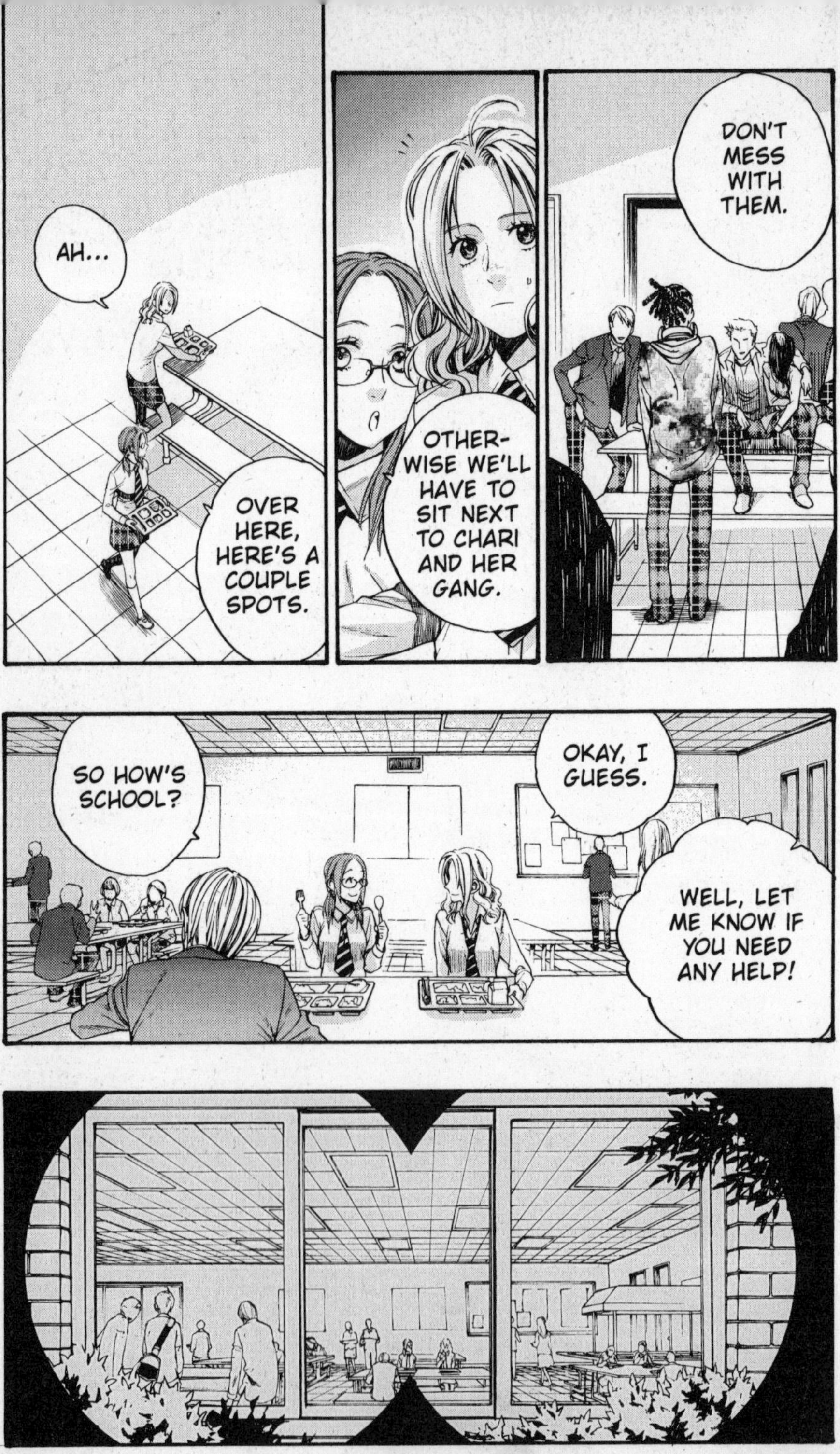
AH...
OVER HERE, HERE'S A COUPLE SPOTS.
OTHER-WISE WE'LL HAVE TO SIT NEXT TO CHARI AND HER GANG.
DON'T MESS WITH THEM.
SO HOW'S SCHOOL?
OKAY, I GUESS.
WELL, LET ME KNOW IF YOU NEED ANY HELP!

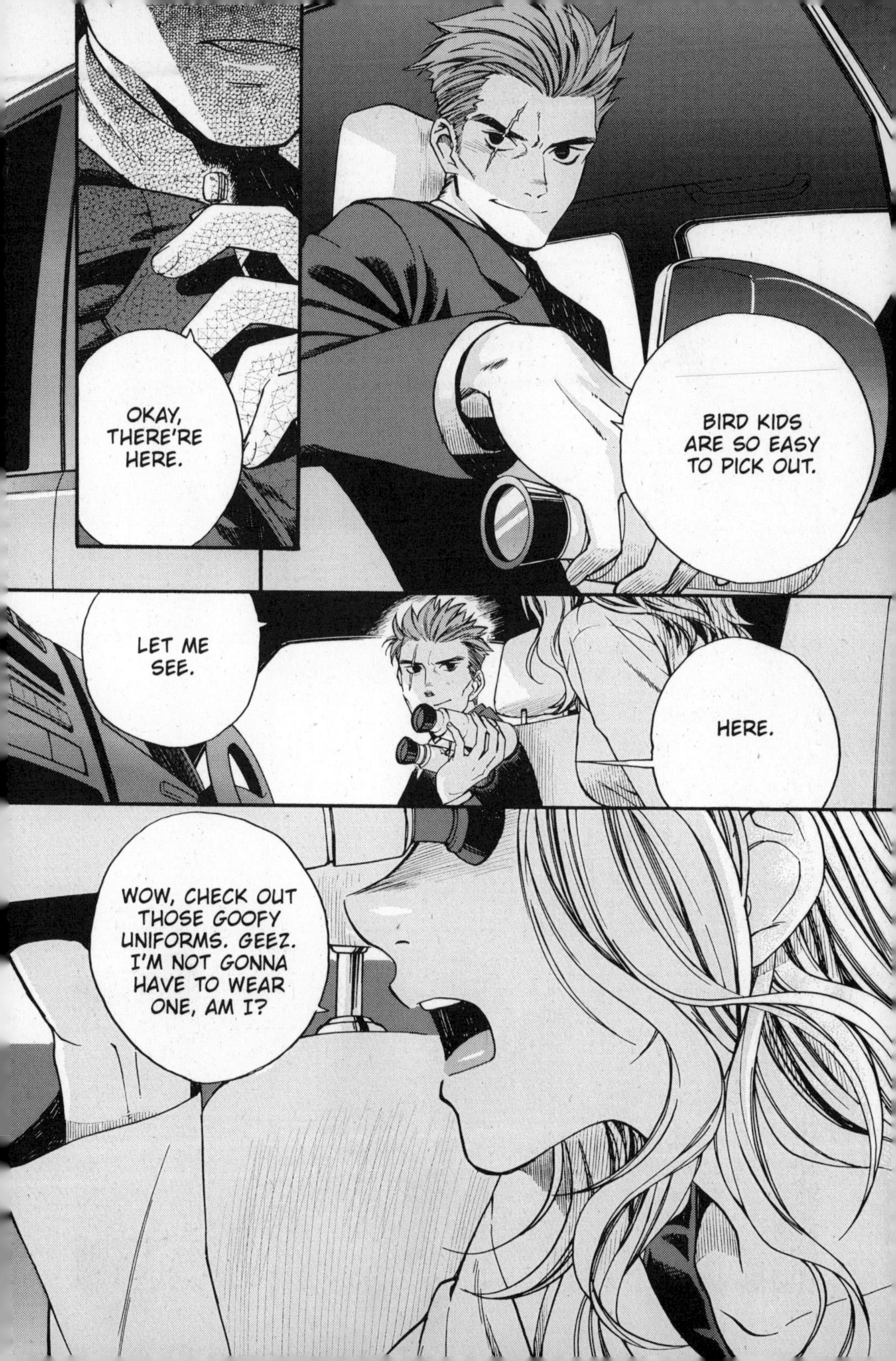
OKAY, THERE'RE HERE.
BIRD KIDS ARE SO EASY TO PICK OUT.
LET ME SEE.
HERE.
WOW, CHECK OUT THOSE GOOFY UNIFORMS. GEEZ. I'M NOT GONNA HAVE TO WEAR ONE, AM I?

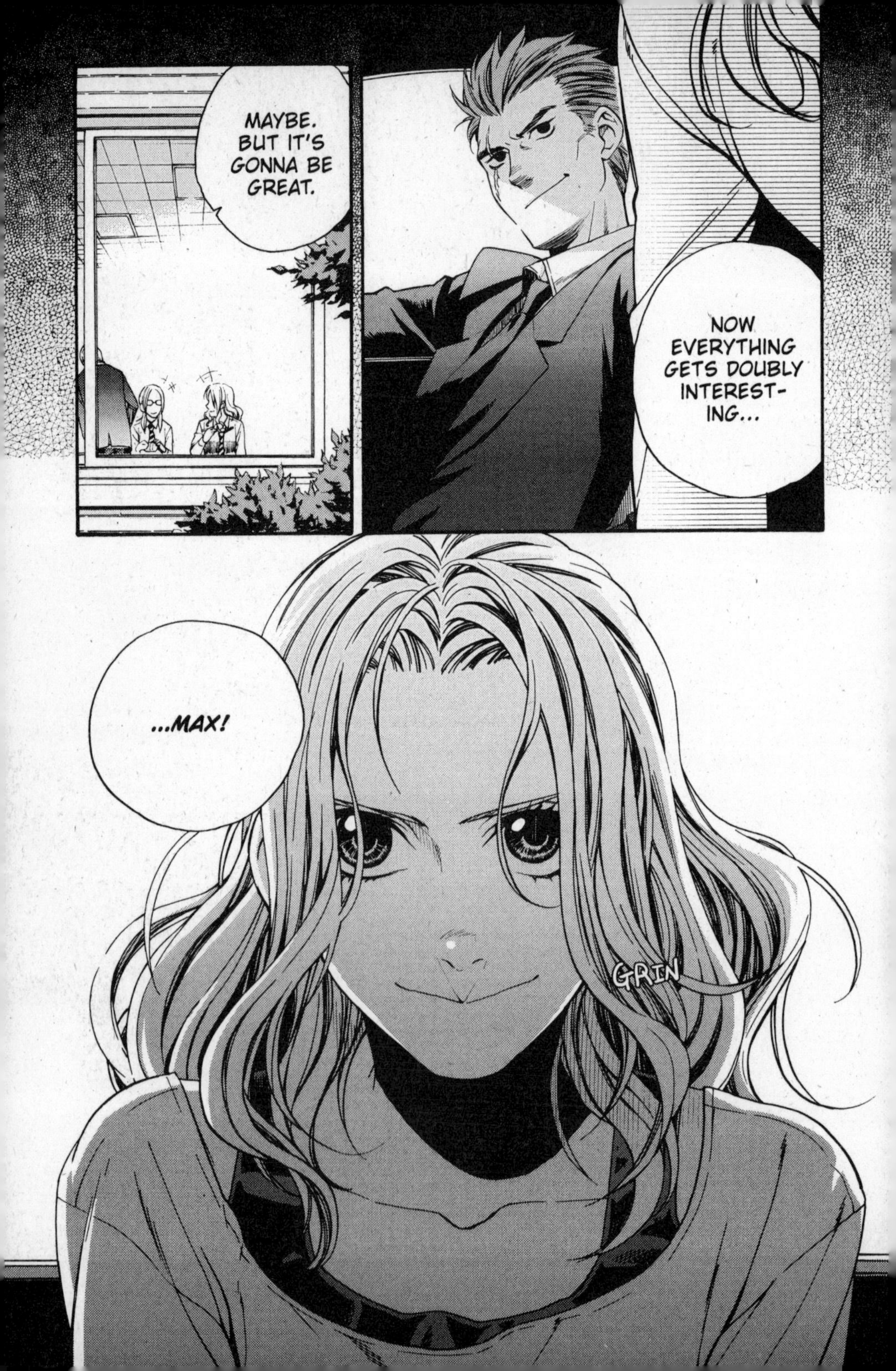
MAYBE. BUT IT'S GONNA BE GREAT.
NOW EVERYTHING GETS DOUBLY INTEREST-ING...
...MAX!
GRIN

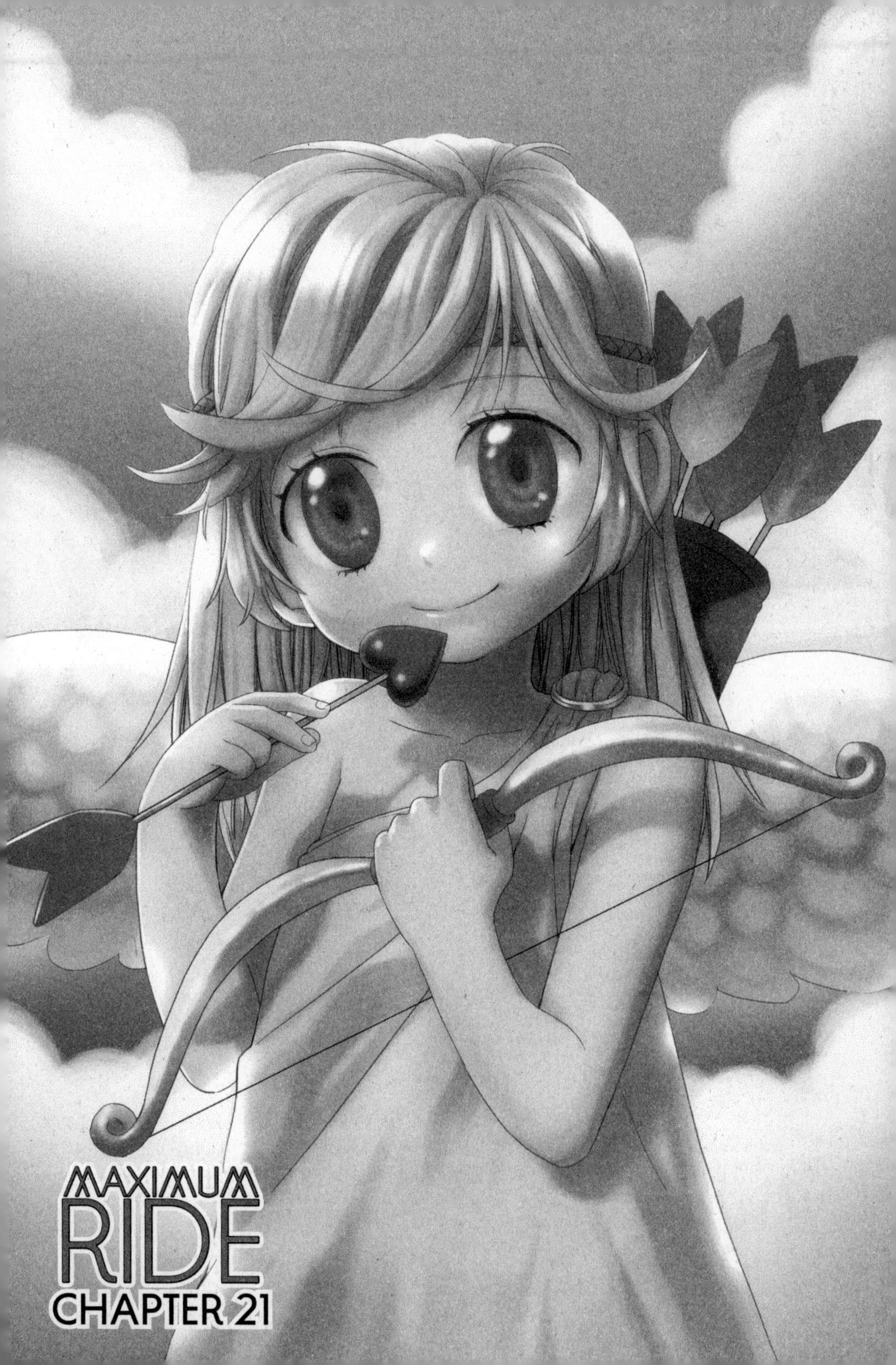
MAXIMUM RIDE
CHAPTER 21

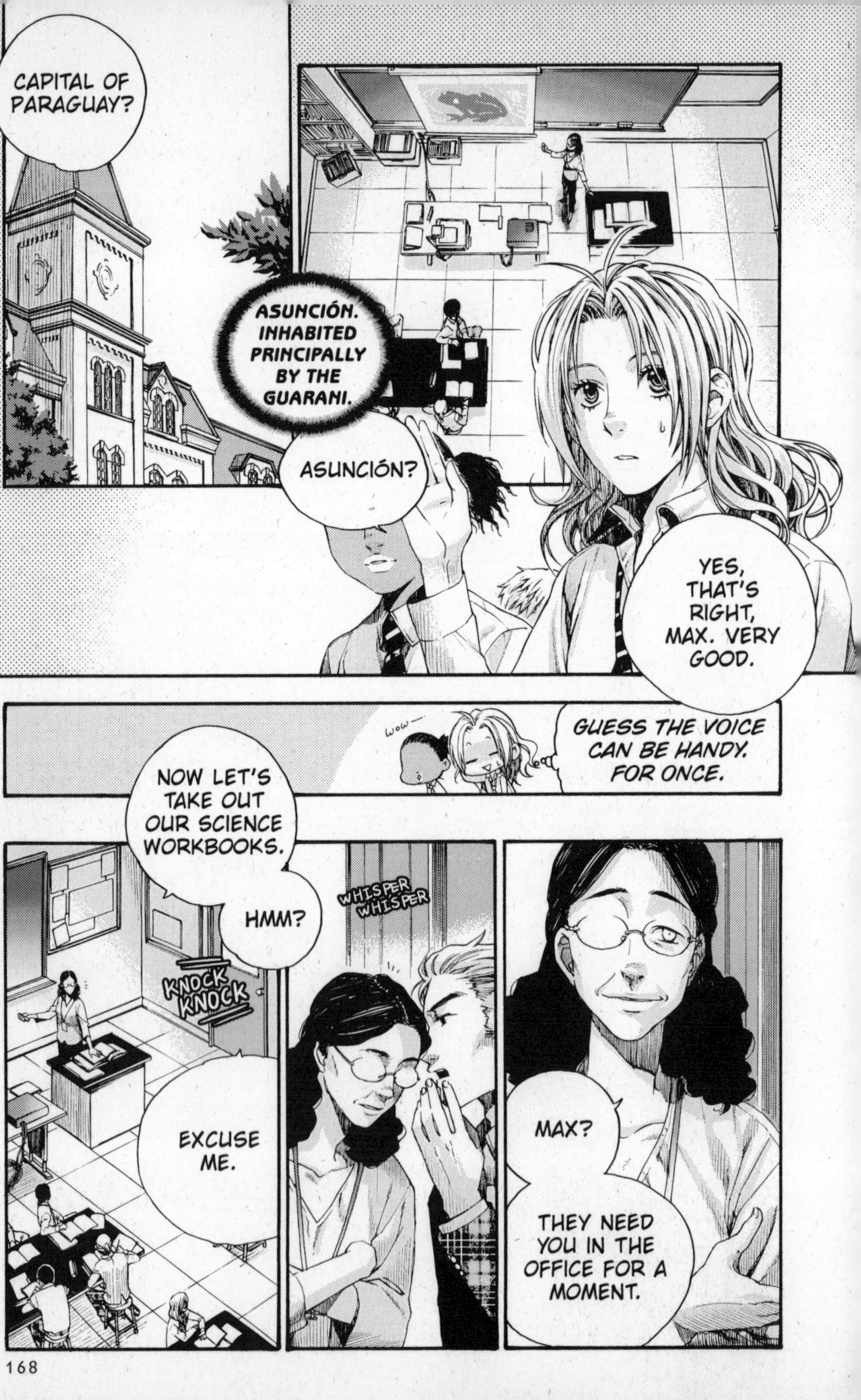
CAPITAL OF PARAGUAY?
ASUNCIÓN. INHABITED PRINCIPALLY BY THE GUARANI.
ASUNCIÓN?
YES, THAT'S RIGHT, MAX. VERY GOOD.
WOW—
GUESS THE VOICE CAN BE HANDY. FOR ONCE.
NOW LET'S TAKE OUT OUR SCIENCE WORKBOOKS.
HMM?
KNOCK KNOCK
WHISPER WHISPER
EXCUSE ME.
MAX?
THEY NEED YOU IN THE OFFICE FOR A MOMENT.

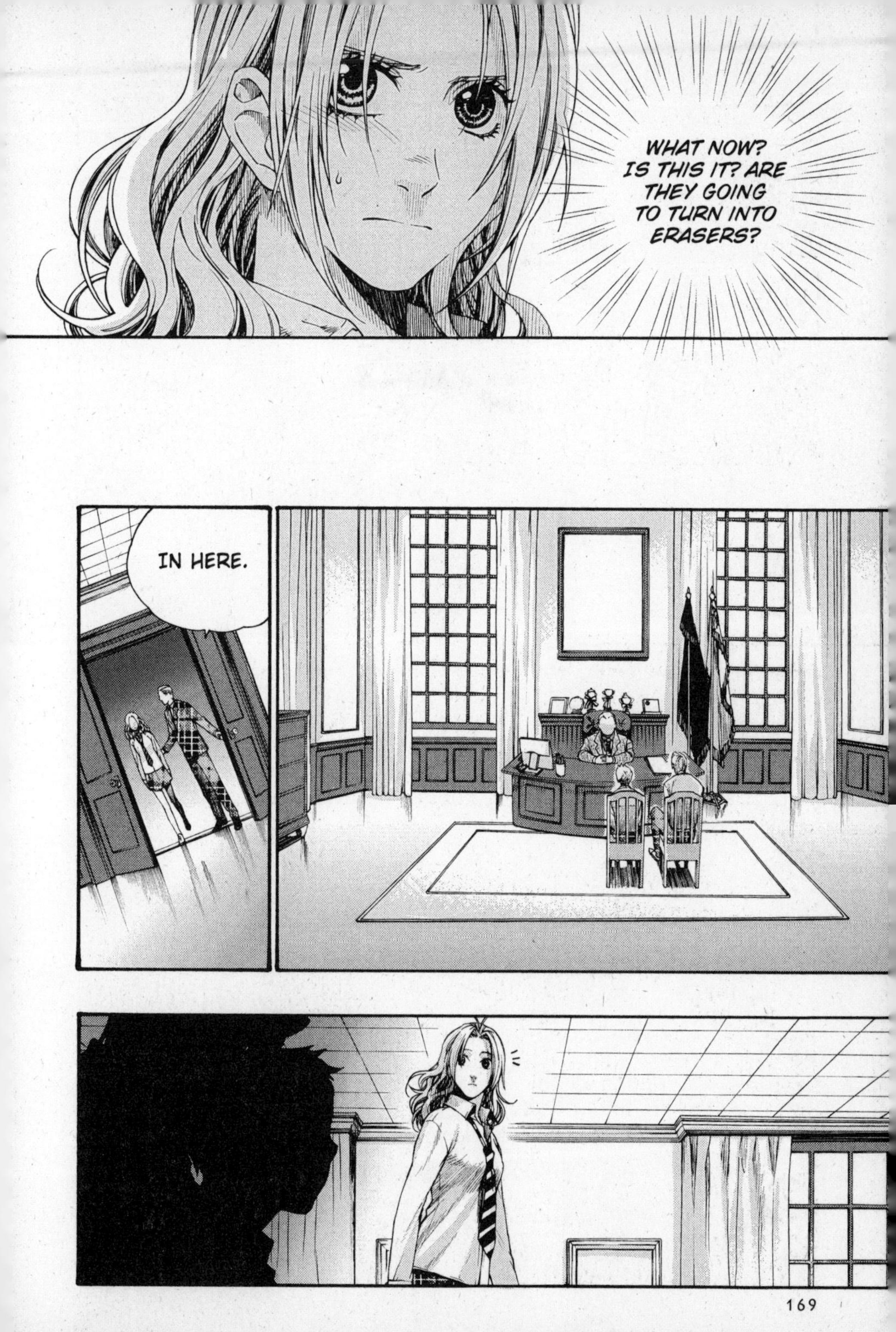
WHAT NOW? IS THIS IT? ARE THEY GOING TO TURN INTO ERASERS?
IN HERE.

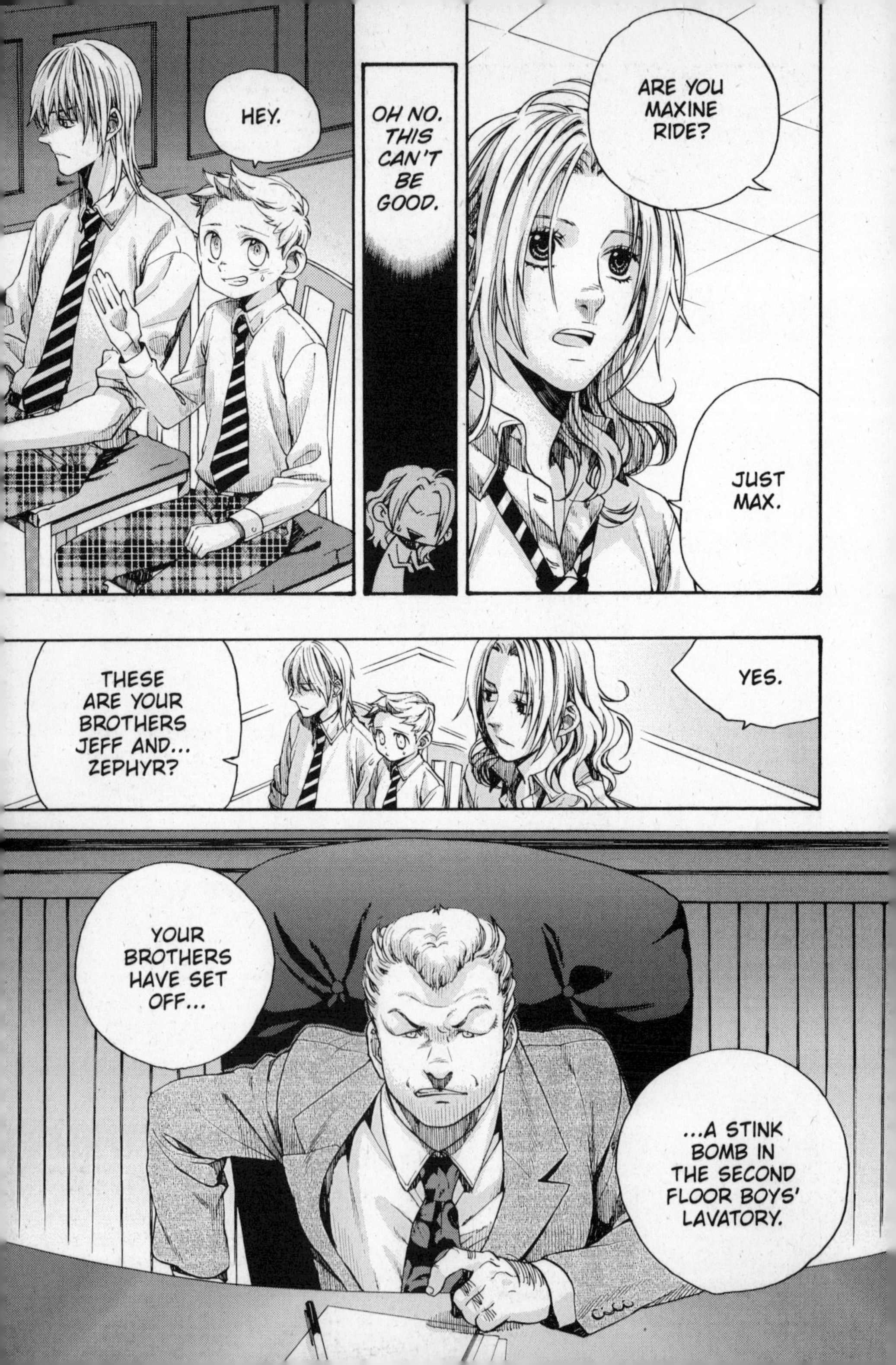
HEY.
OH NO. THIS CAN'T BE GOOD.
ARE YOU MAXINE RIDE?
JUST MAX.
THESE ARE YOUR BROTHERS JEFF AND... ZEPHYR?
YES.
YOUR BROTHERS HAVE SET OFF...
...A STINK BOMB IN THE SECOND FLOOR BOYS' LAVATORY.

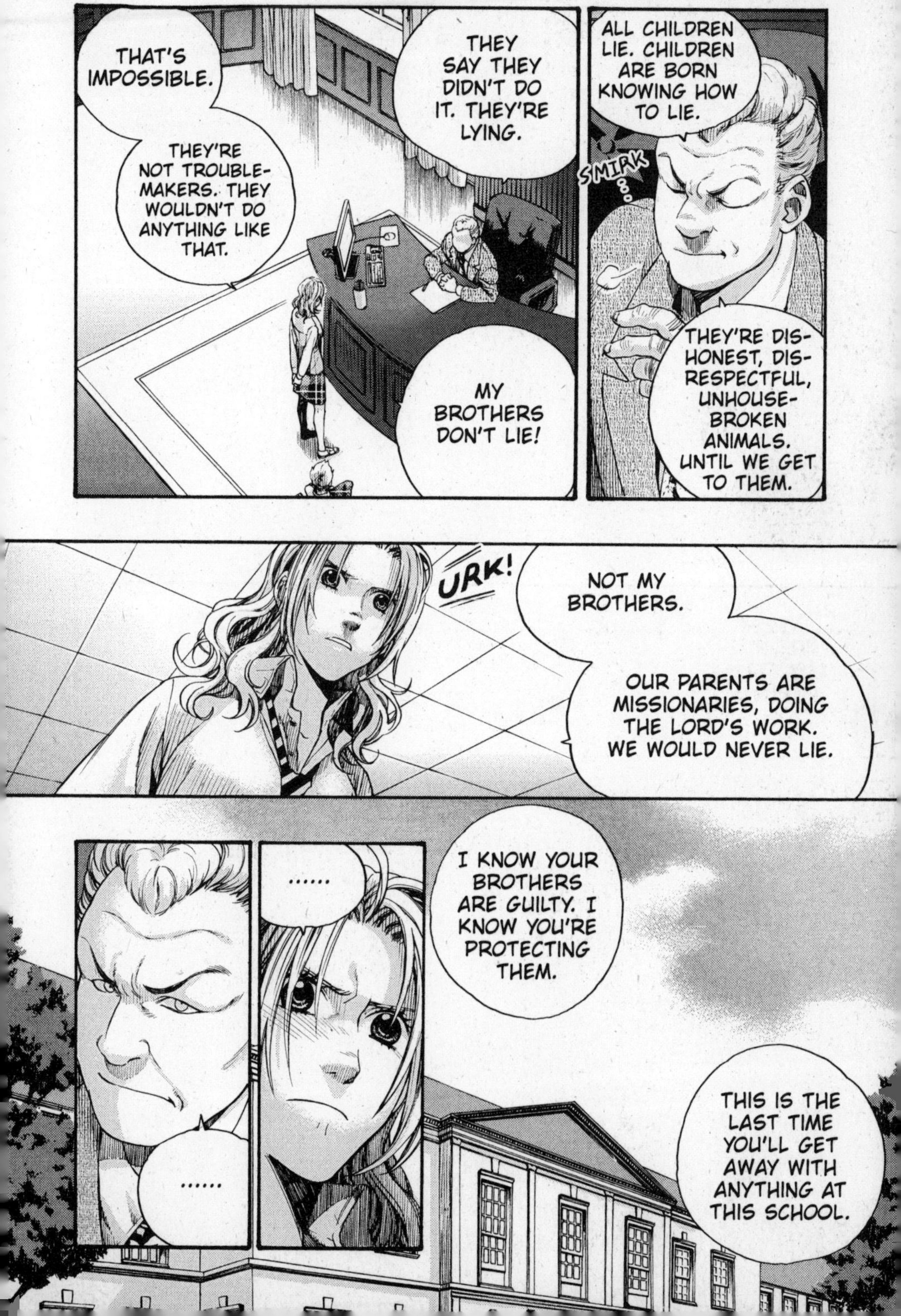
THAT'S IMPOSSIBLE.
THEY'RE NOT TROUBLE-MAKERS. THEY WOULDN'T DO ANYTHING LIKE THAT.
THEY SAY THEY DIDN'T DO IT. THEY'RE LYING.
MY BROTHERS DON'T LIE!
ALL CHILDREN LIE. CHILDREN ARE BORN KNOWING HOW TO LIE.
SMIRK...
THEY'RE DIS-HONEST, DIS-RESPECTFUL, UNHOUSE-BROKEN ANIMALS. UNTIL WE GET TO THEM.
URK!
NOT MY BROTHERS.
OUR PARENTS ARE MISSIONARIES, DOING THE LORD'S WORK. WE WOULD NEVER LIE.
......
......
I KNOW YOUR BROTHERS ARE GUILTY. I KNOW YOU'RE PROTECTING THEM.
THIS IS THE LAST TIME YOU'LL GET AWAY WITH ANYTHING AT THIS SCHOOL.

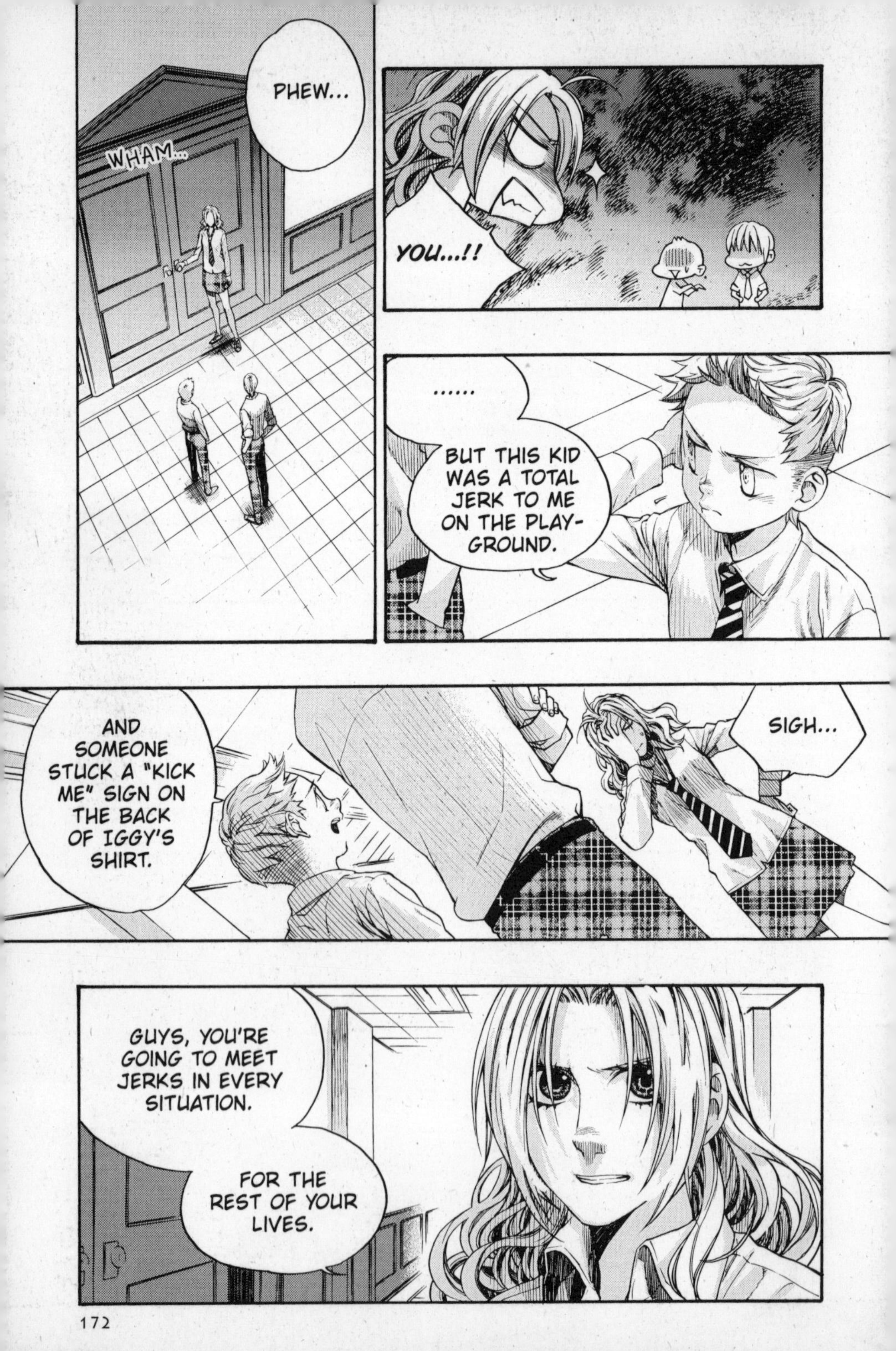
PHEW...
WHAM...
YOU...!!
......
BUT THIS KID WAS A TOTAL JERK TO ME ON THE PLAY-GROUND.
AND SOMEONE STUCK A "KICK ME" SIGN ON THE BACK OF IGGY'S SHIRT.
SIGH...
GUYS, YOU'RE GOING TO MEET JERKS IN EVERY SITUATION.
FOR THE REST OF YOUR LIVES.

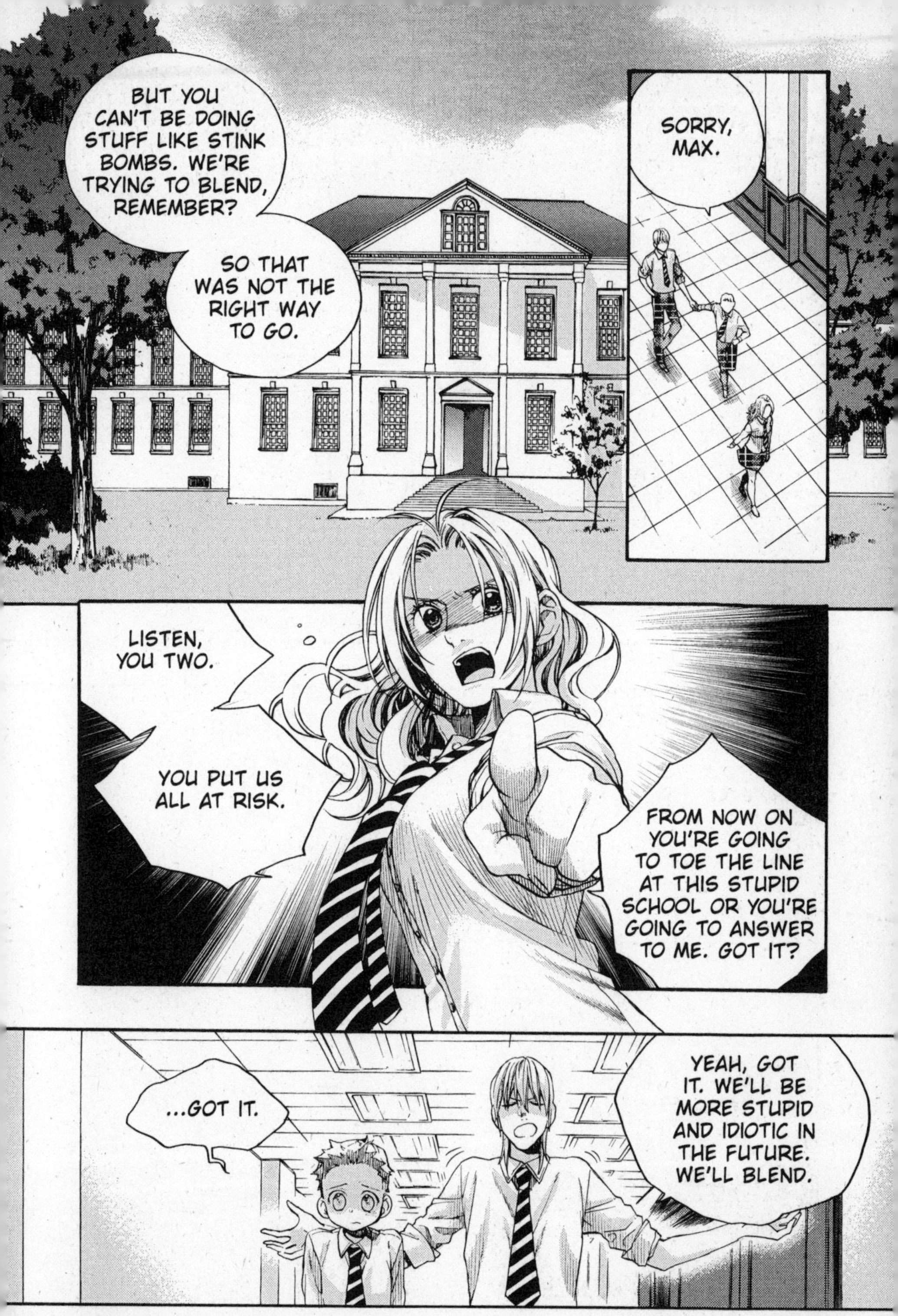
BUT YOU CAN'T BE DOING STUFF LIKE STINK BOMBS. WE'RE TRYING TO BLEND, REMEMBER?
SO THAT WAS NOT THE RIGHT WAY TO GO.
SORRY, MAX.
LISTEN, YOU TWO.
YOU PUT US ALL AT RISK.
FROM NOW ON YOU'RE GOING TO TOE THE LINE AT THIS STUPID SCHOOL OR YOU'RE GOING TO ANSWER TO ME. GOT IT?
...GOT IT.
YEAH, GOT IT. WE'LL BE MORE STUPID AND IDIOTIC IN THE FUTURE. WE'LL BLEND.

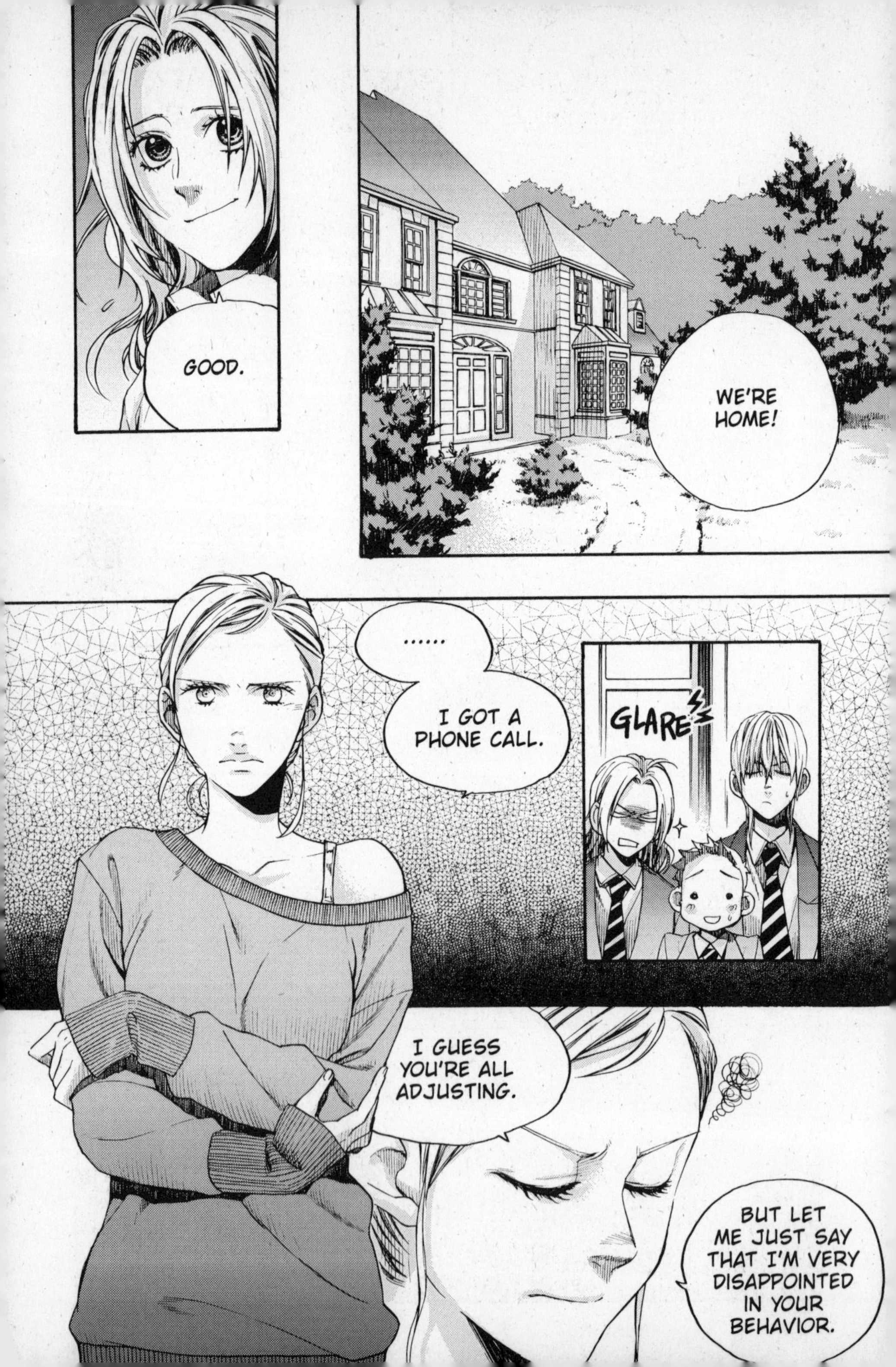
GOOD.
WE'RE HOME!
......
I GOT A PHONE CALL.
GLARE
I GUESS YOU'RE ALL ADJUSTING.
BUT LET ME JUST SAY THAT I'M VERY DISAPPOINTED IN YOUR BEHAVIOR.

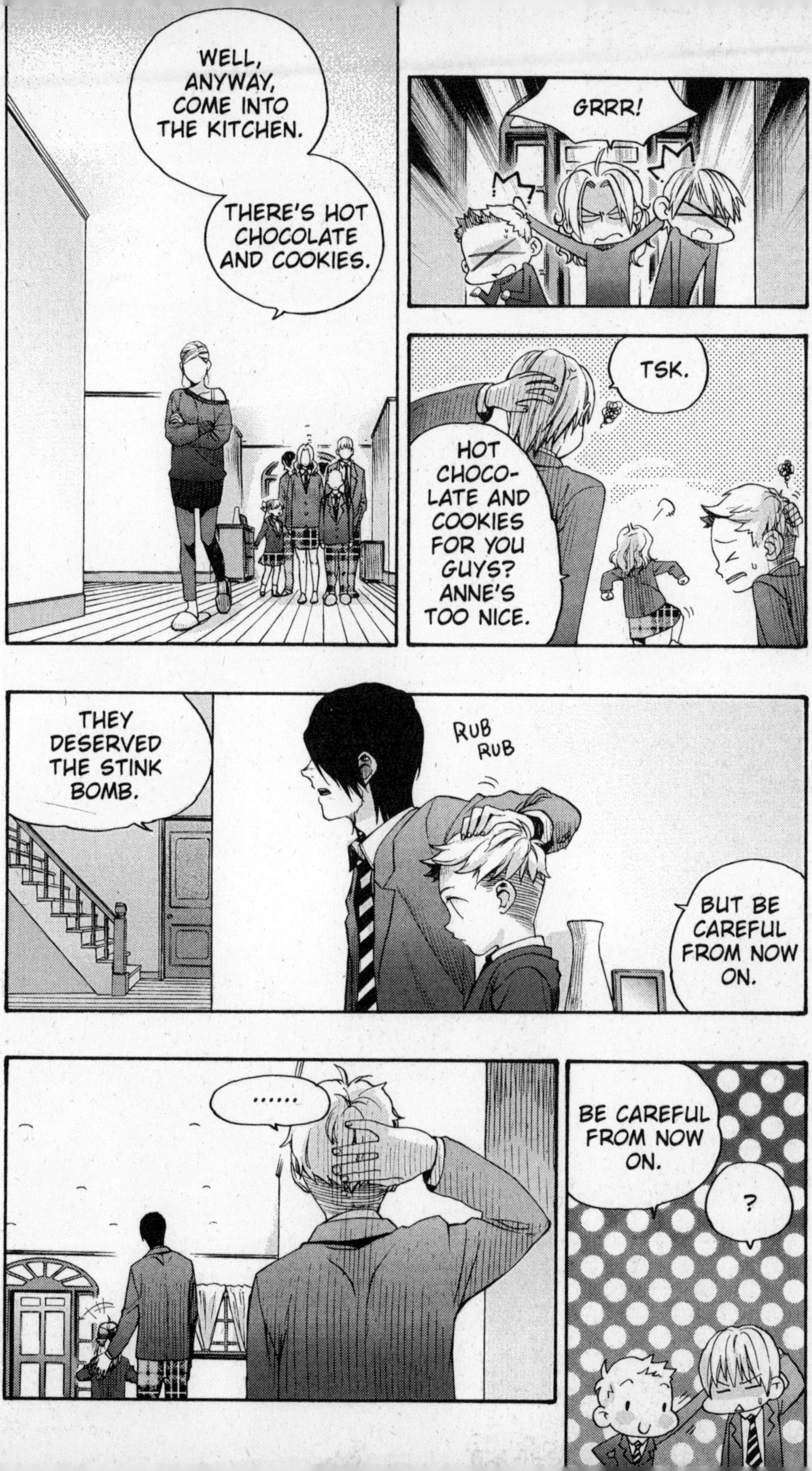
WELL, ANYWAY, COME INTO THE KITCHEN.
THERE'S HOT CHOCOLATE AND COOKIES.
GRRR!
TSK.
HOT CHOCO-LATE AND COOKIES FOR YOU GUYS? ANNE'S TOO NICE.
THEY DESERVED THE STINK BOMB.
RUB RUB
BUT BE CAREFUL FROM NOW ON.
......
BE CAREFUL FROM NOW ON.
?

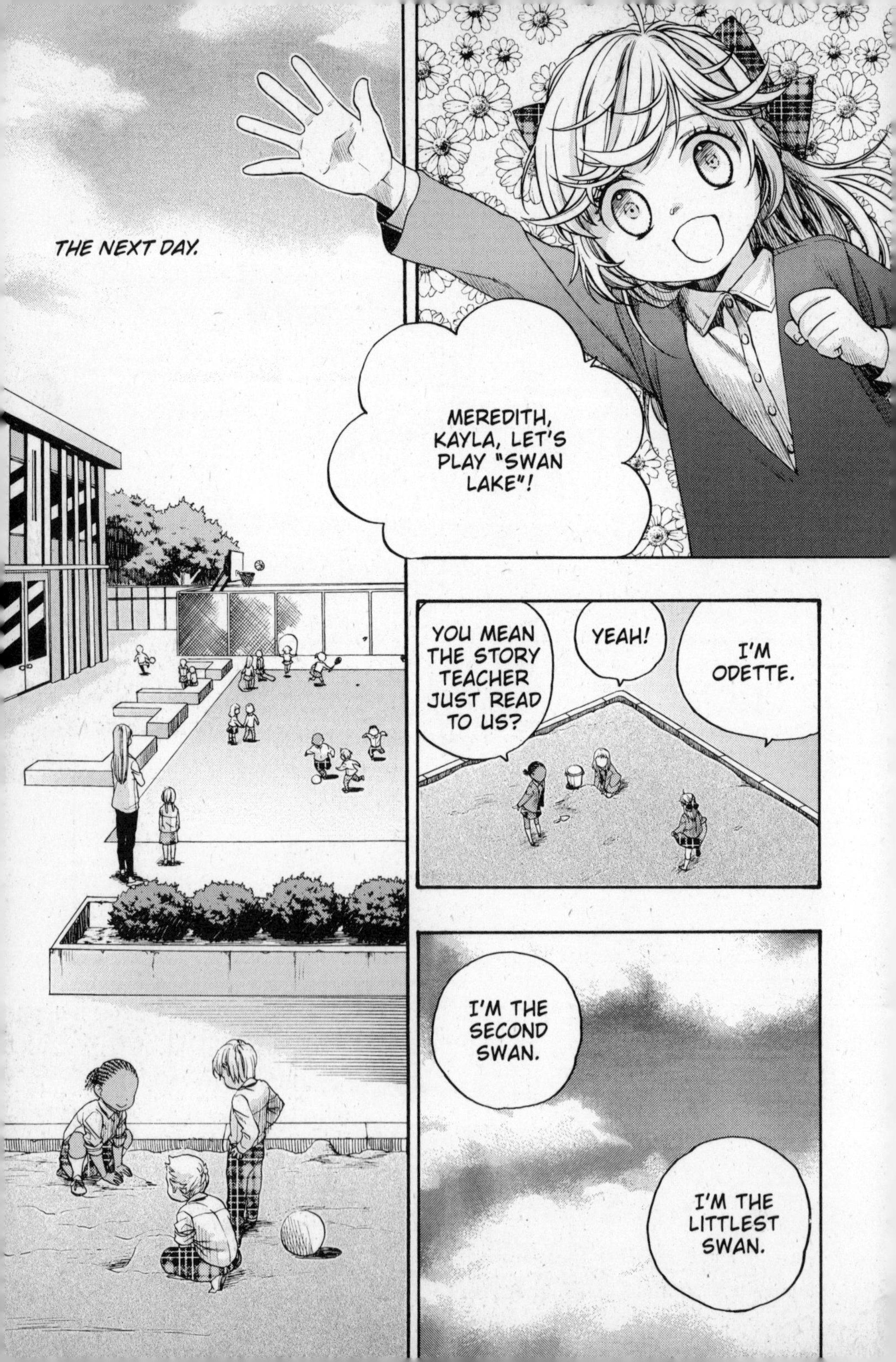
THE NEXT DAY.
MEREDITH, KAYLA, LET'S PLAY "SWAN LAKE"!
YOU MEAN THE STORY TEACHER JUST READ TO US?
YEAH!
I'M ODETTE.
I'M THE SECOND SWAN.
I'M THE LITTLEST SWAN.

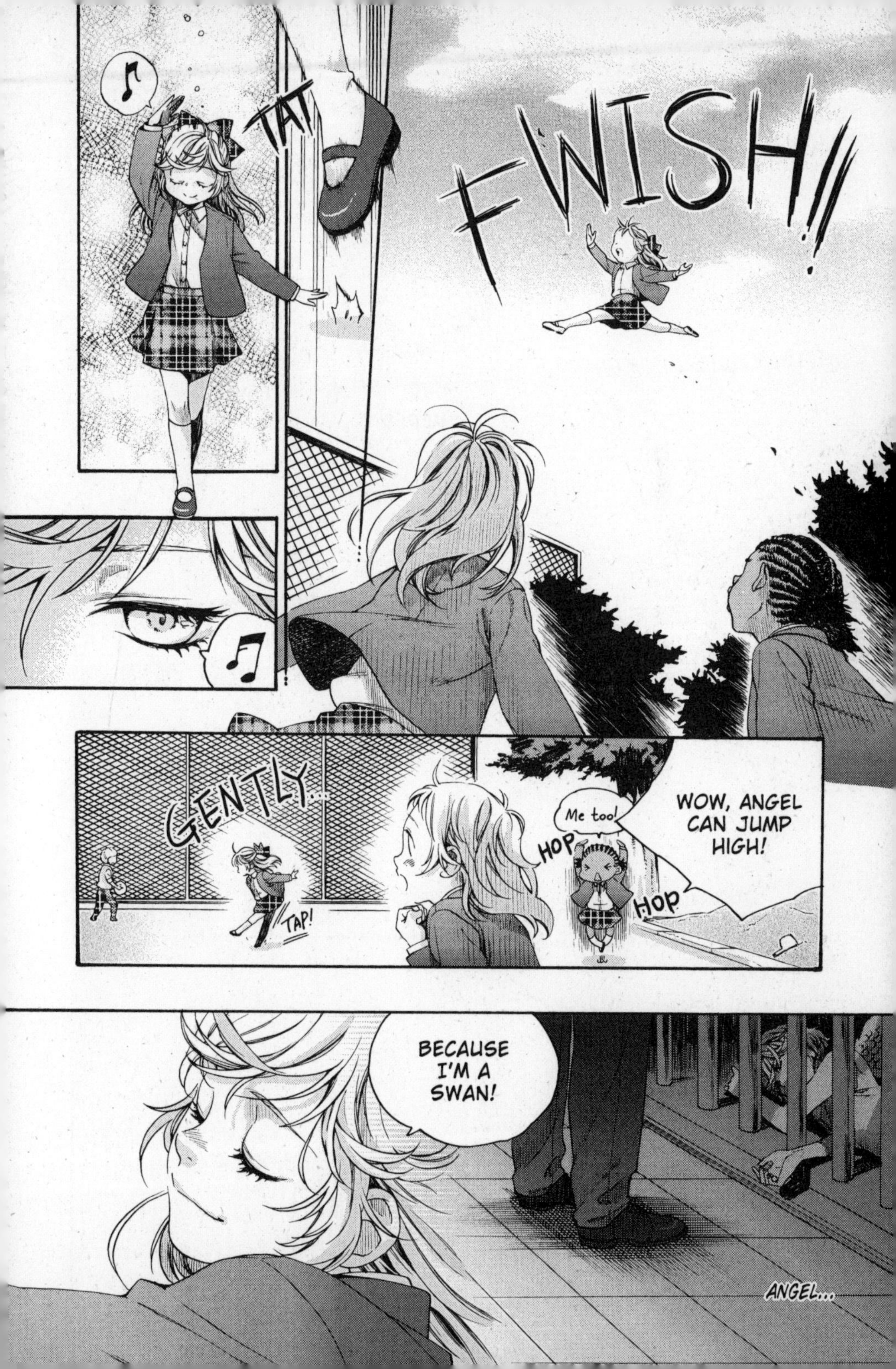
TAT
FWISH!!
GENTLY...
TAP!
Me too!
HOP
HOP
WOW, ANGEL CAN JUMP HIGH!
BECAUSE I'M A SWAN!
ANGEL...

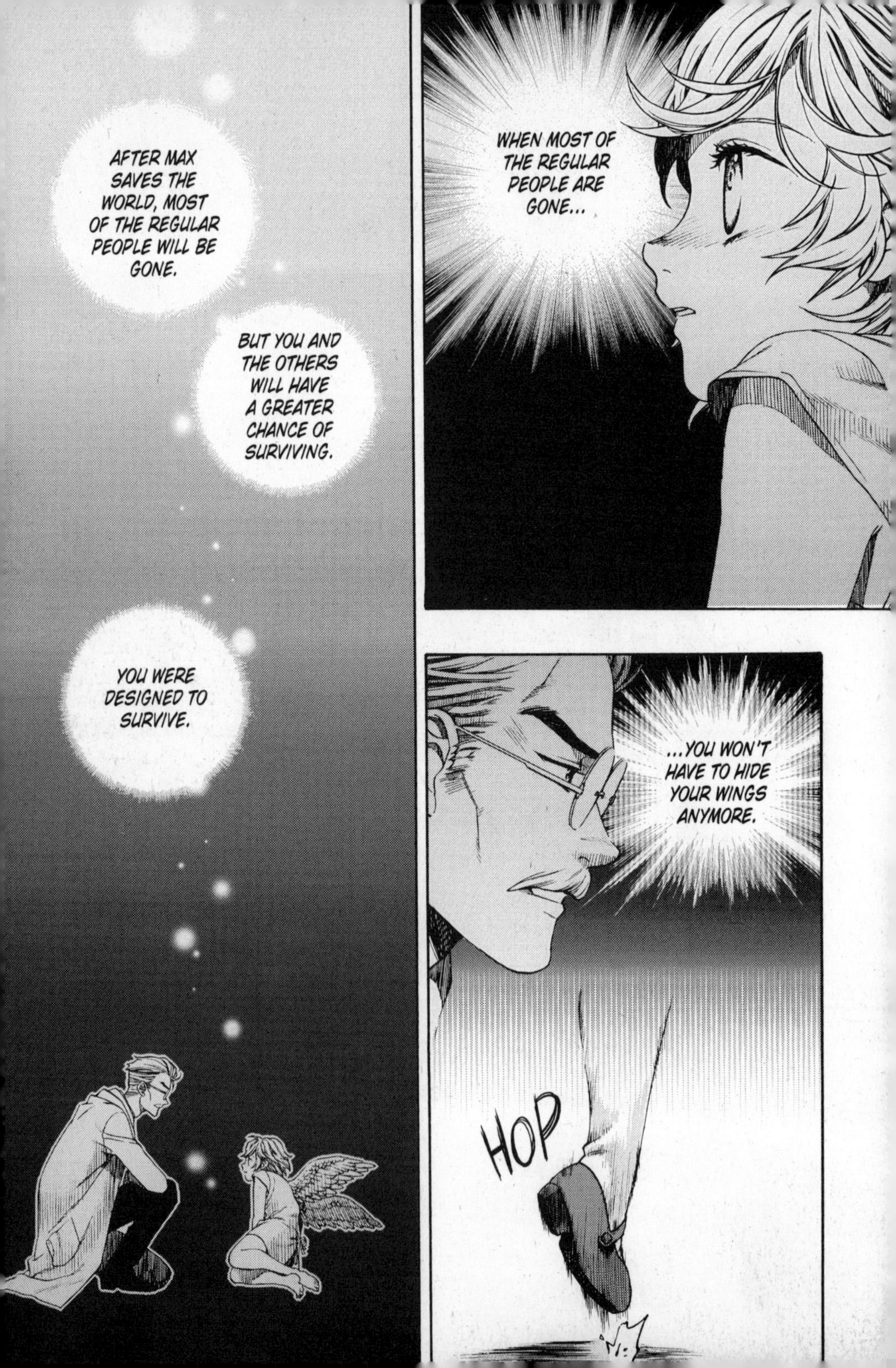
AFTER MAX SAVES THE WORLD, MOST OF THE REGULAR PEOPLE WILL BE GONE.
BUT YOU AND THE OTHERS WILL HAVE A GREATER CHANCE OF SURVIVING.
YOU WERE DESIGNED TO SURVIVE.
WHEN MOST OF THE REGULAR PEOPLE ARE GONE...
...YOU WON'T HAVE TO HIDE YOUR WINGS ANYMORE.
HOP

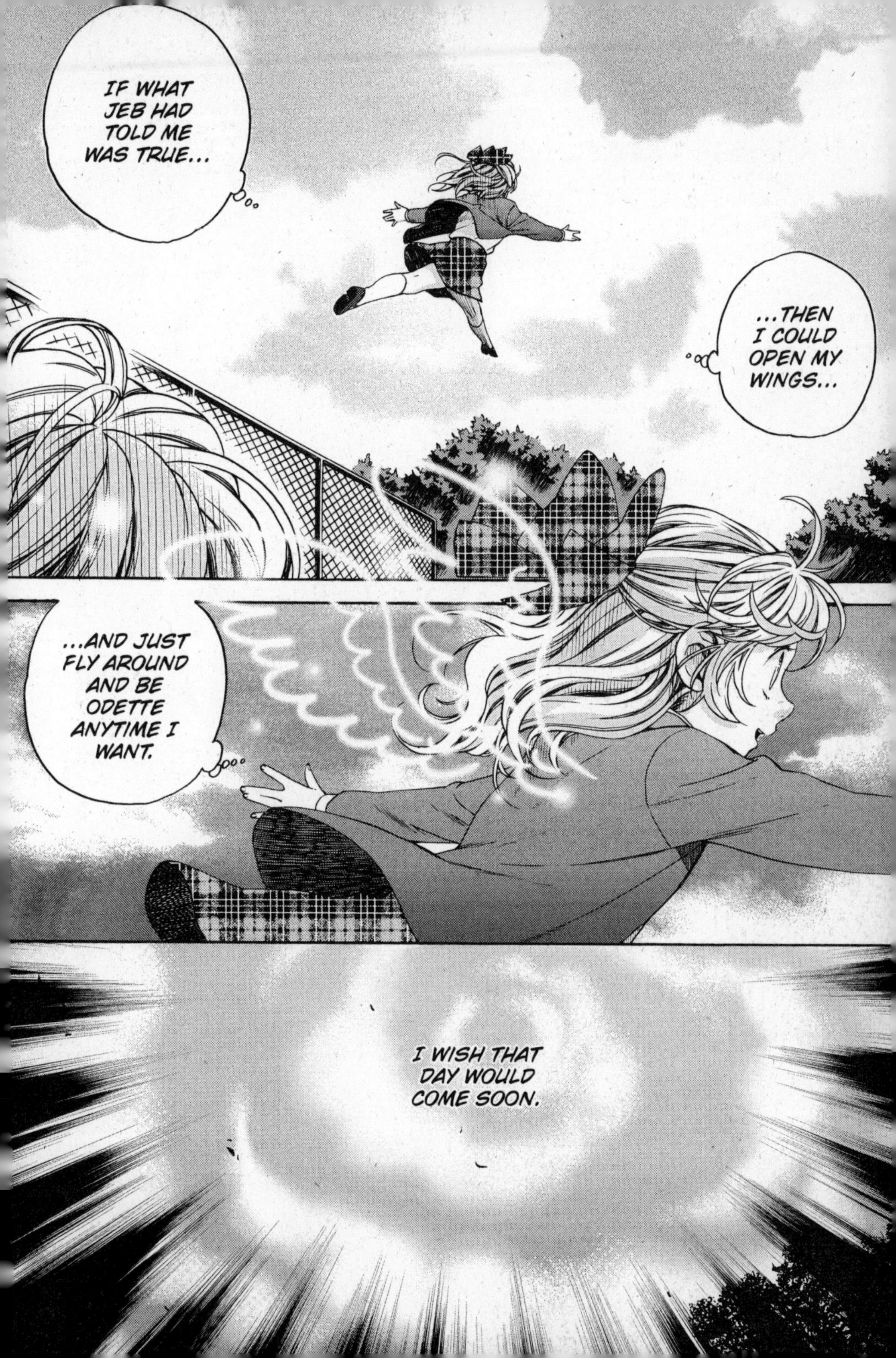
IF WHAT JEB HAD TOLD ME WAS TRUE...
...THEN I COULD OPEN MY WINGS...
...AND JUST FLY AROUND AND BE ODETTE ANYTIME I WANT.
I WISH THAT DAY WOULD COME SOON.

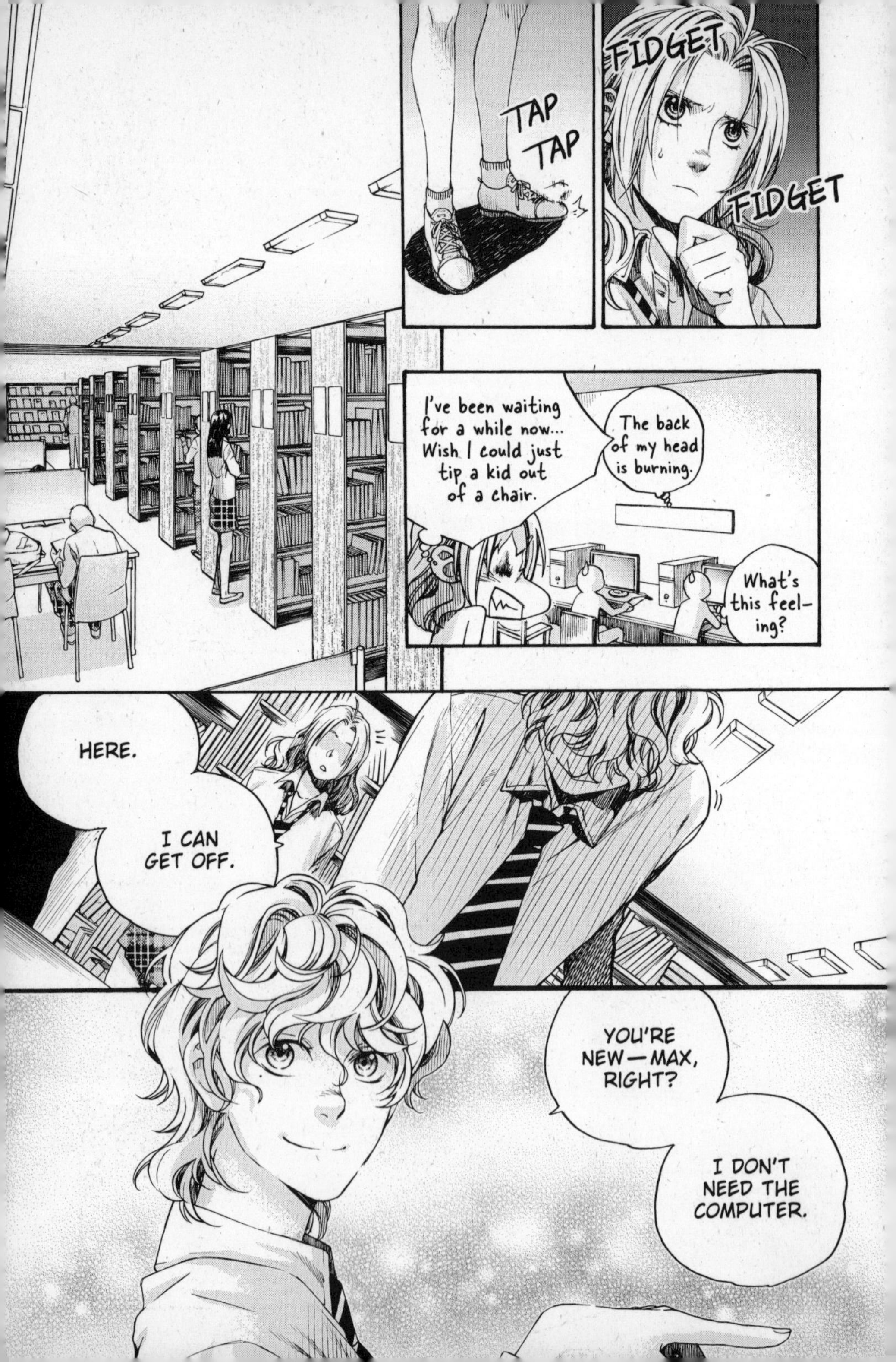
FIDGET
FIDGET
TAP
TAP
The back of my head is burning.
I've been waiting for a while now... Wish I could just tip a kid out of a chair.
What's this feel-ing?
HERE.
I CAN GET OFF.
YOU'RE NEW—MAX, RIGHT?
I DON'T NEED THE COMPUTER.

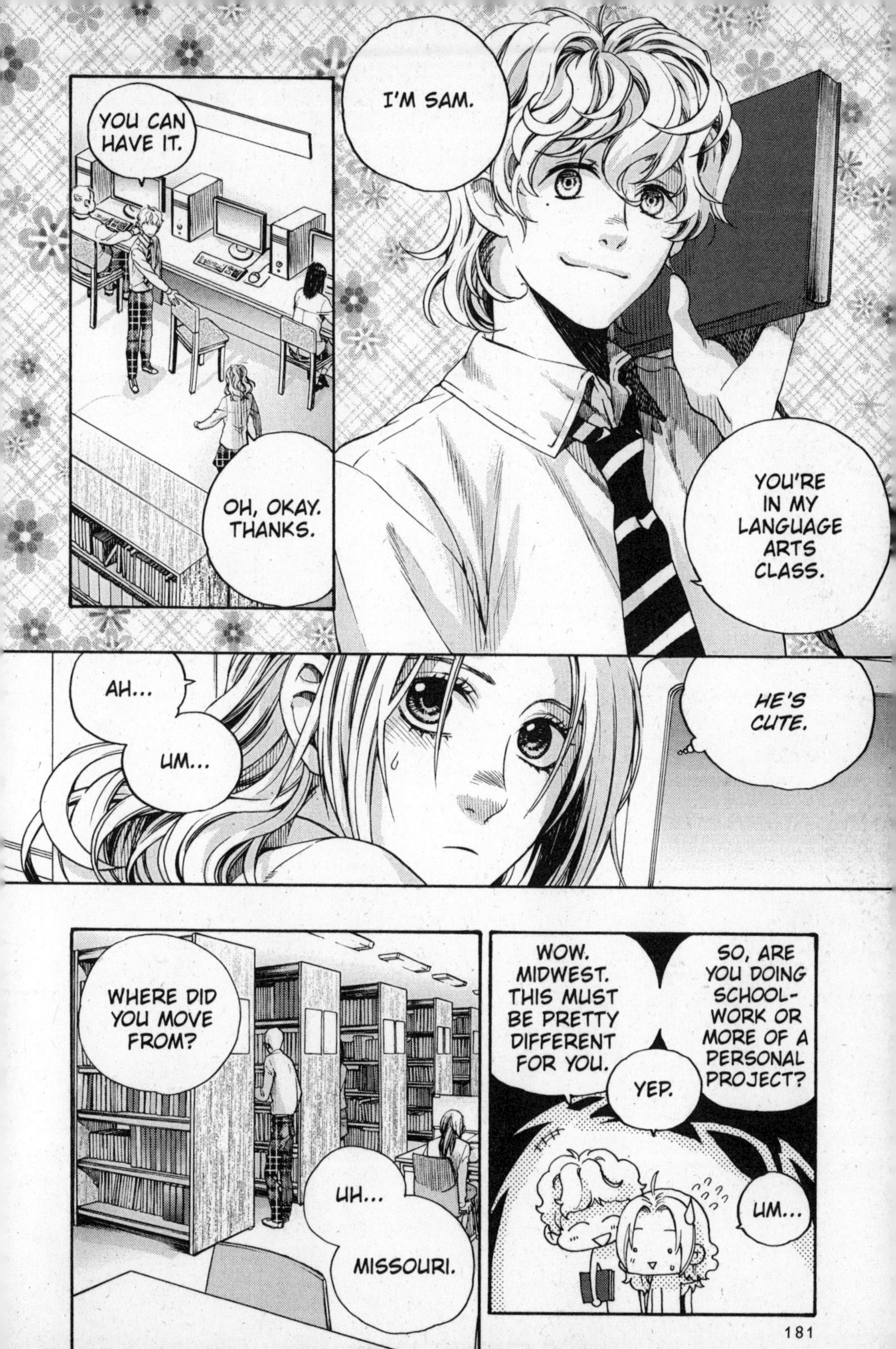
YOU CAN HAVE IT.
OH, OKAY. THANKS.
I'M SAM.
YOU'RE IN MY LANGUAGE ARTS CLASS.
AH...
UM...
HE'S CUTE.
WHERE DID YOU MOVE FROM?
UH...
MISSOURI.
WOW. MIDWEST. THIS MUST BE PRETTY DIFFERENT FOR YOU.
YEP.
SO, ARE YOU DOING SCHOOL-WORK OR MORE OF A PERSONAL PROJECT?
UM...

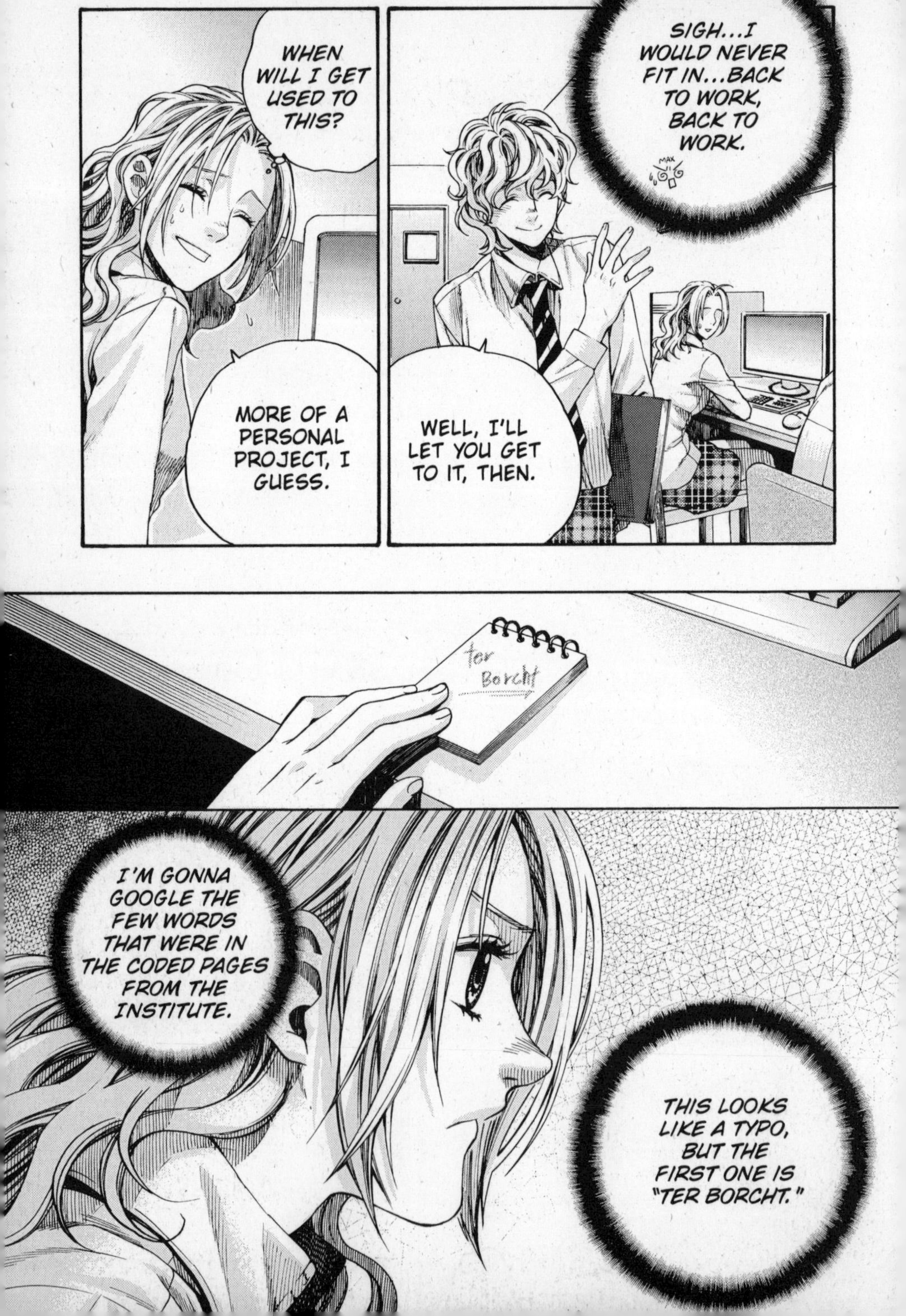
WHEN WILL I GET USED TO THIS?
MORE OF A PERSONAL PROJECT, I GUESS.
SIGH...I WOULD NEVER FIT IN...BACK TO WORK, BACK TO WORK.
MAX
WELL, I'LL LET YOU GET TO IT, THEN.
ter Borcht
I'M GONNA GOOGLE THE FEW WORDS THAT WERE IN THE CODED PAGES FROM THE INSTITUTE.
THIS LOOKS LIKE A TYPO, BUT THE FIRST ONE IS "TER BORCHT."

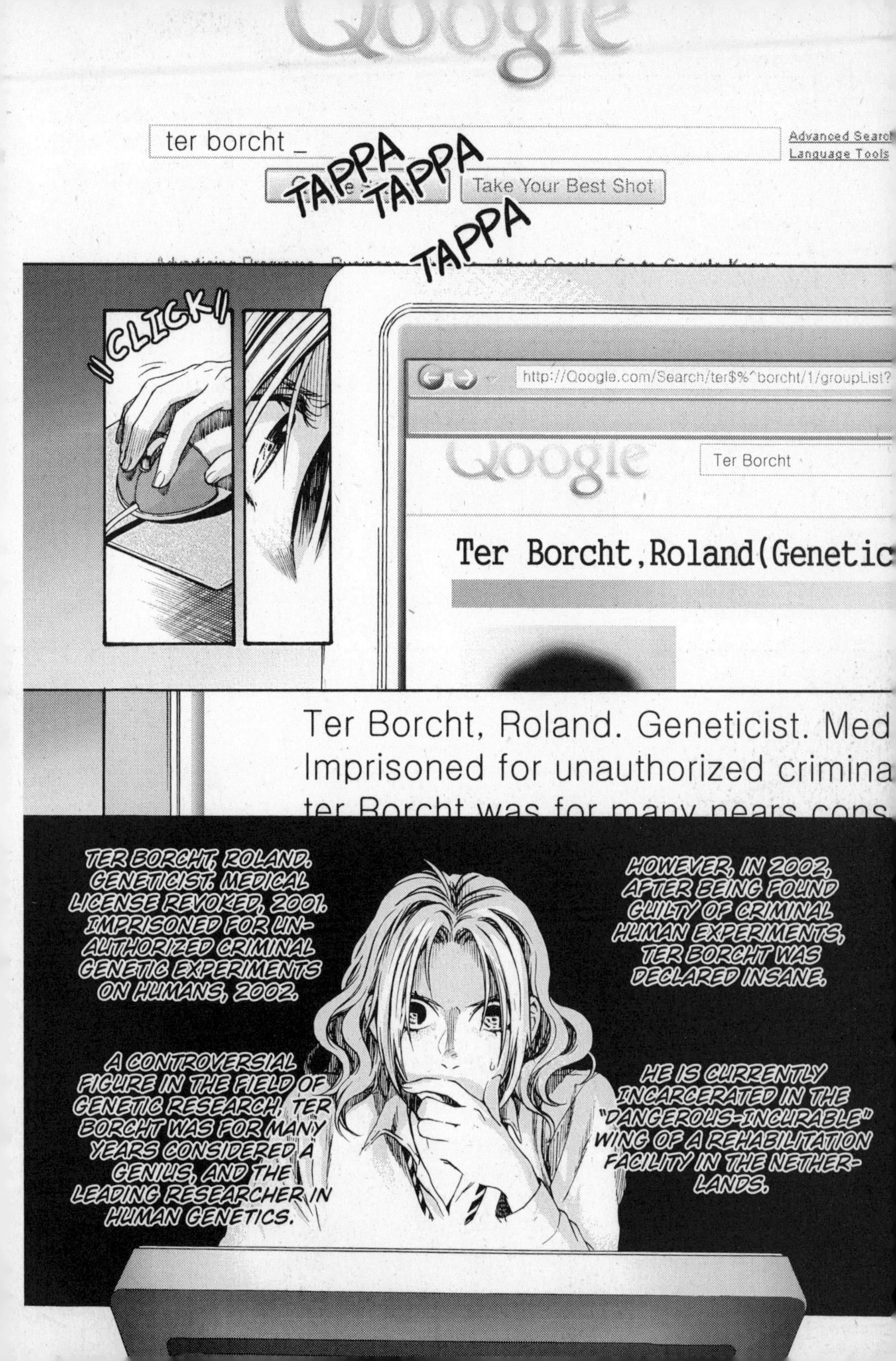
Qoogle
ter borcht _
Advanced Search
Language Tools
Take Your Best Shot
TAPPA TAPPA TAPPA
CLICK
http://Qoogle.com/Search/ter$%^borcht/1/groupList?
Qoogle
Ter Borcht
Ter Borcht,Roland(Genetic
Ter Borcht, Roland. Geneticist. Med
Imprisoned for unauthorized crimina
TER BORCHT, ROLAND. GENETICIST. MEDICAL LICENSE REVOKED, 2001. IMPRISONED FOR UN-AUTHORIZED CRIMINAL GENETIC EXPERIMENTS ON HUMANS, 2002.
HOWEVER, IN 2002, AFTER BEING FOUND GUILTY OF CRIMINAL HUMAN EXPERIMENTS, TER BORCHT WAS DECLARED INSANE.
A CONTROVERSIAL FIGURE IN THE FIELD OF GENETIC RESEARCH, TER BORCHT WAS FOR MANY YEARS CONSIDERED A GENIUS, AND THE LEADING RESEARCHER IN HUMAN GENETICS.
HE IS CURRENTLY INCARCERATED IN THE "DANGEROUS-INCURABLE" WING OF A REHABILITATION FACILITY IN THE NETHER-LANDS.

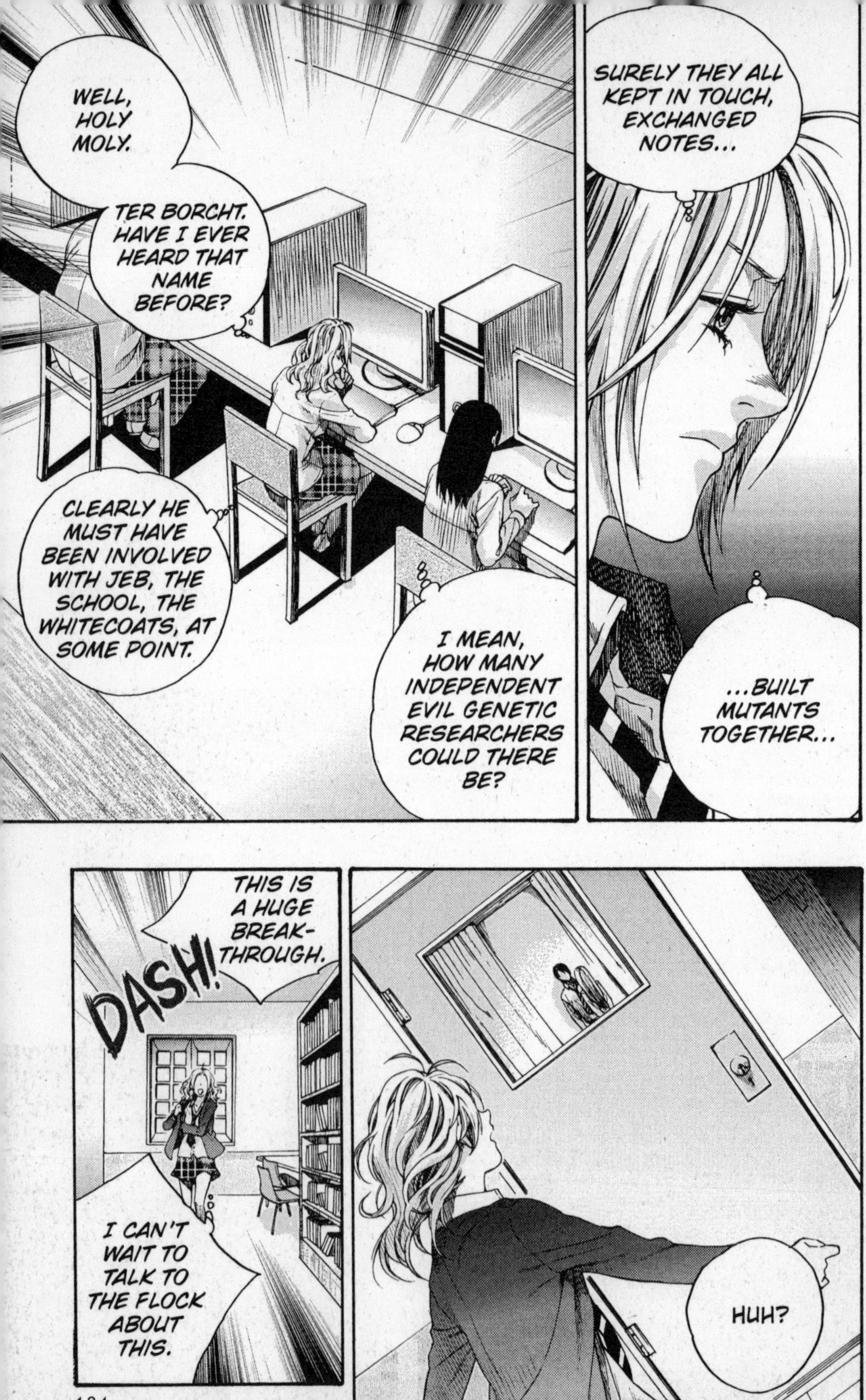
WELL, HOLY MOLY.
TER BORCHT. HAVE I EVER HEARD THAT NAME BEFORE?
CLEARLY HE MUST HAVE BEEN INVOLVED WITH JEB, THE SCHOOL, THE WHITECOATS, AT SOME POINT.
I MEAN, HOW MANY INDEPENDENT EVIL GENETIC RESEARCHERS COULD THERE BE?
SURELY THEY ALL KEPT IN TOUCH, EXCHANGED NOTES...
...BUILT MUTANTS TOGETHER...
THIS IS A HUGE BREAK-THROUGH.
DASH!
I CAN'T WAIT TO TALK TO THE FLOCK ABOUT THIS.
HUH?

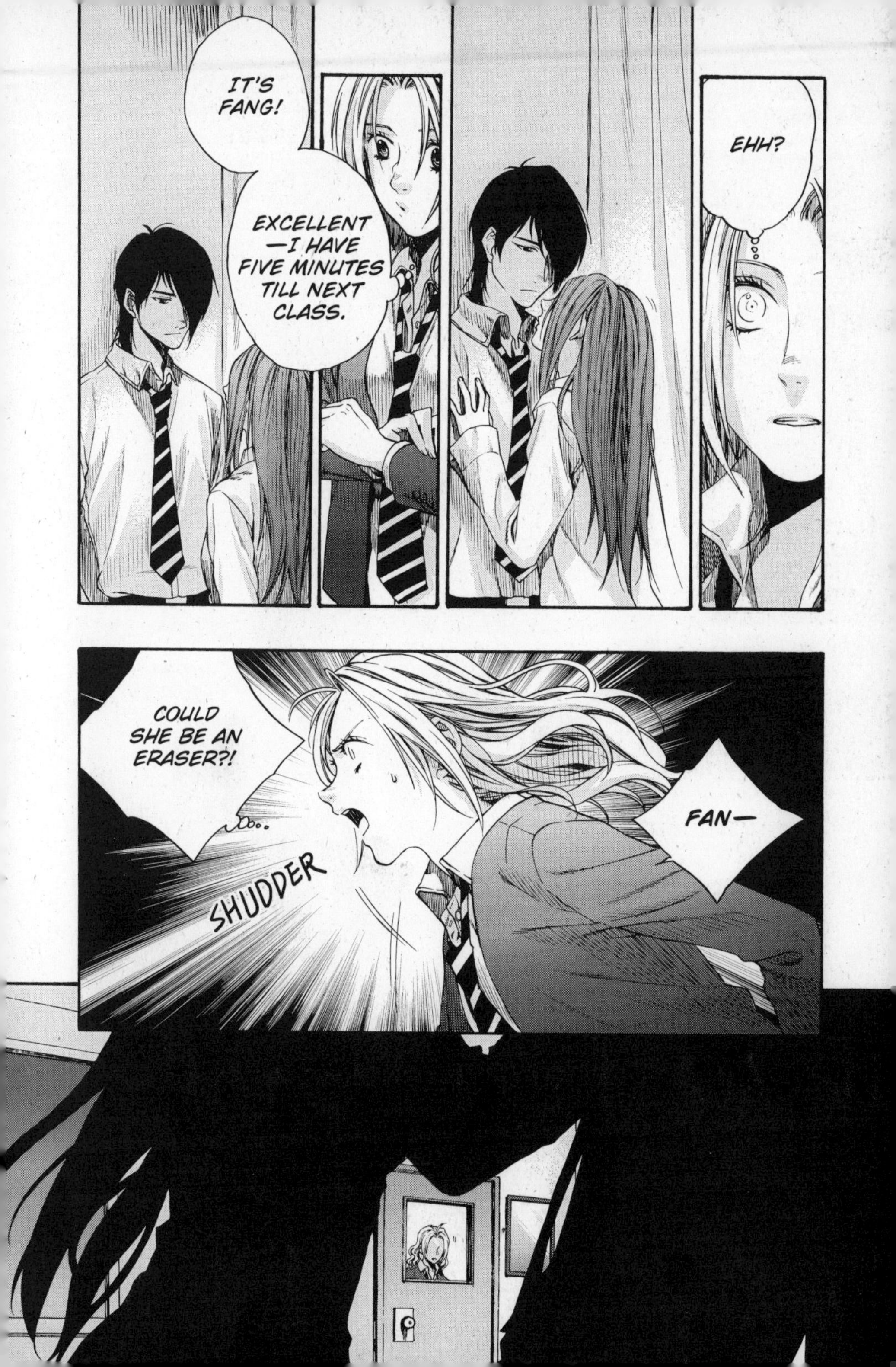
IT'S FANG!
EXCELLENT —I HAVE FIVE MINUTES TILL NEXT CLASS.
EHH?
COULD SHE BE AN ERASER?!
SHUDDER
FAN—

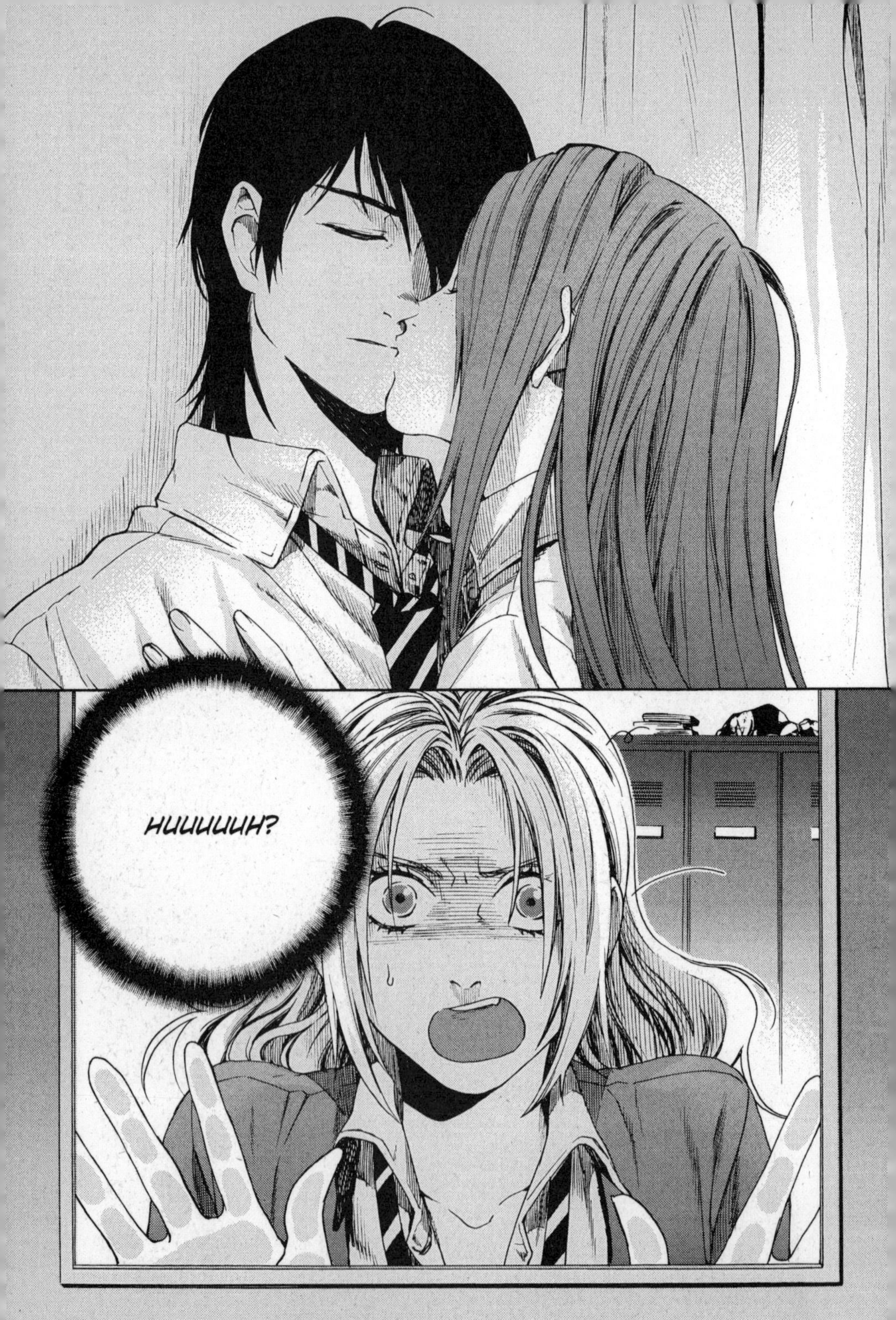
HUUUUUUH?

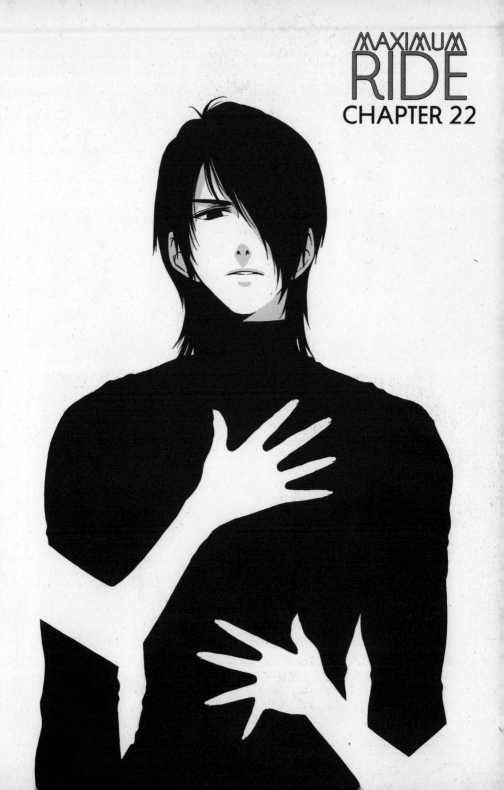

MAXIMUM RIDE
CHAPTER 22

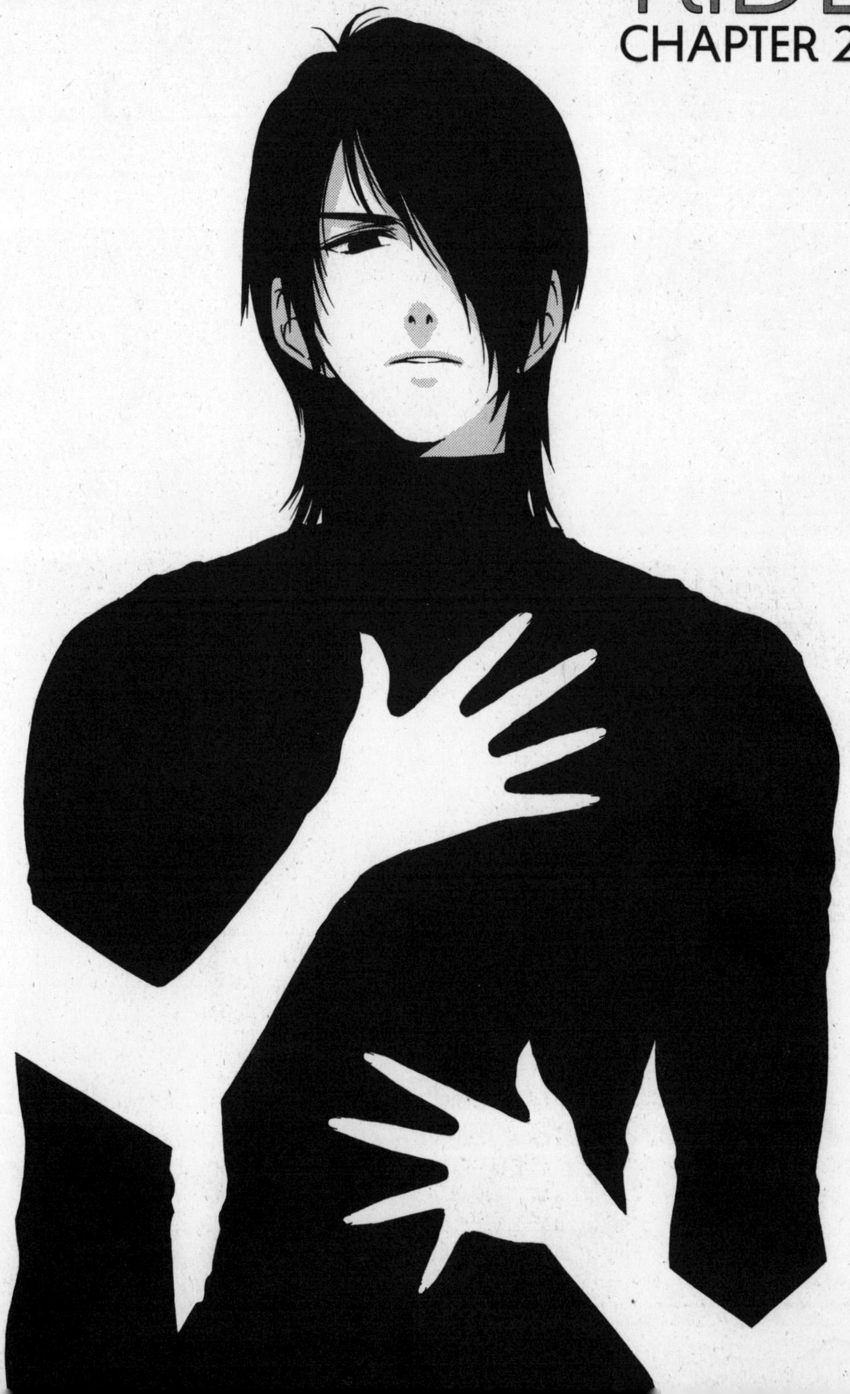

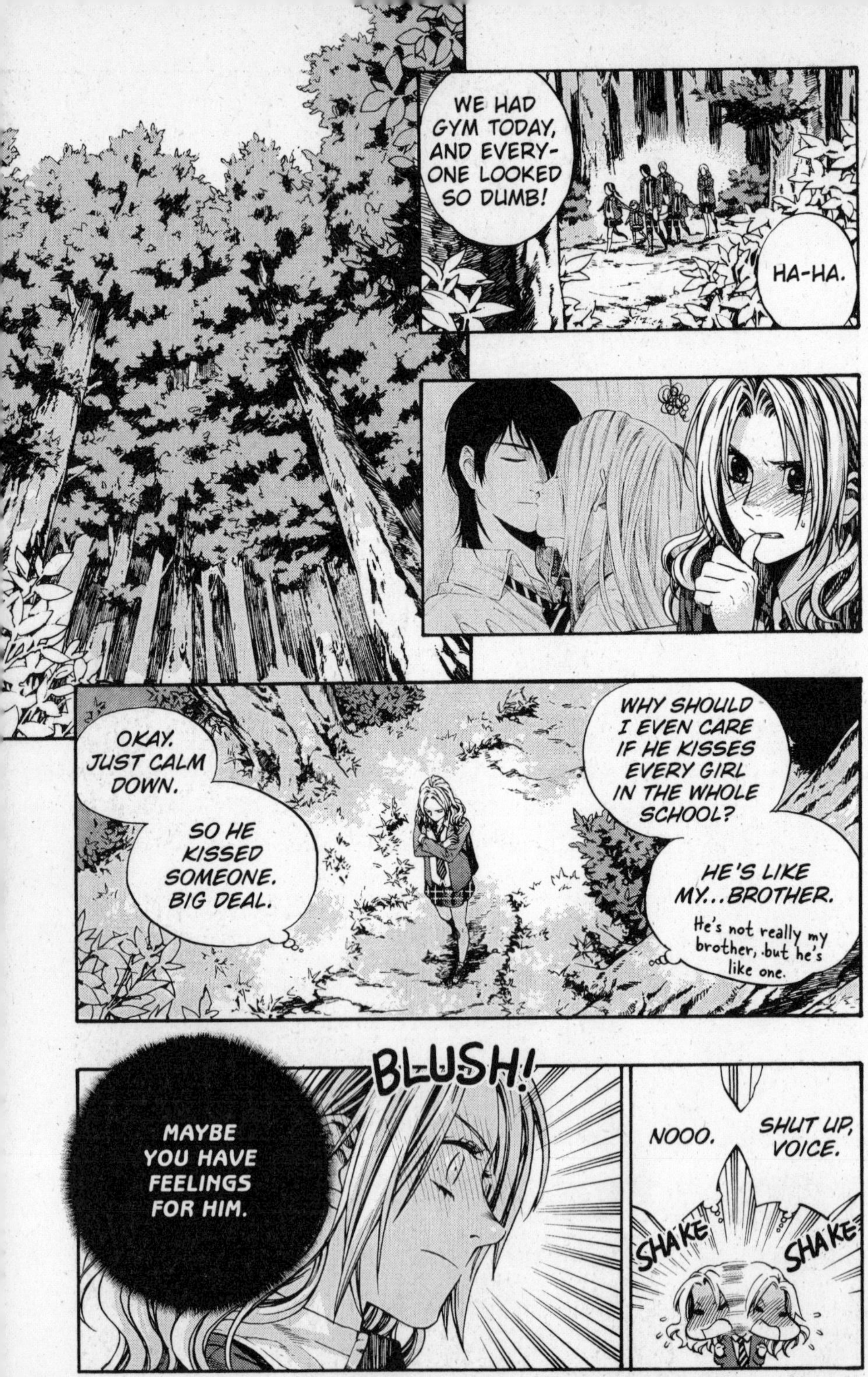
WE HAD GYM TODAY, AND EVERY-ONE LOOKED SO DUMB!
HA-HA.
OKAY. JUST CALM DOWN.
SO HE KISSED SOMEONE. BIG DEAL.
WHY SHOULD I EVEN CARE IF HE KISSES EVERY GIRL IN THE WHOLE SCHOOL?
HE'S LIKE MY...BROTHER.
He's not really my brother, but he's like one.
BLUSH!
MAYBE YOU HAVE FEELINGS FOR HIM.
NOOO.
SHUT UP, VOICE.
SHAKE
SHAKE

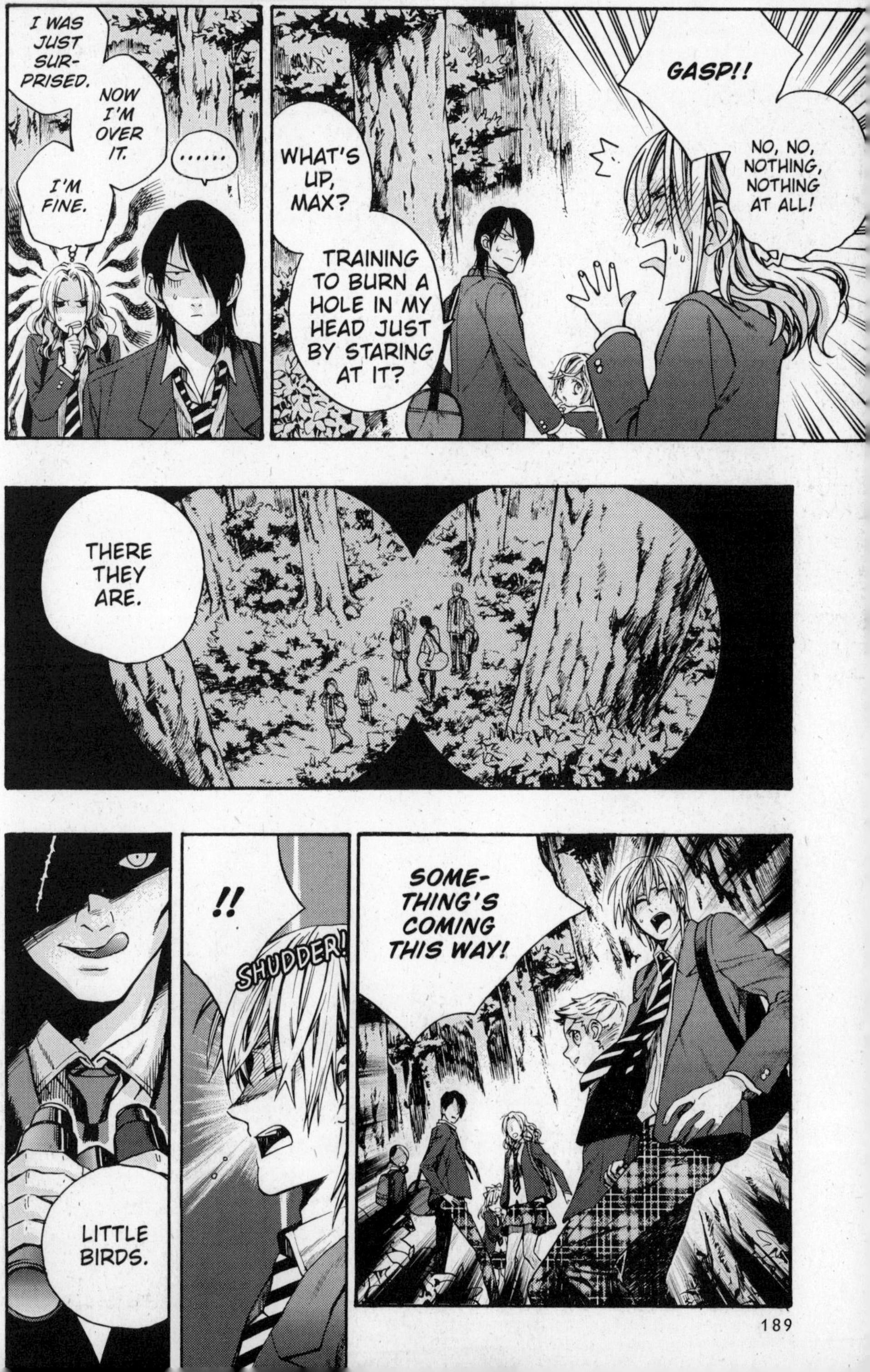
I WAS JUST SUR-PRISED.
NOW I'M OVER IT.
I'M FINE.
......
WHAT'S UP, MAX?
TRAINING TO BURN A HOLE IN MY HEAD JUST BY STARING AT IT?
GASP!!
NO, NO, NOTHING, NOTHING AT ALL!
THERE THEY ARE.
LITTLE BIRDS.
!!
SHUDDER!
SOME-THING'S COMING THIS WAY!

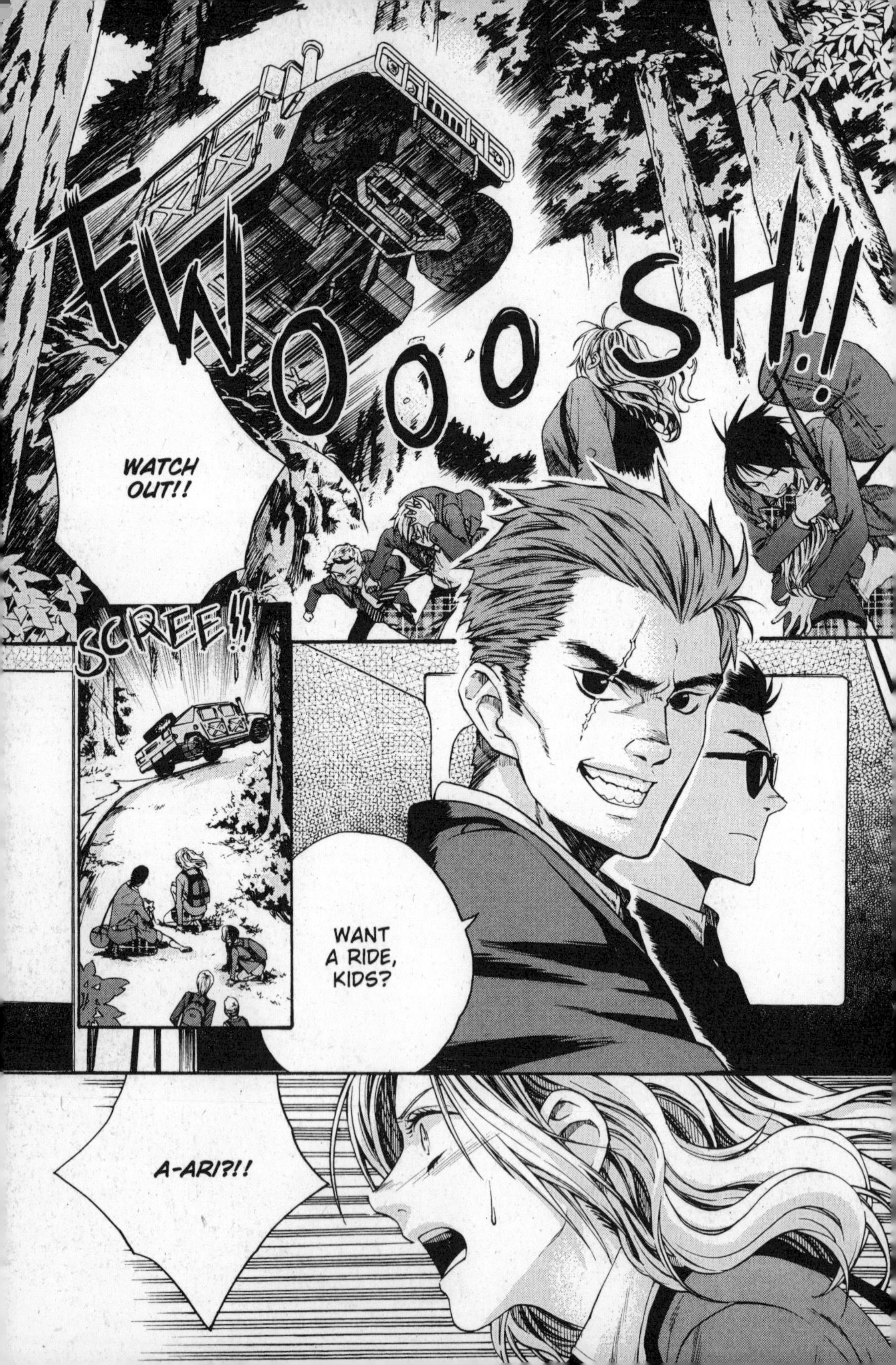
TWOOOSH!!
WATCH OUT!!
SCREE!!
WANT A RIDE, KIDS?
A-ARI?!!

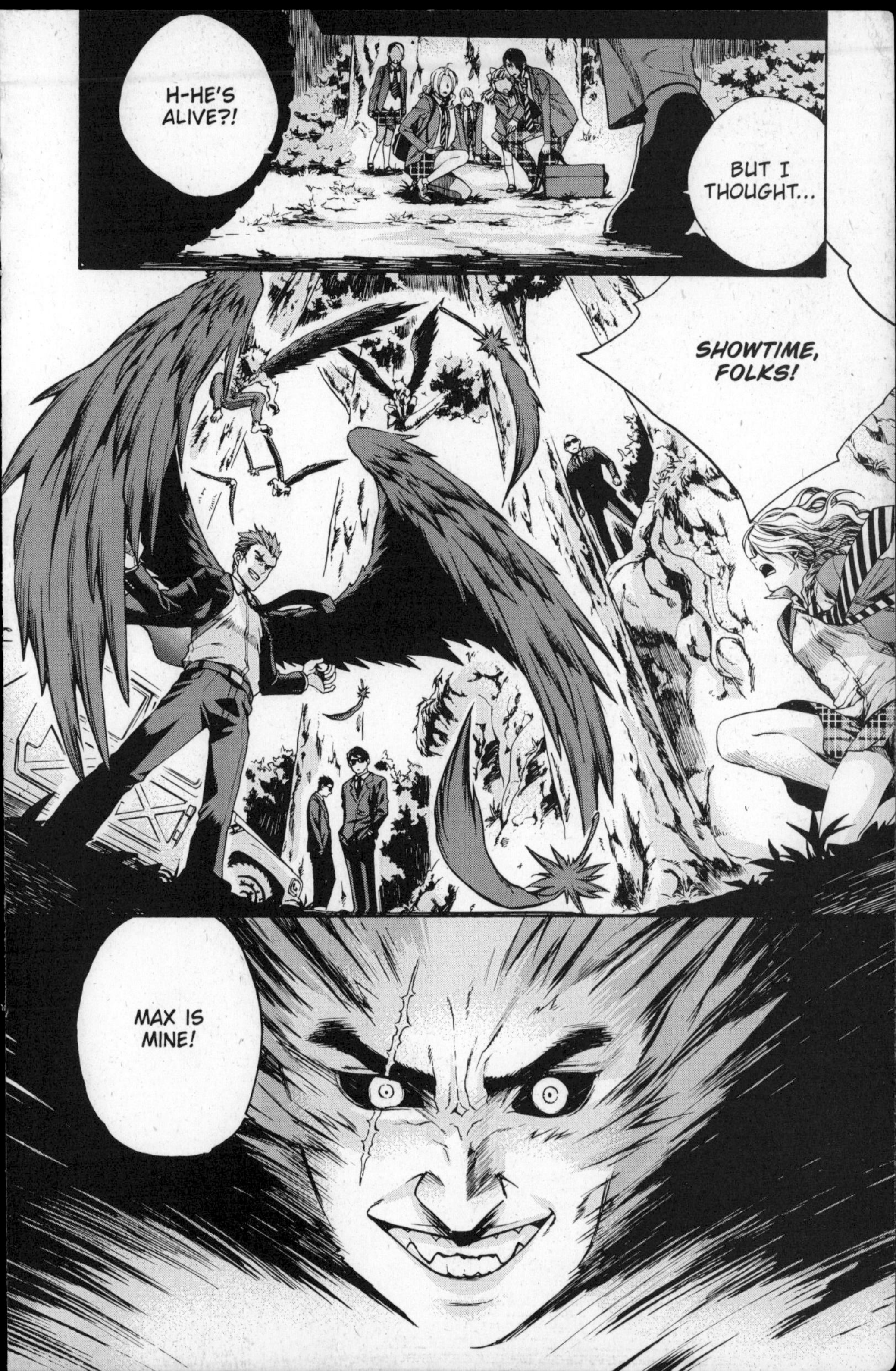
H-HE'S ALIVE?!
BUT I THOUGHT...
SHOWTIME, FOLKS!
MAX IS MINE!

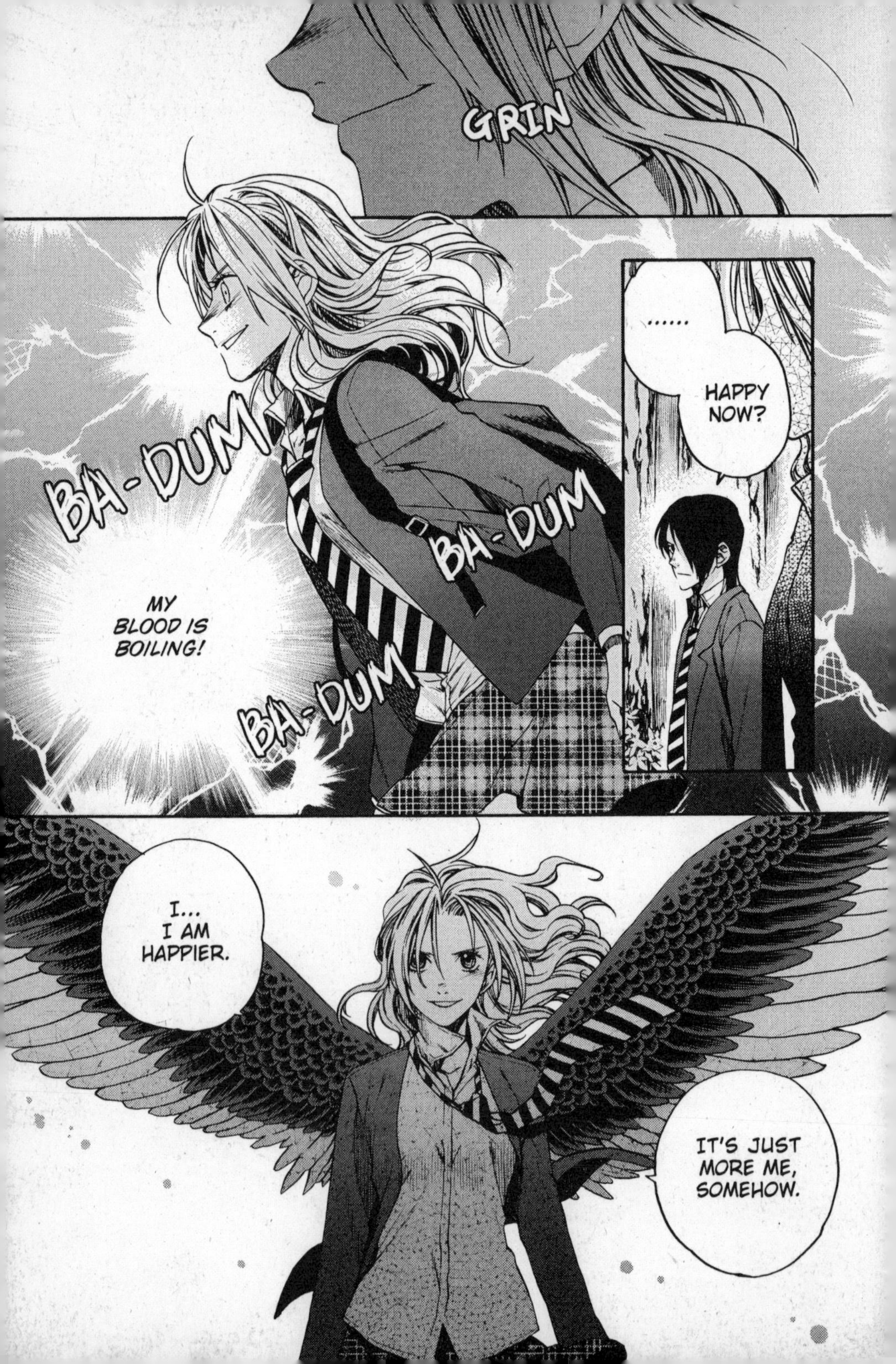
GRIN
BA-DUM
BA-DUM
MY BLOOD IS BOILING!
BA-DUM
......
HAPPY NOW?
I... I AM HAPPIER.
IT'S JUST MORE ME, SOMEHOW.

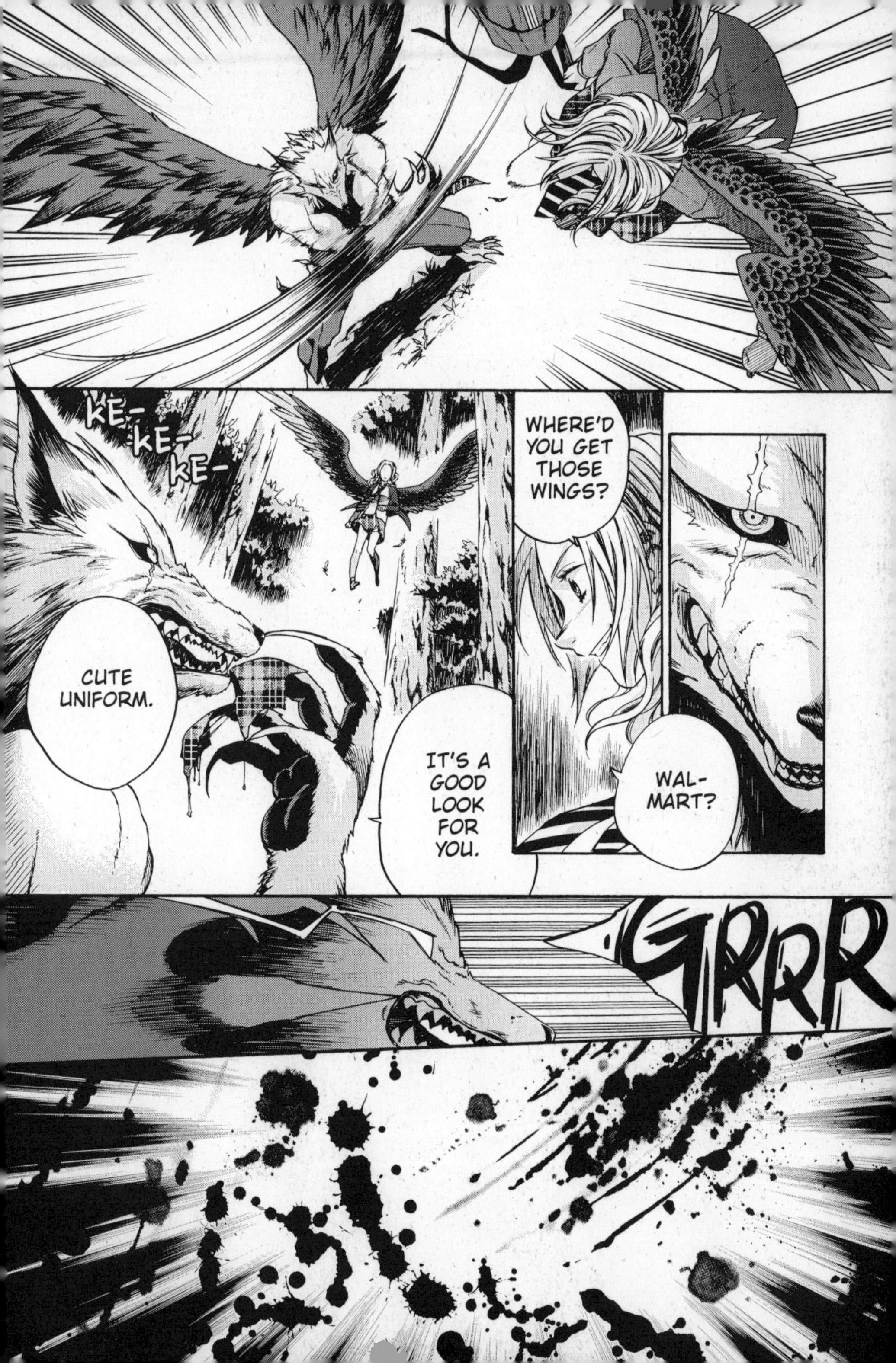
KE-KE-KE-
CUTE UNIFORM.
IT'S A GOOD LOOK FOR YOU.
WHERE'D YOU GET THOSE WINGS?
WAL-MART?
GRRR

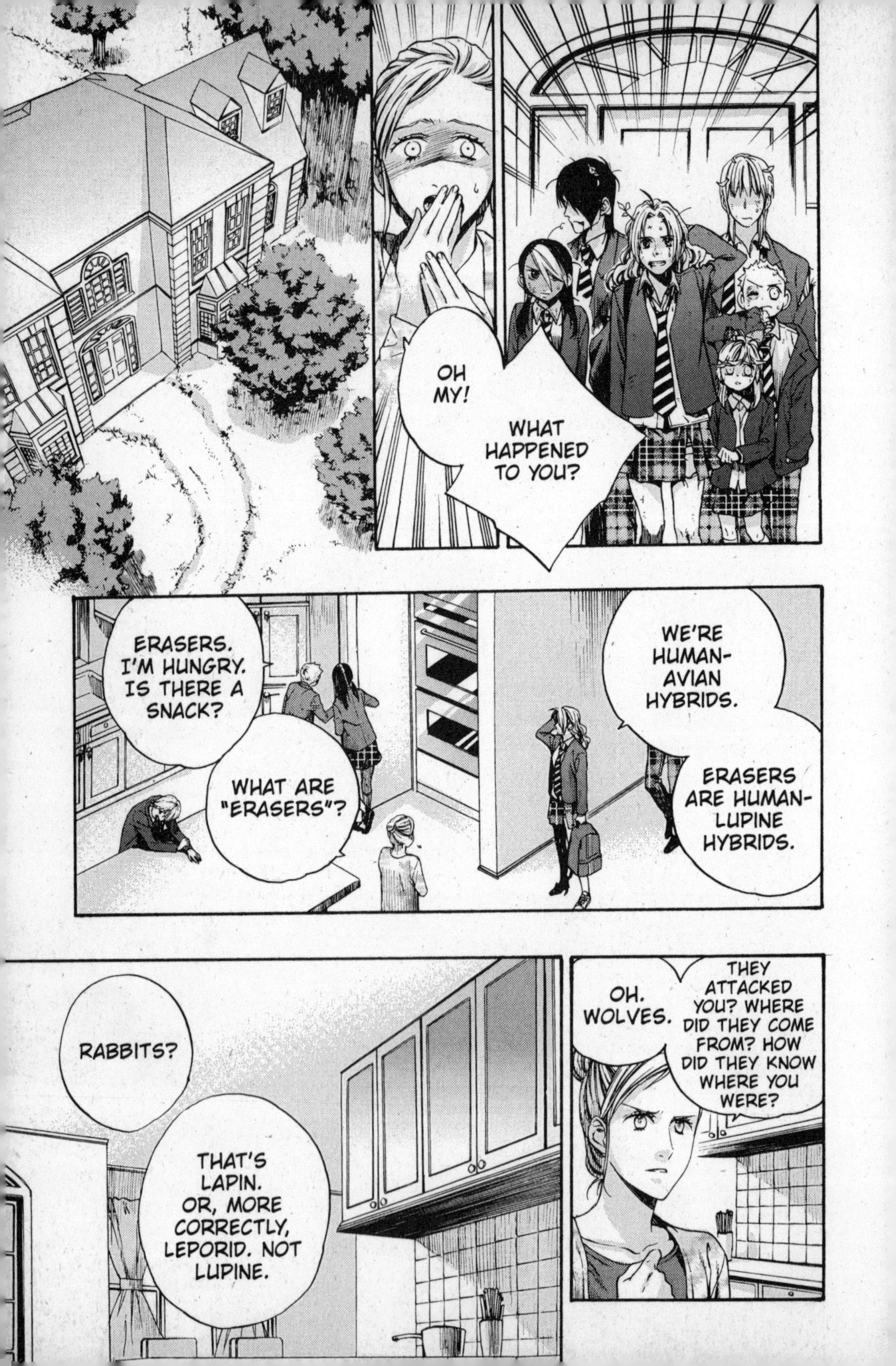
OH MY!
WHAT HAPPENED TO YOU?
ERASERS. I'M HUNGRY. IS THERE A SNACK?
WHAT ARE "ERASERS"?
WE'RE HUMAN-AVIAN HYBRIDS.
ERASERS ARE HUMAN-LUPINE HYBRIDS.
RABBITS?
THAT'S LAPIN. OR, MORE CORRECTLY, LEPORID. NOT LUPINE.
OH. WOLVES.
THEY ATTACKED YOU? WHERE DID THEY COME FROM? HOW DID THEY KNOW WHERE YOU WERE?

?

THEY ALWAYS ATTACK US. THEY'RE EVERYWHERE.

THEY WERE CREATED TO BE...WEAPONS, KIND OF. BACK AT THE SCHOOL, THEY WERE THE GUARDS, THE SECURITY, THE PUNISHERS.

SINCE WE ESCAPED, ERASERS HAVE BEEN TRACKING US.

ISN'T ALL THIS IN YOUR REPORTS?

I WAS WONDERING WHEN THEY'D SHOW UP.

THIS IS THE LONGEST WE'VE GONE WITHOUT THEM FINDING US.

WHY DIDN'T YOU TELL ME?

I REALLY THOUGHT YOU KNEW.

YOU KNEW A BUNCH OF OTHER STUFF ABOUT US.

I MEAN, I WASN'T KEEPING IT A SECRET OR ANYTHING.

WE'D HEARD ONLY VAGUE RUMORS.

THEY SEEMED SO FARFETCHED THAT WE DIDN'T BELIEVE THEM.

WELL, I'M GOING TO MAKE SOME PHONE CALLS.

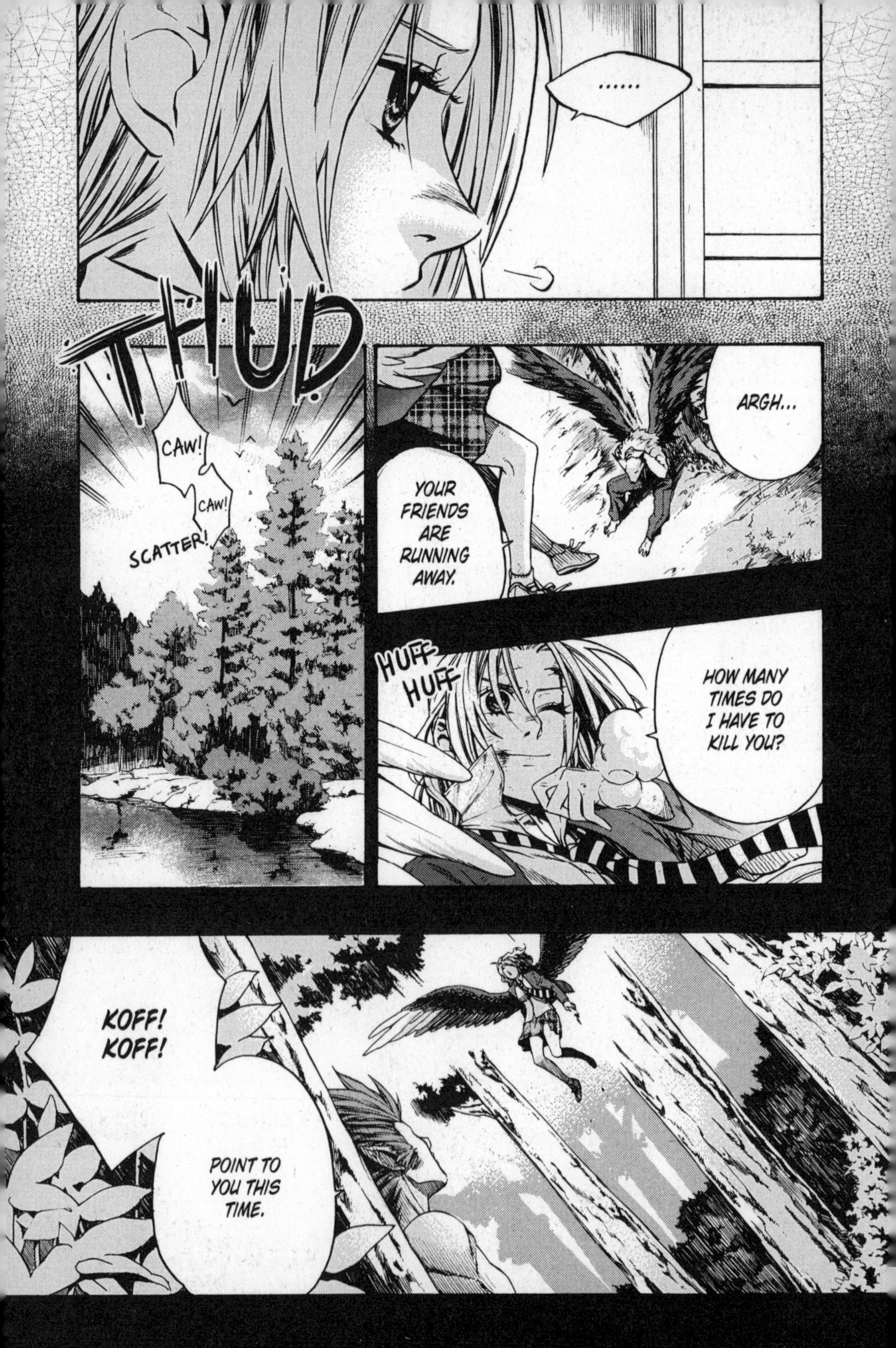
......
THUD
ARGH...
YOUR FRIENDS ARE RUNNING AWAY.
HUFF HUFF
HOW MANY TIMES DO I HAVE TO KILL YOU?
CAW!
CAW!
SCATTER!
KOFF! KOFF!
POINT TO YOU THIS TIME.

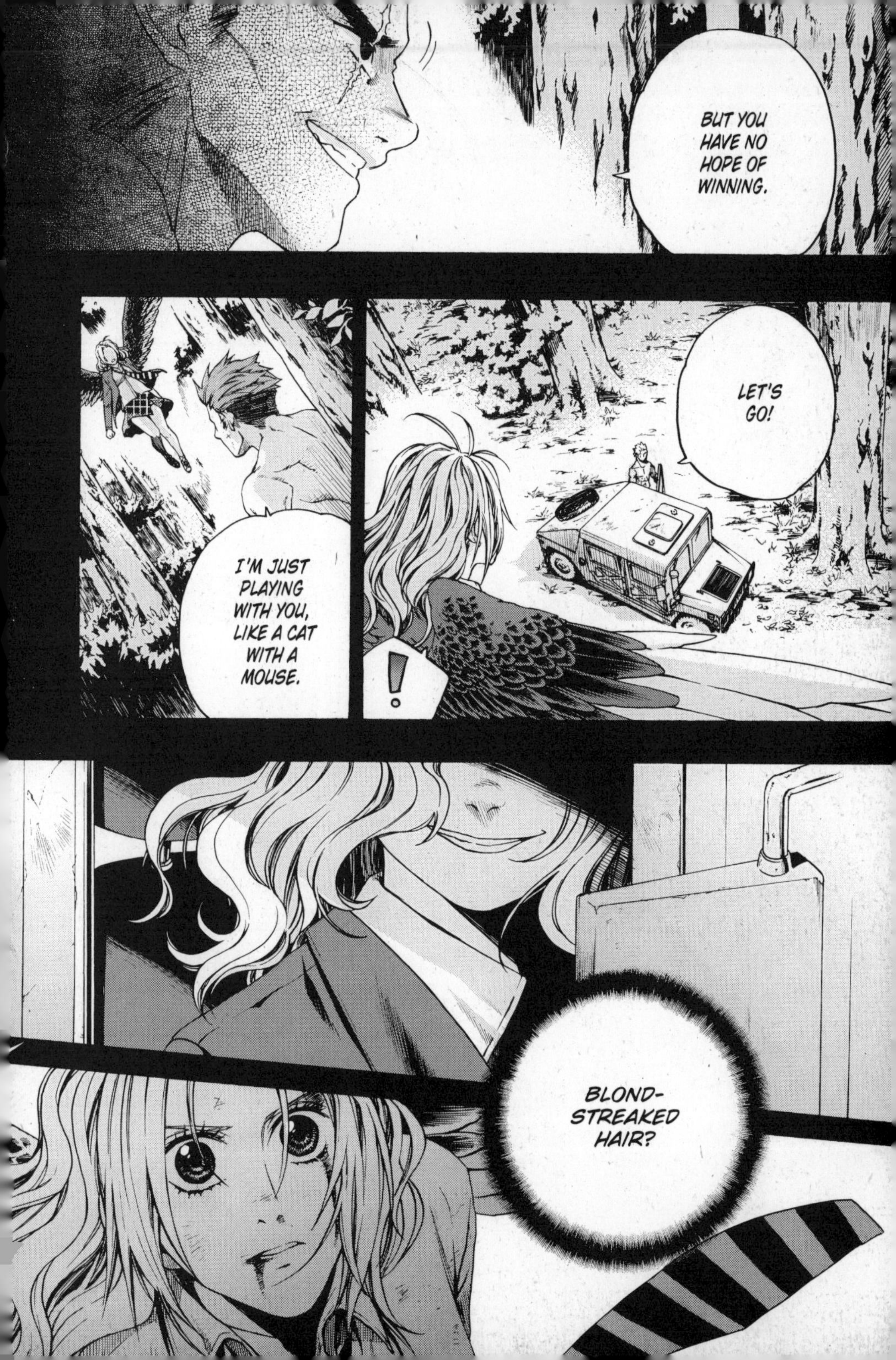
BUT YOU HAVE NO HOPE OF WINNING.
I'M JUST PLAYING WITH YOU, LIKE A CAT WITH A MOUSE.
!
LET'S GO!
BLOND-STREAKED HAIR?

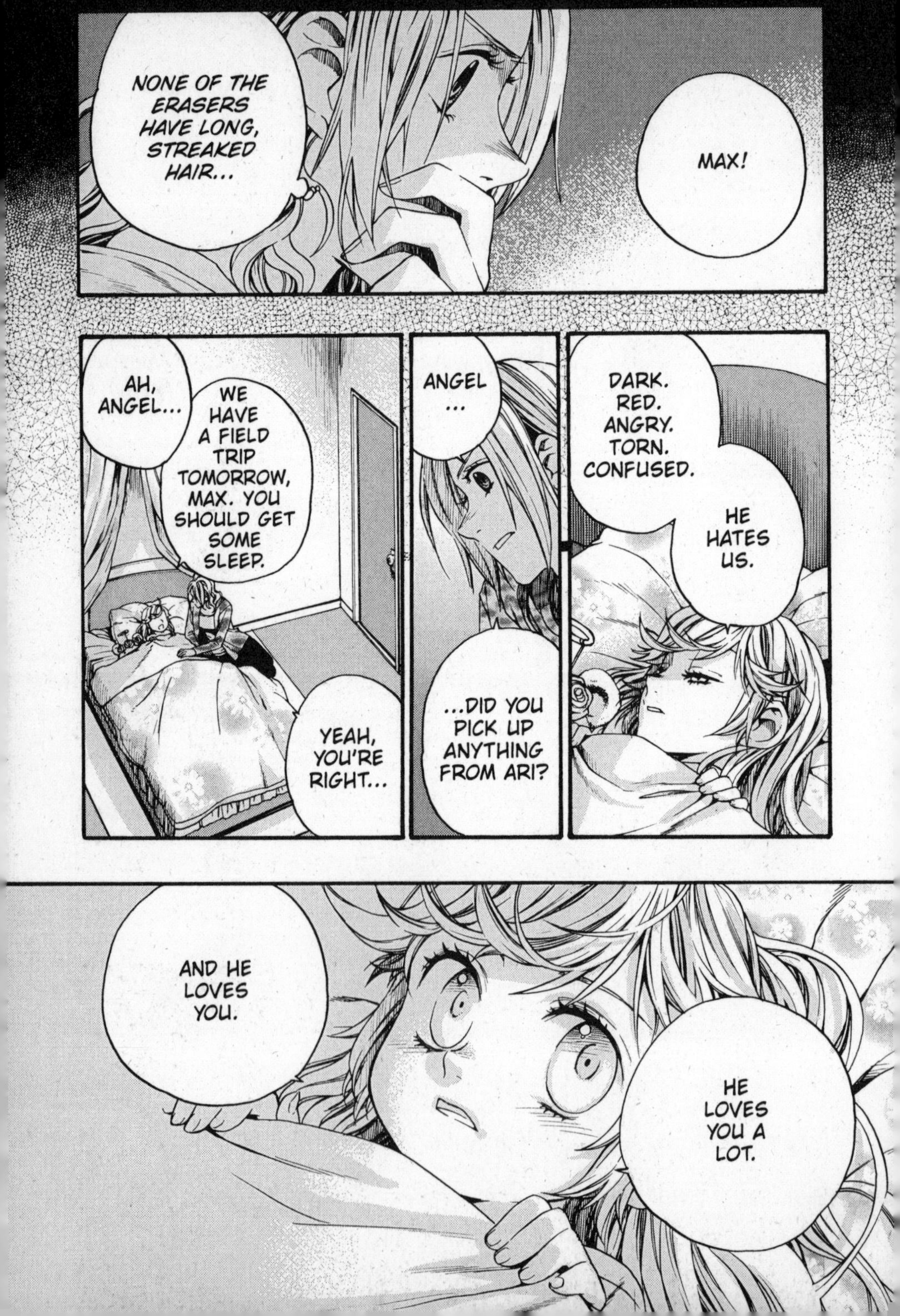
NONE OF THE ERASERS HAVE LONG, STREAKED HAIR...
MAX!
AH, ANGEL...
WE HAVE A FIELD TRIP TOMORROW, MAX. YOU SHOULD GET SOME SLEEP.
YEAH, YOU'RE RIGHT...
ANGEL ...
...DID YOU PICK UP ANYTHING FROM ARI?
DARK. RED. ANGRY. TORN. CONFUSED.
HE HATES US.
AND HE LOVES YOU.
HE LOVES YOU A LOT.

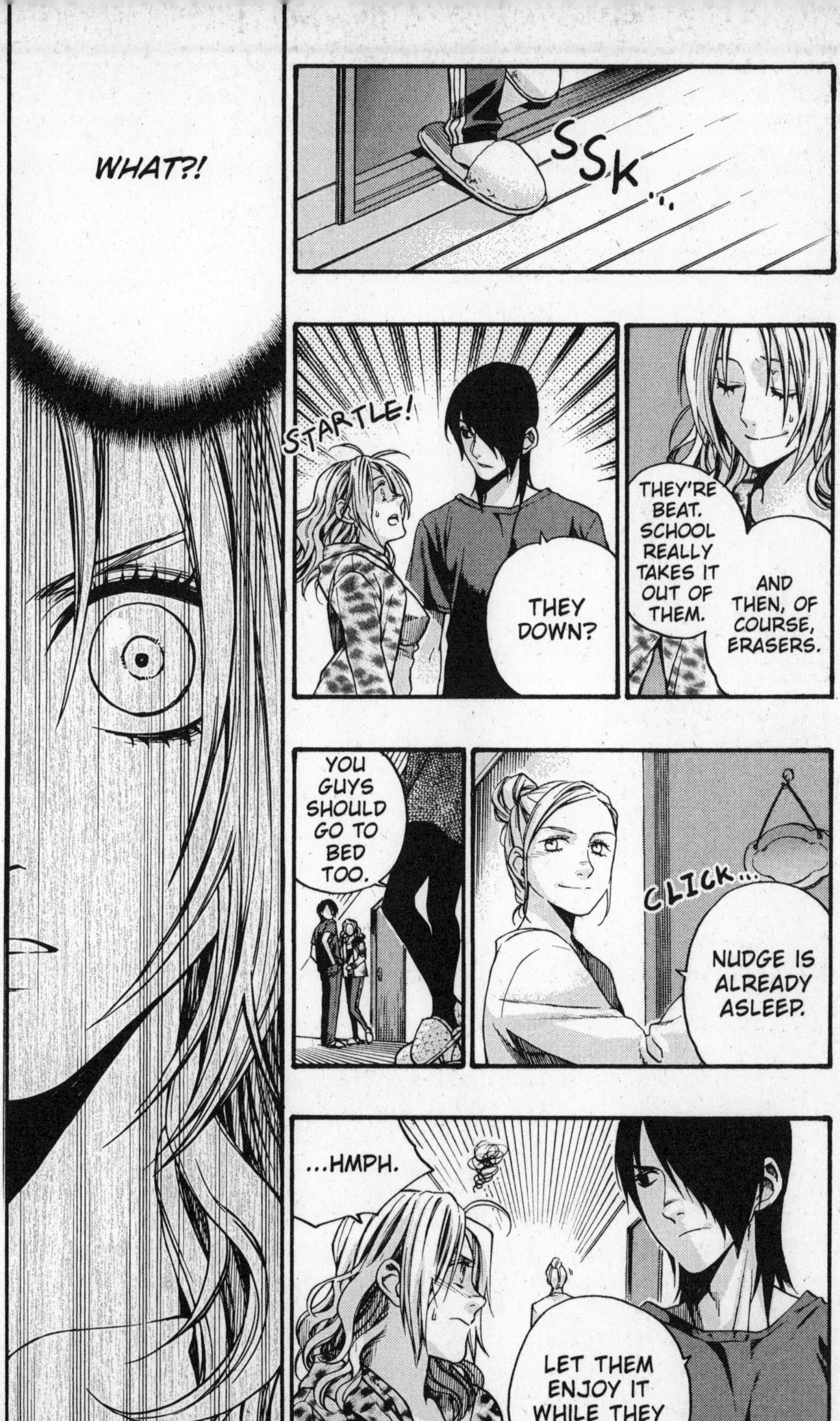
WHAT?!
SSK...
STARTLE!
THEY DOWN?
THEY'RE BEAT. SCHOOL REALLY TAKES IT OUT OF THEM.
AND THEN, OF COURSE, ERASERS.
YOU GUYS SHOULD GO TO BED TOO.
CLICK...
NUDGE IS ALREADY ASLEEP.
...HMPH.
LET THEM ENJOY IT WHILE THEY CAN.

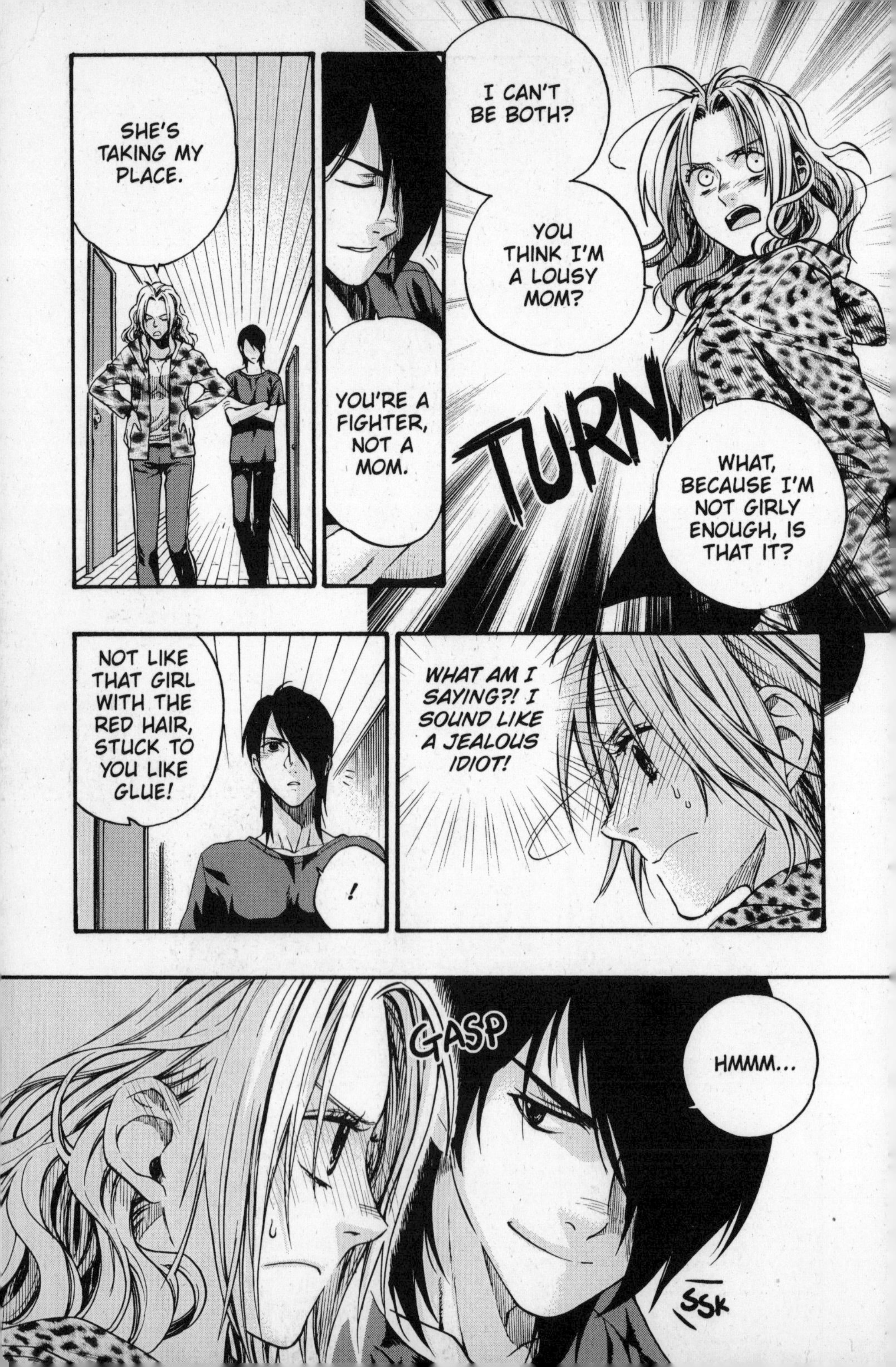
SHE'S TAKING MY PLACE.
YOU'RE A FIGHTER, NOT A MOM.
I CAN'T BE BOTH?
YOU THINK I'M A LOUSY MOM?
TURN
WHAT, BECAUSE I'M NOT GIRLY ENOUGH, IS THAT IT?
NOT LIKE THAT GIRL WITH THE RED HAIR, STUCK TO YOU LIKE GLUE!
!
WHAT AM I SAYING?! I SOUND LIKE A JEALOUS IDIOT!
GASP
HMMM...
SSK

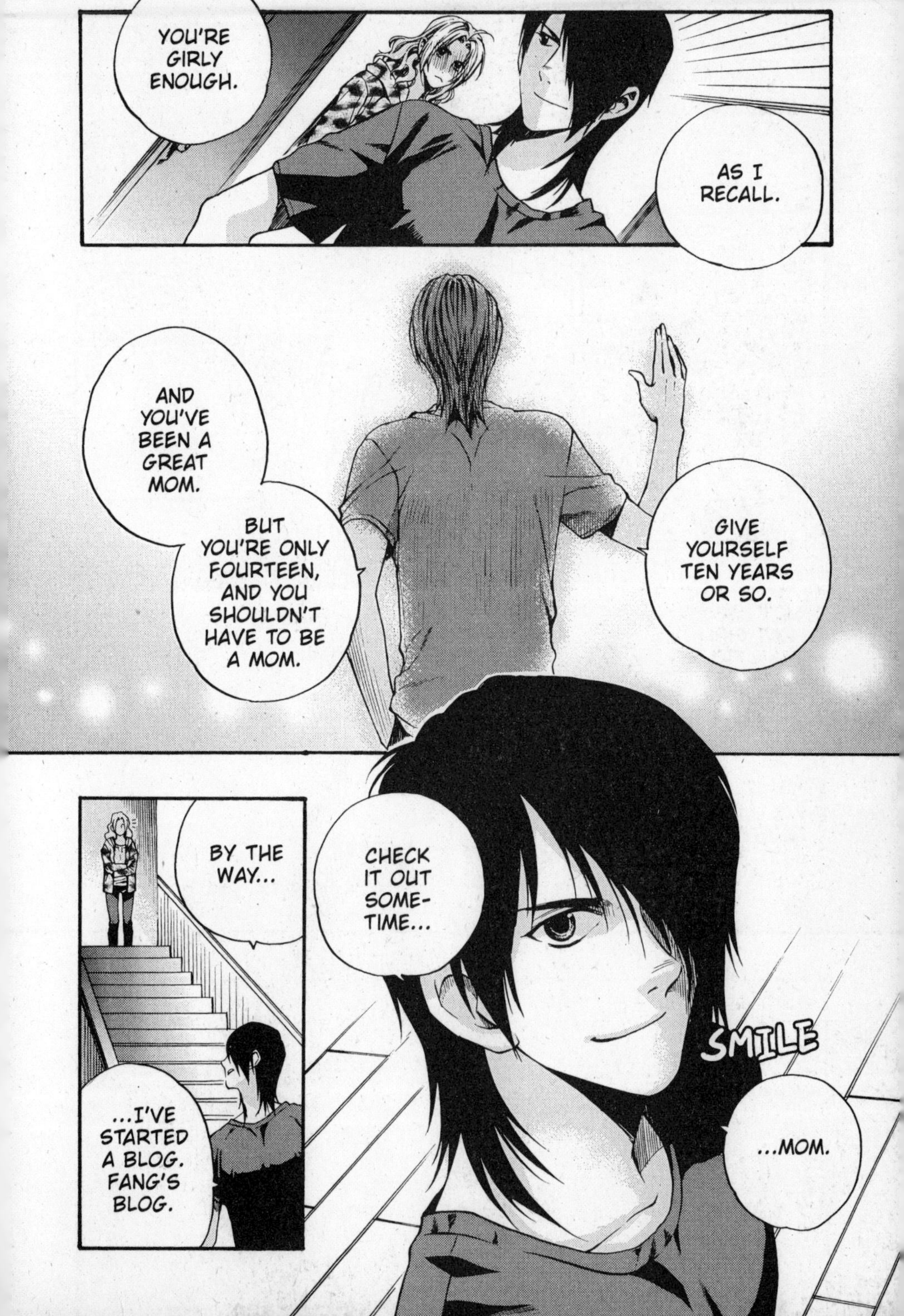
YOU'RE GIRLY ENOUGH.
AS I RECALL.
AND YOU'VE BEEN A GREAT MOM.
BUT YOU'RE ONLY FOURTEEN, AND YOU SHOULDN'T HAVE TO BE A MOM.
GIVE YOURSELF TEN YEARS OR SO.
BY THE WAY...
...I'VE STARTED A BLOG. FANG'S BLOG.
CHECK IT OUT SOME-TIME...
SMILE
...MOM.

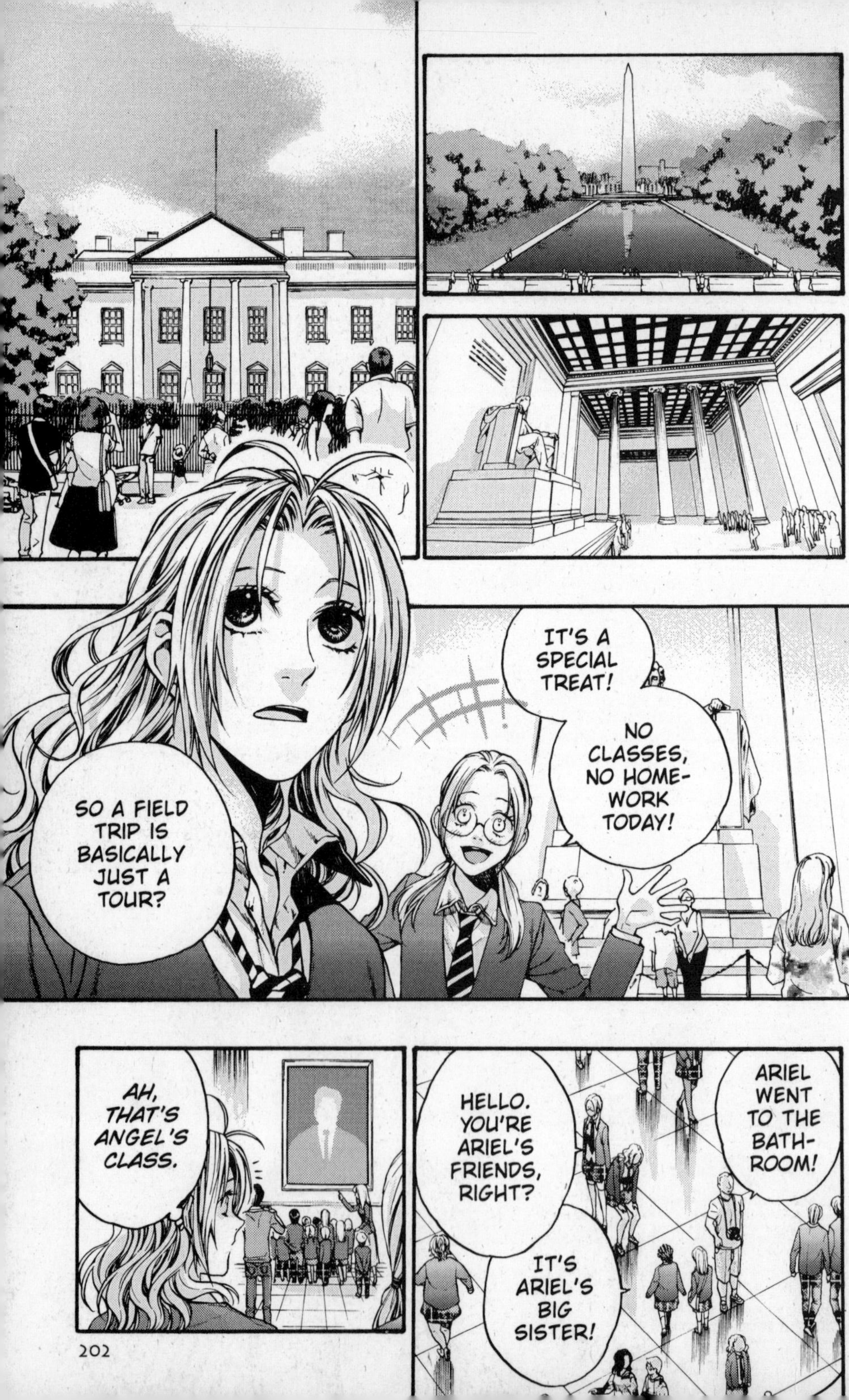
SO A FIELD TRIP IS BASICALLY JUST A TOUR?
IT'S A SPECIAL TREAT!
NO CLASSES, NO HOME-WORK TODAY!
AH, THAT'S ANGEL'S CLASS.
HELLO. YOU'RE ARIEL'S FRIENDS, RIGHT?
ARIEL WENT TO THE BATH-ROOM!
IT'S ARIEL'S BIG SISTER!

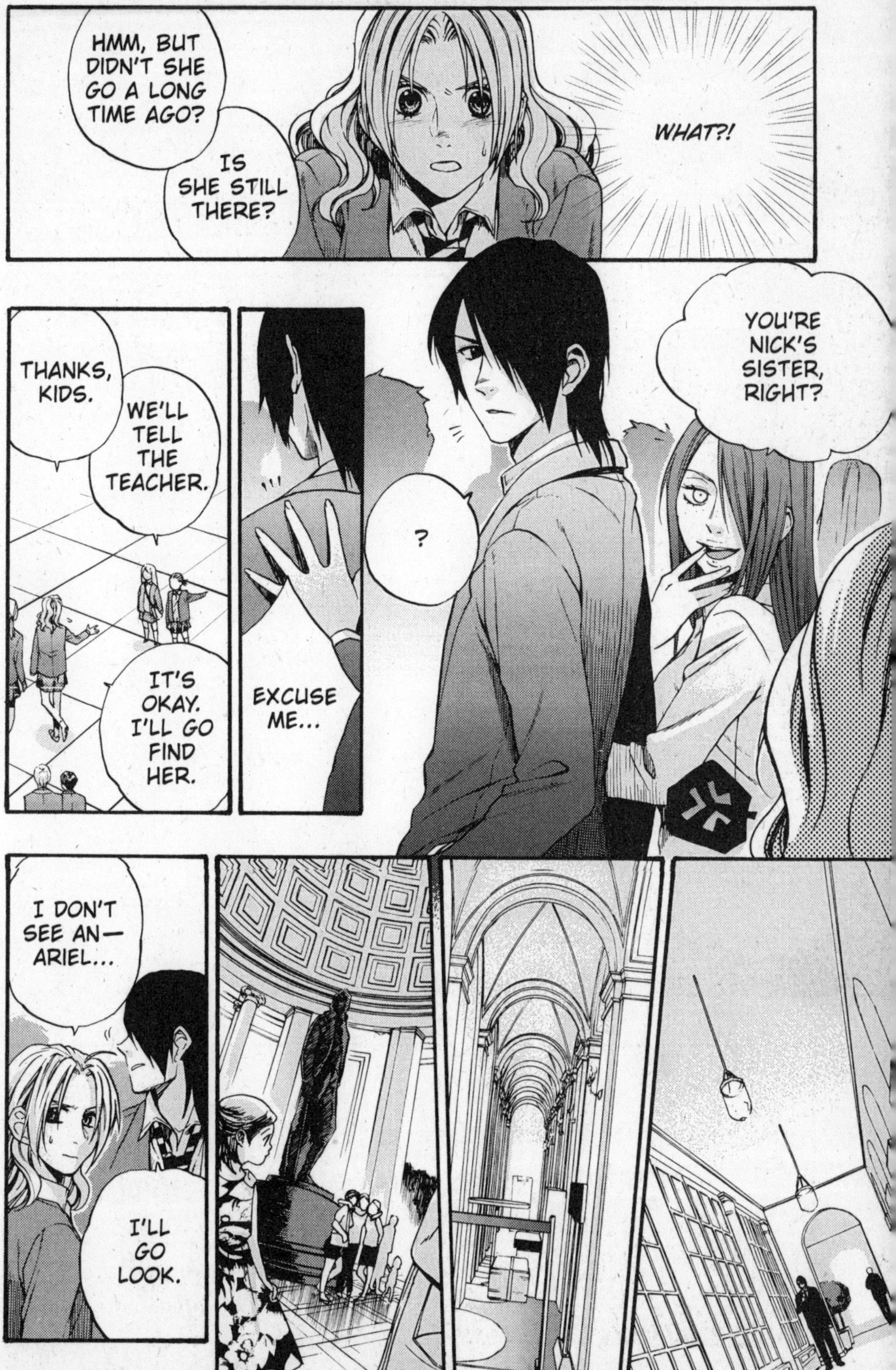
HMM, BUT DIDN'T SHE GO A LONG TIME AGO?
IS SHE STILL THERE?
WHAT?!
THANKS, KIDS.
WE'LL TELL THE TEACHER.
IT'S OKAY. I'LL GO FIND HER.
EXCUSE ME...
YOU'RE NICK'S SISTER, RIGHT?
?
I DON'T SEE AN— ARIEL...
I'LL GO LOOK.

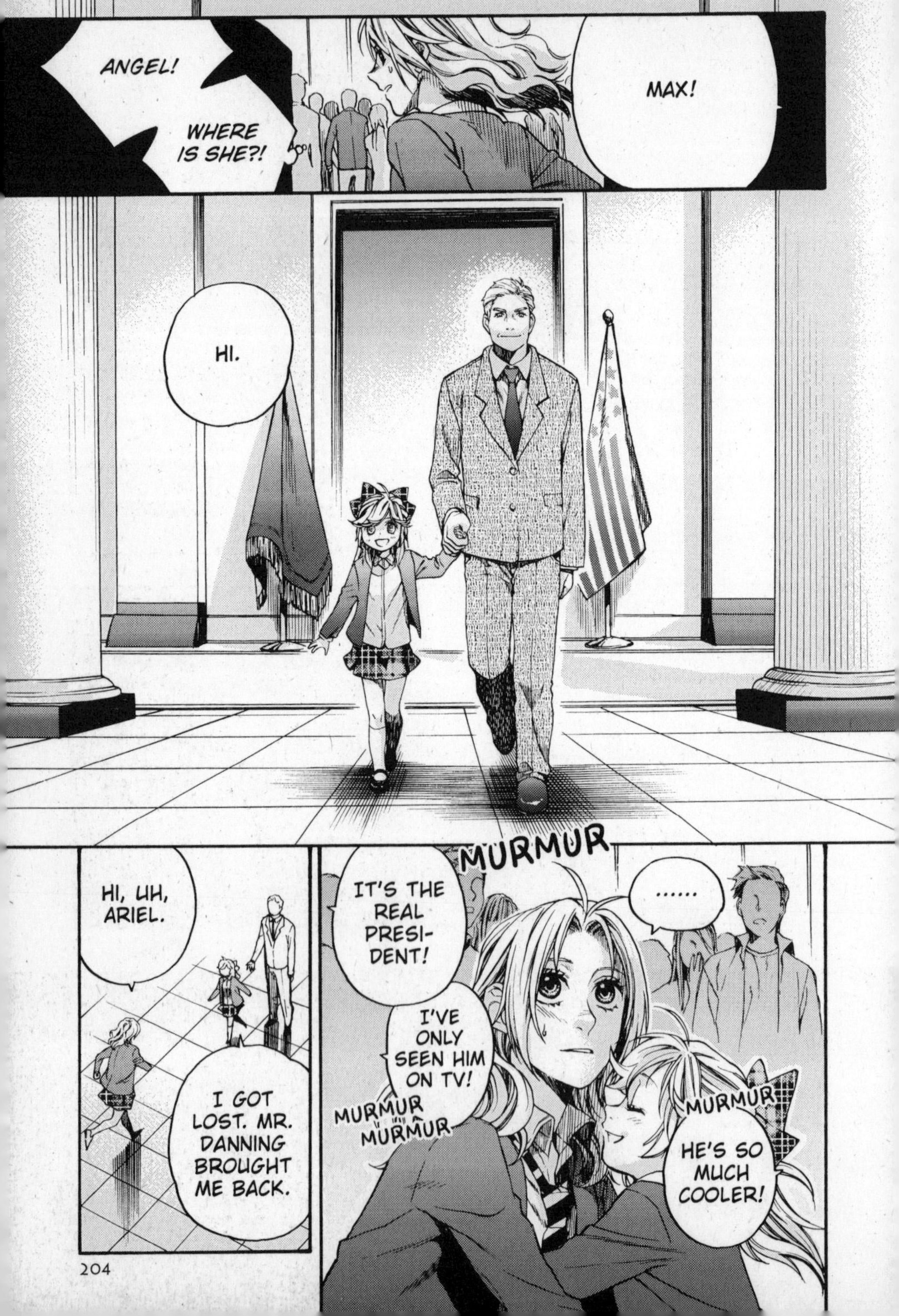
ANGEL!
WHERE IS SHE?!
MAX!
HI.
HI, UH, ARIEL.
I GOT LOST. MR. DANNING BROUGHT ME BACK.
MURMUR
IT'S THE REAL PRESIDENT!
......
I'VE ONLY SEEN HIM ON TV!
MURMUR MURMUR
MURMUR
HE'S SO MUCH COOLER!

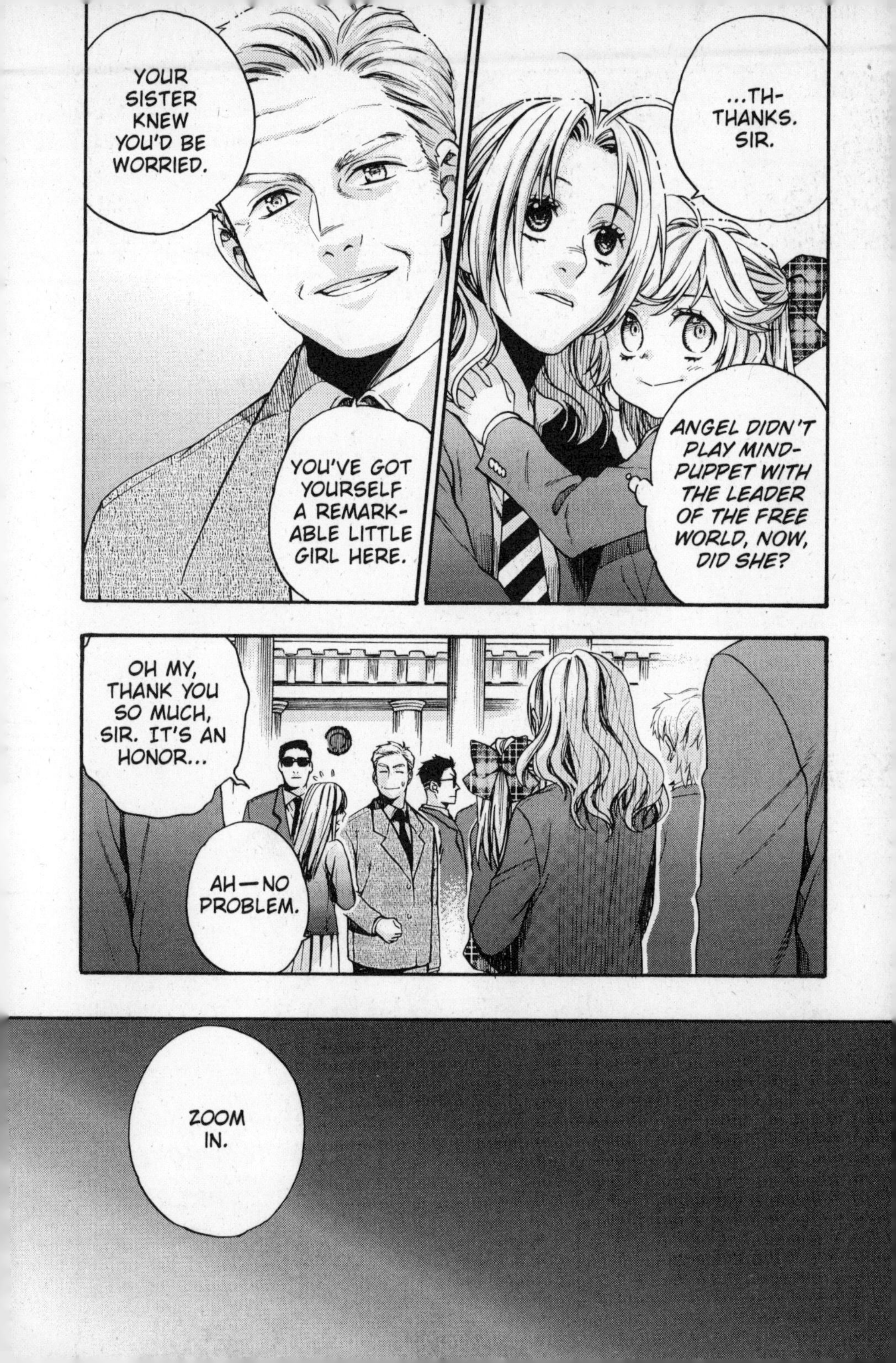
YOUR SISTER KNEW YOU'D BE WORRIED.
YOU'VE GOT YOURSELF A REMARK-ABLE LITTLE GIRL HERE.
...TH-THANKS. SIR.
ANGEL DIDN'T PLAY MIND-PUPPET WITH THE LEADER OF THE FREE WORLD, NOW, DID SHE?
OH MY, THANK YOU SO MUCH, SIR. IT'S AN HONOR...
AH—NO PROBLEM.
ZOOM IN.

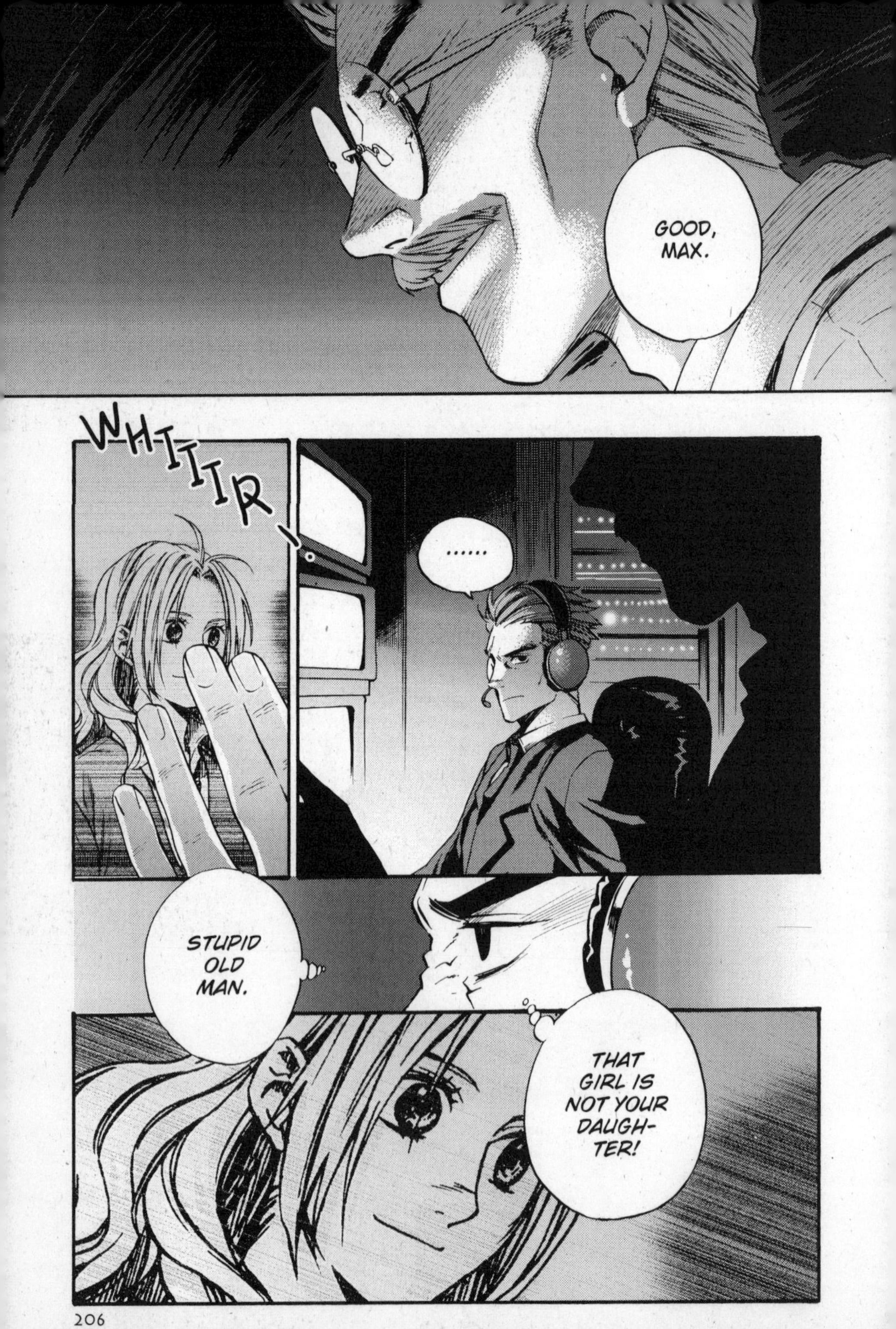
GOOD, MAX.
WHIIIR
......
STUPID OLD MAN.
THAT GIRL IS NOT YOUR DAUGHTER!

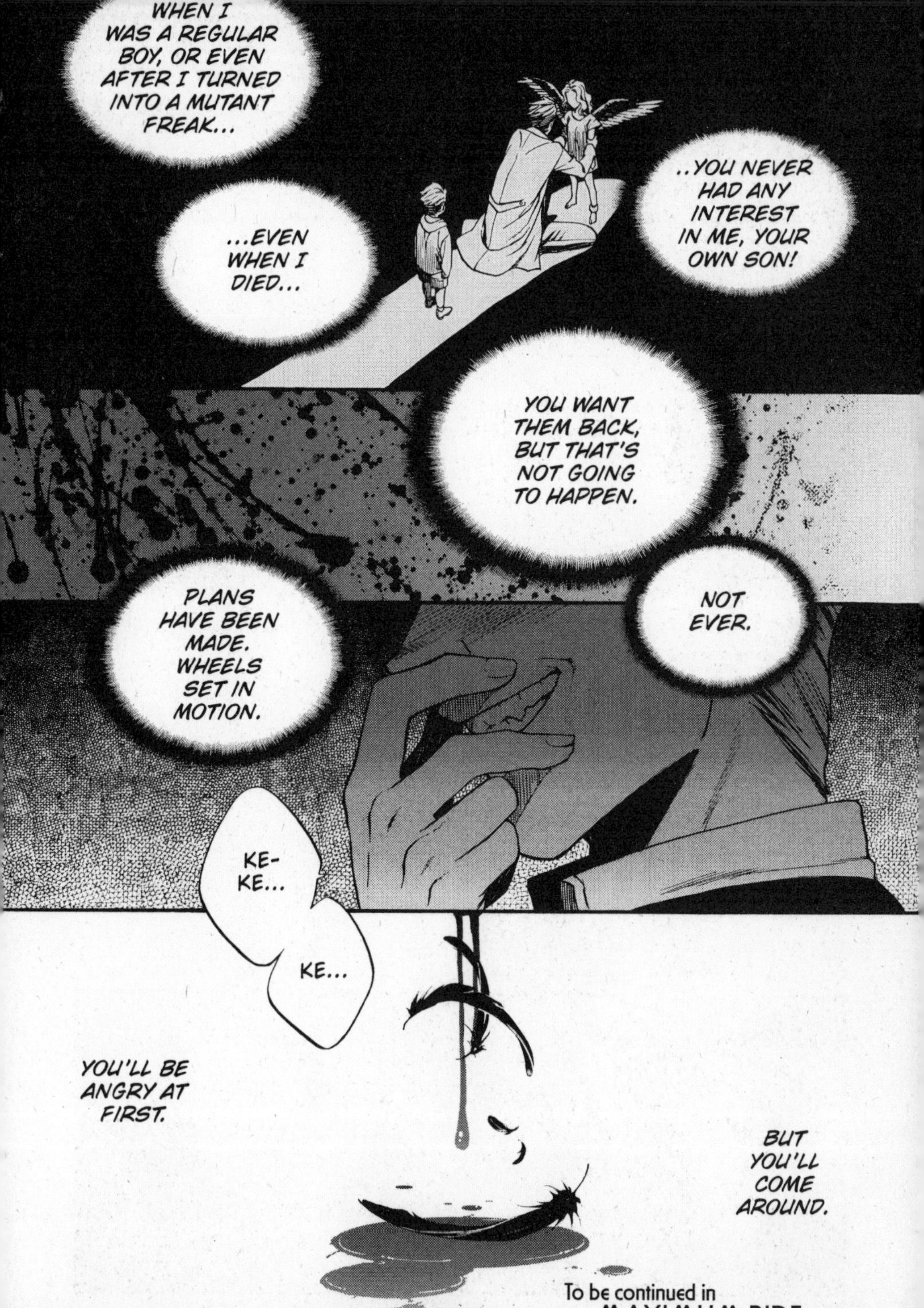
WHEN I WAS A REGULAR BOY, OR EVEN AFTER I TURNED INTO A MUTANT FREAK...
...EVEN WHEN I DIED...
..YOU NEVER HAD ANY INTEREST IN ME, YOUR OWN SON!
YOU WANT THEM BACK, BUT THAT'S NOT GOING TO HAPPEN.
PLANS HAVE BEEN MADE. WHEELS SET IN MOTION.
NOT EVER.
KE-KE...
KE...
YOU'LL BE ANGRY AT FIRST.
BUT YOU'LL COME AROUND.

To be continued in
MAXIMUM RIDE, Vol. 4!

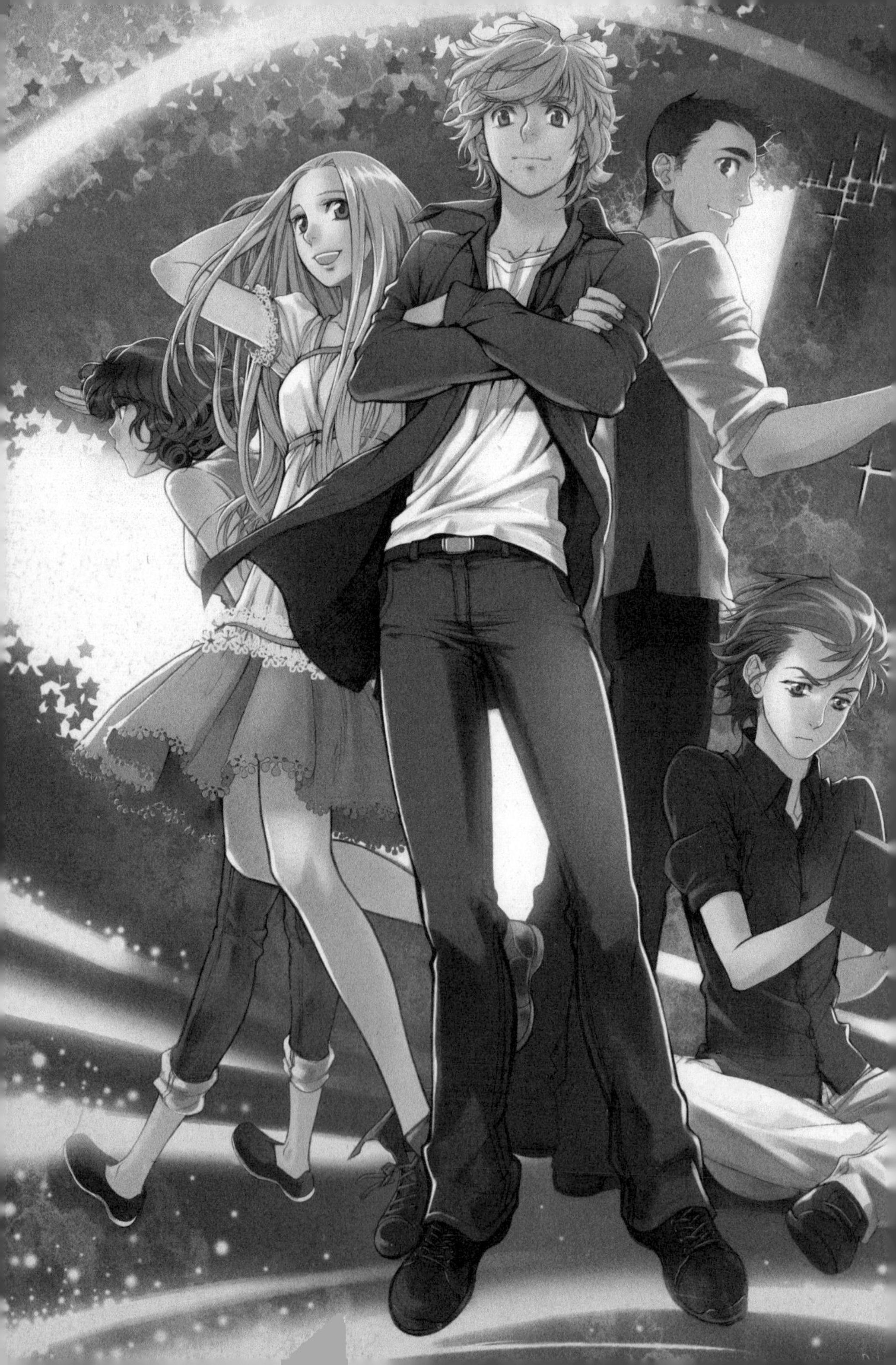

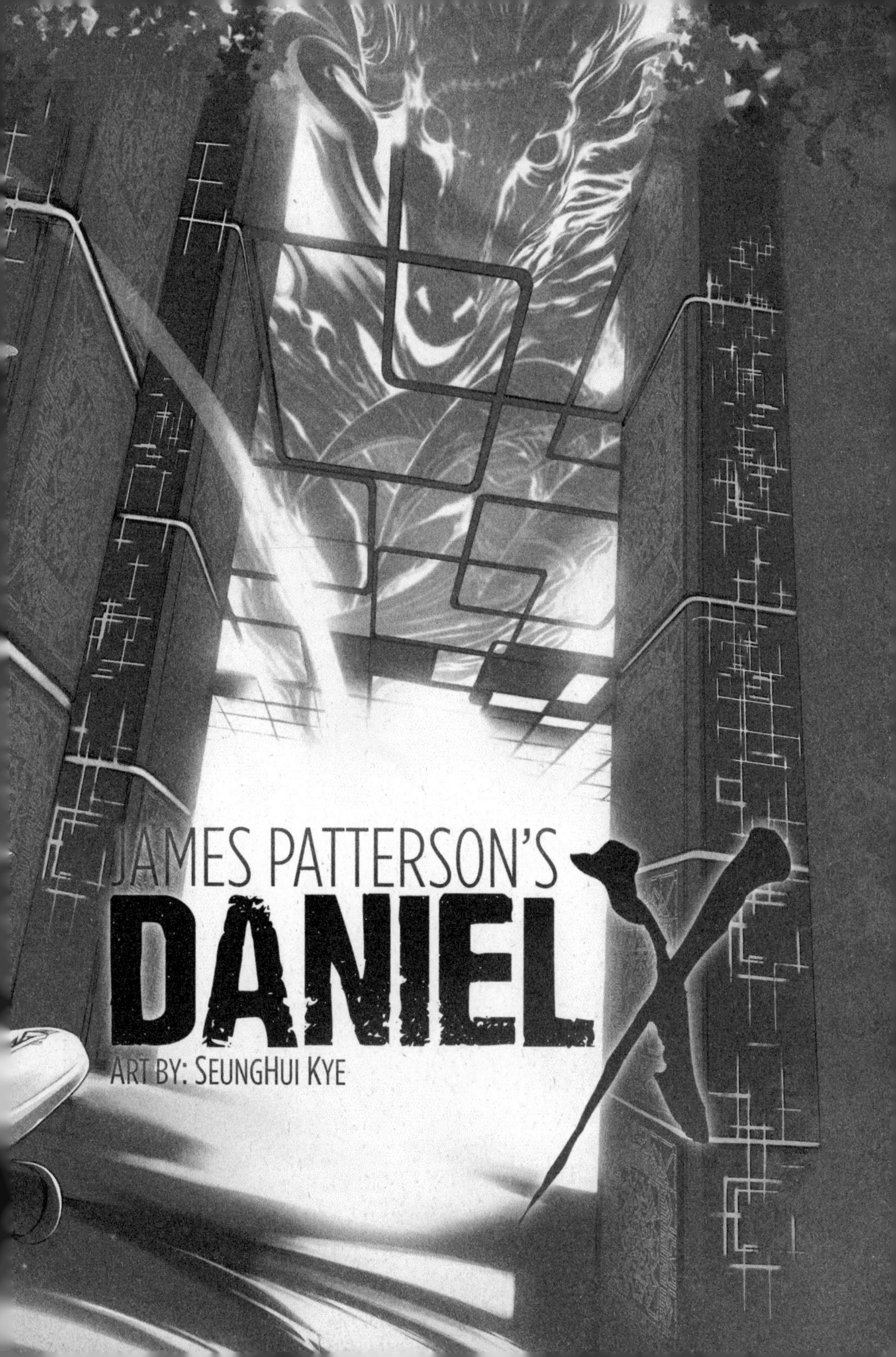
JAMES PATTERSON'S
DANIEL X
ART BY: SEUNGHUI KYE

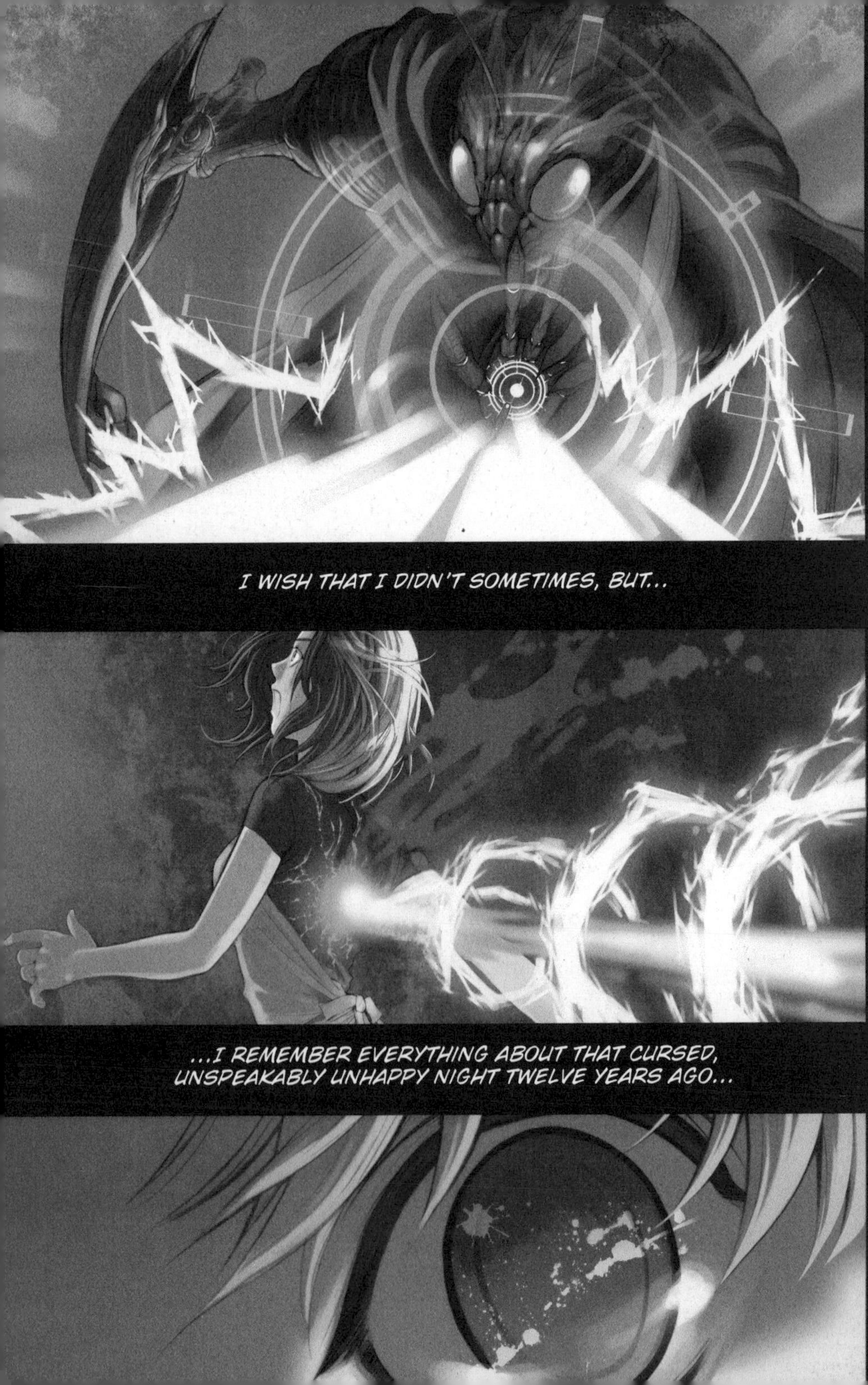
I WISH THAT I DIDN'T SOMETIMES, BUT...
...I REMEMBER EVERYTHING ABOUT THAT CURSED, UNSPEAKABLY UNHAPPY NIGHT TWELVE YEARS AGO...

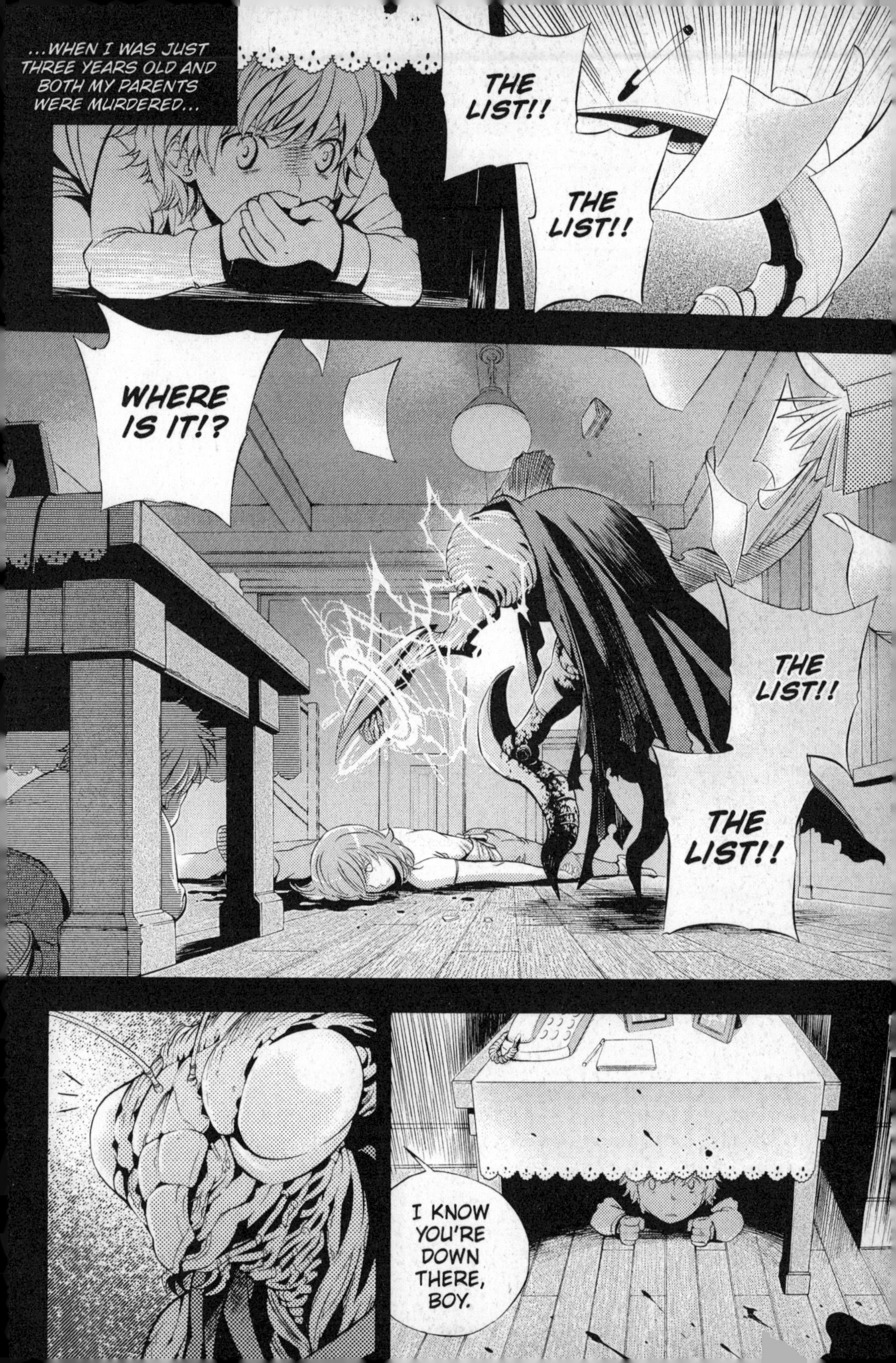
...WHEN I WAS JUST THREE YEARS OLD AND BOTH MY PARENTS WERE MURDERED...
THE LIST!!
THE LIST!!
WHERE IS IT!?
THE LIST!!
THE LIST!!
I KNOW YOU'RE DOWN THERE, BOY.

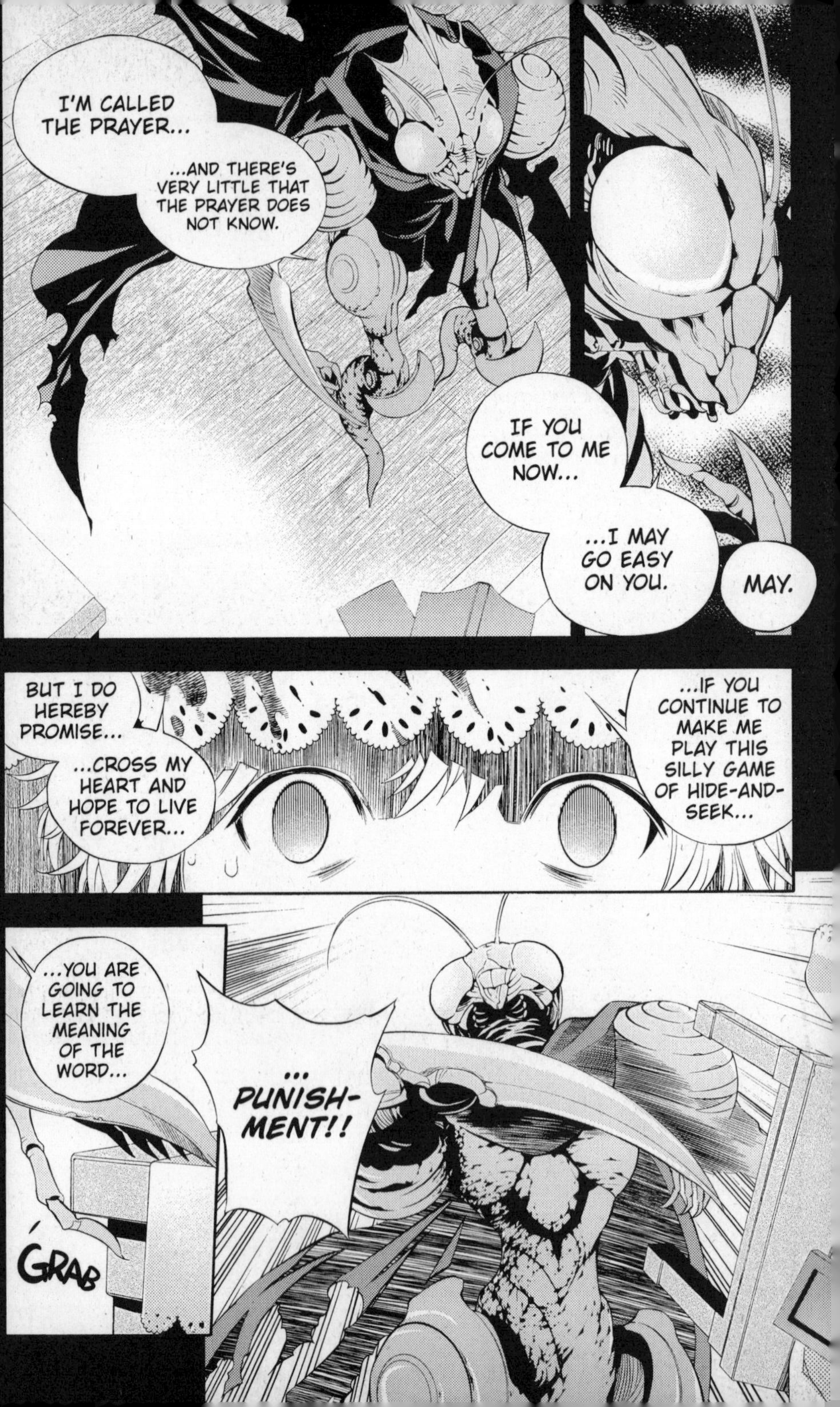
I'M CALLED THE PRAYER...
...AND THERE'S VERY LITTLE THAT THE PRAYER DOES NOT KNOW.
IF YOU COME TO ME NOW...
...I MAY GO EASY ON YOU.
MAY.
BUT I DO HEREBY PROMISE...
...CROSS MY HEART AND HOPE TO LIVE FOREVER...
...IF YOU CONTINUE TO MAKE ME PLAY THIS SILLY GAME OF HIDE-AND-SEEK...
...YOU ARE GOING TO LEARN THE MEANING OF THE WORD...
... PUNISH-MENT!!
GRAB

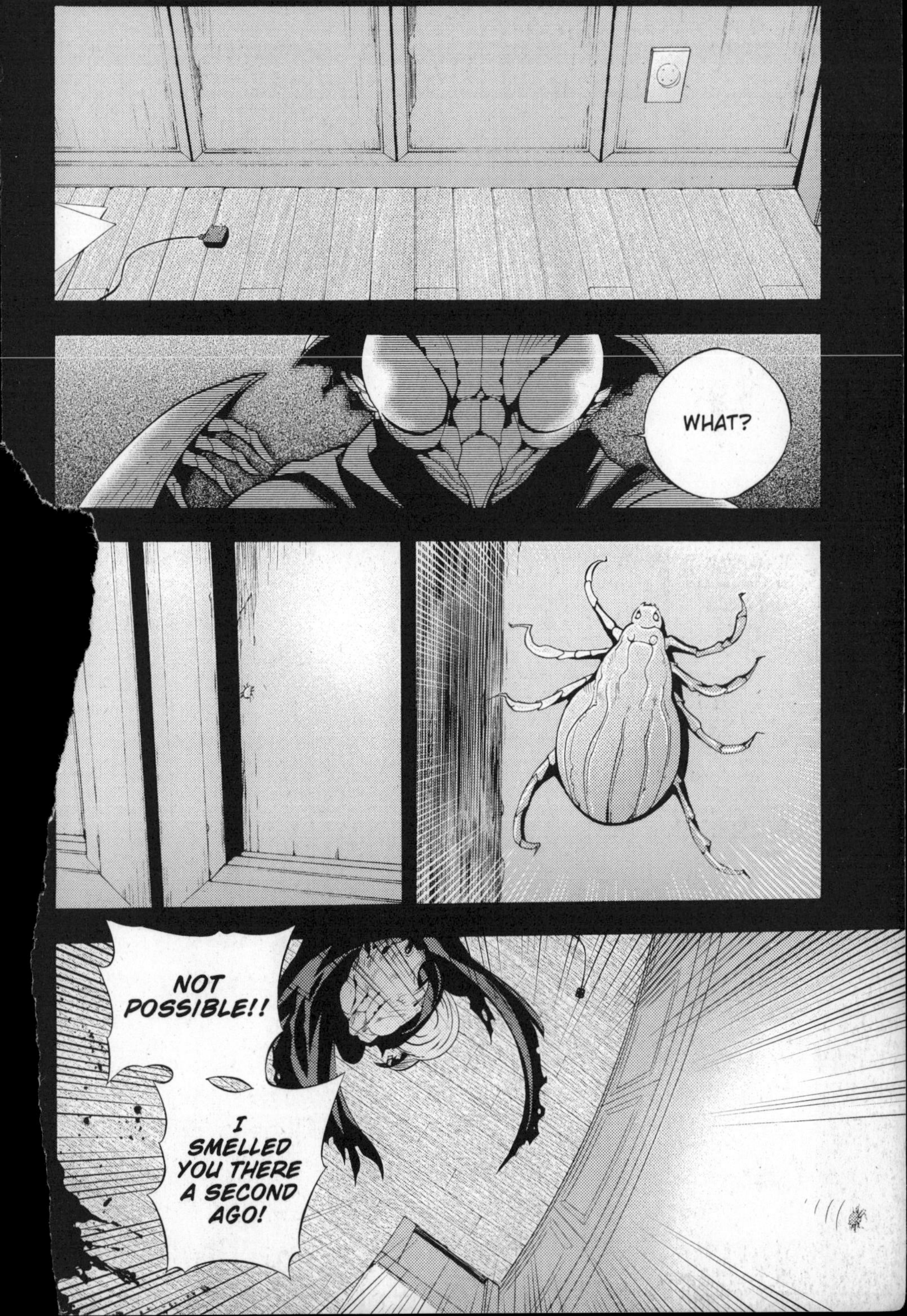
WHAT?
NOT POSSIBLE!!
I SMELLED YOU THERE A SECOND AGO!

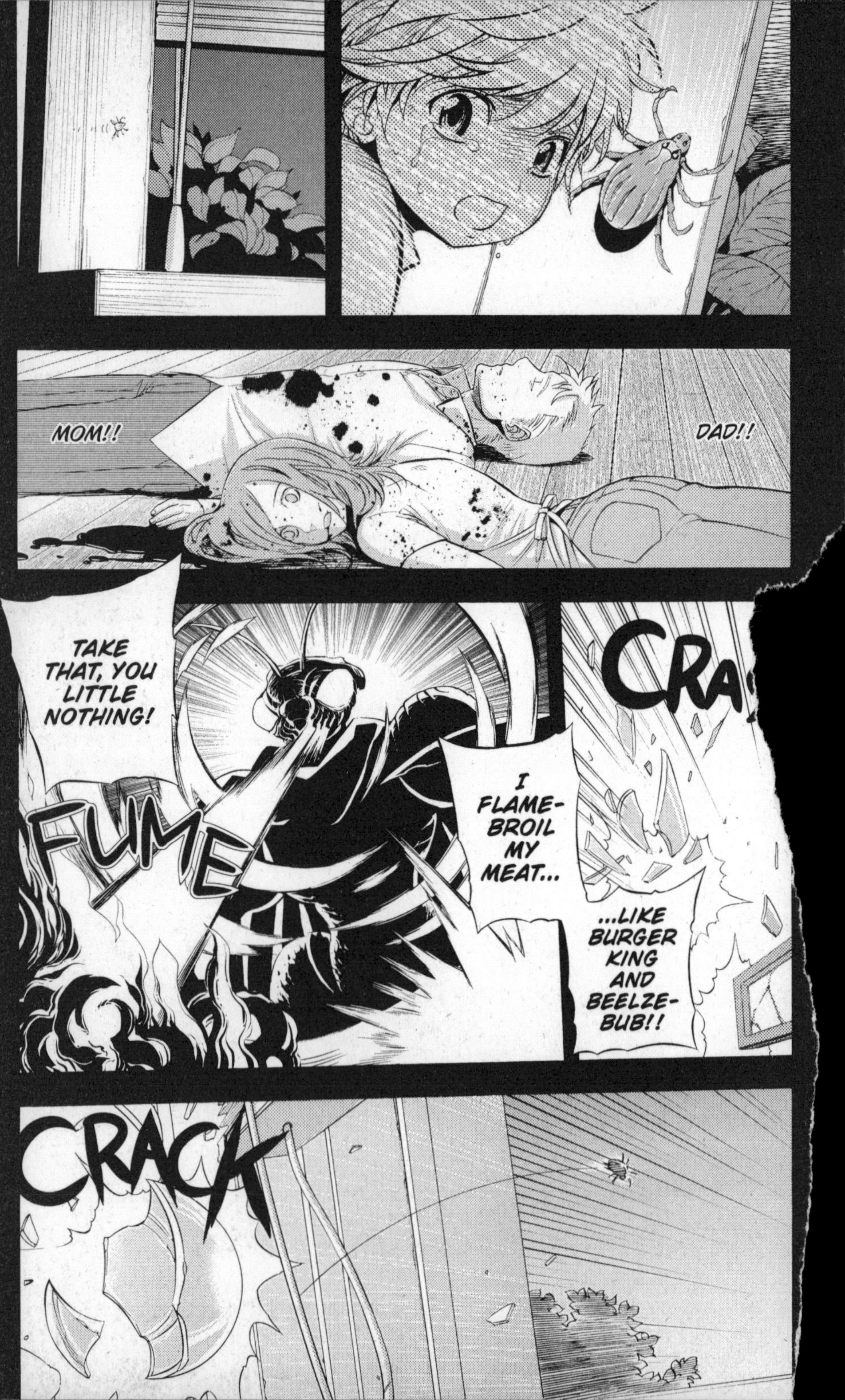
MOM!!
DAD!!
TAKE THAT, YOU LITTLE NOTHING!
FUME
I FLAME-BROIL MY MEAT...
CRA
...LIKE BURGER KING AND BEELZE-BUB!!
CRACK

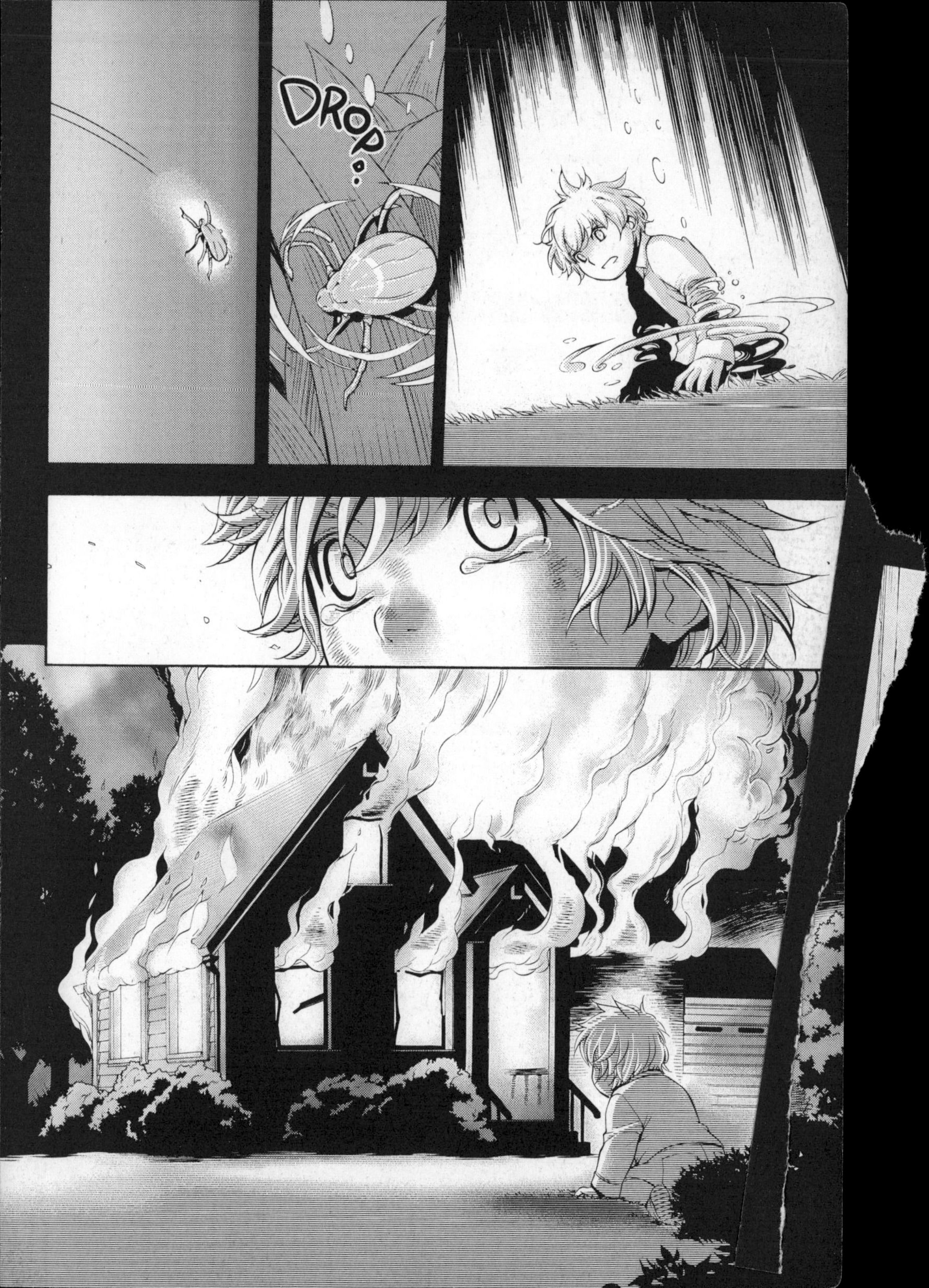
DROP..

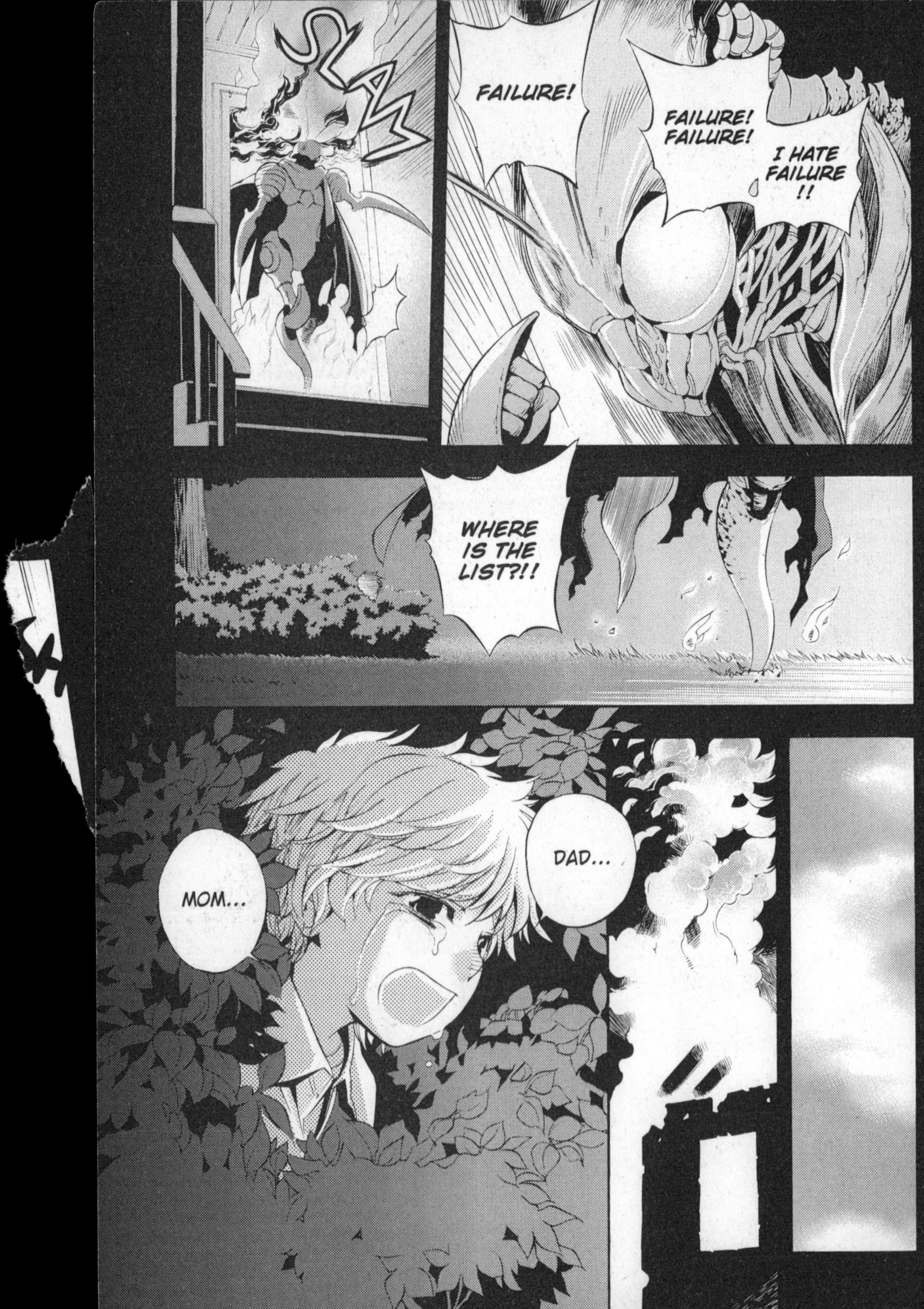
SLAM
FAILURE!
FAILURE! FAILURE!
I HATE FAILURE !!
WHERE IS THE LIST?!!
MOM...
DAD...

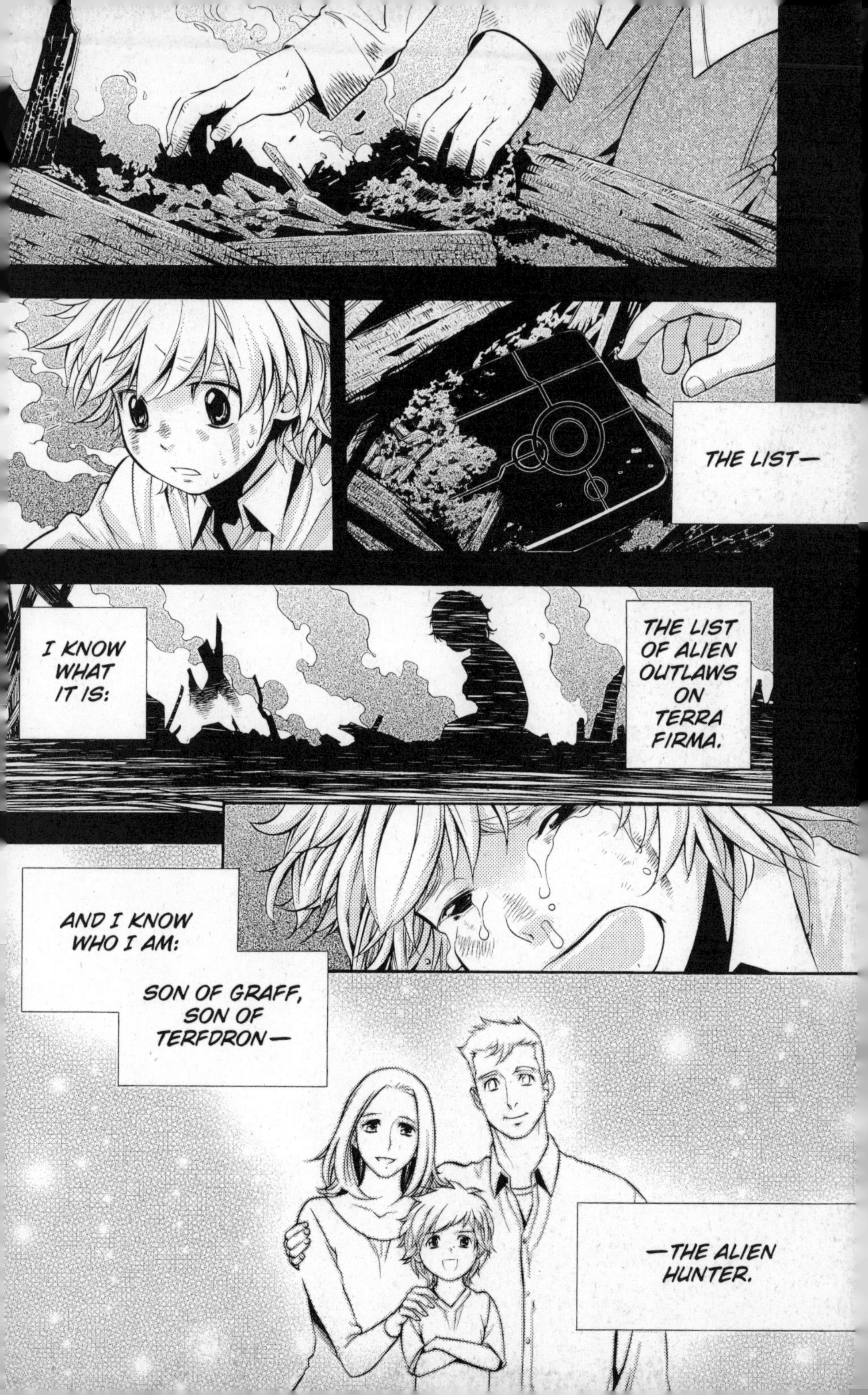
THE LIST—
I KNOW WHAT IT IS:
THE LIST OF ALIEN OUTLAWS ON TERRA FIRMA.
AND I KNOW WHO I AM:
SON OF GRAFF, SON OF TERFDRON—
—THE ALIEN HUNTER.

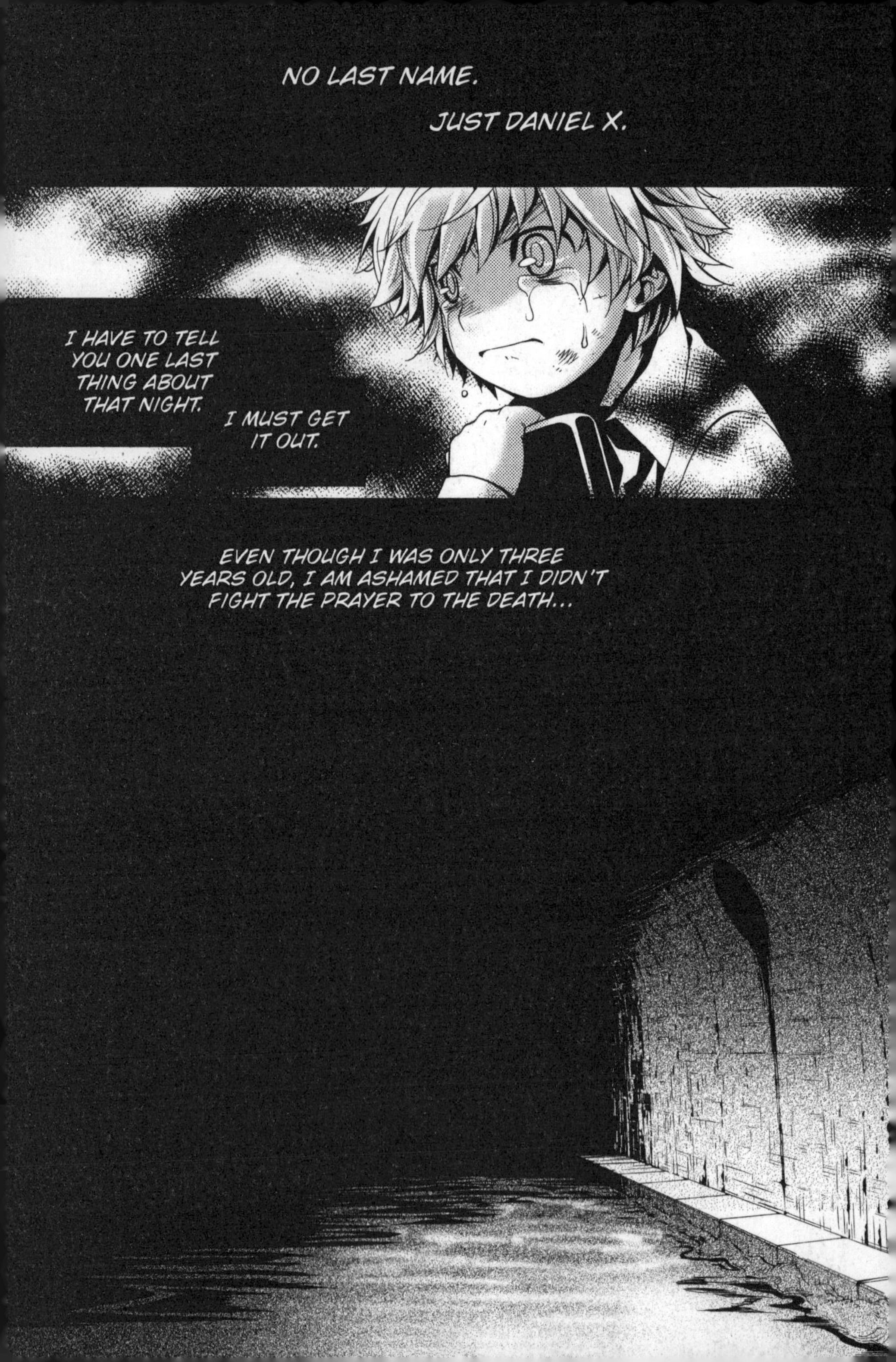
NO LAST NAME.
JUST DANIEL X.
I HAVE TO TELL YOU ONE LAST THING ABOUT THAT NIGHT.
I MUST GET IT OUT.
EVEN THOUGH I WAS ONLY THREE YEARS OLD, I AM ASHAMED THAT I DIDN'T FIGHT THE PRAYER TO THE DEATH...

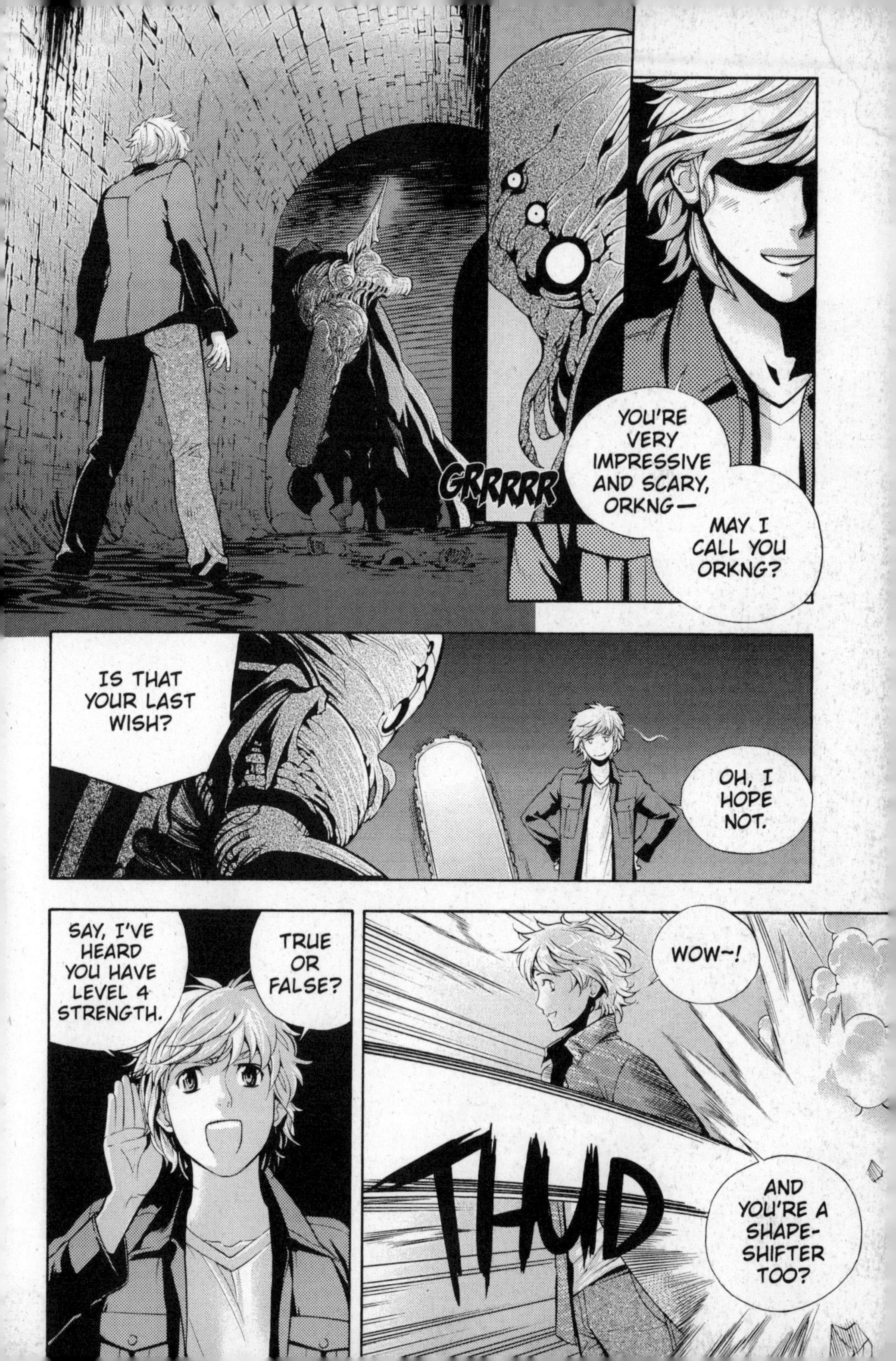
GRRRRR
YOU'RE VERY IMPRESSIVE AND SCARY, ORKNG—
MAY I CALL YOU ORKNG?
IS THAT YOUR LAST WISH?
OH, I HOPE NOT.
SAY, I'VE HEARD YOU HAVE LEVEL 4 STRENGTH.
TRUE OR FALSE?
WOW~!
THUD
AND YOU'RE A SHAPE-SHIFTER TOO?

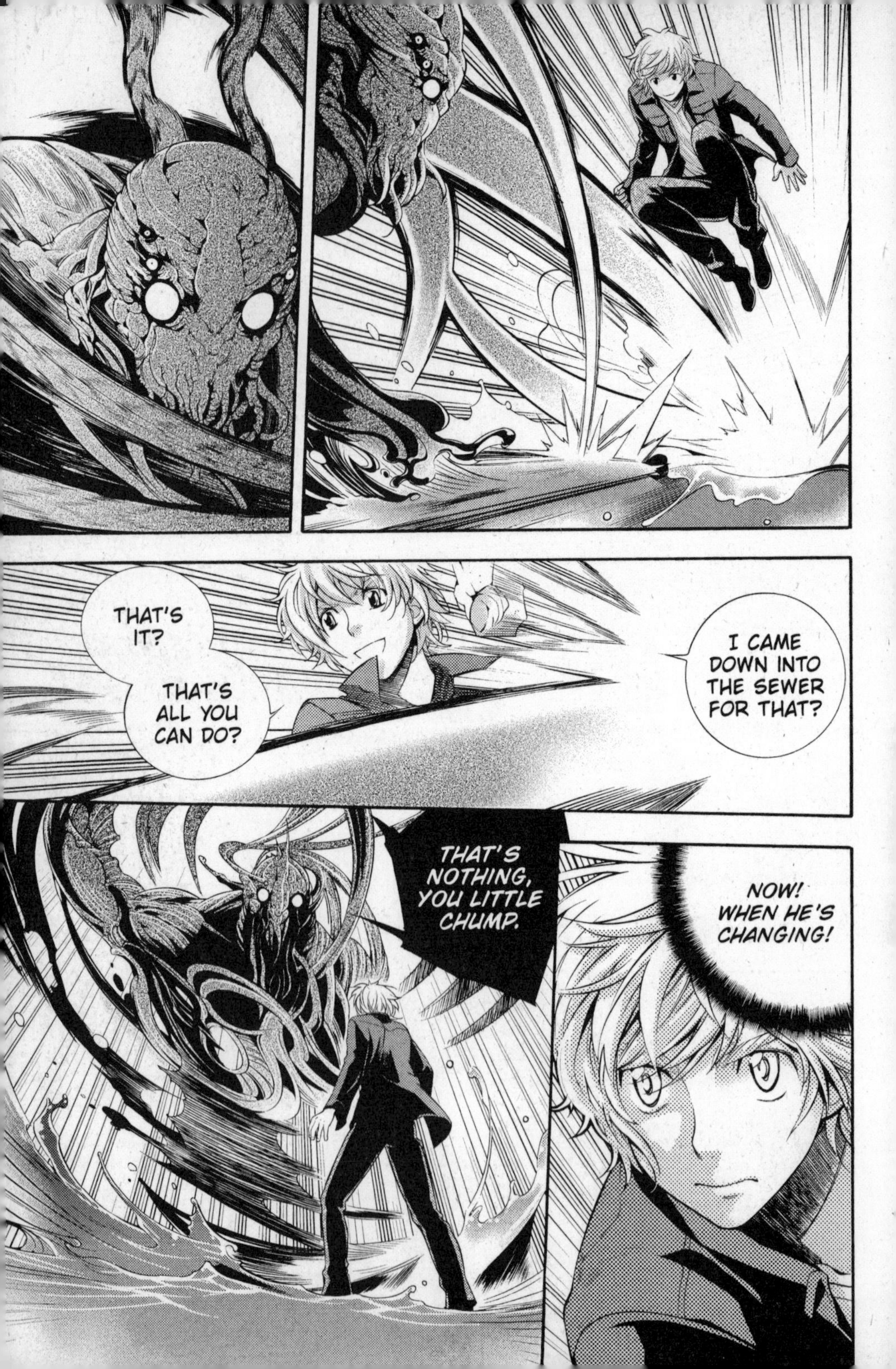
THAT'S IT?
THAT'S ALL YOU CAN DO?
I CAME DOWN INTO THE SEWER FOR THAT?
THAT'S NOTHING, YOU LITTLE CHUMP.
NOW! WHEN HE'S CHANGING!

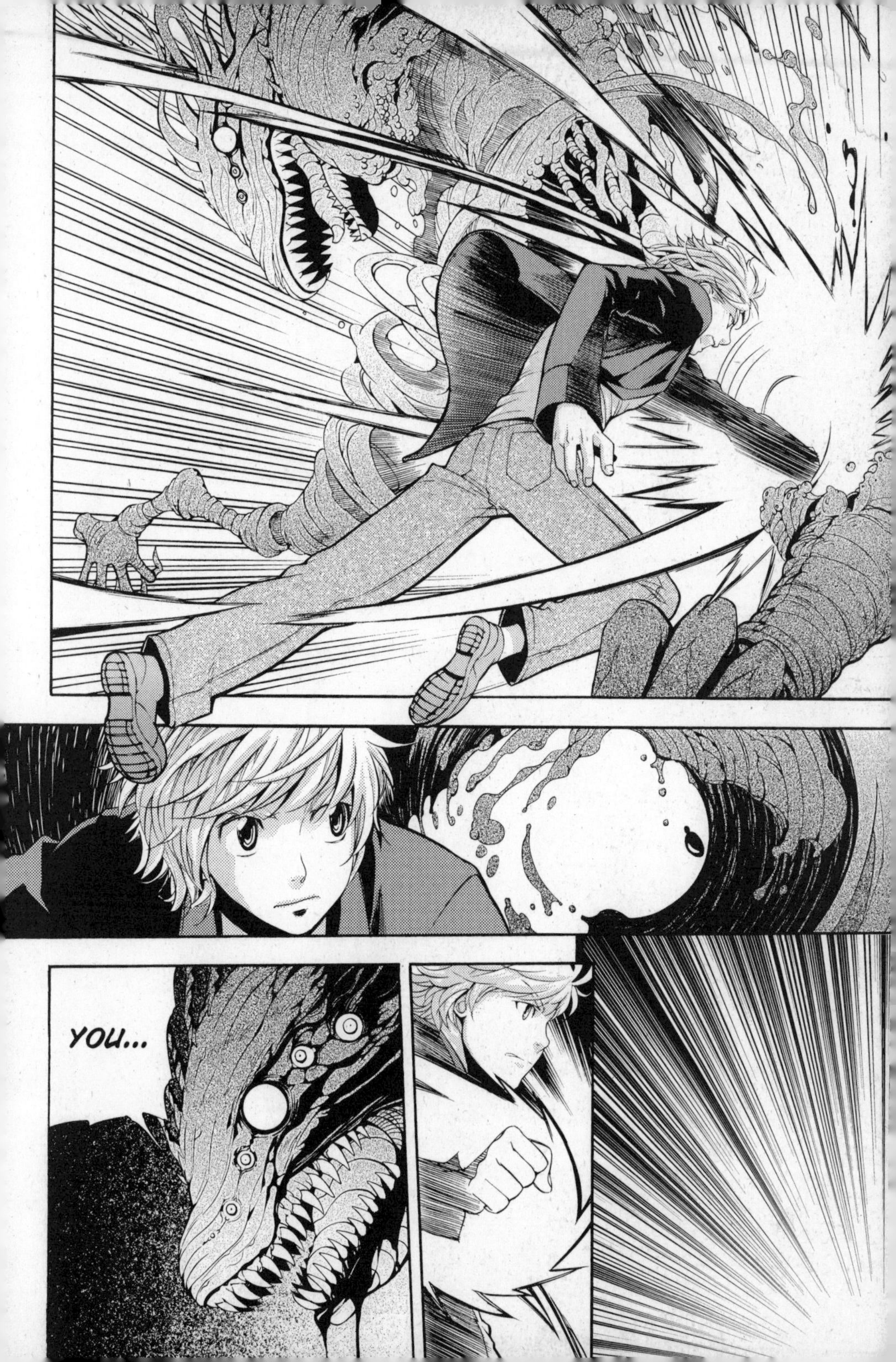
YOU...

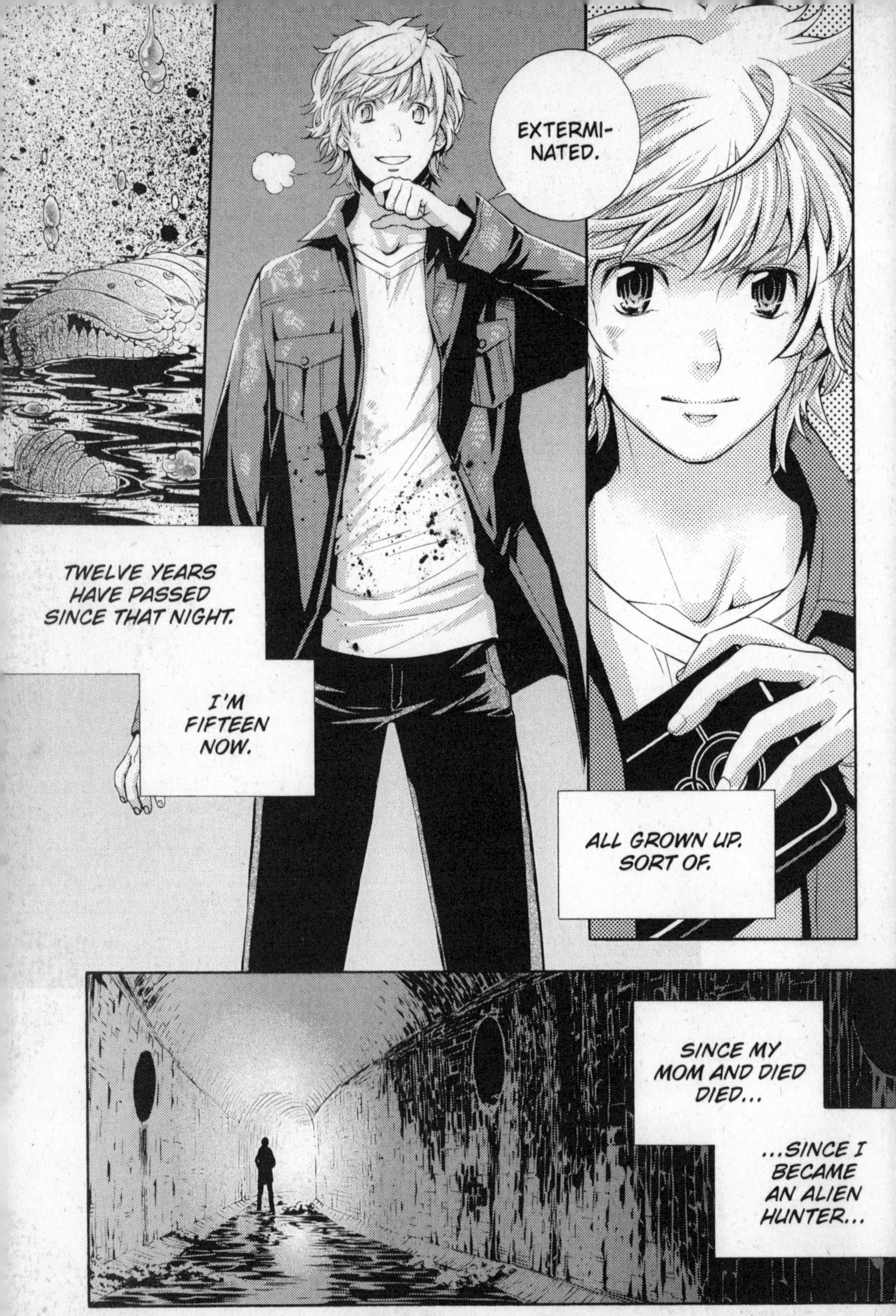
EXTERMI-NATED.
TWELVE YEARS HAVE PASSED SINCE THAT NIGHT.
I'M FIFTEEN NOW.
ALL GROWN UP. SORT OF.
SINCE MY MOM AND DIED DIED...
...SINCE I BECAME AN ALIEN HUNTER...

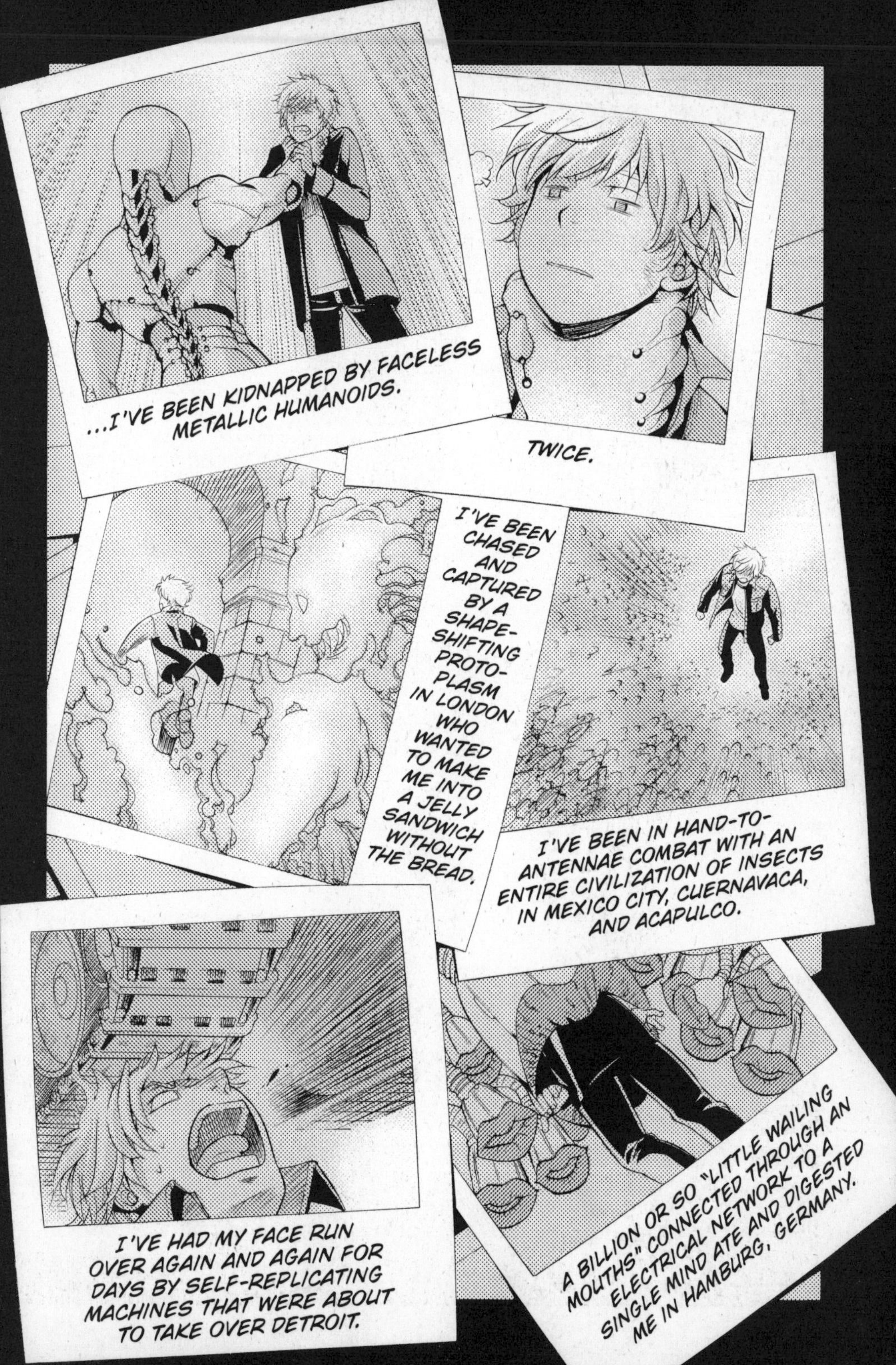

...I'VE BEEN KIDNAPPED BY FACELESS METALLIC HUMANOIDS.
TWICE.
I'VE BEEN CHASED AND CAPTURED BY A SHAPE-SHIFTING PROTO-PLASM IN LONDON WHO WANTED TO MAKE ME INTO A JELLY SANDWICH WITHOUT THE BREAD.
I'VE BEEN IN HAND-TO-ANTENNAE COMBAT WITH AN ENTIRE CIVILIZATION OF INSECTS IN MEXICO CITY, CUERNAVACA, AND ACAPULCO.
I'VE HAD MY FACE RUN OVER AGAIN AND AGAIN FOR DAYS BY SELF-REPLICATING MACHINES THAT WERE ABOUT TO TAKE OVER DETROIT.
A BILLION OR SO "LITTLE WAILING MOUTHS" CONNECTED THROUGH AN ELECTRICAL NETWORK TO A SINGLE MIND ATE AND DIGESTED ME IN HAMBURG, GERMANY.

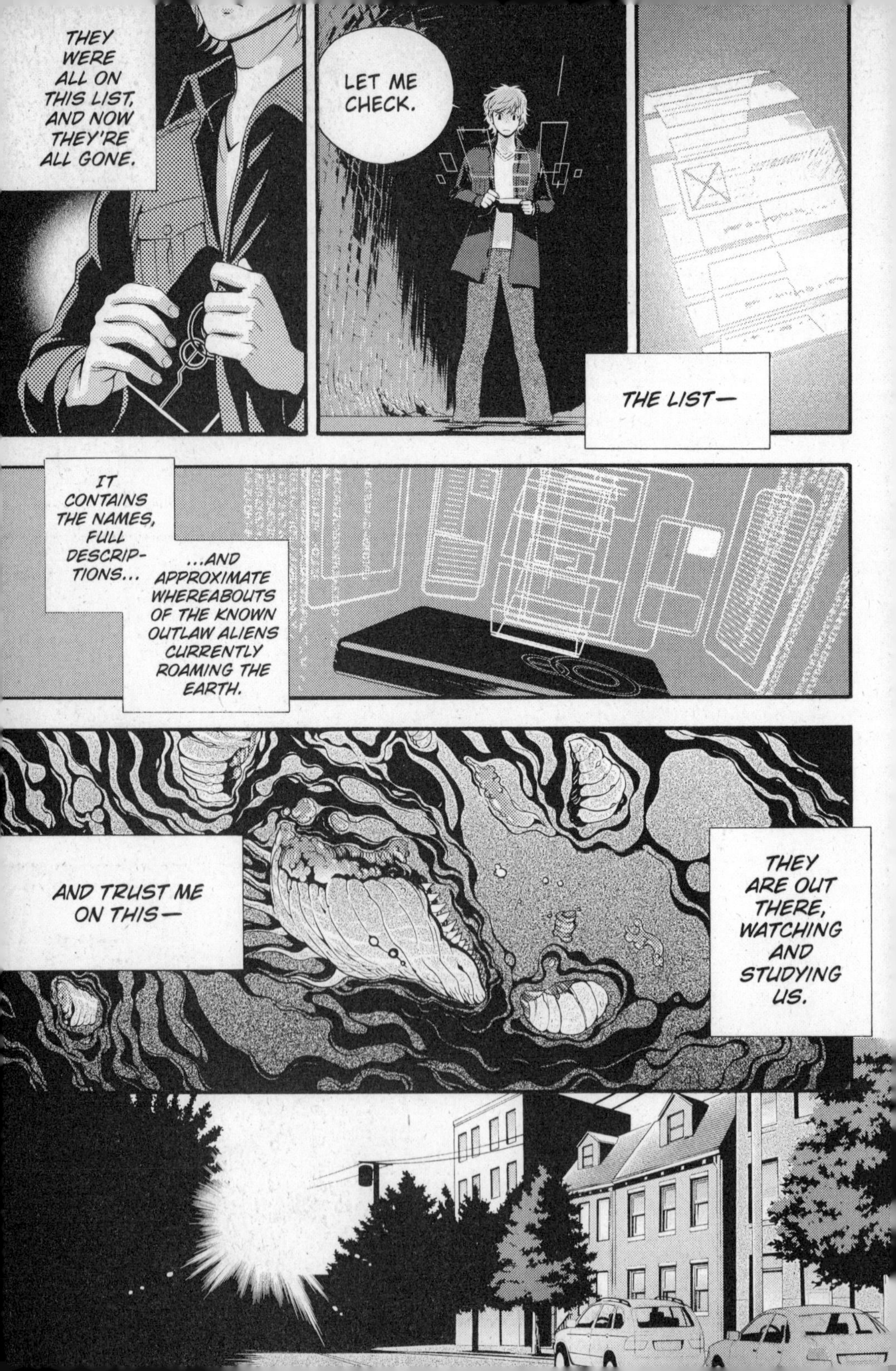
THEY WERE ALL ON THIS LIST, AND NOW THEY'RE ALL GONE.
LET ME CHECK.
THE LIST—
IT CONTAINS THE NAMES, FULL DESCRIP-TIONS...
...AND APPROXIMATE WHEREABOUTS OF THE KNOWN OUTLAW ALIENS CURRENTLY ROAMING THE EARTH.
AND TRUST ME ON THIS—
THEY ARE OUT THERE, WATCHING AND STUDYING US.

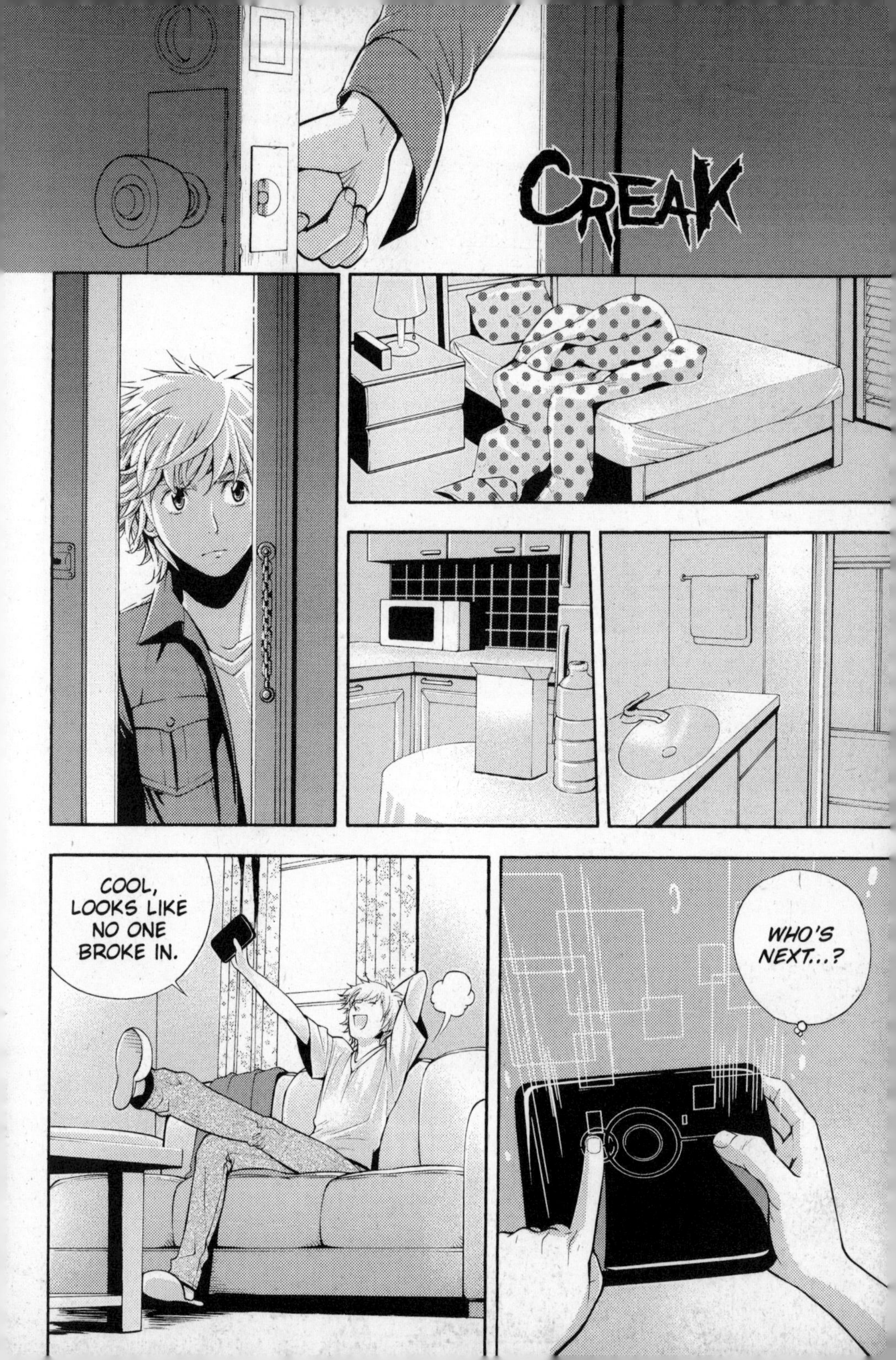
CREAK
COOL, LOOKS LIKE NO ONE BROKE IN.
WHO'S NEXT...?

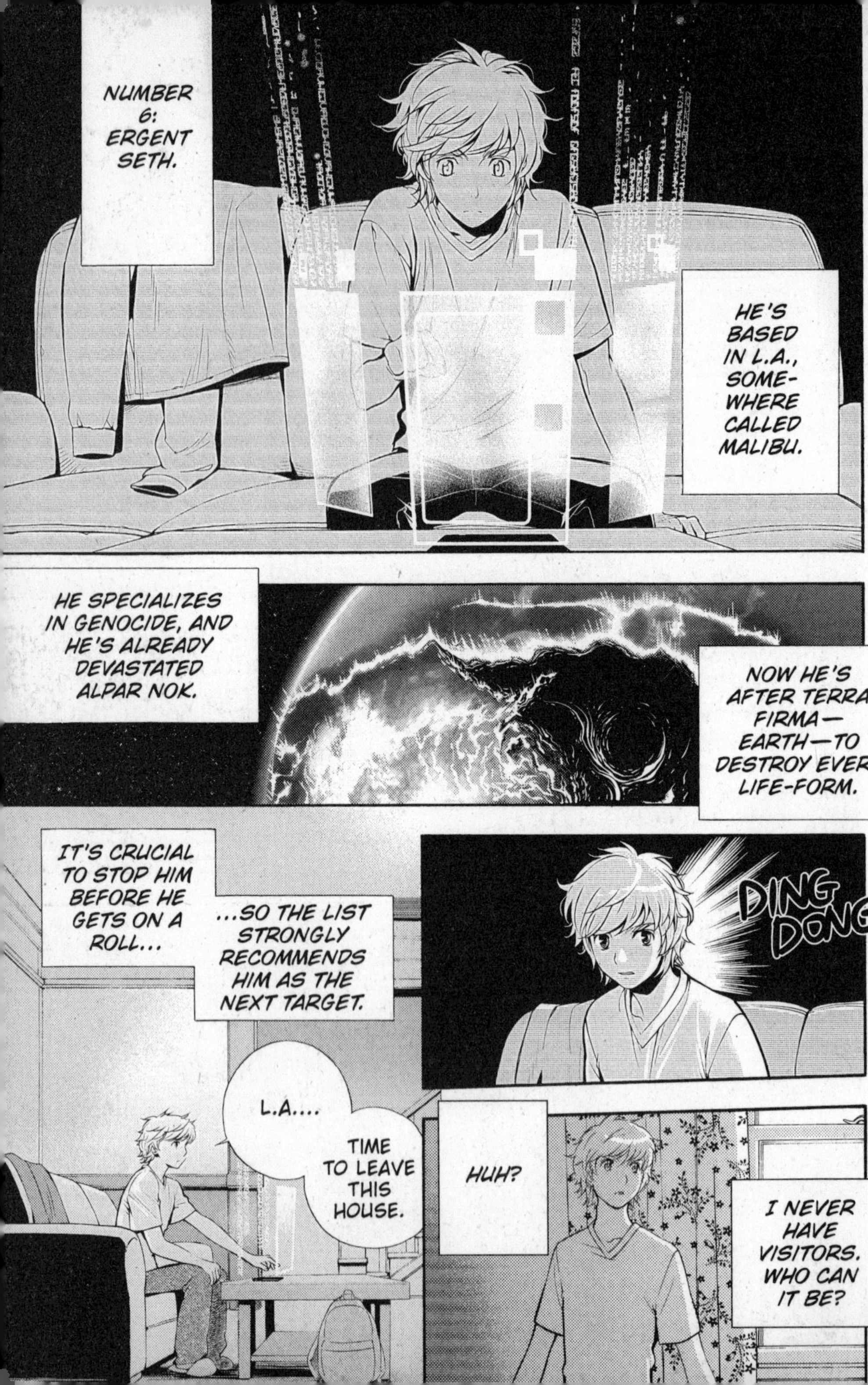
NUMBER 6: ERGENT SETH.
HE'S BASED IN L.A., SOME-WHERE CALLED MALIBU.
HE SPECIALIZES IN GENOCIDE, AND HE'S ALREADY DEVASTATED ALPAR NOK.
NOW HE'S AFTER TERRA FIRMA—EARTH—TO DESTROY EVERY LIFE-FORM.
IT'S CRUCIAL TO STOP HIM BEFORE HE GETS ON A ROLL...
...SO THE LIST STRONGLY RECOMMENDS HIM AS THE NEXT TARGET.
L.A....
TIME TO LEAVE THIS HOUSE.
DING DONG..
HUH?
I NEVER HAVE VISITORS. WHO CAN IT BE?

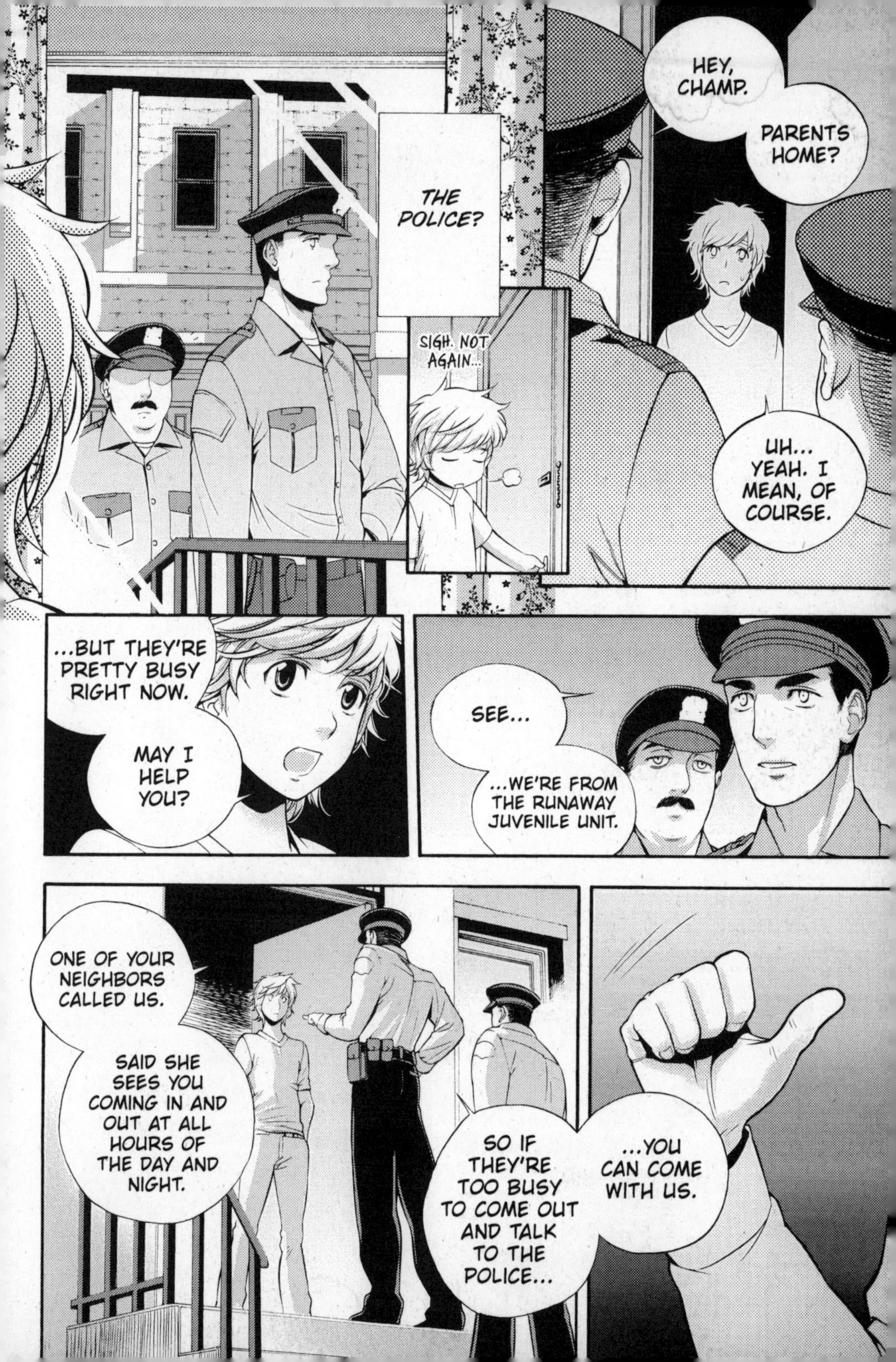
THE POLICE?
SIGH. NOT AGAIN...
HEY, CHAMP.
PARENTS HOME?
UH... YEAH. I MEAN, OF COURSE.
...BUT THEY'RE PRETTY BUSY RIGHT NOW.
MAY I HELP YOU?
SEE...
...WE'RE FROM THE RUNAWAY JUVENILE UNIT.
ONE OF YOUR NEIGHBORS CALLED US.
SAID SHE SEES YOU COMING IN AND OUT AT ALL HOURS OF THE DAY AND NIGHT.
SO IF THEY'RE TOO BUSY TO COME OUT AND TALK TO THE POLICE...
...YOU CAN COME WITH US.

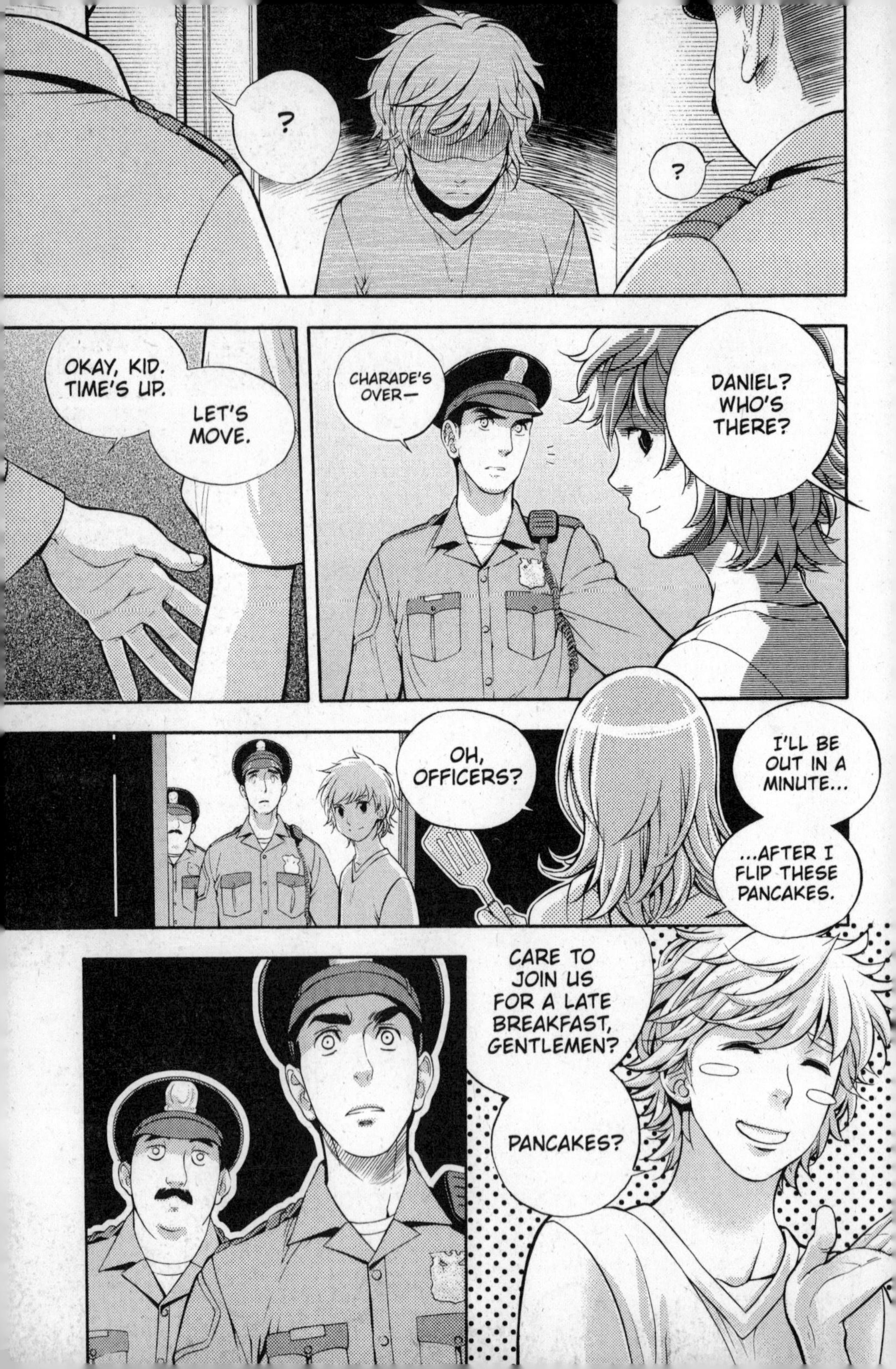
?
?
OKAY, KID. TIME'S UP.
LET'S MOVE.
CHARADE'S OVER—
DANIEL? WHO'S THERE?
OH, OFFICERS?
I'LL BE OUT IN A MINUTE...
...AFTER I FLIP THESE PANCAKES.
CARE TO JOIN US FOR A LATE BREAKFAST, GENTLEMEN?
PANCAKES?

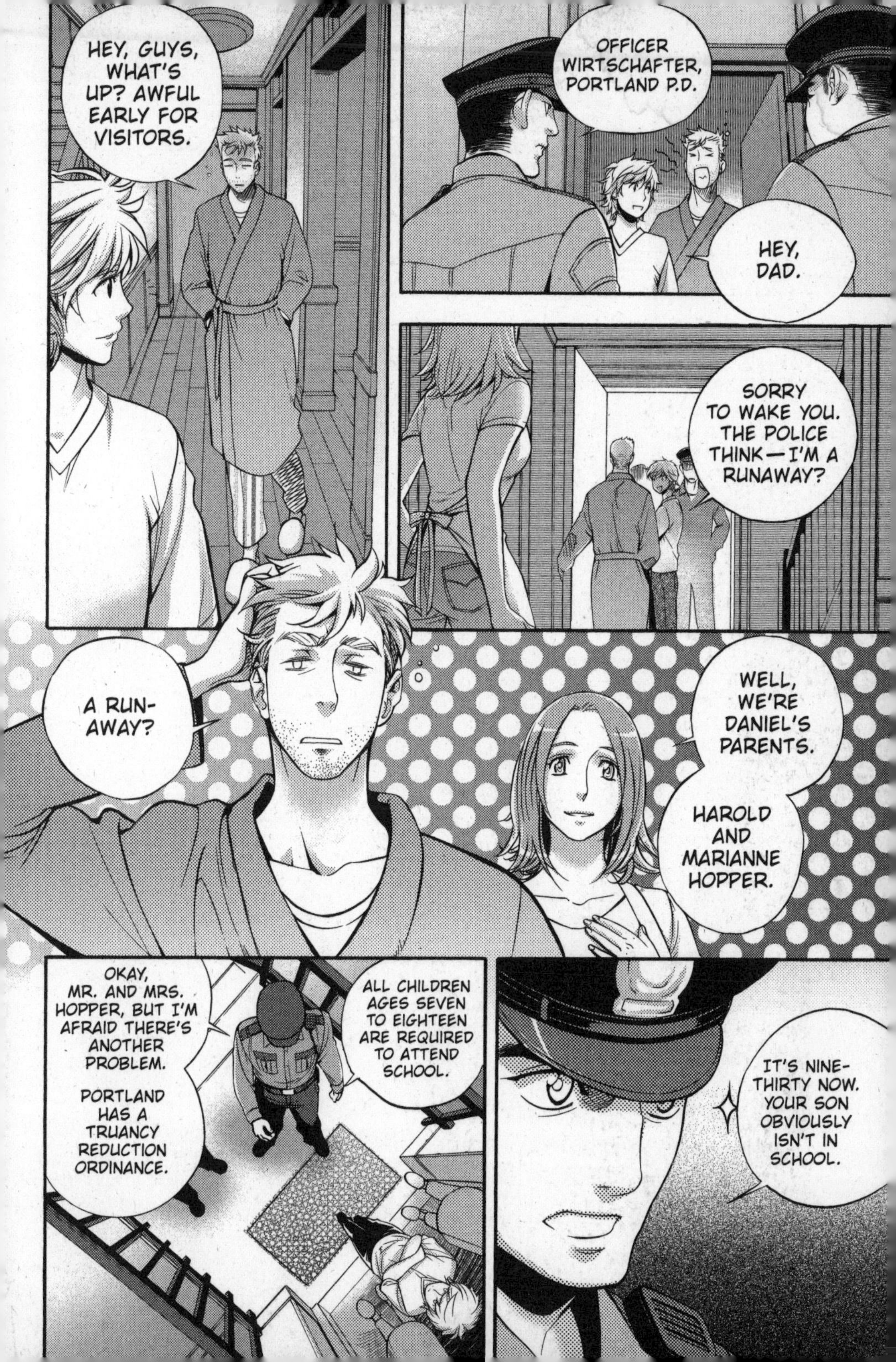
HEY, GUYS, WHAT'S UP? AWFUL EARLY FOR VISITORS.
OFFICER WIRTSCHAFTER, PORTLAND P.D.
HEY, DAD.
SORRY TO WAKE YOU. THE POLICE THINK—I'M A RUNAWAY?
A RUN-AWAY?
WELL, WE'RE DANIEL'S PARENTS.
HAROLD AND MARIANNE HOPPER.
OKAY, MR. AND MRS. HOPPER, BUT I'M AFRAID THERE'S ANOTHER PROBLEM.
PORTLAND HAS A TRUANCY REDUCTION ORDINANCE.
ALL CHILDREN AGES SEVEN TO EIGHTEEN ARE REQUIRED TO ATTEND SCHOOL.
IT'S NINE-THIRTY NOW. YOUR SON OBVIOUSLY ISN'T IN SCHOOL.

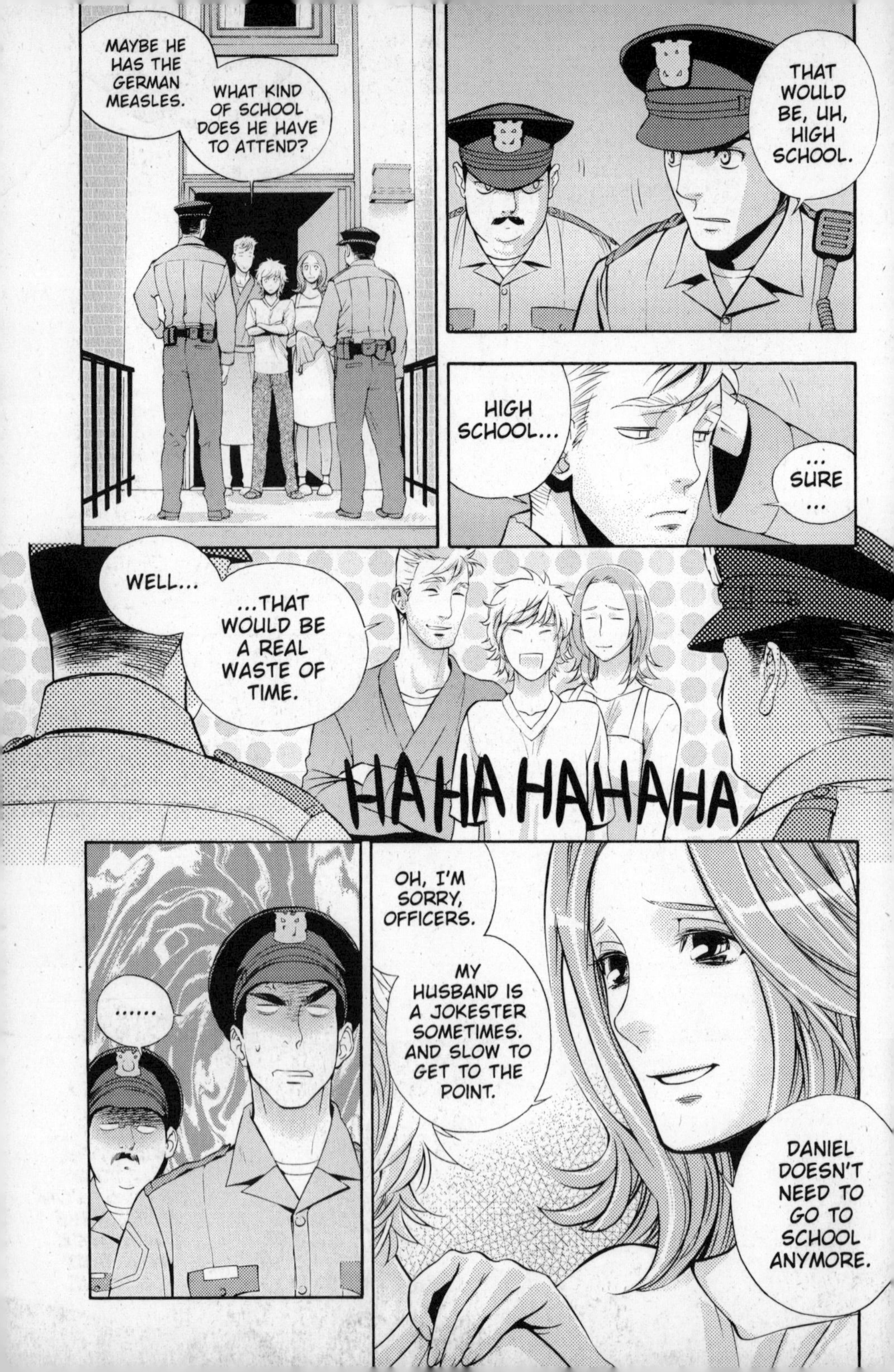

MAYBE HE HAS THE GERMAN MEASLES.
WHAT KIND OF SCHOOL DOES HE HAVE TO ATTEND?
THAT WOULD BE, UH, HIGH SCHOOL.
HIGH SCHOOL...
... SURE ...
WELL...
...THAT WOULD BE A REAL WASTE OF TIME.
HAHAHAHAHAHA
......
OH, I'M SORRY, OFFICERS.
MY HUSBAND IS A JOKESTER SOMETIMES. AND SLOW TO GET TO THE POINT.
DANIEL DOESN'T NEED TO GO TO SCHOOL ANYMORE.

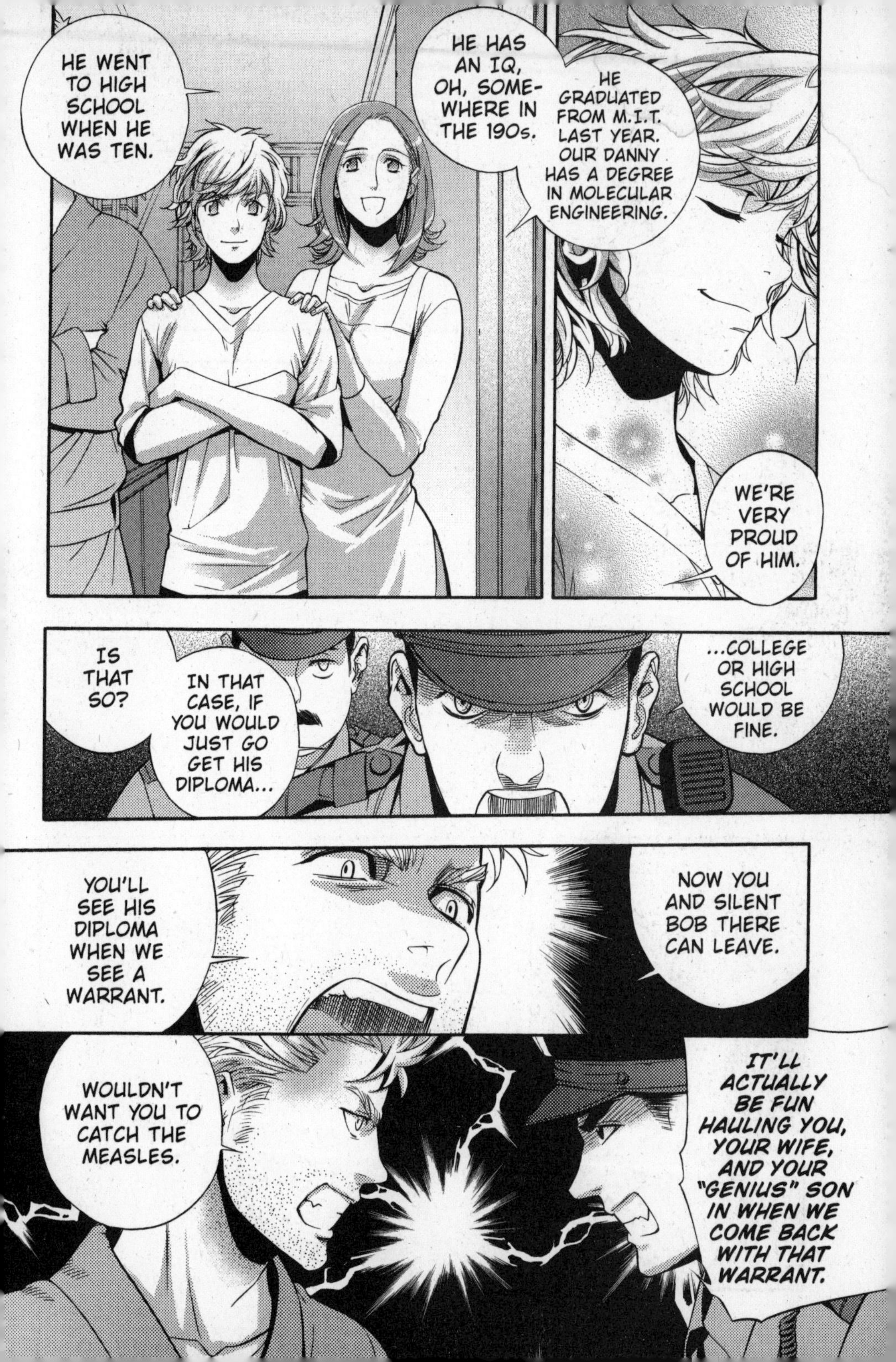
HE WENT TO HIGH SCHOOL WHEN HE WAS TEN.
HE HAS AN IQ, OH, SOME-WHERE IN THE 190s.
HE GRADUATED FROM M.I.T. LAST YEAR. OUR DANNY HAS A DEGREE IN MOLECULAR ENGINEERING.
WE'RE VERY PROUD OF HIM.
IS THAT SO?
IN THAT CASE, IF YOU WOULD JUST GO GET HIS DIPLOMA...
...COLLEGE OR HIGH SCHOOL WOULD BE FINE.
YOU'LL SEE HIS DIPLOMA WHEN WE SEE A WARRANT.
NOW YOU AND SILENT BOB THERE CAN LEAVE.
WOULDN'T WANT YOU TO CATCH THE MEASLES.
IT'LL ACTUALLY BE FUN HAULING YOU, YOUR WIFE, AND YOUR "GENIUS" SON IN WHEN WE COME BACK WITH THAT WARRANT.

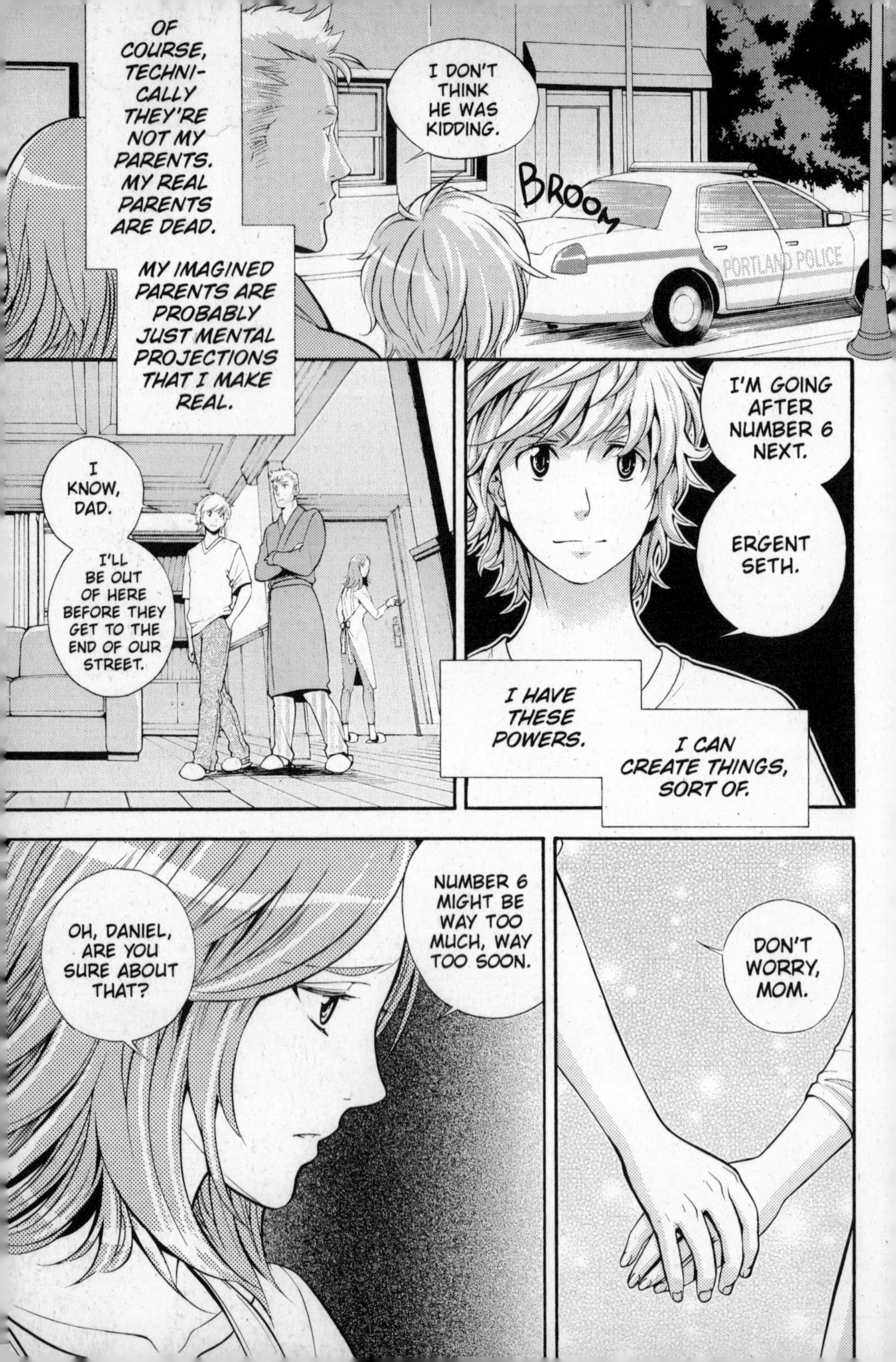
OF COURSE, TECHNICALLY THEY'RE NOT MY PARENTS. MY REAL PARENTS ARE DEAD.
MY IMAGINED PARENTS ARE PROBABLY JUST MENTAL PROJECTIONS THAT I MAKE REAL.
I DON'T THINK HE WAS KIDDING.
BROOM
PORTLAND POLICE
I KNOW, DAD.
I'LL BE OUT OF HERE BEFORE THEY GET TO THE END OF OUR STREET.
I'M GOING AFTER NUMBER 6 NEXT.
ERGENT SETH.
I HAVE THESE POWERS.
I CAN CREATE THINGS, SORT OF.
OH, DANIEL, ARE YOU SURE ABOUT THAT?
NUMBER 6 MIGHT BE WAY TOO MUCH, WAY TOO SOON.
DON'T WORRY, MOM.

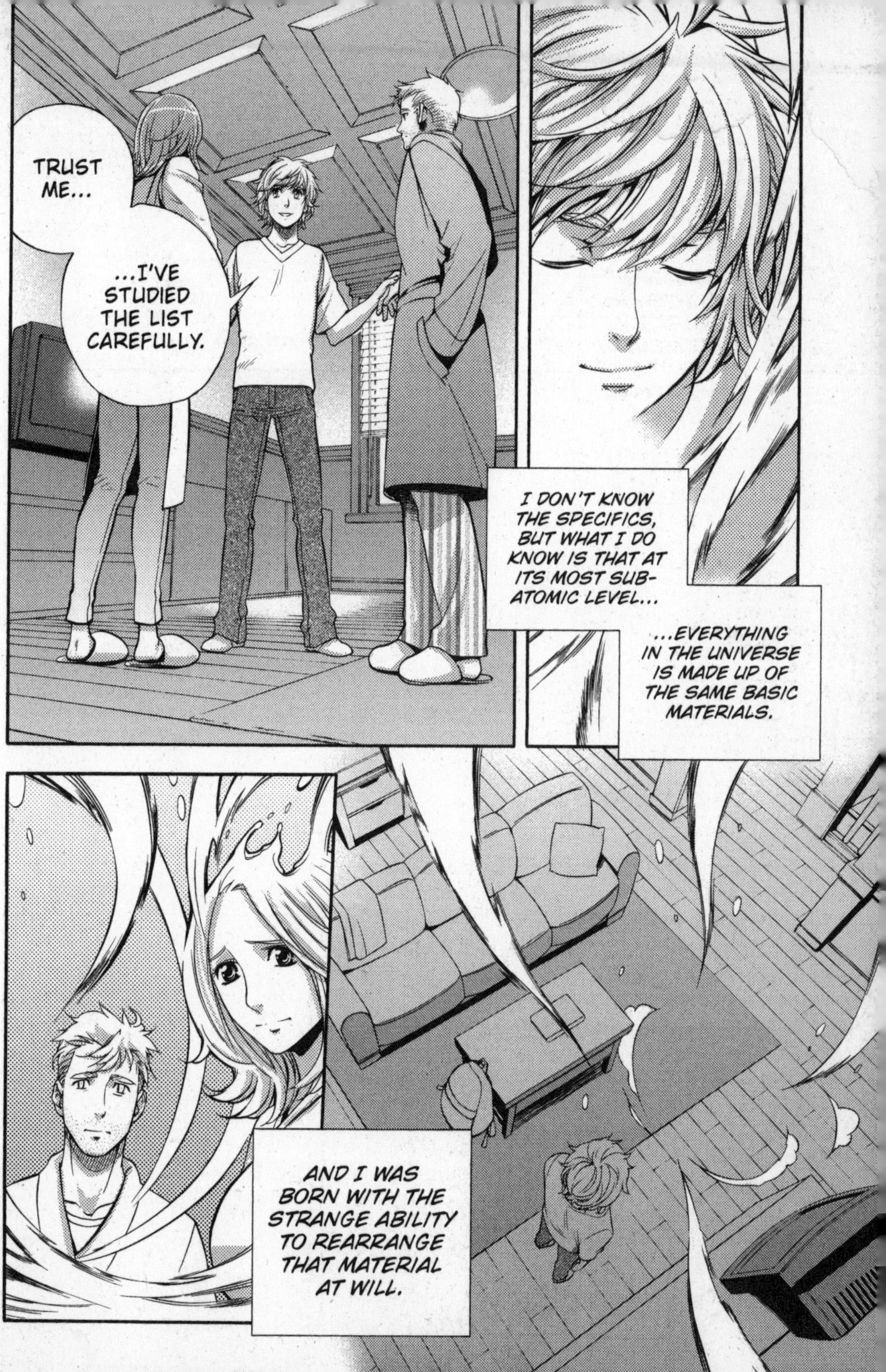
TRUST ME...
...I'VE STUDIED THE LIST CAREFULLY.
I DON'T KNOW THE SPECIFICS, BUT WHAT I DO KNOW IS THAT AT ITS MOST SUB-ATOMIC LEVEL...
...EVERYTHING IN THE UNIVERSE IS MADE UP OF THE SAME BASIC MATERIALS.
AND I WAS BORN WITH THE STRANGE ABILITY TO REARRANGE THAT MATERIAL AT WILL.

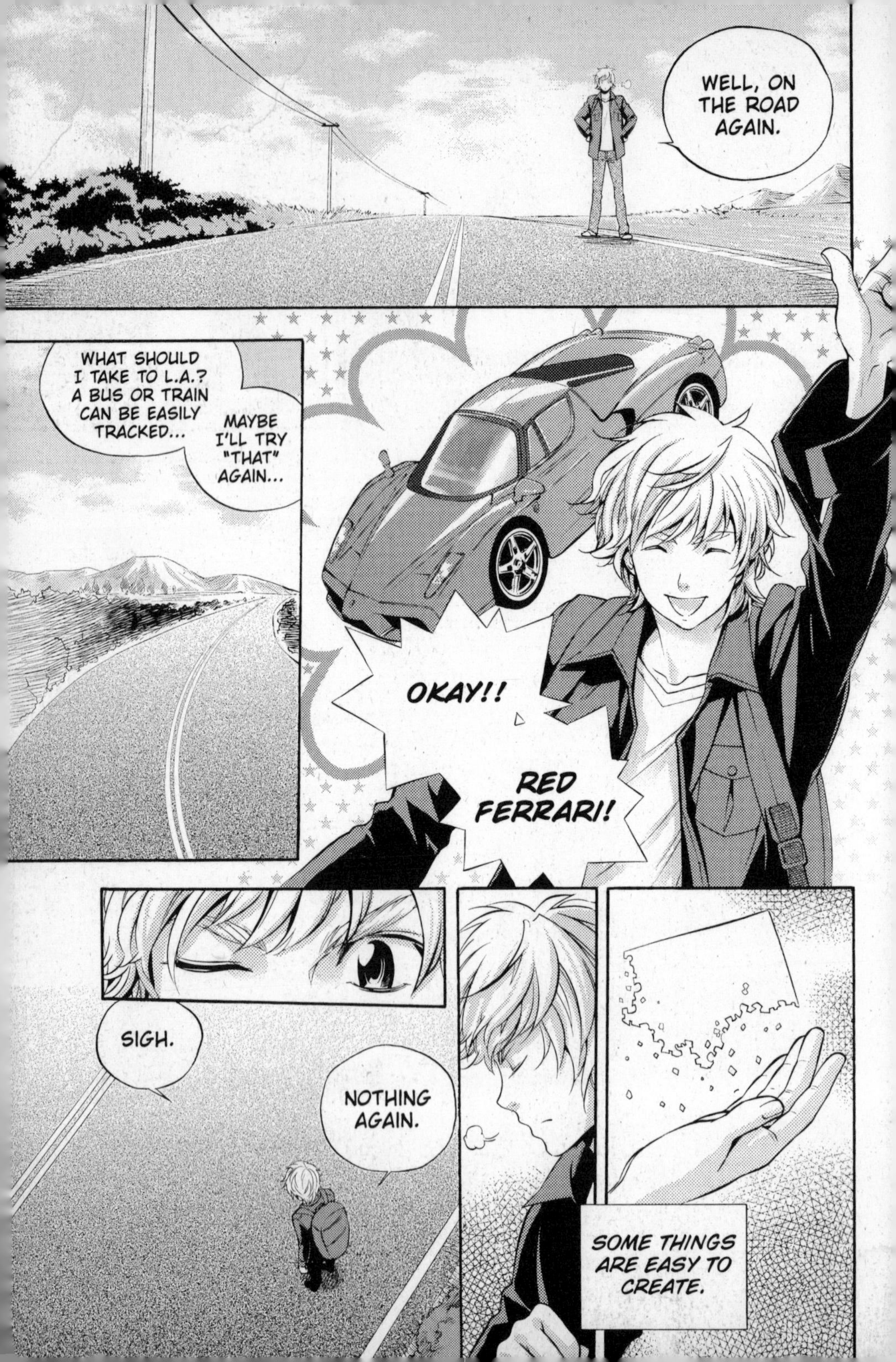
WELL, ON THE ROAD AGAIN.
WHAT SHOULD I TAKE TO L.A.? A BUS OR TRAIN CAN BE EASILY TRACKED...
MAYBE I'LL TRY "THAT" AGAIN...
OKAY!!
RED FERRARI!
SIGH.
NOTHING AGAIN.
SOME THINGS ARE EASY TO CREATE.

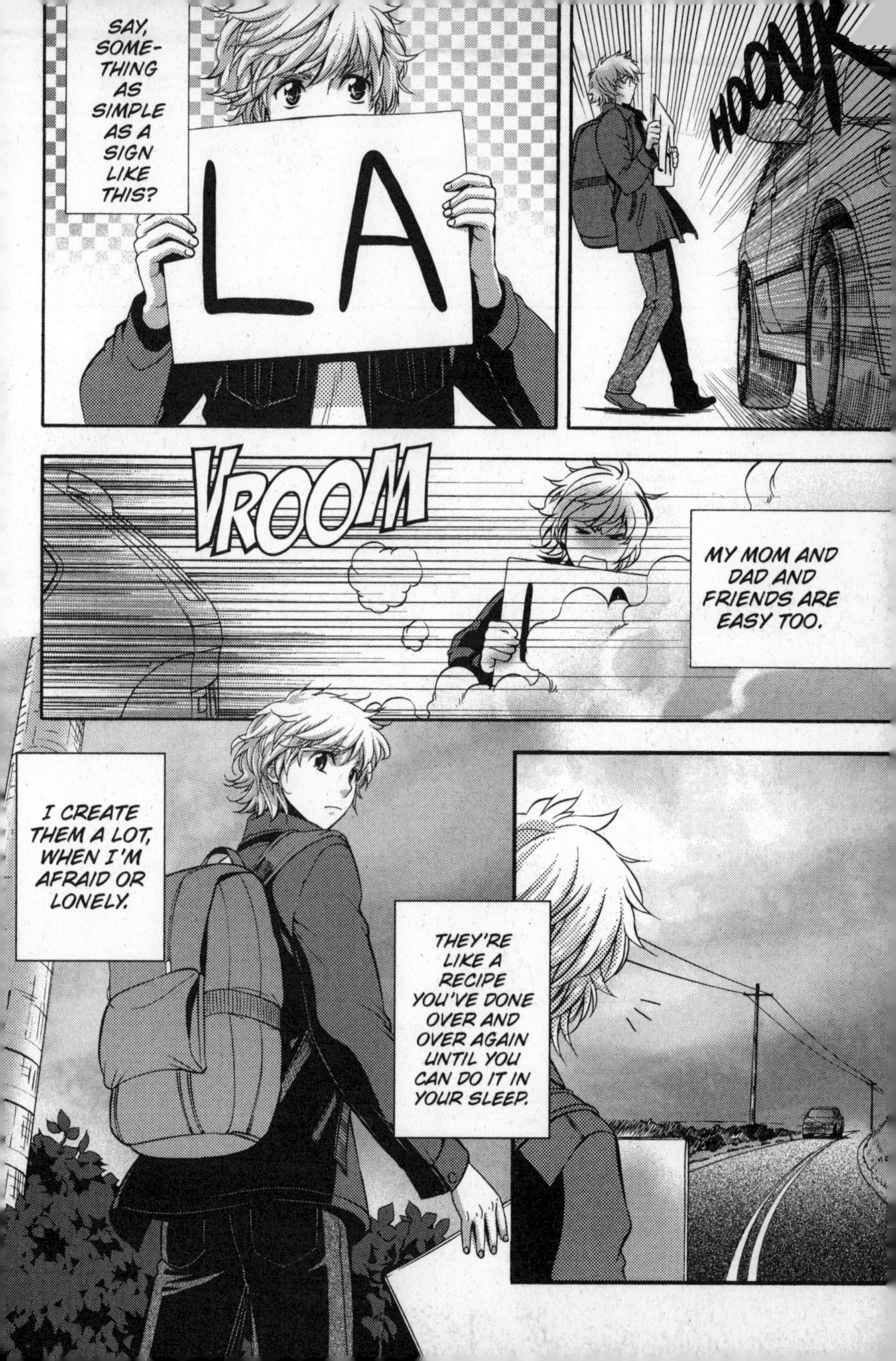
SAY, SOMETHING AS SIMPLE AS A SIGN LIKE THIS?
LA
HOONK
VROOM
MY MOM AND DAD AND FRIENDS ARE EASY TOO.
I CREATE THEM A LOT, WHEN I'M AFRAID OR LONELY.
THEY'RE LIKE A RECIPE YOU'VE DONE OVER AND OVER AGAIN UNTIL YOU CAN DO IT IN YOUR SLEEP.

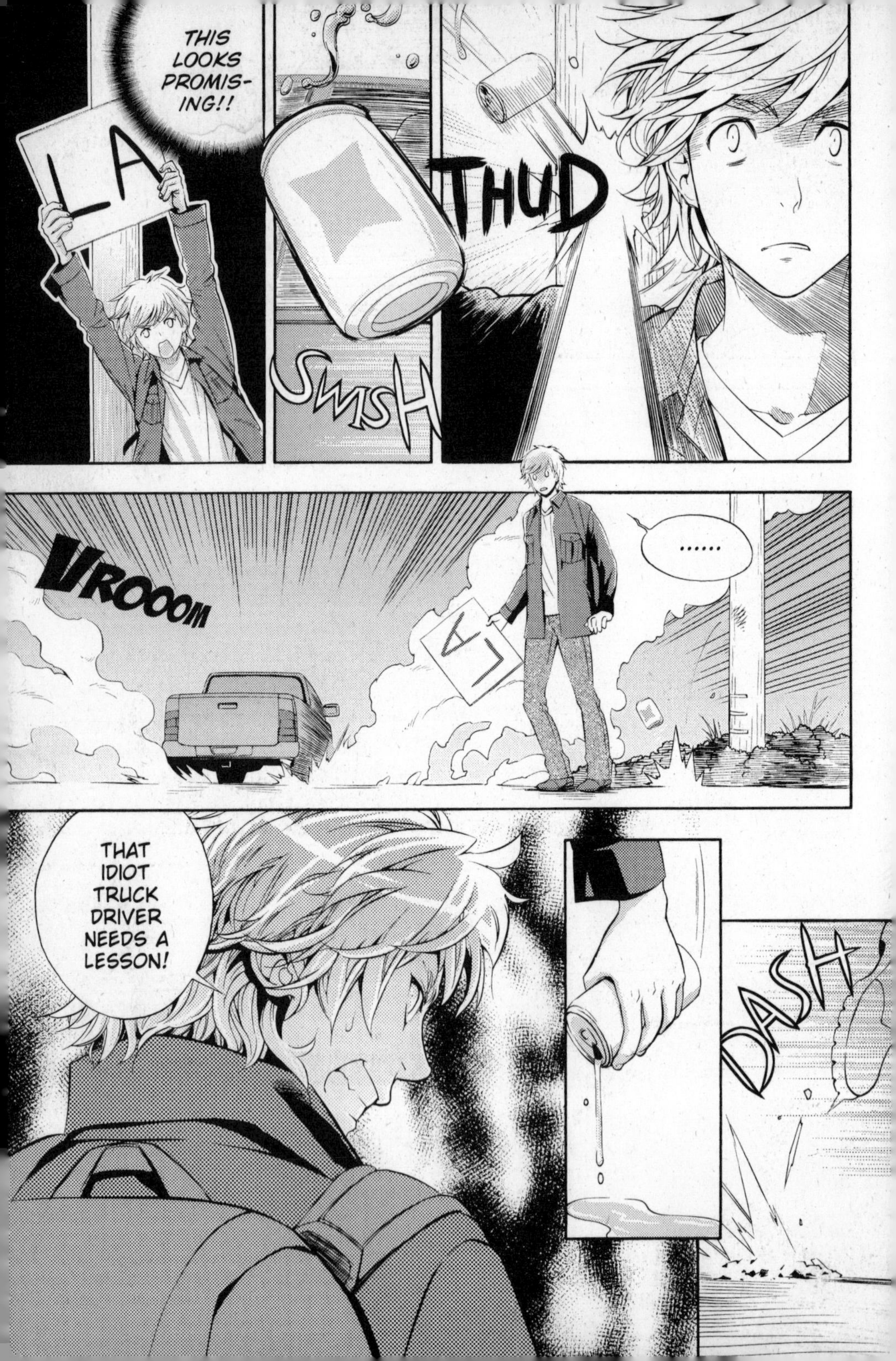
THIS LOOKS PROMIS-ING!!
LA
SWISH
THUD
VROOOM
......
LA
THAT IDIOT TRUCK DRIVER NEEDS A LESSON!
DASH

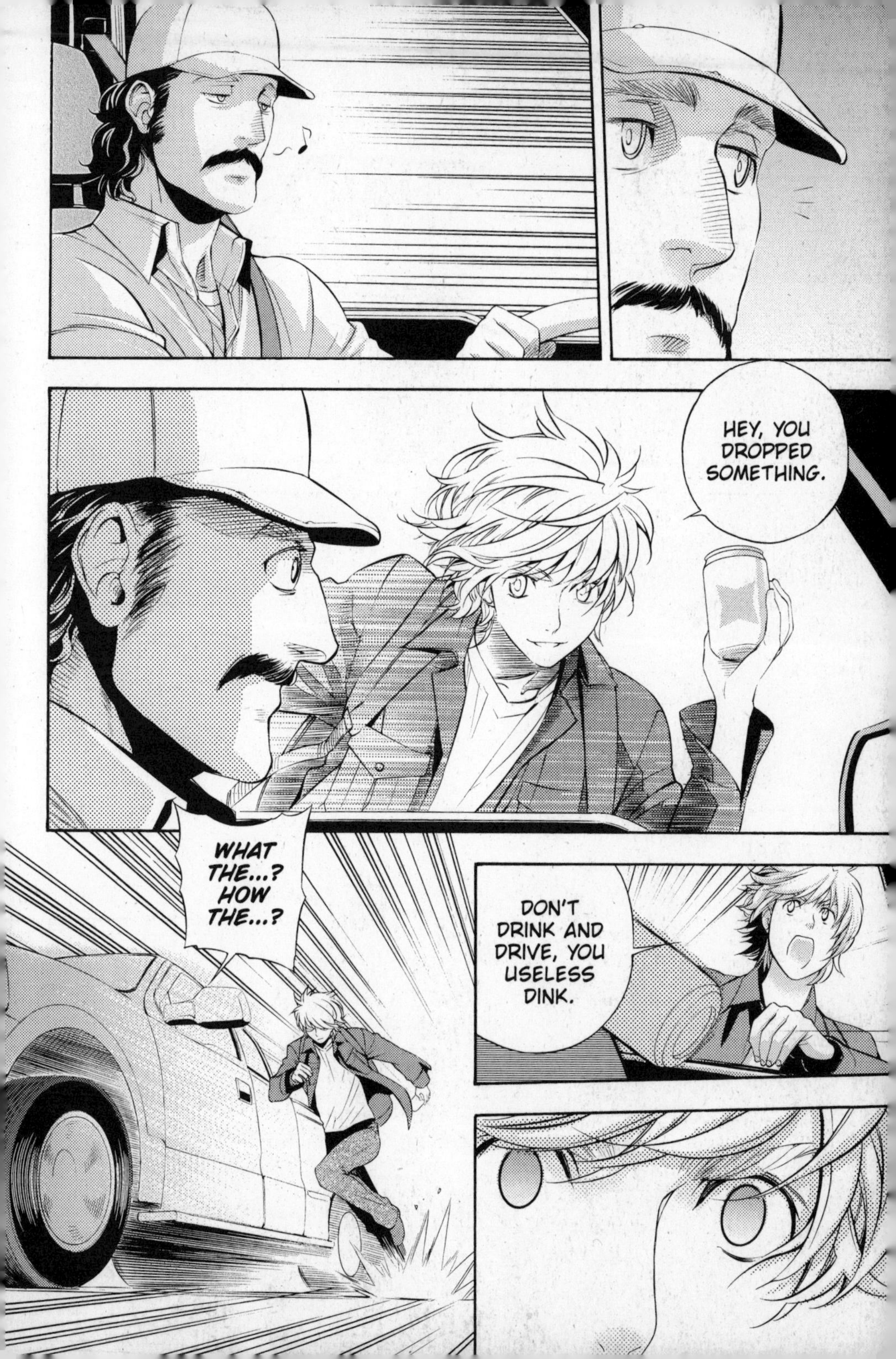
HEY, YOU DROPPED SOMETHING.
WHAT THE...? HOW THE...?
DON'T DRINK AND DRIVE, YOU USELESS DINK.

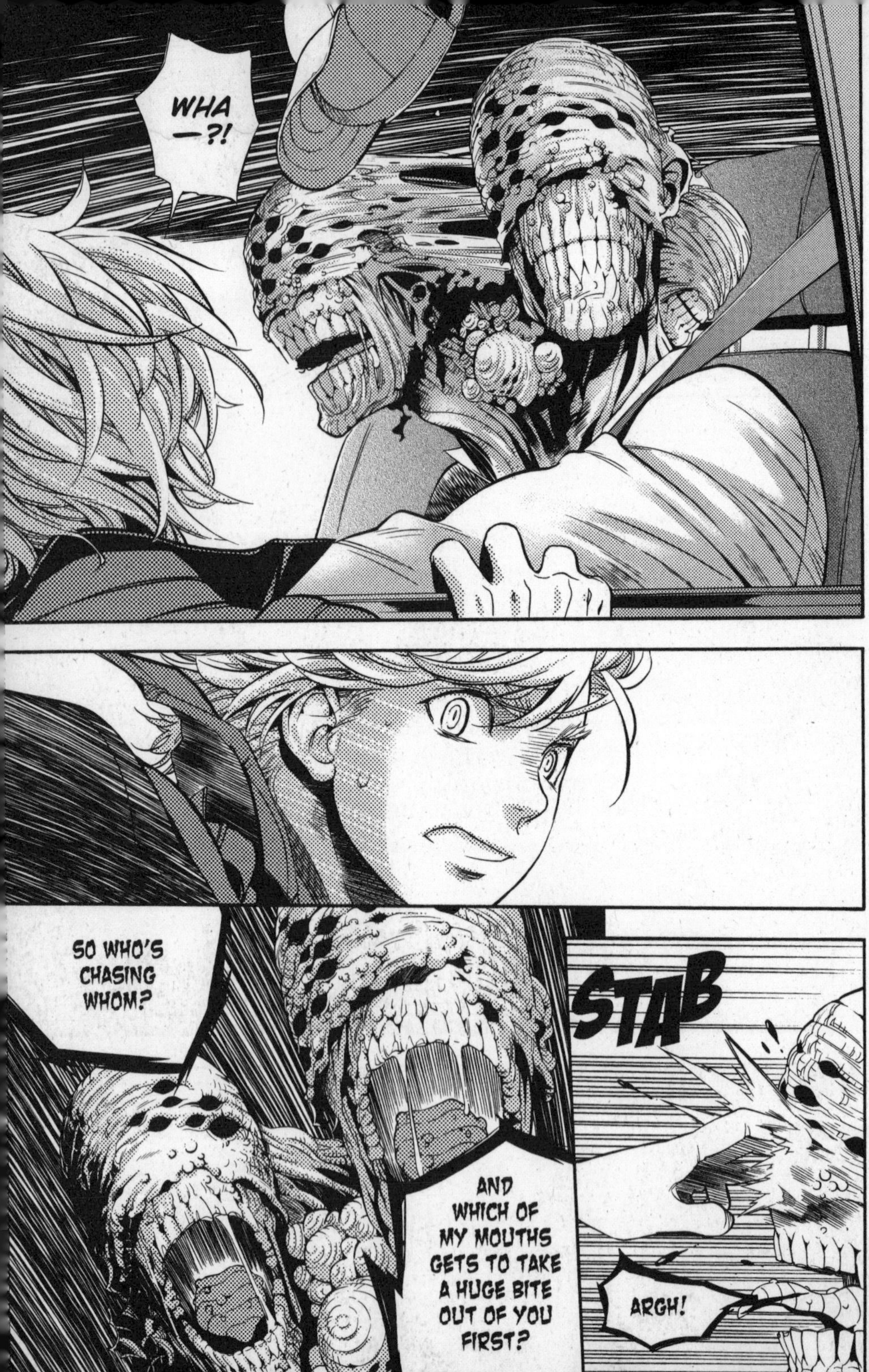
WHA—?!
SO WHO'S CHASING WHOM?
AND WHICH OF MY MOUTHS GETS TO TAKE A HUGE BITE OUT OF YOU FIRST?
STAB
ARGH!

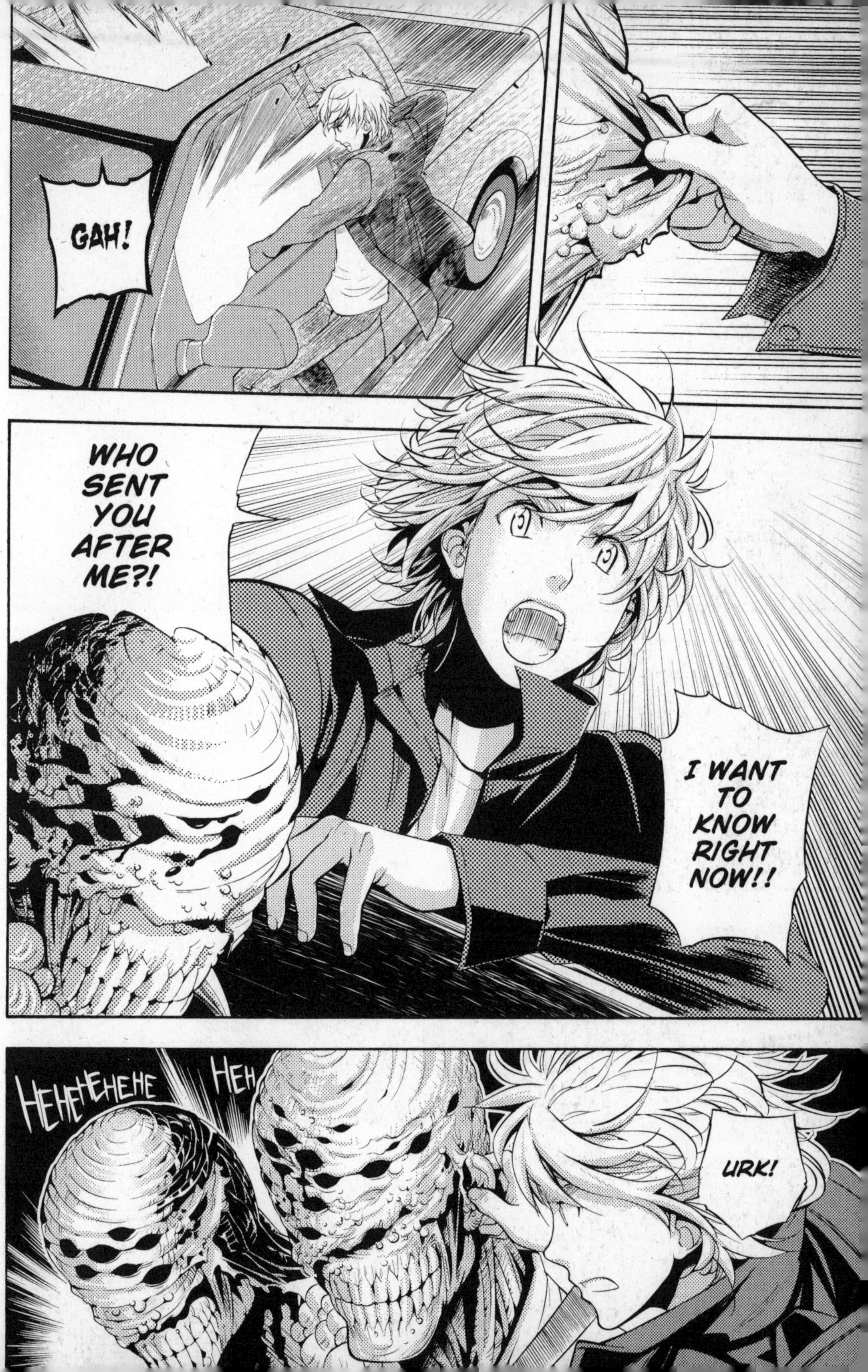
GAH!
WHO SENT YOU AFTER ME?!
I WANT TO KNOW RIGHT NOW!!
HEHEHEHEHE
HEH
URK!

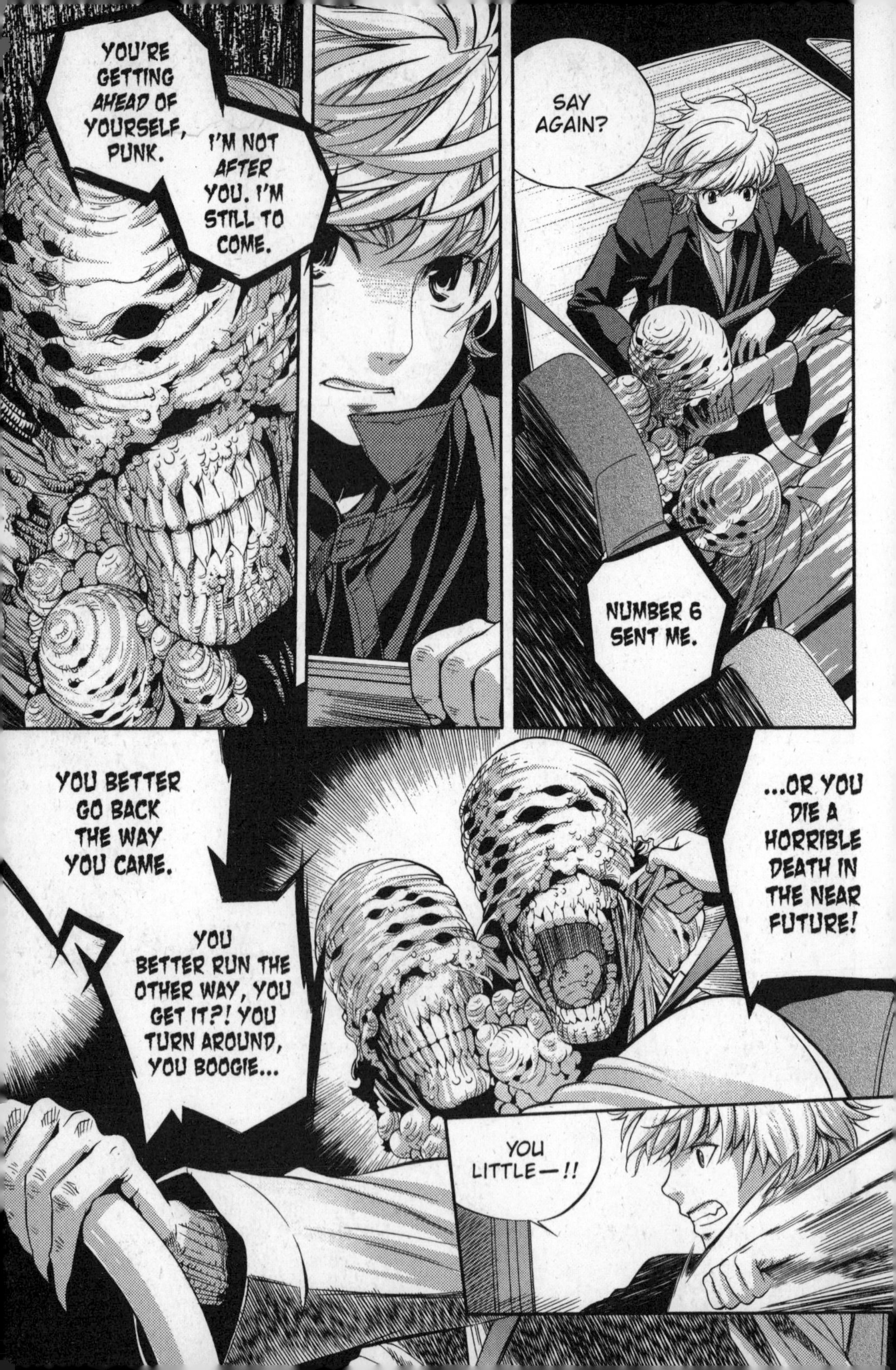
YOU'RE GETTING AHEAD OF YOURSELF, PUNK.
I'M NOT AFTER YOU. I'M STILL TO COME.
SAY AGAIN?
NUMBER 6 SENT ME.
YOU BETTER GO BACK THE WAY YOU CAME.
YOU BETTER RUN THE OTHER WAY, YOU GET IT?! YOU TURN AROUND, YOU BOOGIE...
...OR YOU DIE A HORRIBLE DEATH IN THE NEAR FUTURE!
YOU LITTLE—!!

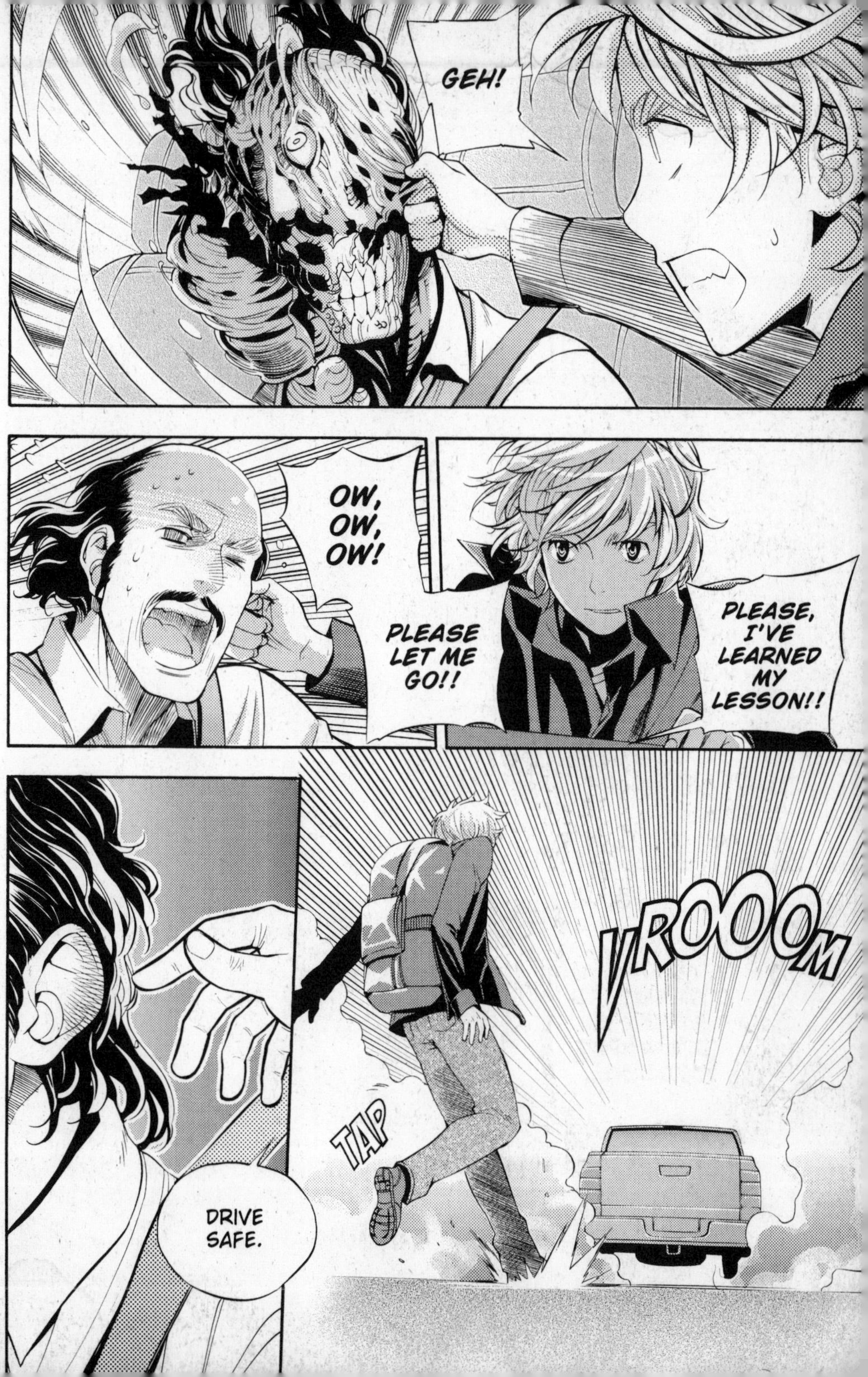
GEH!
OW, OW, OW!
PLEASE LET ME GO!!
PLEASE, I'VE LEARNED MY LESSON!!
DRIVE SAFE.
TAP
VROOOM

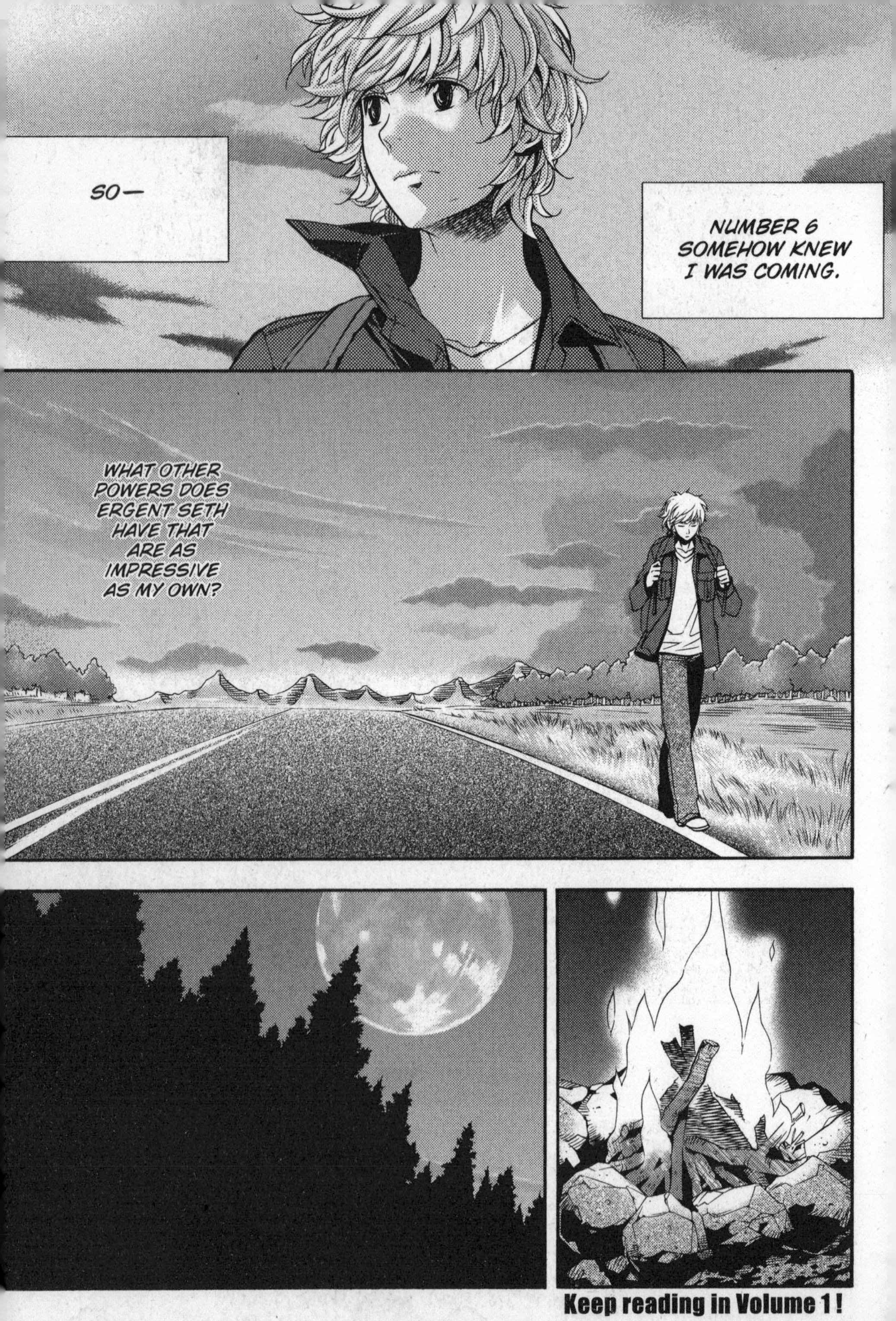
SO—
NUMBER 6 SOMEHOW KNEW I WAS COMING.
WHAT OTHER POWERS DOES ERGENT SETH HAVE THAT ARE AS IMPRESSIVE AS MY OWN?

Keep reading in Volume 1 !

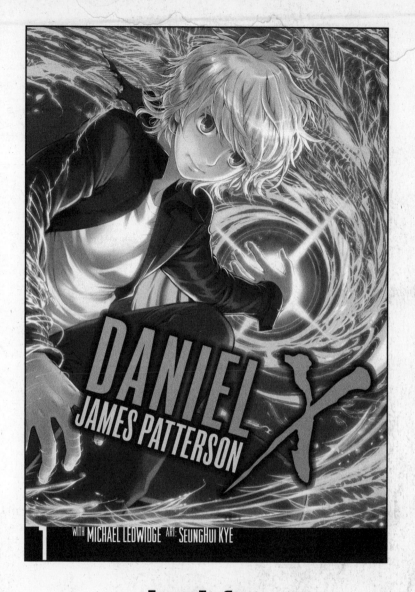

DANIEL X

JAMES PATTERSON

WITH MICHAEL LEDWIDGE ART: SEUNGHUI KYE

**Look for
DANIEL X: THE MANGA Vol. 1
in stores
October 2010!**

MAXIMUM RIDE: THE MANGA ③

JAMES PATTERSON
& NaRae Lee

Adaptation and Illustration: NaRae Lee

Lettering: Abigail Blackman

MAXIMUM RIDE, THE MANGA, Vol. 3 © 2010 by SueJack, Inc.

Illustrations © 2010 Hachette Book Group, Inc.

Yen Press
Hachette Book Group
237 Park Avenue, New York, NY 10017

www.HachetteBookGroup.com
www.YenPress.com

Yen Press is an imprint of Hachette Book Group, Inc. The Yen Press name and logo are trademarks of Hachette Book Group, Inc.

First Yen Press Edition: August 2010

ISBN: 978-0-7595-2969-4

10 9 8 7 6 5 4 3 2 1

BVG

Printed in the United States of America